GREATER PERFECTIONS

PENN STUDIES IN LANDSCAPE ARCHITECTURE

John Dixon Hunt, Series Editor

This series is dedicated to the study and promotion of a wide variety of approaches to landscape architecture, with emphasis on connections between theory and practice. It includes monographs on key topics in history and theory, descriptions of projects by both established and rising designers, translations of major foreign-language texts, anthologies of theoretical and historical writings on classic issues, and critical writing by members of the profession of landscape architecture.

Greater Perfections

THE PRACTICE OF GARDEN THEORY

John Dixon Hunt

PENN

UNIVERSITY OF PENNSYLVANIA PRESS

PHILADELPHIA

10 9 8 7 6 5 4 3 2 1

PUBLISHED BY
UNIVERSITY OF PENNSYLVANIA PRESS
PHILADELPHIA, PENNSYLVANIA 19104–4011

LIBRARY OF CONGRESS CATALOGING-IN-PUBLICATION DATA
HUNT, JOHN DIXON.
GREATER PERFECTIONS : THE PRACTICE OF GARDEN THEORY /
JOHN DIXON HUNT.
P.   CM. — (PENN STUDIES IN LANDSCAPE ARCHITECTURE)
INCLUDES BIBLIOGRAPHICAL REFERENCES (P.   ) AND INDEX.
ISBN 0-8122-3506-1 (ALK. PAPER)
I.   GARDENS—PHILOSOPHY.   I. TITLE.   II. SERIES.
SB454.3.P45H85   1999
712'.01—DC21
                                                    99-17904
                                                        CIP

Frontispiece: Detail, Balthasar Nebot, *Hartwell House, Buckinghamshire*, oil on canvas, 1738. Buckinghamshire County Museum, Aylesbury.

For Nancy

When Ages grow to Civility and Elegancie, Men come to *Build Stately*, sooner than to *Garden Finely*: As if *Gardening* were the Greater Perfection.

   —Francis Bacon, "Of Gardens," 1625

The several arts are composed of two things—craftsmanship and the theory of it.
Of these the one, craftsmanship, is proper to those who are trained in several arts, namely the execution of the work; the other, namely theory, is shared with educated persons. . . . Throughout all the sciences many things, or indeed all, are in common so far as theory is concerned. But the taking up of work which is finely executed by hand, or technical methods, belongs to those who have been specially trained in a single trade.

   —Vitruvius, "De Aedificatio," I, 1, 15–16

According to Hegel, the ancient Greek was amazed by the *natural* in nature; he listened to it continually, and demanded the meaning of springs, mountains, forests, storms; without knowing what all these objects said to him one by one, he perceived in the order of the vegetable world and of the cosmos an immense *frisson* of meaning, to which he gave the name of a god, Pan. Since that time, nature has changed, and become social; all that man encounters is *already* human, including the forests and the rivers that we cross on our journeys. But before this nature became social, which is quite simply culture, the structuralist does not differ from the ancient Greek: he also lends an ear to the natural element in culture, and perceives there all the time, not so much stable, definite, "true" meanings, as the *frisson* of an immense machine which is humanity in the process of moving tirelessly towards the creation of meaning, without which it would cease to be human.

   —Roland Barthes, "Structuralist Activity"

CONTENTS

THIS IS A BOOK about the making of gardens, but it takes a conceptual approach toward what most people consider a practical activity. That is its first challenge—to readers as much as to its author. A second is that the millions who garden, on the one hand, and members of the profession of landscape architects, on the other, are not likely to be interested or impressed by conceptual essays on the making of gardens; at least, that has been the necessary starting point of these inquiries.

Among the gardeners, there is enough to learn and do around the private yard or community garden that little time is left for any reading outside the how-to books, maybe, and the seed catalogs. Their position was nicely represented in the two corresponding panels by Roger de la Fresnaye from 1912–13: one, *L'Arrosoir*, used a watering can to signal the active theme of gardening, while the other, *Emblems*, displayed a globe, violin, and books as emblems of the contemplative life.[1] Among the professionals, contrariwise, garden-making enjoys a fairly low profile and certainly low esteem; they have bigger fish to fry, more ways to deploy their acquired and sophisticated technical skills that also give them a higher profile in the community or on the environmental stage.

So gardeners get on with gardening, and rightly so, except that it seems they are afforded little opportunity by publishers, magazines, and the majority of their fellows to consider their activity more conceptually. Landscape architects, the body legally registered to intervene and reshape the environment, has far less excuse. The profession will argue, rightly, that it is preoccupied with a range of important decisions and reworkings of territory, often of regional scope and extent, and that the garden seems both insignificant and a distraction,

best left to landscape contractors or the careful readership of do-it-yourself publications. It will also argue that conceptual matters, of the sort touted here,[2] have little impact on its day-to-day activities.

But landscape architecture is fractured as a profession partly because it is obliged to divide its energies among a daunting variety of projects. Above all, it has largely lost touch with whatever conceptual or thoughtful understanding of its activities was available to earlier generations of practitioners, and it has lost touch, too, with gardens not as items to be designed and built but as models or ideas for larger enterprises. Landscape architecture is uncertain of its way and at the same time profoundly skeptical of intellectual demands upon it.[3]

Of course, theory and practice can be separate and distinct activities; but theory *as opposed to* practice is not what this book explores. It is, instead, the far older idea of theory as contemplation, the deep scrutiny and understanding of praxis from within.[4] It has been argued that the beginnings of architectural practice were tied to the birth of speculative thought or philosophy.[5] Nothing like the same alliance can be traced to the origins of landscape architecture, but in my search for the guiding principles and conceptions of this related practice I intend to seek comparable moments of speculation: the roots of landscape architectural theory inevitably lie in the soil of its developing practice, just as its best practice has been forced to contemplate—even if intuitively rather than conceptually—the sustaining principles of its activities. Further, if a theory of gardens functions as a standard or paradigm of landscape architecture, it measures specific designs at the same time that the theory itself is monitored by such practice.[6]

There is a misplaced, if understandable, apprehension of theory today, not simply because it is likely to be abstruse and arcane, but because it tends to remove itself too far from the activity that is contemplated. In particular, theory often seems to work to eliminate the mystery that adheres to the actual production or consumption of an activity such as garden-making. Indeed, nowhere is this resentment of theoretical endeavor, this anti-intellectual stance, more sharply felt than in the sphere of gardening, where the divide between practical concerns and theory is immense and apparently unbridgeable.

This modern divide between theory and gardening practice has two aspects: it is a chasm between the activity of making and maintaining gardens on the one hand and (outside the pragmatic, horticultural guides) the activity of writing about them on the other. And within this latter group, there is a further schism, no less regrettable because it is less obvious, between different approaches to garden history: between those who are content to document specific sites and perhaps locate them in some standard narrative of garden history, and those who try and understand the cultural resources that were and are accessed as well as realized through garden-making. And within the latter group should be included those who, increasingly, are concerned with how garden history should be conducted, itself as much a cultural construction as garden-making. For, given both the sheer amount of garden-making and the range of human interests that gardens can literally host, it seems extremely odd that the activity of their making, which goes back thousands of years, has not attracted more thoughtful analysis. The paradox is that gardens are hugely important, as places and as an idea, to thousands of people; yet we know next to nothing about why and how that is so.

Though it may be an absurd ambition, as anyone who well knows the circles of garden history and garden writing will attest (on whatever side of those chasms he or she stands), I want to direct this theoretical inquiry precisely at those who will say they do not want it. It

is not my intention to neglect the undeniable mystery, even mystique, at the heart of garden-making. Indeed, I wish eventually to celebrate it: "it is through wonder that men now begin and originally began to philosophize."[7] So our theoretical contemplation of landscape architecture will begin in and must never lose contact with our wonder at its best and most exciting productions.[8]

I am also concerned to address landscape architectural professionals, for whom a renewed dialogue between their practice and its theoretical possibilities is long overdue. For them more particularly have I chosen this book's first two epigraphs. That from Bacon, cliché though it is, is to remind them that their work may indeed constitute a greater perfection than that of architects, and this being so, it is worth being more proud of, more involved in, its intellectual achievements. That from Vitruvius (in the absence of any classical landscape architectualist) underlines the tradition of connections, reciprocal rather than confrontational, between theory and practice, even as he works to define their distinct and separate arenas. The concentrated technical skills required for the practice of any of the "several arts," in which we will specifically include—though Vitruvius does not—landscape architecture, are not the same as those of the theorist. Here the wide range of a general education is apt—the more so in garden art because it draws together many different skills, among which are architecture itself, botany, arboriculture, chorography, verbal and visual languages, and philosophy. And somebody like myself, who has in Vitruvian terms no "technical" training in the "single trade" of gardening let alone of landscape architecture, must rely instead on the more general education that I bring to bear upon theorizing about that practical craftsmanship.

Nevertheless—or perhaps precisely because of being a generalist—I have many debts to acknowledge since I came permanently to the United States in 1988 and, in a new career, was able to devote myself full-time to studying landscape architecture, at which point I started work on this book. My first obligation is to the many other writers I have read along the way, which I hope my notes and bibliography will make clear; this endeavor has been nothing if not a collaborative enterprise. And in trying out versions of this book upon a variety of audiences, I have also enjoyed useful discussions in many institutions and at many conferences: the most notable were the IFLA Conference in The Hague in 1990; various audiences at the Center for Studies in Landscape Architecture at Dumbarton Oaks, Washington, D.C.; the Collège de France, where I was privileged to be the first visiting professor to talk about landscape architectural matters;[9] the Department of Landscape Architecture at the Université de Montréal, where I was able to try out more or less complete versions of my main arguments; the Architectural Association, where for some years before I left England I gave occasional seminars on the history of landscape architecture; the Centro Studi Giardini Storici e Contemporanei, in Pietrasanta, Italy; the Massachusetts Institute of Technology; and the Graduate School of Fine Arts at the University of Pennsylvania.

Friends, colleagues, and students, especially at the last named institution, have also participated—sometimes more than they can ever know—in the completion and revision of the text over the last few years. Above all, I have been constantly encouraged by the positive responses from practitioners to my endeavor to construct a conceptual basis for landscape architecture.

Among those from whose comments the final version has materially benefited I want to acknowledge Marina Adams, Michel Baridon, James Corner, Stanislaus Fung, Edward Harwood, Peter Jacobs, Bernard Lassus, Michael Leslie, Therese O'Malley, Robin Middleton, Nancy Patterson Ševčenko, Alessandro Tagliolini, Marc Treib, and Robert Williams. In particular, I must thank David Leatherbarrow, Laurie Olin, and Michel Conan for their careful, detailed, and helpful readings of a final draft of this book. Yet it is always important to add that their collective good advice cannot be held responsible for my errors or misjudgments. Finally, without the care and intelligence of Jo Joslyn at the University of Pennsylvania Press, neither this book nor the series of which it forms part would have been possible.

CHAPTER I

"First Principles" or "Rudiments"

THE FIRST PROFESSIONAL practitioner of landscape architecture in England to publish any explicitly theoretical account of his work was Humphry Repton. In the preface to his last book, *Fragments on the Theory and Practice of Landscape Gardening* (1816), he remarked that "the art of landscape gardening . . . is the only Art which every one professes to understand, and even to practise, without having studied its Rudiments" (p. vii). Yet he himself, while formulating rules and precepts, never really succeeded in setting out anything like "the first principles" in which he felt the discipline was lacking (p. viii). Indeed, he chose to present himself on his trade card (Figure 1) as the practical man, busily surveying the terrain. Repton is not alone in this reluctance to conceptualize. Landscape architecture even today lacks any body of theoretical writings, despite its being a field that now echoes to lamentations for "the present theoretical vacuum."[1]

The term *landscape architecture* was basically an invention of John Claudius Loudon in 1840.[2] It is odd and unhappy, seeming to signal the unease and lack of focus with which the modern profession views its activities. These exist somewhere inside the space bracketed by architecture and landscape: the first term gestures toward the older, more established, and theoretically grounded discipline of architecture; the latter—given the derivation of the term *landscape*—to the fine art of painting.[3] *Landscape*, alternatively and no more happily, increasingly came to be taken as referring to the unmediated natural world. But within the parameters that their formal title designates, the activities of professional landscape architects nowadays consist of a whole swathe and range of activities from management

and planning of natural resources to environmental and ecological refurbishments, from complex analyses of land and its uses at regional scale to small interventions in (usually) the urban fabric.

I would provisionally define landscape architecture as exterior place-making;[4] at that simplest level, place-making is to landscape architecture what building is to architecture. Place-making may sometimes take its cue from architecture, being established vis-à-vis some important building or even some building that in its turn acquires importance from that place-making. But professional landscapers' inclusion of the word *architecture* in their description seems largely the result of a feeling of acute inferiority, an inferiority that many architects have done little to relieve by their rather patronizing assumption that landscape architects are the ones who put the flowers and shrubs around *their* finished buildings. Nor has landscape architecture much more to do with "landskip" in the original sense of a painted image of some territory; indeed, the current reaction against anything "scenic" in landscape design has taken the profession even further from that original link with painting. Again, I suspect that the lure of this word is the implied salute by practitioners to a senior and respected partner in the pantheon of beaux arts, landscape painting. While that reference bolstered the status of place-making in the eighteenth and nineteenth centuries, the continuance of the term signals a lingering nostalgia for the picturesque (a word that enjoys an astonishingly virile existence). At the time that place-making acquired aesthetic status in the years around 1800, it also derived (somewhat mistakenly) a formal vocabulary and syntax from painting that it has

FIGURE I. The engraved trade card of Humphry Repton. Private collection.

not entirely thrown off. Yet another more recent use of *landscape* by professionals (along with the general public) tends conversely to infer a neutral world of topography, a zone of "nature," that is deemed to be their concern.

Landscape architecture is, then, an activity of exterior place-making. This activity may include buildings within its remit; it may also look to pictorial art for inspiration, but it occurs essentially in the space *between* buildings/architecture and paintings/*landskip*. It may include elements of what conventionally we call nature—in other words, organic materials like trees, shrubs, and grass and inorganic like water and rocks. Place-making is fundamentally an art of milieu;[5] it creates a "midst" in which we see or set ourselves, places to be lived in, hence its concern to environmentalists, whose business is with our environs or surroundings. The milieu involves not only inhabitants and users but the history of the place that is made or remade, the story of the site over time. Time and process lie at the very heart of landscape architecture and therefore, as we shall see in later chapters, accommodate themselves very readily to narrative. The stories of place-making engage innumerable narrative strategies and modes, for there are, after all, many sorts of fiction.

The awkwardness of the term *landscape architecture,* combined with the profession's current lack of interest in any conceptual account of its activities, at best ensures it a fuzzy profile in the larger world. While everybody has a general idea of what architects do— they design buildings—no such popular formula exists for the landscape architect; schoolchildren may want to grow up to be architects, but virtually none have even heard of the other exciting opportunity. Furthermore, architecture is a largely professional affair, for which training, accreditation, and licensing are required. Landscape architecture, too, requires of its practitioners the same professional rigor; the term *landscape architect* (first used by Olmsted and Vaux in 1862) is legally restricted to members of professional organizations like the American Association of Landscape Architects (founded 1900) or the British Institute of Landscape Architects (1929). But unlike most architecture, landscape architecture is also "practiced" by a range of nonprofessionals. And all these practitioners, whether certified as landscape architects or working simply as landscape designers or contractors, share their turf with millions of enthusiastic amateurs: it is estimated that thirty million residents of the United States are gardeners.[6] This, which has consequences for the literature about landscape architecture, also contributes to the lack of clear professional identity for landscape architects as makers of place.

Perhaps as a result of its tighter professional focus, architecture has accrued a considerable corpus of theoretical as well as technical literature.[7] That tradition began early, at least with the Roman architectural writer Vitruvius, and subsequent cultures have vied to produce their own versions of his treatise. Landscape architecture never enjoyed that classical jump-start,

and for a variety of reasons. Until the late eighteenth-century, its proponents were not identifiable as a distinct profession; place-making was done by—among others—architects, engineers, poets, estate managers or stewards, farmers, and gardeners, physicians. But that situation in its turn derived from the essentially mixed work that went into what we now call landscape architecture—part agriculture (at least in its origins), part horticulture; part hydraulics, part building; part symbolic expression and cultural rhetoric on behalf of a patron, part pragmatic planting and maintenance.[8] Consequently, there was never a body of specialists to compose treatises specifically for what we have come to call landscape architecture, as Vitruvius did for architecture. What observations were made on this topic were incorporated in treatises on those other activities. Thus Alberti includes some splendidly acute but largely incidental paragraphs on place-making in *De re aedificatoria,*[9] and Agostino Gallo's various works on agriculture and estate management in the Veneto, the *Giornate dell'agricoltura,* treat of garden-siting and the ornamentation of gardens and orchards within the larger scope of agrarian business. It is entirely typical of the traditional assumption that the topic of place-making was the province or specialty of no particular specialist that the Latin poet Virgil, writing on matters of agriculture and husbandry in his *Georgics,* announced that, though the topic of gardening was within the scope of his topic, he would leave it to be taken up by others.

This classical lacuna—the lack of any work equivalent to Vitruvius for landscape architecture or garden art[10]—became a source of some concern after the Renaissance when gardens began to assume great importance. There were even specific attempts to remedy the situation, first by the Frenchman René Rapin, whose Latin poem in four books, *Hortorum Libri IV* (1665), was modeled on Virgil's *Georgics.* So important did Rapin's endeavor seem that in the absence of new attempts at a conceptual overview of the art of garden-making the Frenchman's Latin poem was made available in two English translations, even though Rapin's perspectives hardly suited activities across the English Channel. Eventually William Mason refashioned the Virgilian poem into another verse treatise, *The English Garden*, during the 1770s, and this specifically addressed the English situation in the late eighteenth century.[11]

Meanwhile, various prose treatises had been produced in northern Europe which addressed the technical, aesthetic, and conceptual aspects of place-making.[12] That specialist treatises were produced first in northern Europe rather than Italy suggests, as with the case of Rapin, that theoretical formulations derived from a need to understand and schematize the new "italianate" gardening as it came northward and settled in France, Germany, and the Low Countries. Italian publications, too, seem to have been retrospective attempts to codify established practice.

Even so, many publications were necessarily focused only partly on landscape architecture, like Agostino Gallo's volumes (1550 et seq.), Charles Estienne and Jean Liebault's *La Maison rustique* (1564, with an English edition in 1606), or even the earliest garden book for German-speaking peoples, Johann Peschel's *Garten Ordnung* (1597). The first treatise formally and wholly dedicated to garden art was Jacques Boyceau's *Traité du jardinage selon les raisons de la nature et de l'art* (1638), although Bernard Palissy's recipe for the making of a fine (and Protestant) garden appeared as part of his *Recette véritable* in 1563.[13] But, important as Boyceau's book or the subsequent works by the Mollet family were,[14] they scarcely answered the need for a work with the scope and seriousness of Vitruvius' *De Architectura* or its Renaissance successors in Italy like Alberti's treatise. John Evelyn's ambitious project "Elysium Britannicum" may perhaps be considered the first and only attempt to survey the whole territory of garden art, garden history, garden theory, and garden practice. That it was left unfinished at his death in 1706 suggests the hugeness of the enterprise he contemplated.[15]

Evelyn was himself a gentleman virtuoso, what might still be termed an amateur. Landscape architecture, as we have briefly noted—and in this it is quite unlike architecture—continues to attract the attention of virtuosi; this shows itself most noticeably in writings on the subject, some of which hanker after addressing the full scope of the subject.[16] In keeping with place-making's appeal far beyond professional circles are the awe-inspiring book making and book consumption of present-day gardenists. The shelves of bookstores groan with garden books. The click of art photographers' cameras resounds through the shrubbery as yet more elegant imagery is prepared to outflank the text of yet more garden books. One volume on a topic seems no impediment to more on the same theme, whether this is water gardens, creating period gardens, or garden tours; they reappear each spring with the innocence of daffodils. Their readership is clearly ensured both by the gardeners and by the many thousands more who visit gardens. Though professional landscape architecture may reflect the ups and downs of regional and world economies, the enjoyment of DIY (do-it-yourself) garden creation, garden maintenance, and garden writing knows no remission among the population at large. Indeed, gardens seem to bloom and fade with little attention to economic or global problems, and publications keep happily in step with these natural cycles.[17]

The demand for and supply of writings on the garden have, however, largely neglected any theoretical or contemplative concerns. This was not always the case, as images of practical gardening and conceptual projections from the same culture clearly testify (Figures 2 and 3). From the end of the eighteenth century, matters of practical horticulture were treated as largely distinct from design theory. Given the market for garden publications, this is wholly understandable, since the pragmatic demands of garden-making and maintenance leave little leisure, as they create little need, for such considerations—"Gardeners being only guided by Experience, are seldom led to make any Reflection upon the Principles of their Art."[18]

Yet there are contrary stirrings. Gardens, if not the

FIGURE 2. Title page of Jan van der Groen, *Le Jardinier Hollandois*, Amsterdam, 1669, showing work in the garden. Private collection.

FIGURE 3. Laurent de la Hyre, *Arithmetica*, oil on canvas, 1650. Hannema de Stuers Fundatie, Heino.

larger reaches of landscape architecture, are again being taken seriously as an object of study, with an agenda of concerns ranging from their formal poetics to their capacity for meanings, from their status as an art to their staging of cultural concerns.[19] It is unclear whether this revival of interest in all gardenist matters, largely within institutes of higher education, will rival the period when Evelyn began to interest himself in theoretical garden matters. Those were the heady days of the Samuel Hartlib circle during the last months of the Commonwealth and, after the Restoration of the monarchy in 1660, the early years of the Royal Society, with its Georgical Committee (taking its name from Virgil's poem) upon which Evelyn served (see Chapter 7). While a revival of serious intellectual consideration of garden art will not, of course, distract many toilers along the herbaceous borders, the separate worlds of gardening *tout pur* and of garden theory and history will in the end only benefit from an exchange of perspectives. Further, the role of the garden, or the idea of the garden, may also be fostered within the wider range of landscape architectural practices. It is in the interests of these dialogues that this book attempts to raise some theoretical issues about landscape architecture.

The chapters that follow focus on specific topics that must have a high priority within any theory. As David Leatherbarrow has argued for architecture,[20] the "permanence of any architecture topic results from its essential correspondence with a recurring and fundamental human situation"; topical thinking—i.e., thinking about these recurring topics—"is inventive and productive because it creates new forms of agreement and unity." Topics are thus a "formal generative principle, something 'empty' capable of being 'filled' with ever new arguments."

The topics that will be addressed in the following chapters are the privileged position of the garden in landscape architecture; the definition of a garden and its etymology; the range of representations of gardens

in both verbal and visual arts, and what these can tell us about both the idea of the garden and the experiences of actual gardens; a consideration of the role within landscape architecture of what we loosely call nature; the extent to which landscape architecture is itself an art of representation and, if so, what is being represented in any one instance; how different cultures express themselves through landscape architecture; what contribution the historian of those expressions can make to theoretical concerns; and how the history of landscape architecture can best be reconstructed so that the full potential of garden-making in human society can be realized afresh, which is, in other words, to ask what uses can be found for theoretical contemplations of the garden in the future practice of landscape architecture.

By way of introduction and to clarify the larger scope of the project, it may be useful to set out some of my overall motives and my reasons for undertaking it and even (for those readers already immersed in the subject) to set the subject of landscape architecture in the context of a larger intellectual discourse. I offer, therefore, by way of arriving at my main topic, seven theses or theorems.

1. The subject of landscape architecture has no clear intellectual tradition of its own, either as a history, a theory, or even a practice. This is, in fact, its great advantage, and it is to be welcomed (as many involved in it are quick to declare), but it also has drawbacks. Its territory is adjacent to, even contested with, geography, anthropology, geology, botany, engineering, architecture, philosophy, fine arts, and literature. If we enlarge our lens to take in the uses to which gardens have been put, then the fields of theater, museology, sport, musicology, and zoology (to add a few more) would be drawn into the proper study of gardens. This range of matters pertinent to place-making and place-usage is nothing new: when Evelyn and his colleagues discussed the contents lists of their projected volumes on gardens in the last years of the seventeenth century, their

categories included many items that we would find odd today.[21] What, however, is new and to be regretted as hampering efficient study of landscape architecture is the compartmentalized structure of academic learning during the twentieth century; this significantly curtails the diversity of interest in—as well as the potential contributions to—landscape architecture. Nobody can bring to the subject a full repertoire of competences; conversely, anyone who crosses subject boundaries to tackle gardens is inevitably going to arrive with some colonizing instinct. Art historians have made gardens sites of iconography; philosophers parry and thrust over definitions of garden art without much commitment to its actual messy, material, and changeful world; literary critics take gardens as texts of deep meaning and significance; arborculturists cannot see the wood for their trees. A similar diversity of skills is suggested by the very location of university departments of landscape architecture, which are engaged in training professionals: they can find themselves in schools of design, agriculture, environmental studies, horticulture, architecture, or (in my own case at the University of Pennsylvania) fine arts. Probably the best compliment one could pay a specialist in the study of gardens is to be puzzled as to where, academically, he or she has come from.

2. Given this amorphous intellectual structure of the subject, it is unsurprising that, though much has been written about the garden, none of it satisfies even the basic requirements of a theoretical position. In her long poem on the intellect, "The Vain Life of Voltaire," Laura Riding wrote, "What reconciles the garden / Does not reconcile the mind." Wonderful gardens have been created, coherent and fully achieved within their sites. Yet such total works of art and culture, *gesamtwerken*, have elicited no adequate conspectus of theoretical writing. Some valuable concepts about garden art—that is to say, some disjunct elements of a possible theory—have been variously enunciated in the past; others can usefully be extrapolated from otherwise nontheoretical accounts by reading between the lines of de-

scriptions of informed visitors to gardens or by studying verbal and visual descriptions of gardens in different cultures and periods. But a coherent view of garden-making and of its place in human life and society is frustrated by the special claims upon it of too many specialties, each of which is too *parti pris*, too committed to its own agenda, to take on the larger picture.

Conversely, some recent attempts to establish such a larger perspective are inhibited by their distance from, even their apparent lack of acquaintance with, a sufficient range of actual gardens.[22] Yet adequate generalization presupposes a suitable distance from actual examples. Nowhere in any fine garden is the visitor permitted an adequate view of the whole—the process of understanding even the smallest territory and its changes through hour and season militate against that, except in the more generous spaces of our minds and memories. So, too, in the study of gardens and the complex traditions out of which they have come and to which they contribute: it is only by provisionally stepping back from the rich materiality of gardens that we can understand them better. However, it is hoped that readers of this book will sense that a sufficient familiarity with a wide range of gardens in all their palpable forms warrants my generalizations.

3. Any attempt, then, to offer theories about landscape architecture will need to acknowledge two sets of paradoxical constraints (the garden, as we shall see, is no stranger to paradox). First, a theoretical essay will draw upon every possible range of expertise—it must call into play as many possible specialties as an individual writer can summon—and yet be beholden to none of them. Second, it will need to establish a complex dialogue between generalization and exemplification—a theory exists to get a handle on particular cases just as its theoretical efficacy must be judged in its turn by the usefulness of that handle on other specific examples.

One major defect of my own endeavor will probably prove to be its exclusive focus on western garden art. I

have derived a few insights into various aspects of eastern art at second hand and felt able to include them;
but I am too distant as a cultural historian from Chinese and Japanese gardens to treat them with the same
confidence as western examples. That will necessarily
restrict the validity of any theoretical proposals I shall
make.[23]

The main title chosen for this book obviously alludes
in the first instance to Bacon's well-known suggestion
that, since gardens have always come after buildings,
they were a "greater perfection." Yet it also mischie-
vously implies that the practice of theory can be a
"greater perfection" than garden-making. In some circumstances, it will indeed be so: the articulation of
some "first principles" must be founded on an adequate
experience of a wide range of different examples.

4. Lest one develop too firm a commitment to any
one perspective—literary, art historical, philosophical,
horticultural, and so on—the garden theorist must in-
vent the subject anew. This slightly perverse proposal
—as if garden art and landscape architecture had not
by now established themselves sufficiently and independently—involves recognizing them as sui generis
to the extent that it will be difficult if not impossible
to apply to them theoretical formulations from outside
the discipline. Above all, I believe this to mean that
the necessary conceptual reinforcement of landscape
architectural practice should not come entirely if at all
from such theoretical masters as Freud, Lacan, Der-
rida, Foucault, Barthes, et al. Rather, we must discover
within the activities of garden art and landscape architecture themselves the grounds of an adequate theory.[24]
Since we need to excavate this possibility from within
the theoretic traditions of landscape architecture itself,
this necessitates a detailed and strategic dialogue between theory and practice, the history of both of which
must be systematically reviewed. Landscape architecture today has strong and healthy roots; these, as any
tree specialist knows, are the essential prerequisites of
a flourishing canopy of branches.

5. Landscape architecture is a fundamental mode of
human expression and experience. Although the term
is of relatively recent coinage, the activity it designates—what at its most generic I call place-making—
can be traced to the earliest civilizations. Men and
women have always intervened in their immediate environment to shape and create (open-air) surroundings for themselves and for a given society or culture.
This activity will necessarily take local forms, scope, or
even names—the professionalization and institutional-
ization of place-makers, for instance, marked a particularly decisive development in the procedures and
scope of this kind of work. Despite the cultural differences of its activity at different times and places,
it can usefully be thought of as an "art of milieu," a
term borrowed and adapted from the French geographer Augustin Berque.[25]

Berque's concept of milieu contains two related ingredients. The first is that the production of "landscape," whether urban, suburban, or rural, is not simply
a question of environment (or environmentalism), but
the *mediation* of environment. In other words, a milieu
is not just objective, physical surroundings, but involves
the inscription on that site of how an individual or a
society conceives of its environment. It is not simply
a place made but a place that we register as having been
made or as continuing to be made. "Milieu" is literally what we are in the middle of and surrounded by;
but it is we ourselves (or those whom we choose to
employ) who have constituted and continue to modify
these surroundings.

The second point follows: that landscapes, whether
we focus on their making or the experiencing of them
long after their creation, are a combination of object
and subject, of the place made and the place-maker
or place-user. It is, in effect, impossible to distinguish
between these elements of the total landscape. They
are neither geomorphological realities nor a "given" set
of territorial facts; nor are they just what we impose
on them—by way of association, sentiment, or fantasy.

Rather, landscape comes into being as the creative coupling of a perceiving subject and an object perceived.[26]

This explains the peculiar richness of landscape architecture (as, mutatis mutandis, of all manner of landscape experience, which is Berque's own concern). It allows full weight to the facts of each physical site at the same time that it admits the modifying or mediating input of the human being. As such, landscape architecture rehearses a central modern dilemma: how to endow the world with value, without falling into the error of arguing either that value adheres in the world or that the world is devoid of value.[27]

If the dilemma has received significant modern attention, its existence as an essential element of place-making has been long-standing. It is precisely this ambiguous process of combination that Alexander Pope addresses in his famous lines on the "genius of the place";[28] the phrase may seem to imply noumenous rather than phenomenal aspects of the site (i.e., that value, significance, preexists in a given place). But the context of Pope's phrase makes clear that he addresses specifically the physical disposition of the ground and then the place-maker's creative response to the phenomena. First, the "genius of the place"—

   tells the waters or to rise, or fall,
Or helps th'ambitious hill the heav'ns to scale,
Or scoops in circling theatres the vale;
Calls in the country, catches op'ning glades,
Joins willing woods, and varies shades from shades.

Then, since it is the genius of the place that "tells" how to treat each feature of the ground or that "Now breaks, or now directs, th'intending line," Pope further implies the contribution of the human designer, responding to what the physical conditions tell him or her. But what his lines marvelously enact is the coming together of a new whole, the melding of the object (ground) and the subject (designer) into a place newly made. And if Pope is primarily concerned here with place-making, his account also implies a model for visitors to a place already made: at Rousham, Oxfordshire, or at Stowe, Buckinghamshire, places that Pope probably helped to design, today's visitors also make them anew in their creative exchanges with the site (Figure 4).

The richness of landscape architecture is further augmented by the fact that each human being also brings to making or to visiting a landscape a double set of resources: first, those cultural, social, and historical determinants which have gone into the making of the human subject; second, the individual's tastes, memories, and what Berque calls the "dispositions du moment" (p. 28). It is, then, the complexity of the human being as historical, cultural, and individualized subject that is engaged instrumentally in making and, later, experiencing the landscape; but the landscape itself is an ever-changing object of no mean scope in its own concentration of natural and cultural resources.

6. This way of looking at landscape architecture draws into prominence its paradoxical nature. Place-making comprises both object and subject, but also nature and culture, product and process, praxis and theory, visual and verbal, private and public, real virtues and virtual realities, order and chaos, materiality and psychology, or an insistent physicality and a traditional accommodation of metaphysics. And the art of making places renews itself always on the basis of well-established criteria.

But prime among those paradoxes of garden art—as also more largely of landscape architecture—is its constitution by two prime constituents: what we loosely call "nature," but which are really the unmediated ingredients and processes of the physical world, organic and inorganic;[29] and what we call art or culture, by which those "natural" elements are mediated. Gardens are arguably unique among the arts in this combination—only the dance and body painting otherwise come to mind as arts that actively involve a living, organic, and changing component. Further, the parallel between place-making and place-makers is obvious,

FIGURE 4. Modern visitors in the Elysian Fields at Stowe, 1989 (photograph: Marina Adams).

both enjoying the binary structure of nature and culture. This perhaps explains why human beings alone among all the animals create gardens.[30]

7. The most sophisticated form of landscape architecture is garden art. This is a claim that will be considerably substantiated later on; here, though, it still needs to be rigorously defended—not to those millions who practice their own gardening and visit examples of other peoples', but to professional landscape architects for whom the private worlds of garden space are no longer the preferred site of activity. What is at issue here is not (necessarily) the creation of more gardens, but the understanding that this particular mode of place-making is still paradigmatic for landscape architecture. The "idea" of the garden, rather than versions of the garden per se, needs to be reactivated; I suspect, too, that behind many ideas of landscape in the modern world also lurks an idea of its most concentrated version, the garden.[31]

Gardens certainly have been privileged sites. Though they may have derived their forms and their methods, at least in part, from agriculture, they have in every culture come to transcend or refine those origins, just as the pleasure garden came to be valued over the more pragmatic spaces of *potager* and orchard, even if in practice their boundaries remained blurred. And the devices and effects of gardens were carried into the design of larger spaces during the late eighteenth, the nineteenth, and the twentieth centuries—public parks, cemeteries, or those peculiarly American inventions, the college campus and corporate park. Many of these newly invented sites would not or could not emulate the quantity or quality of devices that wealthy private patrons had enjoyed; yet they were still inspired by the idea of the garden that retained its aura of a special site, a paradigm of milieu valued for the extra art and care devoted to it and so for the concentration, this time of effort, that went into it. The usage of the word *garden*, often in contexts that do not involve planting or garden-making, continues to reflect the special regard in which it is held.

Gardens are privileged, then, because they are concentrated or perfected forms of place-making. This concentration takes various shapes: the representation of many topographical features (valleys, hills, plateaus, springs) or the display of various organic and inorganic forms (shrubs, woods, waters, rocks, earth) can achieve that sense of plenitude which has been associated with gardens ever since the first one (Eden contained, of course, "every tree that is pleasant to the sight").[32] Special kinds of garden—botanical, sculptural, or zoological—aim to gather as many specimens as possible within their walls, or as many as seems apt for the given space (one statue does not make a sculpture garden, nor one exotic beast a zoo). Yet crowding in everything possible (Figure 5), as many gardeners learn to their cost, is not the answer: that way, cemeteries like Père Lachaise or Mount Auburn would become the acme of design, the sculpture garden cum memory theater par excellence. No, as Thomas Jefferson attested when confronted with the abundant flora and fauna of the New World, the concentration of landscape architectural effects does not necessarily mean their multiplication or addition; the *subtraction* of elements could also leave a site concentrated in the sense of being more carefully focused.[33] What happened in that case, as with Capability Brown's best work, was that the designer highlighted the essence or idea of a place as much by removing extraneous or distracting elements (Figure 6) as by supplying those that were needed to fill out the whole scene. Either way the garden concentrated its effects.[34]

Gardens focus the art of place-making or landscape architecture in the way that poetry can focus the art of writing. Not everyone wants to write poetry, nor do its modes of expression suit every occasion or topic (people probably don't use verse to make up shopping lists). But the poet's formal and creative skills, technical resources, linguistic inventions, and (especially relevant to the highly atavistic art of garden-making) uneasy relationship with the demanding traditions of his or her art—all these make poetry among the most concentrated and demanding of literary expressions; this quality of compactness, concentration, is especially conspicuous in lyric poetry, where the scale is relatively small. The same claim can arguably be put forward for garden art, which of all forms of open space design draws on a richly constituted repertoire of effects, motives, and traditions. Undoubtedly, novelists will object to the terms of my analogy—rightly, too, in that the greatest novels achieve that concentration of effect that is aptly called "poetic"; similarly, landscape architects who work at the scale of regional planning could create effects the subtlety or density of which mirror some of the best historical achievements in garden art (indeed, it would be exactly my proposition to them that they do this more deliberately).

Thus, throughout this study, gardens will be taken as the prime territory of and for investigation; this implies, inevitably, some value judgments, some acknowledgment of a hierarchy of sites. But it is otherwise a

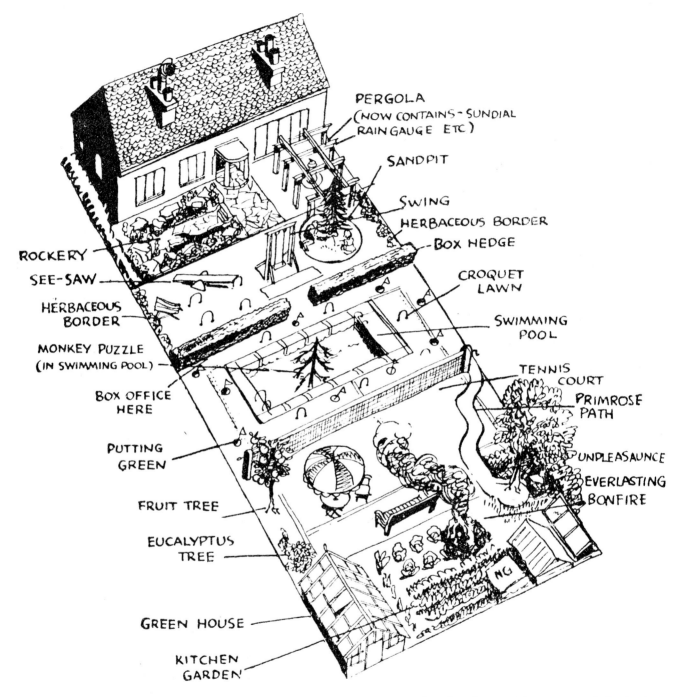

PERGOLA
(NOW CONTAINS - SUNDIAL
RAIN GAUGE ETC)

SANDPIT

SWING

HERBACEOUS BORDER

BOX HEDGE

ROCKERY

SEE-SAW

HERBACEOUS
BORDER

MONKEY PUZZLE
(IN SWIMMING POOL)

BOX OFFICE
HERE

PUTTING
GREEN

FRUIT TREE

EUCALYPTUS
TREE

GREEN HOUSE

KITCHEN
GARDEN

CROQUET
LAWN

SWIMMING
POOL

TENNIS
COURT

PRIMROSE
PATH

UNPLEASAUNCE

EVERLASTING
BONFIRE

FIGURE 5. A garden where much is concentrated; drawing by
Stephen Dowling, reprinted from R. J. Yeatman and W. C.
Sellar, *Garden Rubbish* (London, 1936).

FIGURE 6. The landscape at Blenheim in 1989, designed by
Capability Brown.

decision intended mainly to facilitate experiment and
analysis by focusing on a paradigmatic form of landscape architecture.

These seven theses define both the challenges and the
problems of practicing garden theory. It seems to me
that we need what might provisionally be understood
as an anthropology of the garden.[35] This would explore the many cultural versions of the idea or essence
of the garden, what (borrowing from Berque) we could
call the different "symbolic performances of milieu or
médiance."[36] The garden is a medium that has been
with us more or less since the beginning of recorded

civilizations; widely different cultural systems have invoked gardens in their sustaining narratives and have
elaborated myths of garden creation and garden consumption. The garden, then, must presumably reflect,
answer, even create certain human needs and concerns.
Indeed, its recurrence makes it precisely what J. B. Jackson calls an archetype, a continuing and recognizable
concept, yet subject to constant reinterpretation both
in treatises and upon the ground through many different periods and cultures.[37] It is appropriate, therefore,
first to review what different etymologies can tell us
about the garden and then to ask what are the human
concerns to which this archetypal creation responds,
and what does garden-making reveal to us about our
own human makeup and existence.

CHAPTER 2

What on Earth Is a Garden?

Les jardins traversent sans bruit notre histoire.
— Michel Conan

I

That question "what on earth is a garden?" may seem unnecessary, naive, or perhaps off-puttingly intellectual. After all, the poet tells us, "A garden is a lovesome thing, God wot,"[1] and we know that all the world loves a garden. Some people can get along without definitions. To Reginald Arkell, for all practical purposes, it is obvious what a garden is—

> What is a garden?
> Goodness knows!
> You've got a garden,
> I suppose.[2]

The doyen of French garden historians, the Comte Ernest de Ganay, after some of the most perceptive analysis of gardens on record, simply opines that a garden is what it is ("un jardin est ce qu'il est").[3] Others mistrust definitions, arguing that important aspects of whatever is being defined will escape their net. Or they might invoke the argument against essentialist definitions that has been powerfully expressed by Ludwig Wittgenstein in his *Philosophical Investigations*, where he writes that "phenomena have no one thing in common which makes us use the same word for it." The example he chooses is games (*Spiele*): having explored the diversity of experiences to which the word refers, he understands it only as "a complicated network of similarities, overlapping and criss-crossing."[4]

As with games, there are many kinds of gardens. So many, in fact, that what distinguishes them from each other may be more important than whatever they may have in common (indeed, is it not just the word *garden* that is shared?). There are flower gardens, vegetable gardens, botanical gardens, landscape gardens, public gardens, community gardens, allotment (or victory) gardens, peace gardens, cloister gardens, pleasure gardens, edible gardens, therapeutic gardens, rock gardens, water gardens, bog gardens, dry gardens, winter gardens, container gardens, nursery gardens, truck gardens, beer gardens, tea gardens, parking-lot gardens, gardens of remembrance, zoological gardens, wildlife gardens, workplace gardens.[5] We could extend the list by including translations from the German, like tree gardens, *kindergarten*, animal gardens, wine gardens, and even corpse gardens.[6]

Nevertheless, in spite of Wittgenstein's eloquent argument against essentialist definitions, and perhaps rather more in the spirit of his own apparent conviction that garden paths must be of a certain width,[7] it seems worth trying to define what the "garden" is. If a subject is to be fully and seriously considered, it is arguably useful to know its parameters and its essential constituents; one prime element of such analysis must be definition. From the specific terms of a definition other elements of the inquiry, including exceptions, will necessarily proceed. Thus, without further ado, a garden may be described provisionally as follows:

A garden will normally be out-of-doors, a relatively small space of ground (relative, usually, to accompanying buildings or topographical surroundings). The specific area of the garden will be deliberately related through various means to the locality in which it is set: by the invocation of indige-

nous plant materials, by various modes of representation or other forms of reference (including association) to that larger territory, and by drawing out the character of its site (the genius loci). The garden will thus be distinguished in various ways from the adjacent territories in which it is set. Either it will have some precise boundary, or it will be set apart by the greater extent, scope, and variety of its design and internal organization; more usually, both will serve to designate its space and its actual or implied enclosure. A combination of inorganic and organic materials are strategically invoked for a variety of usually interrelated reasons —practical, social, spiritual, aesthetic—all of which will be explicit or implicit expressions or performances of their local culture. The garden will therefore take different forms and be subject to different uses in a variety of times and places. To the extent that gardens depend on natural materials, they are at best ever-changing (even with the human care and attention that they require above all other forms of landscape), but at worst they are destined for dilapidation and ruin from their very inception. Given this fundamental contribution of time to the being of a garden, it not only exists in but also takes its special character from four *dimensions. In its combination of natural and cultural materials, the garden occupies a unique place among the arts, and it has been held in high esteem by all the great civilizations of which it has been a privileged form of expression.*

A few extra notes are in order at this point, glosses (etymologically, tongues) to set out elements of the necessarily concise and interconnected description just offered.

First, it is worth observing that, while the term *art* is used, the definition does not plead especially for the garden as art. It is obvious to me that the making of places we call gardens is an art, but an art of a special sort in that (above all) it involves the inclusion of "natural materials" which are to some extent beyond the control of the designer. In this respect it resembles the dance, as Giulio Carlo Argan explains: "The fundamental element of the dance is also natural, but its esthetic legitimacy is not questioned."[8] Philosophers

especially have worried away at the issue, but the artistic status of the garden hardly abides their question.[9] In the meantime, other more important and yet much less vexed issues get neglected.

Second, the special place of place-making among the arts seems linked to the special value that has been placed on gardens as the most sophisticated or refined versions of that activity. This value in its turn may be explained by the coincidence between humans (unique among animals in their affinity for gardens) and gardens themselves—for both are the result of a melding of nature and culture.

Third, the definition works in two distinct ways, a dual focus that will be maintained throughout this book and which follows logically from a point already argued. As an art of milieu, a site exists both as a physical object and as a place experienced by a subject. So gardens will be conceived, first of all, in the abstract (their ontology, or essence); but that idea of a garden is at the same time paradoxically composed of the perception of gardens in many different ways by different people and different cultures and periods.

Finally, it is intended that the definition will be taken as a whole, that the removal of any one element will jeopardize its efficacy. Nevertheless, the remainder of the book will isolate specific aspects of the definition in order to develop their contribution to the whole and thereby refine it. Specifically, I shall consider later in this chapter the etymology of *garden* and then in a subsequent chapter the ways gardens have been represented visually and verbally. Both of these inquiries support, qualify, and complicate such crucial elements of the definition as the role of time or process in garden creation and experience, a garden's enclosure, or the relationship of its special space to differently handled zones outside its boundaries. The combination of natural and cultural elements will also be refined by a detailed look at some historical attempts around the year 1700 to understand the exact extent of their different roles in place-making. The ways in which different cultures have realized the potential of garden imagery as

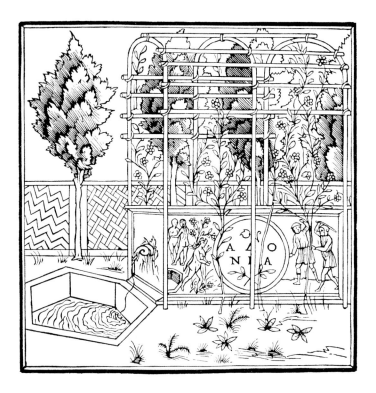

FIGURE 7. Fountain and pergola garden, woodcut from
F. Colonna, *Hypnerotomachia Poliphili*, 1499.

a form of self-expression, as statements of some relationship with space and nature, are usually the subject-
matter of histories of garden art; here, though, they
can be invoked to call into question the habitual narratives of garden development that try to privilege one
mode—nature or culture—over another.

II

Mine is, of course, by no means the first attempt to define gardens. The shock of cultural surprise,
when gardens were encountered in strange locations or
in fresh forms, has elicited definitions of a sort. The
curiosity of the Greeks, for instance, was aroused in
540 B.C. by the walled and elaborated parks of the Per-

sians, the term for which Xenophon famously translated into Greek (and thence it arrived in English) as
paradise and which he also explains: "There are 'paradises,' as they call them, full of all the good and beautiful things that the soil will produce . . . a fine stock
of trees. . . . Now Lysander admired the beauty of the
trees in it, the accuracy of the spacing, the straightness
of the rows, the regularity of the angles and the mul-
titude of the sweet sounds that clung around them as
they walked."[10]

One is struck here by the recognition of the com-
pleteness, the beauty of the ordering, and the appeal
to the senses. A further surprise for the Greek visitor, Lysander, was to be told by his host, King Cyrus,
that he had personally measured and set out the whole
paradise, thus introducing the idea of the great care
required in design and maintenance. Or the anonymous author of the *Hypnerotomachia Poliphili* (Venice,
1499) lets the dreamer ponder in awe and intricate detail his encounter with a whole series of gardens;[11] this
work registers a fresh Renaissance wonder at the art
of place-making, where gardens draw on the repertoire of classical precedent and contemporary developments (Figure 7). No less astonished were early northern, especially English, visitors to Italian gardens in the
sixteenth and seventeenth centuries,[12] recording their
delight in word and image (Figure 8). Similarly, foreign
visitors to England during the eighteenth century acknowledged and came to terms with fresh modes of designing the landscape. In each case the experience of a
new kind of place-making elicited, even required, fresh
definitions of the garden. More routinely, ever since
the second half of the eighteenth century when what
we now call landscape architecture began to take itself
seriously, other definitions have been offered, especially
in professional treatises on its theory and practice; several of these will be invoked later as the provisional
definition is glossed and augmented.

But too many definitions are either incidental, so
minimalist that they exclude necessary considerations
(perhaps because they are taken for granted within the

context), or they are shaped in the interests of an already determined agenda. Often, attempts at definition betray the practical occasions of their formulation: thus in *The Illustrated Dictionary of Gardening* we read that "'garden' . . . is usually understood to mean a piece of land of any description or size, adjacent to, or connected with, a residence, and set apart, either for the purpose of growing vegetables and fruits for the supply of the household, or for the cultivation of plants and flowers for the embellishment of any part of the house or the Garden itself."[13] Not surprisingly, it turns out to be written by the curator of the Royal Botanical Gardens at Kew; despite its useful emphasis on "set apart" and "embellishment," it is biased toward the garden's botanical role, without any further acknowledgment of either design or the cultural significance of the activities noted. Likewise, to take a further example, in the early twentieth century the landscape architect Willy Lange surreptitiously furthers his own concerns for a racially pure German "nature garden," at once culturally tendentious and manipulatively horticultural, in the brief statement that "a garden is a piece of ground set aside for the raising of plants."[14] Another perspective—something legally and bureaucratically instrumental—was needed by those bodies which oversee the conservation of historical gardens and landscapes; yet many so concerned feel that the definitions of gardens and sites offered by the ICOMOS Florence Charter are wholly inadequate, in part because it does not go beyond the self-evident.[15]

Some definitions, like Lange's, work by eliminating elements that would not further their unstated ends. Some elements, conversely, are included precisely to be rejected: the philosopher Mara Miller cites one from the *Shorter Oxford English Dictionary*—not on the face of it a likely source of more than etymological scope—largely to be able to object to it from "the philosophical point of view."[16] Her objections, legitimate in themselves, are nevertheless determined by her need to focus on gardens as an art: thus the dictionary's definition is deemed too "generous," because it would include

agricultural land and privilege cultivation, and yet too "narrow," because it excludes many plants, objects, and structures usually associated with gardens. Her own four-line definition works specifically to exclude what she calls metaphorical gardens (Noguchi's courtyard at Yale)[17] or interior gardens (like orangeries): "A garden is any purposeful arrangement of natural objects (such as sand, water, plants, rocks, etc.) with exposure to the sky or open air, in which the form is not fully accounted by purely practical considerations such as convenience" (p. 15). Rightly and usefully, Miller comments that "from the philosophical point of view" it is the excess of form over "practical considerations" that is "interesting and requires study." Her definition seems both insufficiently concerned with the garden's relationship to other zones of human activity like agriculture and architecture (hence presumably her omission of inorganic materials) and intolerant of the garden as a form of expression let alone representation. Philosophy, in fact, does not seem the only or even the best perspective from which to view the garden, not least because so much energy is expended on arguing with other statements rather than looking at both actual gardens and the pronouncements of those who have made them.[18]

III

Comparative etymology affords some useful perspectives on the basic meaning and definition of the garden as it recurs in different times and cultures; one of the most persuasive contributions of etymology is to stress the fairly constant requirement that garden space, in its various guises, always be enclosed or somehow marked off from its surroundings.

Humphry Repton, the landscape designer who by the end of his career in 1818 had effectively countered the openness of the "Capability Brown" park and reaffirmed the garden's enclosure, was very confident that "the most important of all things relating to a garden, is that which cannot contribute to its beauty, but without which a garden cannot exist; the fence must be

FIGURE 8. Paul Brill, Month of May. Promenade on the terrace of a villa, pen and wash, 1598. Louvre, Cabinet des Dessins.

effective and durable." Earlier he had begun his definition of a garden by writing that it was "a piece of ground fenced off from cattle, and appropriated to the use and pleasures of man: it is, or ought to be, cultivated."[19] Repton's confidence in the necessity of enclosure for a garden is supported by much etymological evidence that predates the cultural conditions that influenced his own theory and practice.

As Anne van Erp-Houtepen has clearly demonstrated, all European, Indo-European, and Slavic languages derive their words for gardens from roots that signify enclosure.[20] A small sampling of her examples will illustrate this vividly. But furthermore she has shown that other words which etymologically derive from meanings of enclosure, such as yard, court, park, and (in days of fortification) town, have each at some stage become involved with words that betoken gardens or garden-related structures. For instance, *yard* (from Indo-European *gher* = fence, or old English *geard* = fence) has yielded *boomgaard* (orchard) in Dutch, *ogorod* (vegetable garden) in Russian, and *gradina* (garden) in Bulgarian, and still sustains the North American usage of *yard* for garden. *Court* from the Indo-European *ghort* (= enclosure) slipped into the Latin *hortus* (= garden) and the English *courtyard*; *court* is semantically equivalent to the Dutch *hof*, which sustains in its turn idioms like *huis en hof* (house and garden) and also produced the term *hovenier* (gardener). *Town* from Old High German *tun* (= fence), Old English *tun* (= enclosure), and Middle English *tounne* (= village) has yielded the Dutch word for garden, *tuin*. Similarly the French *ville* (town) is cognate with the Latin *villa* (country estate) and its later Italian and English usages. *Park*, related to Old English *pearroc* (= enclosure), yields the modern Dutch *perk*, flowerbed.

What is interesting about all these slippages between words that carry with them notions of enclosed space is that at one point or another of their existence they all converge on gardens. The Greeks were fascinated with the Old Persian *pairidaeza* (from *pairi* [around] and *daeza* [wall]); hellenized as *paradeisos*, this effectively introduced the word *paradise*, meaning a wonderfully enclosed ground, into several modern languages.[21] And that Paradise which Genesis celebrates was guarded, we are told, at least after Adam's and Eve's expulsion, by walls.[22] Thus etymology strongly hints at the fashion in which the garden summarizes many activities, all of which share a basic human need for protective reassurance.

The word *garden* itself puts down its etymological roots to words for enclosure and has in its turn spawned many derivatives. It comes from the same root as the Old English *geard* (= fence), Indo-European *gher* (= fence), and *ghort* (= enclosure). Thus it travels into vulgar Latin as *gardinum* (= enclosure), into Old Norman French as *gardin*, into Middle English as *gardyne* (first recorded around 1300), and thence into the Italian *giardino* and the French *jardin*. It has spawned descendants in many languages, like the Spanish *huerto* and Greek *chortos*. Nor is this identification of garden with enclosure simply a western phenomenon: for one Chinese commentator in the Ming period, "That which has a hedge is called a *yuan* [garden]."[23]

IV

Etymology, then, certainly supports the idea that gardens have always been perceived as enclosed spaces. All definitions, however, provoke or elicit exceptions, which may nonetheless prove the rule. A few are worth considering.

An obvious counter example to the idea that a garden is essentially enclosed, as its etymology seems to proclaim, would be the so-called English landscape garden at its high point under Capability Brown in the 1760s. A less obvious exception, but one that, recently proposed, seems nonetheless very compelling in that it concerns a garden which might be thought of as a prima facie case of clear distinction from its surrounding territory, is André Le Nôtre's Vaux-le-Vicomte; allegedly this "eludes containment."[24] Or, as a third

possible exception to the etymological straitjacket, the famous gardens at Cleves created from the late 1640s by Johan Maurits van Nassau-Siegen had no clear lines of enclosure.[25] Doubtless, readers will think of other exceptions.

There are responses to all these objections. A Capability Brown landscape, for example, might well still be protected by a surviving ha-ha, the sunken ditch which effectively separated the garden from agricultural territory without obstructing the view. But it would be possible also to see a Capability Brown landscape garden as circumscribed simply by the limits of its own sophisticated art (here I refer to discussion elsewhere about the garden's concentration of effects, whether concentration by reduction or addition).[26] Though it was objected at the time that Brown's work was indistinguishable from the common fields, a remark more applicable to his lusterless imitators,[27] Brown's landscapes may always be distinguished by their design, by his application of art to specific spaces and not to those beyond them.

The example of Vaux-le-Vicomte, so the authors of *The Poetics of Gardens* argue, marks a "profound revolution [in garden design] . . . here, for the first time, the pattern garden, previously cut off from a hostile world by a clear and definite edge, plunges through that edge and invades nature, while it eludes containment" (p. 198). Their analysis is not convincing: the canal does not "vanish out of the manicured garden." Indeed, at one end it is elegantly shaped into a hemicycle, probably designed to allow pleasure boats to turn, while the other, uncompromisingly linear, is marked by pavilions, and to walk around the canal in either direction is to experience a distinct sense of containment by the strict woodland on the land side.

The exploration of the enclosure at Vaux certainly involves a complex adjudication of many spatial experiences;[28] but they are all based on a clear sense of within/beyond, which, incidentally, the handsome axiometric drawings of Vaux provided in *The Poetics of Gardens* do much to support. These drawings effec-

FIGURE 9. Aerial view of Vaux-le-Vicomte (photograph: Amis de Vaux).

tively record the garden's boundaries, registered specifically in the regularity within them of tree planting. Inside the woodland borders, the gardens offer a series of differently modulated zones of regularity, on a scale that stretches from the topiary and embroidery of the parterre immediately adjacent to the chateau,

where artful intervention dominates the natural ingredients, to the open glades around the statue of Hercules, from whence a goose-foot of avenues branches off into the surrounding forests (Figures 9, 10). We are always made aware of the control within the gardens, whatever the ratio of art:nature at any one spot: the more intricate parterre echoes the formal shapes of the chateau's architecture and interior furnishing in materials that, further away, are allowed their natural

FIGURE 10. View across the parterre, Vaux-le-Vicomte.

shape;[29] the pools of water are strictly shaped, yet reflect the untouchable and mobile sky; the alcoves and groves on either side of the parterre are reiterated less rigidly in the opening and closing glades of the hillside where Hercules now stands. And those final *radiating percées*, essentially avenues for hunting, also establish corridors where the spatial control of the gardens is still vestigially maintained and extended, and in so doing the avenues mediate between "polish'd garden" and "wilderness." "Nature" here is "invaded," but the containment of the garden is not compromised.

The third potential exception, Cleves, is an example of how the location of gardens within a larger landscape establishes their own privileged space—like a campfire, its circle of security is nonetheless precise and felt for being invisible.[30] At Cleves, where the views out are one of the garden's raisons d'être, the designed spaces are demarcated by their being constituted as the privileged sites which authorize that looking (Figure 11). More conventionally, the two blocks of gardens to west and east of the castle, though linked to distant features by sightlines and sometimes avenues, are distinctly wrought areas, more conspicuously wooded and criss-crossed with paths than the adjacent lands.[31] Contemporary illustrations of Cleves (Figure 12), too, indicate—even if they were not apparent from within —that fencing did enclose the spaces of the Sternberg and the Amphitheater (thus constituting a prototypical ha-ha).

Another objection to the criterion of enclosure or marking of territory is that it is not an exclusively human phenomenon; animals will mark out ground that has palpable if (at least to humans) insensible edges. What is unique to the human experience of gardens are the deliberation with which some space is colonized as well as the artistic intentions that have directed both the enclosing and its interior elaboration; there is, further, the perception by the user or visitor that these effects have occurred. It is the interior elaboration that marks the descriptions of gardens by the Mughal emperor Babur:

> Those were the days of the garden's beauty; its lawns were one sheet of trefoil; its pomegranate-trees yellowed to autumn splendour, their fruit full red.[32]

Any insistence on a garden's walls is far less important to Babur than celebration of the interior spaces; indeed, James L. Wescoat suggests that "rows of Tents and portable textile enclosures" probably marked the "separation between one plot of land and the next." Yet famous illustrations to the *Baburnama* (Figure 13), executed eighty years after the emperor's death and therefore to be interpreted cautiously as evidence for what Babur's gardens were really like, reveal the striking difference between the rich gardenscape, on the one hand, and the orchards and precipitous mountains in which it is located; by this stage in Mughal gardening, walls have become a prominent feature of its strategy, drawing attention to the relationship of garden area to its locality.

The examples of Brown, Vaux-le-Vicomte, and Cleves make a further point about lines of demarcation or enclosure. Gardens change our perceptions of the landscape in which they are set, enabling discriminations of the scales of human intervention in nature (a topic to be addressed in the next chapter). Even though —as at Cleves—the gardens draw the larger landscape into their magnetic field, we still know how to distinguish between them. What Chinese gardeners term "borrowed landscape" or what Alexander Pope was to urge for the English garden—that it "call[s] in the country"[33]—by no means obscures a sense of boundary, a sense of difference between gardens and territory beyond; indeed, it helps in appreciating that difference.

The forms that garden enclosure can take are limited, but our experience of it can vary considerably, not least as a result of the size of a site. And like that other essential element of garden experience, the art:nature ratio, the extremes of enclosure/openness, by isolating one feature at the expense of the other, serve to reaffirm their necessary and habitual dialogue. A cloister garden allows no views of the surrounding world—it

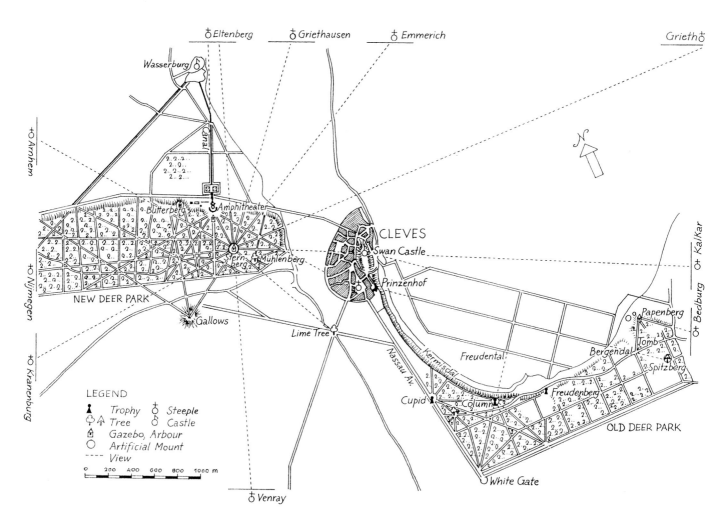

FIGURE 11. Plan of the Cleves garden landscape. By kind permission of Wilhelm Diedenhofens and Dumbarton Oaks Studies in Landscape Architecture.

privileges only the eloquent and symbolic sky—yet its studied enclosure affirms by denying the world elsewhere. Conversely, an apparently boundary-less English landscape garden usually recalls us to the garden's habitual enclosure, to the notional center of the open spaces. This is why so many painted representations of landscaped parks, reversing the Baroque view outward from the mansion and its regular garden spaces toward a distant wilderness (see Figures 19–21), turn and look back toward the mansion, the still point of the park's turning world (see Figures 24, 26).

The history of the English landscape garden, indeed, suggests that there were many who could not live without a more tangible sense of boundary. This perhaps explains certain generally unremarked aspects of the English landscape garden history—the relative brevity of the vogue for the best work of Capability Brown as well as its limited territorial reach;[34] the awful inepti-

FIGURE 12. C. Elandts, etched view of the Sternberg in the New Deer Park, Cleves, 1670. Leiden, Universiteits-biblioteek, Collectie Bodel Nijenhuis.

tude of lesser artists who aped him and yet could not imply the enclosure/openness dialectic without which the open spaces made little sense; and the closed forms into which the reaction against the Brownian style returned the garden.

V

Actual or implied enclosure may exist to keep things in or keep things out. A part of Virginia known as Burke's Garden, a circular basin of nearly forty square miles (20,000 acres) rimmed entirely by one continuous mountain, apparently derived its name from the sprouting of a potato garden from peelings left over by the first party of explorers:[35] but for this strange topographical feature, which first excluded white men and now preserves within it, even if precariously, a small agrarian society, the name and idea of a garden

FIGURE 13. *The Emperor Babur Laying Out a Garden at Kabul*, c. 1600, Victoria and Albert Museum, London.

FIGURE 14. Glimpses of gardens, Venice, 1985.

are wholly apt even if Burke's Garden only encloses an agricultural community. From natural to "magical walls": the anthropologist Bronislaw Malinowski has written of Trobriander peasants who protect their yam gardens with coral fences that "gleam like gold among the green of the new growth."[36]

The designed pleasure garden works more deliberately than either of these examples, as Brown knew perfectly well, to exclude accidents and to eliminate the contingencies and happenstance of the organic and inorganic world. However, even these may be involved in the design and thereby become part of its art, like the rocks chosen in the wild for setting up in Chinese or Japanese gardens or the inclusion of some topographical feature within the design of a site.

Gardens also convey to the "insider"—be they resident or visitor—that various hazards are kept outside; they also represent unattainable desires to the outsider who cannot gain admission. Those West London squares, into whose gardens only the surrounding inhabitants may enter by key, are a prime example of this sense of how a garden's fence excludes as well as incorporates (versus those other garden squares, say, in Bloomsbury, which are now public arenas). Gardens in the city of Venice, inaccessible and often all but unnoticed behind high walls (Figure 14), are for most people similarly unattainable zones, as Aschenbach realizes in Thomas Mann's *Death in Venice*: "They passed little gardens high up the crumbling wall, hung with clustering white and purple flowers that sent down an odour of almonds."[37] Gardens suggest seclusion, privacy, and safety (ironically for Aschenbach, who dies after eating strawberries from the gardens of Venice). Garden visitors, if they are lucky, temporarily participate in these privileges, vicariously enjoying a protection from annoyance and harm that is a garden's special gift (hence the appalling violation of its space, mythically, by the serpent of Eden, or horticulturally by pests and unwanted animals).

All this may also be true of a building, but then other elements of the idea and effect of boundary and what it encloses come into play with architecture. Architecture does not achieve either so strongly or so readily what is one of a garden's most important and characteristic forms of exclusion, reference to a world beyond its own confines.[38] Garden enclosures both define their spaces and appeal across boundaries—by way of representation, imitation, and allusion—to a world dispersed elsewhere. Enclosure, it has been rightly observed, "appeals to our imagination as well as to our senses."[39]

Isamu Noguchi has frequently used his sculpture/gardens to allude to territory beyond their own immediate space and scope. In 1933, there was his unexecuted *Monument to the Plough*, conceived as a plough for erection on the Great Plains, an early essay in putting a jar upon a hillside and "enclosing" the surrounding territory anew in the imagination.[40] However, Noguchi has also worked, more predictably, with actual enclosures: the symbolic forms in the marble courtyard of the Beinecke Library at Yale (Figure 15) gesture to large cosmic forces, while "A California Scenario" (1982) at Costa Mesa in Southern California invokes regional references. Here, in the quadrangular space between an L-shaped parking garage and two green glass, high-rise bank buildings, are dotted forms that provide the "scenario" for this piazza or plaza. They all refer to typically Californian topography—desert, forests, watercourses, mountains—and to contemporary ecological concerns that are sometimes thought to be most domi-

nant in the western United States. A fountain, thick with plushing water shaped as a cylinder atop a hemisphere with an anemonometer, is the Energy Fountain. A large, flat pyramid is named Water Use; a long, flat granite block on a grassy hillock is called Land Use (with maybe some satiric play in its coffinlike shape, just as the Energy Fountain manifests a supreme excess). A pile of brown rocks is the Spirit of the Lima Bean, a pile of earth with cacti, the Desert Land. A water chute feeds into a channel that meanders across the sandstone plateau of the piazza, mimicking valued river courses through arid land. There is a mound with tall grass and flowers around which a horseshoe-shaped path takes the stroller to a bench on its summit (Figure 16): this is the Forest Walk.[41]

The wit and contrivance of it all may not suit every taste, though the mockery and the spirited elaboration of the average American downtown urban vacuum is undeniable; but this attempt to ensure that a confined public enclosure speaks of everything that is beyond the glass walls of the banks and the blank walls of the parking garage is an extreme example of how a garden at its most vital will always refer beyond its enclosure.[42] It is this outward reference and gesture from within gardens that sustains their or, more precisely, their users' frequent invocations of mythic places beyond human realization: locations in Eden, Arcadia, Elysium, Tempe, Paradise,[43] even—for workers of Costa Mesa—the *idea* of California.

This chapter began with the etymological evidence of words for garden and for other enclosed structures related to gardens. It has brought us back and in more detail to a fundamental aspect of place-making at its most concentrated, namely, the scope and the extent of its disposition. For it is not just the enclosure of the garden that distinguishes it from, say, fields or buildings, but the organization of those interior spaces by which you know that you are in a garden. It was this perception which elicited one of the first moments of Renaissance garden theory, which we must now explore.

FIGURE 15. Isamu Noguchi, courtyard of the Beinecke Library,
Yale University (photograph: Marc Treib).

FIGURE 16. Isamu Noguchi, *California Scenario*, showing hill,
Lima Bean, and "river" (photograph: Marc Treib).

CHAPTER 3

The Idea of a Garden and the Three Natures

L'industria d'un accorto giardiniero, che incorporando l'arte con la natura fa che d'amendue ne riesce una terza natura.
— Bartolomeo Taegio

It is only the scholar who understands why the raw wilderness gives definition and meaning to the human enterprise.
— Aldo Leopold

I

Long before any complete treatise was devoted to the art of making pleasure gardens, their increasingly conspicuous place in sixteenth-century life attracted the attention of commentators. Some addressed largely practical concerns, like Agostino Gallo in his books on agriculture, or the authors of *La Maison rustique*. Gallo discourses largely on the management of a country estate, but also focuses on the siting of a garden within that estate, on its soils, its planting (especially fruit trees), and the ornamentation of orchards and gardens. Charles Estienne and Jean Liebault, the French text of whose *Maison rustique* was published in 1564, are also concerned with the whole gamut of life and work in the countryside; but they, too, take time to discuss the compartments and decoration of *parterre* gardens adjacent to the farmhouse with their knots, *treillage*, and *berceaux*.

Other writers at about the same time as Gallo, Estienne and Liebault tried to come to terms conceptually with this new art form. Their theoretical concerns mirrored a turn from horticultural efficiency to ideas of the garden as luxurious display and consumption.[1] In France, for example, Bernard Palissy, a ceramics artist, garden designer, and Protestant polemicist,[2] set out his recipe for a delectable garden that combined instructions for its design and layout with arguments for its conceptual purpose; he imagined his intricate garden as a glorification of God's creation, an understanding of which by a Protestant craftsman like himself was enshrined in the design.

But it is a couple of Italian humanists who offered one of the most interesting conceptual handles on garden art. Independently of each other, or so it seems, Bartolomeo Taegio and Jacopo Bonfadio coined the same term for gardens: a "third nature."[3] In offering this seemingly neologistic formulation they were drawn to that central feature of garden art characterized in the previous chapter as a special combination of nature and culture. Taegio was writing in his treatise on *La Villa*, published in Milan in 1559, while Bonfadio was crafting an epistle to a fellow humanist in August 1541;[4] the latter is the more interesting because it is the most explicit text for our purposes.

Describing his country retreat on Lake Garda to a friend left behind in the city, Bonfadio uses a highly self-conscious and rhetorical style — a medley of hyperbole and literary allusions, some of which are couched in at least graphic hints (of fabulous giants, mythical persons, pastoral dance). But its most sophisticated ploy is to emulate the ekphrastic mode of the famous letter of Pliny the Younger,[5] describing to a friend in similar circumstances his country seat in Tuscany; not the least part of this conceit, perhaps, is that Bonfadio's correspondent was himself named Plinio Tomacello.

From his opening ekphrastic promise ("I shall describe to you") Bonfadio seeks to emphasize what is to be seen. His ill humor is cured "instantly simply by the sight of this lake and this shore," he writes. "Here you will see an open sky, bright and clear, and with a living splendour that, as if smiling, invites us to be cheerful." But—as there—what is seen, the fleeting changes of light, as well as the smells, are only the occasion or promise of something unseen and permanent ("eternal light, infinite peace"). In a crucial acknowledgment of the movement from visual to verbal/conceptual and back, Bonfadio writes, "Many things can be seen there that require a diligent eye and much consideration. Thus it happens that no matter how often a man returns there, he finds new marvels and new pleasures." The very process of considering or theorizing about what he sees is thus linked to the continuing stimulus of the site/sight itself.[6] Not surprisingly, one rhetorical strategy of the letter is to claim—in that slippage from material thing to mental idea that lies at the heart of landscape experience—that his words are inadequate and that the scenery must be visualized by his friend. But the imagination of Plinio Tomacello, as that of Bonfadio himself, is sustained by an array of literary allusions to Aristotle, Catullus, Lucretius, and Virgil as well as to a series of images that have literary origins themselves—"Venus in her favourite dress, Zephyr accompanied her, and her mother Flora goes about distributing flowers and life-giving scents."

It is two-thirds of the way through his epistle that Bonfadio, turning his glance toward the lake shore and hillsides, first specifically notices gardens. By way of both hyperbole ("fruitful, happy, and blessed") and the invocation of classical precedent ("those [gardens] of the Hesperides and those of Alcinous and Adonis"), he arrives at local examples:

> Per li giardini . . . la industria de' paesani ha fatto tanto, che la natura incorporata con l'arte è fatta artefice, e connaturale de l'arte, e d'amendue è fatta una terza natura, a cui non saperei dar nome. (p. 96)

> For in the gardens . . . the industry of the local people has been such that nature incorporated with art is made an artificer and naturally equal with art, and from them both together is made a third nature, which I would not know how to name.

This is, I believe, along with a virtually identical formulation by Bartolomeo Taegio quoted as an epigraph to this chapter,[7] a hugely important passage. Though Bonfadio's final remark seems casual and the phrase *terza natura* is apparently thrown out without much thought, I doubt whether anything in this epistle is unstudied; in particular, "third nature" is emphatically neologistic. After he has cited so many classical authorities, it is at the very least an oddity to hear Bonfadio claiming to be baffled or nonplussed. In fact, it is very doubtful that he is floundering on his own: he alludes—I believe—to a remark of the Roman writer Cicero in the treatise *De natura deorum*, a well-known classical text that circulated in at least a dozen manuscripts and had already been printed four times in the years leading up to these two occasions in which the phrase *terza natura* was coined by Bonfadio and later by Taegio.[8]

Cicero, in describing landscape, writes of what he calls a second nature: "We sow corn, we plant trees, we fertilize the soil by irrigation, we dam the rivers and direct them where we want. In short, by means of our hands we try to create as it were a second nature within the natural world." This second nature is what today we would call the cultural landscape: agriculture, urban developments, roads, bridges, ports, and other infrastructures. Cicero uses the phrase *alteram naturam*, an alternative nature, or second of two; his etymology therefore implies that there is also a first nature. This is "the natural world" to which he refers at the end of the passage quoted above and "within" which his second is created; for the Cicero of *De natura deorum* this primal nature is both the raw materials of human industry and the territory of the gods.[9]

If I am right about Bonfadio's, and presumably Taegio's, allusion to Cicero, theirs are far less casual maneuvers than appear at first sight: they are placing the new art of gardens not only within an obligatory mythological framework but also within classical traditions of cultural history and explanation.[10] Gardens now take their place as a third nature in a scale or hierarchy of human intervention into the physical world: gardens become more sophisticated, more deliberate, and more complex in their mixture of culture and nature than agricultural land, which is a large part of Cicero's "second nature." By implication, the first nature becomes for Bonfadio the territory of unmediated nature, what today we might (provisionally and awkwardly) call wilderness.[11]

Bonfadio, indeed, reads the whole landscape, with its gardens, as exactly this trio of natures.[12] Following his reference to gardens as a third nature, he returns to what Cicero would have labeled the second, the world of citrus and olive groves, orchards and "green pastures," and then to their "enemy" or "opposite"—the "tall, arduous, steep, sloping, and menacing mountains" that surround the Italian lakes to their north. This mountainous zone of first nature may seem, in Bonfadio's rhetoric, to be culturally absorbed into what we would now term a sublime experience[13]—"horrifying the observer, with caves, caverns, and cruel cliffs, shelter to strange animals and hermits," its summits threatened by "fiery flashes and fogs in the shape of giants." But the force and meaning of this mountainous zone in Bonfadio's survey of the landscape is its lack of any physical reworking by the cultural forces that organize agriculture, human habitations, and gardens in the countryside below.

Bonfadio is probably less interested than some other *cinquecento* writers in gardens for their own sake; but his concern for the territory as a whole is precisely what is useful to us. Modern garden and landscape architectural writings from roughly the mid-eighteenth century

to the present have generally neglected this view of gardens as part of a larger landscape; as a result we tend to miss the importance of setting and understanding the garden in a context that is at once topographical and conceptual.[14] Bonfadio's intuition of the physical and conceptual place of garden art springs jointly from his description of its topographical location and from his classical reading—a maneuver that interchanges horticultural and agrarian practice with theory, visual with verbal. And in a final rhetorical coda, Bonfadio's letter sees the three natures that he has posited as "representing" in miniature the history of human development—from the "wild, hard people [who still live in the mountains, who are] . . . made as much of stone and oak as of man, and who live on chestnuts the greater part of the year," down to the "civilized people, gentlemen and *signori* who live on the shore." This history lesson constitutes the final claim for the "nobility and perfection" of his region, which he has been justifying to his friend back in the city.

II

The idea of a series of interventions in the landscape, diminishing or accelerating according to your point of view, implied by the concept of a "third nature," is variously manifest during the Renaissance, but it becomes especially palpable a century or so after Bonfadio and Taegio. Its hierarchical implications are apparent, for example, whenever we encounter the application of perspective to garden design or to the experience of designed landscapes. Though there are earlier examples of the control of territory through spatial vision,[15] it became de rigueur for the Renaissance and post-Renaissance garden to be established along and on either side of a sightline that began in the center of the mansion associated with the garden. Before this, medieval gardens would have been established in any location that the exigencies of defense or other building and land use directed (Figure 17). But the Renaissance garden saw the establishment of axial

FIGURE 17. Bernardo Martorell, detail of *St. George Killing the Dragon*, tempera on panel, late 1420s. Art Institute of Chicago. Gift of Mrs. Richard E. Damielson and Mrs. Chauncey McCormick.

lines of sight leading from the geometry of the central palace or villa and through gardens where the regular forms associated with architecture and its decoration were applied (Figure 18). Eventually this line would be extended outward, past perhaps less clearly formalized spaces of groves, orchards, or "wildernesses," into agricultural land and even into relatively untouched countryside where the axis would usually discover its other termination in some distinctive feature of the topography (see Figure 19). In this way, as we shall see, the garden's order and harmony were experienced at a strong focal point near the house, at one end of a scale of human control of the natural world, the other end of which might be wild territory beyond even agrarian intervention.

It must be emphasized that the arithmetic of "three natures" is symbolic, not literal and certainly not prescriptive, nor does it necessarily privilege the third over the other two natures. It is meant to indicate—after the manner of Taegio and Bonfadio—that a territory can be viewed in the light of how it has or has not been treated in space and in time. Historically it may mean the gradual colonization and elaboration of spaces for dwelling. But this temporal process also manifests itself spatially on the ground, which can be zoned in different ways and with diminishing artistry, usually as it recedes from the building. On certain sites these "three" zones

FIGURE 18. Giusto Utens, *The Medici Villa of Castello*, tempera on canvas, 1559. Museo Firenze Com'era.

may be abbreviated or extended, according to the financial and topographical exigencies of their location; their sequence on the ground may also be "scrambled," for similar reasons. But distinct, palpable, and meaningful distinctions, declensions or gradations of intervention, are clear in virtually every instance. It is this phenomenon, not necessarily a particular number of zones in the landscape, which the idea of "three natures" codifies.

The seventeenth century was particularly engaged in understanding how landscape was experienced. Among writers, draftsmen, and especially professionals engaged with the land (geographers, cartographers, military en-

gineers), the fascination with distance becomes marked at this time. And, as Thierry Mariage has demonstrated, this fuels a corresponding concern to understand and name its component spaces: thus captions to Claude de Chastillon's engravings in the *Topographie Française* distinguish between *paysage prochain* (nearby land), *paysage contingent* (contingent or adjacent land), and *paysage circonvoisin* (the land that surrounds the other types).[16]

This organization or perception of space became most conspicuous around the year 1700 in the vogue throughout Europe for engraved views of country seats.[17] These Baroque representations are the most eloquent testimony to the idea of three natures (Figures 19–21). Different treatments of territory are usually

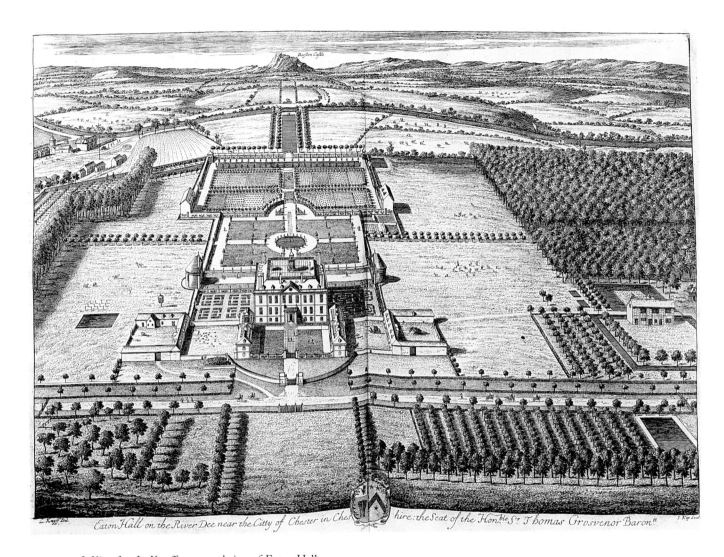

Eaton Hall on the River Dee near the Citty of Chester in Ches——hire: the Seat of the Hon.ble S.r Thomas Grosvenor Baron.tt

FIGURE 19. J. Kip after L. Knyff, engraved view of Eaton Hall, near Chester, from *Nouveau Theatre de la Grande Bretagne*, London, 1724–28. Dumbarton Oaks Research Library and Collections.

FIGURE 20. An engraved view of a "princely seat" from Matthias Diesel, *Erlustierende Augenweide*, Augsburg, 1717–23. Dumbarton Oaks Research Library and Collections.

drawn into a conceptual program by the simple device of a strong axial line that bisects the whole landscape — a central path through the parterre, then tree-lined avenues across agricultural land, often aligned upon some conspicuous feature in the far distance. (Occasionally, as in Figure 21, the juxtaposition of zones is eloquent enough without the axial sightline.)

Many writers concentrated on the correct implementation of this axis on the ground. In general terms, as with Leonard Meager, the garden needed to be sited where it would yield "Prospect from your House";[18] then, it was essential not to curtail that prospect by poorly scaled sightlines — so Moses Cook demanded, "Do not . . . vail a pleasant Prospect (as too many doe) by making the walkes too narrow."[19] That the axis existed for reasons beyond itself — for more than the pleasure of drawing a straight line across the land — is clear from much contemporary commentary, which

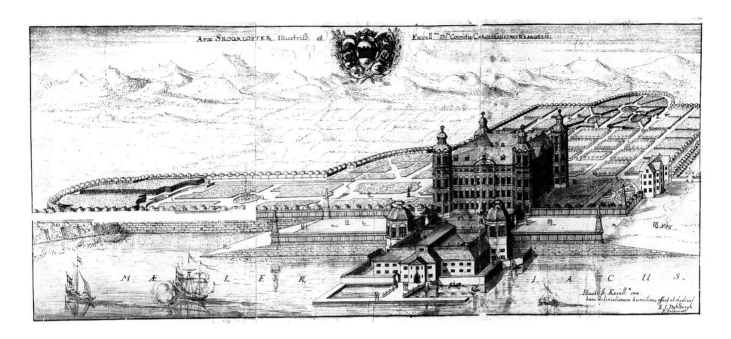

FIGURE 21. Count Erik de Dahlbergh, drawing of Skogkoster,
early eighteenth century. National Museum, Stockholm.

explored the techniques of its establishment: Evelyn's
Sylva insisted that avenues not "terminate abruptly,"
while his "Elysium Britannicum" required a garden
walk to be "much protracted by Arte"—presumably by
deliberate planting or even by *trompe-l'oeil* paintings
(see Figure 118).[20] Stephen Switzer explained the role
of these axes in 1718 as relating parts to whole; they
connected the "beauty and Magnificence of the Garden" to the whole estate.[21] Above all, the axis enforced
a perspective—both a line of sight and an organization of things within that sight for purposes of better
understanding: in his *Elements of Architecture* (1624) Sir
Henry Wotton made one of his precepts for architecture (and by implication landscape architecture) what
he called "optical": "Such I meane as concerne the
Properties of a well chosen Prospect: which I will call
the Royaltie of Sight. . . . There is Lordship likewise
of the Eye (as of the feet) which being a raunging and

Imperrious, and (I might say) an usurping Sense; can
indure no narrow circumscription; but must be fedde,
both with extent and varietie." He further notes that
this visual mastery of a landscape cannot work with
vast and indefinite views.[22] On the other hand, a significant extent is needed for us to appreciate the variety
of forms included therein.

The axis, then, functioned both as a physical feature across the land and as a sign of a more conceptual
perspective. This is expressed clearly if rudimentarily
in the frontispiece to the Abbé Pierre Le Lorrain de
Vallemont's *Curiositez de la Nature et de l'Art* (*Curiosities of Art and Nature in Husbandry and Gardening*)
(Figure 22), a popular book that was issued in Paris
in 1705, with five subsequent French editions as well
as Spanish and English translations. What catches our
eye first is a regular garden, its main feature a central fountain. This "third nature" is succeeded by agricultural fields, again designated with the simple signs
that recall Cicero's second nature—a man plowing and
another scattering seed. Further away the view is termi-

FIGURE 22. Frontispiece, *Curiositez de la nature et de l'art* by l'Abbé de Vallemont, Paris, 1705.

nated with a lumpish hillside from the bottom of which gushes a natural spring. In the other direction—back toward the viewer—the sequence is similar: first the ordered garden, then a grove of trees regularly planted (we see only their tops), then the waste ground on which sit two women.

It is under their aegis that this whole scene is presented to us. Their roles are announced by labels on the ground in front of each: they stand for Art (including what we would now call Science and Technology) and Nature. Their occupation of a space of rough ground above and in front of the garden answers in some fashion to the Muses who, we now recognize, form the group upon the distant hillside. There is more to this rather naive, almost diagrammatic image (as we shall see in the next chapter); but here it is important simply to register that the frontispiece appeals clearly to some notion of a landscape divided into territories in each of which the collaborations of the two presiding figures of Art and Nature will be different.

By the end of the seventeenth century, this perspectival structuring of our vision of the natural world and man's control over it had clearly become a commonplace. And it went along with a related understanding of how such control could be exercised in different intensities and modes. Both the topic of physical layout and its related concepts are invoked by Anthony Ashley Cooper, the third Earl of Shaftesbury, in his philosophical treatise, *The Moralists*. As a frontispiece to the second edition of his *Characteristics* (1714), to which *The Moralists* had been added, was attached an engraving by Simon Gribelin after portraits of the author by John Closterman, but the original backgrounds of those earlier paintings have been replaced by a glimpsed vista down a garden out into wooded countryside (Figure 23). As David Leatherbarrow has shown, this image of a garden, where control or geometry diminishes as we move further away from the arcade where Shaftesbury is standing, seems to be offered as a gloss upon one of Shaftesbury's essential philosophical remarks—

FIGURE 23. Detail of the background of a portrait of the Earl of Shaftesbury, engraved by S. Gribelin after John Closterman, from Shaftesbury's *Characteristics*, 2nd ed., 1714.

that nature's inherent perfections or characters can be learned by regarding them first in the artificial world of a garden where man has cultivated the nascent taxonomy of natural forms.[23] What Shaftesbury calls the "several orders . . . into which it is endeavoured to reduce the natural views" are instituted so that the person "who studies and breaks through the shell" or exteriority of the world will "see some way into the kernel" and appreciate the "genuine order" of the natural world.[24]

Shaftesbury's point could be made so succinctly at that time because in so many contemporary gardens, as we have seen, the sight was guided down a central vista that bisected and yet linked in sequence different kinds of human management of grounds. Indeed, Shaftesbury instructed his own gardeners in precisely these terms to organize sightlines from within the ordered garden out into the fields and toward ancient trees that nobody had trimmed: "Only for yᵉ guiding of yᵉ Eye up that Hill and so to yᵉ end of yᵉ reset Fields where yᵉ great old Yew Tree stands."[25]

III

Now this diagrammatic world of three natures would be less significant for a theory of gardens if its scope and influence were historically limited. But it wasn't. Its significance was certainly highlighted by the fashion for bird's-eye views in the seventeenth century, where visually distinct zones are rendered so palpably; and this format for imaging the countryside did lose favor during the eighteenth century. Yet even as painters lowered their viewpoints (often to ground level),[26] in response partly to new attitudes toward the natural world and partly to new design moves on the ground, what is here termed "the idea of the three natures" tenaciously survived the cycles of fashion. This suggests the enduring need for some conceptual formulation of landscape experience: this was a dual concept—gardens were best understood in relation to the larger landscape and, when these zones became less dis-

tinct or even overlapped, a varied treatment and use of terrain were still seen as essential to designed space. We may encounter these concepts or assumptions at work throughout the eighteenth century: thus the approach to Bateman's Grove House in the 1750s took visitors through a farm, down a pergola tunnel that skirted a meadow, where they glimpsed the first flower garden in a temple grove; or Walpole, when visiting Redlynch in 1762, responded to its gardens in relation to the surrounding agricultural land.[27]

New design ideas certainly modified the concept of a series of differentiated natures—their sequence, for instance, seemed less crucial than their presence. Similarly, of course, design developments were themselves inaugurated as a result of fresh philosophical inquiries into human relationships with nature. These shifts have been the basis of oft-repeated clichés in landscape architectural history that charts a steady movement toward the "natural." But some aspects of this narrative have gradually been challenged, and it now needs to be revisited. Such reexamination must bypass the sterile stylistic dualisms of "formal" and "informal," "ancient" and "modern," and "French and English"[28] in order to isolate more clearly the topics that guided and may continue to guide landscape architecture.

After the heyday of the Baroque country house views, the axis became less fashionable and was often eliminated or muted; furthermore, in the work of Capability Brown, green sward could be swept right up to the walls of the mansion (Figure 24), and with its arrival all sense or imagery of gradation of effect across the landscape could be lost. But, as Mark Laird has shown,[29] our sense of the ubiquity of this design formula—lawn, groves, and clumps—must be thoroughly revised; the immediacies and particularities of the flower garden and shrubbery were maintained, even if now scattered through the grounds rather than set out as the first segment of a scaled artifice. In other words, visual formulations of the idea of three natures changed, sometimes radically, but its conceptual basis survived intact.

To start with, the mode of landscaping associated

FIGURE 24. Wilson after Griffith, engraved view of Llanerch, late eighteenth century. National Library of Wales.

with Capability Brown did not, as has long been the accepted orthodoxy, eliminate all the older layouts in England. While many landowners opted for the fashionable Brownian sweep of green sward right up to the walls of their mansions, as many others continued to gaze out over some sector of carefully organized gardenscape near the house, then across orchards, fields, and other agricultural land (some of it probably newly en-

closed) toward a "first nature" of unmediated scope.[30] The Reverend William Hanbury presumably addressed such landowners in his 1770 book, *A Complete Body of Planting and Gardening*: the "eye," he argued, "must be carried on to a distance," and nothing should block these distant prospects. He advised as to "where the pleasure-ground is to cease, and the pasture is to commence" (being also concerned that "the lawn . . . must always be proportioned to the extent of the ground"); while in managing the transitions within the grounds, he was particularly concerned that among the sequence

FIGURE 25. William Tomkins, *The Elysian Garden at Audley End*, 1788 (photograph: Department of the Environment, London).

of plantations the "wilderness" (in this case, the garden feature so called) should "have first place."[31]

Uvedale Price, not usually considered one of Brown's most enthusiastic supporters, actually credited him with extending the scale of natures about the house, even if he neglected its immediate surroundings: "Mr. Brown has been most successful in what may properly be called the garden, though not in that part of it which is nearest the house. The old improvers went abruptly from the formal garden to the grounds, or park; but the modern pleasure garden with its shrubs and exotics [Figure 25] would form a very just and easy gradation from architectural ornaments, to the natural woods, thickets and pastures."[32] Furthermore, the duration of the Brownian vogue, understood as a blanket of green sward right up to the house, was remarkably brief; probably the shortest vogue for any one style in the history of landscape architecture was effectively terminated by a return to sequences of differently zoned layouts in the early nineteenth century.

Even Thomas Whately, the influential author of an authoritative exposition of the new landscaping, *Observations on Modern Gardening* (1770), who showed a conventional hostility toward artifice and regularity at the start of his work, nevertheless still addressed the "whole range of nature from parterre to the forest."[33] And in discussing how the landscaped site might be distinguished from surrounding territory, as we have seen a fundamental aspect of garden experience, Whately also argued that "the marks of distinction must be borrowed from a garden . . . as evidence of the domaine."[34] And in his specific analyses of actual sites he repeatedly made clear that the "excellencies both of a park and of a garden are thus happily blended at Hagley," or that "the park and the gardens at Painshill . . . mutually contribute to the beauty of the several landskips," in part because around the house there were a parterre, orangerie, and flowers.[35]

The theoretical arguments used against the modish Brownian designs suggest the continuing desirability of a landscape that featured what Whately (even) found valuable in this "whole range of nature." William Chambers protested the similarity of Brown's work to "common fields," disparaging a uniformity of effects. And however novel were Chambers's own proposals in the "Chinese" taste, he was perfectly conventional in his division of landscape into three different modes—pleasing, enchanted, and sublime—which corresponded to the long-established triad of three natures that were, in his case, pleasing fields, enchanted gardens, and wild landscapes.[36]

In *The Tory View of Landscape*, Nigel Everett shows how objections to Brownian improvements were based on appeals to "some degree of equilibrium in the landscape, a balance of both scale and equity" (p. 82). This was especially pronounced in the picturesque reaction at the end of the eighteenth century.[37] A common assumption about the picturesque is that it sought to replace bare Brownian green sward with "one huge picturesque forest," a misconception founded largely on the evidential weight given to the two engravings of such alternatives by Thomas Hearne annexed to Richard Payne Knight's 1794 poem, *The Landscape*.[38] But as Knight tried to explain in its second edition a year later, he was more concerned with a landscape composed

of different zones that stretched from human haunts through "accidental mixtures of meadows, woods, pastures, and corn fields" to "shaggy hills . . . left to rude neglect." Though he may have been skeptical about old-fashioned versions of third nature, with their "despotic" topiary, Knight noted that they had at least not invaded the "open grounds of nature"; those gardens had, so to speak, known their place in the ensemble of a country estate. And William Gilpin, in his *Three Essays* of 1792, continued to identify three zones of landscape, even if their order was, like Chambers's, somewhat skewed: "the park, the forest, or the field."[39] And the landscape gardener Repton, caught up and swayed by the arguments of the picturesque theorists, came increasingly to emphasize zoned landscapes in his designs. His last publication, *Fragments on the Theory and Practice of Landscape Gardening* (1816), was praised by the *Quarterly Review* precisely for its grasp of this observance of scale and variety: "The very name, the *English garden*, suggests ideas of cheerfulness and comfort unknown in every other country. Indeed the heart-enlivening prospect, over the pleasure ground, the park, the woods and the well tenanted farms surrounding the country residence of an English gentleman, gives a favourable impression of the spirit of freedom and independence of its possessor."[40]

As that quotation implies, design was intimately linked with larger social issues. The idea of a varied scenery was as likely to be advanced in writings on social and moral matters as in treatises that focused specifically on matters of shrubbery design. Uvedale Price, another picturesque commentator, attacked Brown for what the latter had called his "levelling Business"; it was a term fraught with political and social implications dating back to the seventeenth-century Levellers. Its use by Brown to convey his work at eliminating the different zones of older estates could not escape Price's attack on the civil and moral consequences of the repression of different natures.[41]

Those who championed a scale of effects were numerous, and they were not just landscape designers or

FIGURE 26. Anonymous, watercolor of an unidentified house, The British Museum, London (Add MS 5671, 26 top).

theorists; their variety suggests that the motives were more than simply formal. Thomas Gisborne, author of *Enquiry into the Duties of Men in the Higher and Middle Classes* (1794) and the poem *Walks in a Forest* (1794-96), consistently emphasized the immediate garden around the house and its extension, not into the Brownian parkland but into farmed land, after which came "the wilds" that were not subjected to "needless interference."[42] A similar emphasis on the harmony of well-maintained gardens diffused throughout the "whole domain" can be found in Wordsworth's *The Excursion* (1814).[43] William Cobbett's preference for mixed landscapes found room for gardens, fields, and wild places ("coppices, trees, corn-fields, meadows . . . gardens, flowers, neat houses").[44] More metaphorically, in S. T. Coleridge's "The Statesman's Manual" (1816) the skills honed by the skillful gardener extend across all zones of the estate.[45]

Visual representations of country houses in the late eighteenth century and early nineteenth century radically alter the format of the Baroque bird's-eye view engravings. The mansions depicted have often been set down modishly in wholly "natural" landscapes, green

FIGURE 27. Michael Angelo Rooker, *Jennings Park*, oil on canvas, 1776. Leger Gallery, London (photograph: Prudence Cuming Associates, Ltd.).

to the very door (Figure 26). Evidence already cited may lead us to be skeptical of the actual extent of such new designs; commissioned portraits of country estates may have boasted its owner's hopes and ambitions rather than any actual layout. But it is also worth noting that since the viewpoint of some of these house portraits is now lower and gives less opportunity for sightings across a variety of terrain, we cannot always be sure whether such features did not still survive on the ground. Indeed, some country house portraits, carefully scrutinized, provide just such evidence. Michael Angelo Rooker's painting of Jennings Park (1776), for instance, appears to show off the modish grass up to the walls of the house; but, more closely inspected, it also reveals immediately around the building slight but sufficient tokens of the third nature—a gazebo, shaded by trees, an urn on the sloping lawn beside the stable yard, and a walled garden in full view of the users of the gazebo (Figure 27). And even the various images produced of Hafod, that quintessential picturesque property in Wales, reveal—though not in the diagrammatic sequence of Baroque layouts—a mixed triadic vocabu-

FIGURE 28. John "Warwick" Smith, *Hafod*, watercolor, 1795.
National Library of Wales.

lary of platform for the Gothick mansion, new agricultural land, and the expected wildness (Figures 28, 29).

But enough instances continue to occur of houses set
conventionally within a distinct series of zones to suggest that the idea of "three natures" was not entirely
neglected. J. M. W. Turner's view from a terrace of a
villa at Niton (Figure 30), significantly painted after
sketches by the garden's owner, reaffirms a tripartite
view of the natural world: from the orderly and archi-

tectural space of the terrace, with its flower border, col-
umns, and urns, we look down some invisible slope to
a grove where what seems to be a fountain spurts into
the air, and we then extend our gaze over wilder coastal
scenery.

IV

The concept or symbolic arithmetic of "three
natures" is useful above all for its dual reminder that
the interventions of landscape architecture are distinct
from other territory and that one mode of intervention
is not necessarily privileged over another. The English

FIGURE 29. Thomas Jones
of Pencerrig, pencil view in
the grounds of Hafod, 1786.
Private collection, courtesy
the Hafod Trust.

landscape garden and its enthusiastic proponents and historians largely lost sight of that essential relativism, which the previous generation of gardenists had celebrated.[46] In fact, the insistence is not wholly lost among more practically minded persons in the later eighteenth century. Hanbury in 1770 insists on "variety of situations" that in their turn necessitate "as many different plans";[47] an engraved plan of Leyton Grange in Essex also suggests an appreciation of this various treatment of ground (Figure 31). By the early nineteenth century, a gradated scale of interventions had been reinstituted, often for reasons that went far beyond design fashion:

FIGURE 30. J. M. W. Turner, *View from Niton, Isle of Wight*, oil on canvas, 1826. Museum of Fine Arts, Boston.

the *Gardener's Magazine* urged, "We must engraft upon our own romantic harshnesses something that will accord better with the equipment of the interior of our houses, something like furniture and ornament, and not leap from our windows into jungles, and steppes, and wildernesses, where the lion and panther would be more at home than the 'lady with her silken sheen.'" [48]

Here, I must briefly anticipate an argument of the next chapter, that landscape architecture represents the other zones of nature. We must not only understand gardens as zones of what is being termed third nature and therefore as being juxtaposed to other kinds and levels of intervention. We must also learn to see how gardens from all periods represent within their own area that scale of natures.

A clear example occurs at Wilton House in the mid-seventeenth century (Figure 32): here the elaborate parterre of embroidered beds and shaped trees is closest to the house (where the artist stands). Beyond are two further and distinct zones: one, an amphitheatrical space surrounded by carefully spaced trees and bracketed by two elaborate, architecturally shaped arbors; another, composed of dense groves of trees and simple tunnel arbors, that is cut through by a small river that seems to follow its natural, slightly meandering course. If we curb our modern instinct to lump all of this into one contrived whole and instead register three distinctly different treatments of space, we shall appreciate that the seventeenth century was aware of how there existed different modes or "performances" of cultural control over natural materials. The Wilton garden, however, does not offer these zones in a sequence—3, 2, 1. That would demonstrate a strict declension; rather, given what is clearly a design decision to incorporate the river in its "natural" course through the middle of the garden, the zones have been reordered as 3, 1, 2. This suggests that different handling of natural materials was a recognized part of landscape experience and landscape architectural practice; it also confirms (what has already been suggested) that topographical exigencies could readily be accommodated without losing sight of the essential concept.

And this notion—that the garden could represent versions of a tripartite nature within its own articulation of the third one—is not lost, as might be expected, after the Baroque period. For example, designs by Frederick Law Olmsted and Calvert Vaux for both Central Park (Figure 33) and Prospect Park in Brooklyn include within the overall designed landscape the same scale of "natures" that were laid out at Wilton. Here again they are not in sequence, but nonetheless clearly

differentiated (regular, pastoral, wild).[49] Thus gardens can be both exemplifications of a third nature as well as capable and sometimes explicitly concerned to display all of these zones.

There are considerable advantages in continuing to affirm the idea of a garden, of any piece of landscape architecture, as being one of several available "natures," even when the prospects into differentiated territories, upon which the idea of the three natures was based around 1700, are virtually unobtainable on modern landscape architectural sites. To retain this habit of thinking has many advantages: it actively discourages the belief that nature is normative rather than culturally constructed, it allows place-making to be seen as essentially related to its immediate topography, and by virtue of its emphasis on graduated modes of mediation, it urges more subtle adjudications of landscape architecture than the habitual ones of "formal" and "informal." It therefore seems imperative to experience and to discuss designed sites as the result of choices made within a structure of possibilities, what I have termed "the three natures." This will be taken up again briefly in the final chapter; here, the better to understand the interrelation of this triad and the place within it of the third (my prime subject), it is worth adding a separate commentary, part historical and part topical, on each of these natures.

First nature. This is an extremely complex topic, which it is neither possible nor necessary to explore fully here.[50] It is important only to insist that some notion of a first nature, of wilderness, or of a territory of the gods seems to have been an essential ingredient in the ways that humans viewed and treated the physical world; it helped them organize their experiences. Indeed, first nature or wilderness is inevitably constructed by a given culture as a means of differentiating kinds of identity or behavior, or of protecting parcels of territory for special purposes. Thus versions of this wild, unknown, or "other" zone could be invoked by writers such as

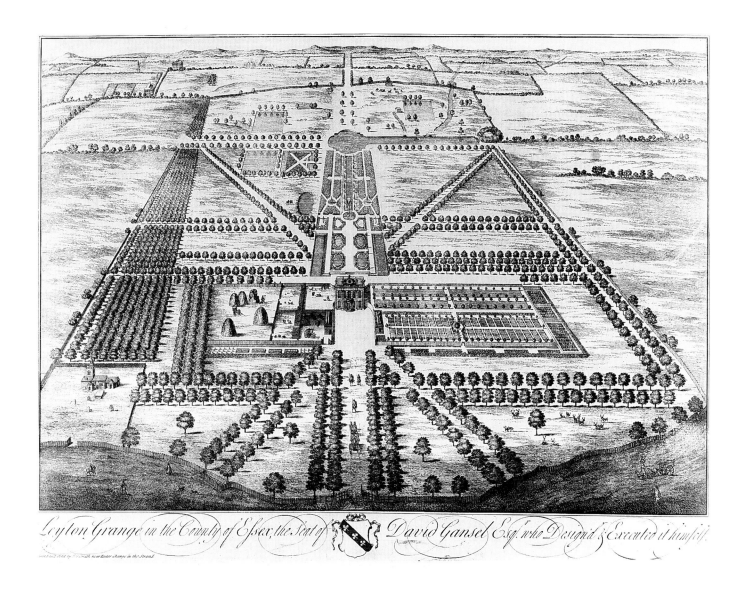

Leyton Grange in the County of Essex, the Seat of   David Gansel Esq.r who Designd & Executed it himself.

FIGURE 31. Engraved view of the estate of Leyton Grange, Essex, (?)1730s. The Bodleian Library, Oxford (Gough Maps 8, folio 59B).

(*facing page*) FIGURE 32. Isaac de Caus (?), engraved view of Wilton House gardens, late 1640s. Private collection.

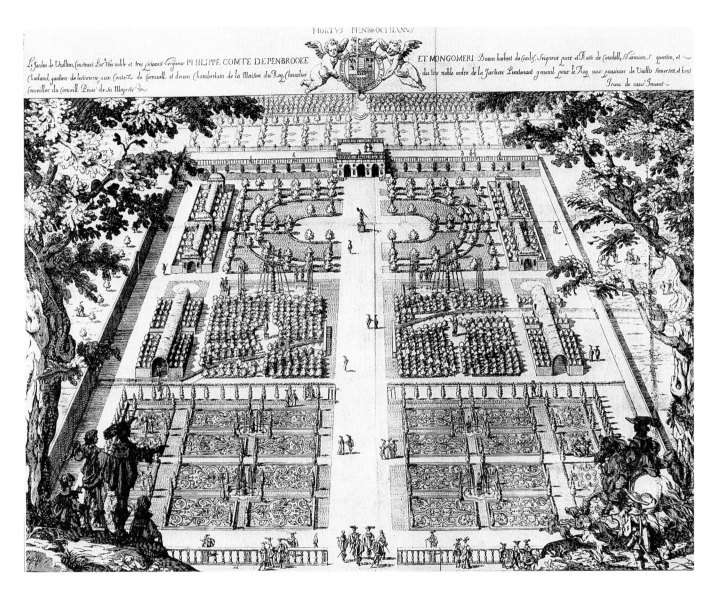

Cicero as places to locate the mysterious and sometimes fearful presence of the gods; the Greeks had located their gods on the heights of Mount Olympus—a spiritual zoning that seems to have persisted well into our own day, if the extremely belated ascent of this imposing peak is considered.[51] Likewise, the wilderness in Christian thought could also be "the ground itself of the divine being."[52] Alternatively, many societies have made wilderness the place where the wicked, the criminal, or other outcasts were banished to perish in its inhospitable wastes.

For Max Oelschlaeger, the idea of wilderness was derived significantly from that period of human development when hunting-gathering gave way to herding-

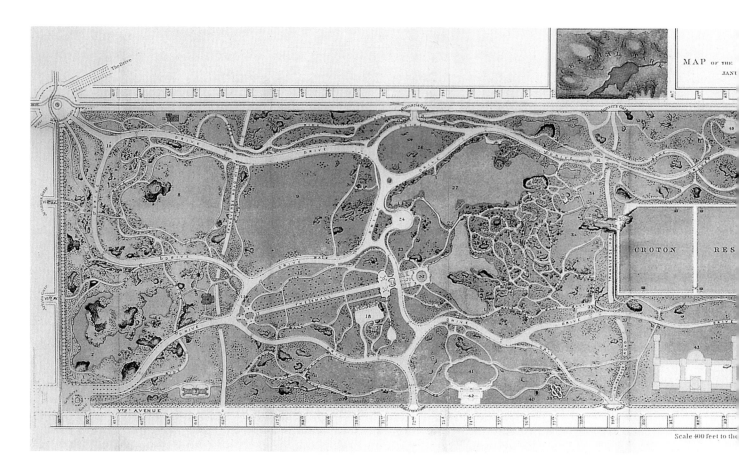

FIGURE 33. Calvert Vaux and Jacob Wrey Mould, map of Central
Park, New York, 1870.

farming; then the need for a second nature of fields
and enclosures isolated and identified the idea of a first.
"Once the agricultural turn was made," he writes, "philosophy and theology sprang forth with a vengeance,"
and the idea of wastelands, badlands, hinterlands, and
wilderness was born.[53] Conversely, in the twentieth
century, once wild parts of the globe rapidly disap-
peared or were threatened with elimination, "wilderness" areas became valued once again. Different cultures will identify the first nature differently; within

complex cultures there will even be wide divergencies
of interpretation—one person's wilderness is another's
backyard. It seems therefore too simplistic to blame all
human dominance of nature on Judeo-Christian tradition—after all, as George Seddon points out,[54] the
Psalmists, even the Book of Genesis, celebrate a world
of wonderful natural creation antecedent to human
claims on it.

In the late twentieth century, many want to believe in
the existence of "true wilderness." Yet few examples of
first nature survive, as least in western Europe, without
any trace of human intervention. Some of the highest
mountain regions or the deserts might count, but the

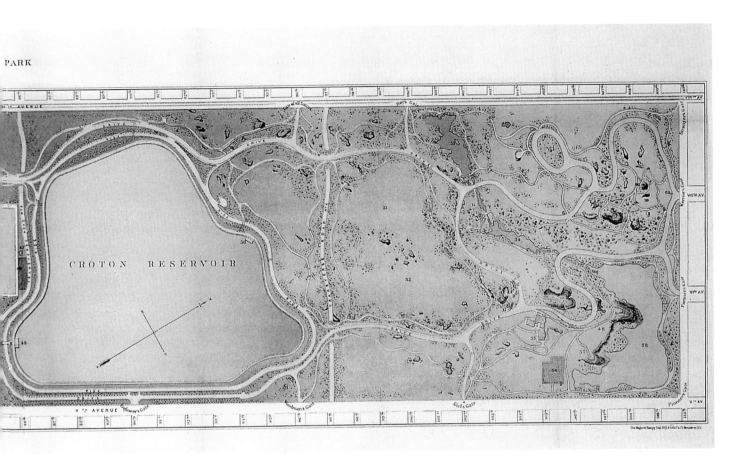

PARK

CROTON RESERVOIR

summit of Mount Everest, with its abandoned oxygen canisters and dead bodies, is an eloquent reminder of how first nature can be colonized (not to say corrupted) physically as well as metaphysically. The problem—environmental and philosophical alike—is that once we get there to see, it will no longer be, the wilderness. If we have reached the mountains or the desert, it is likely to be via airplane or automobile (Figure 34). The very highway and any other means by which remaining wildernesses are made accessible to human presence, or even to human consumption in photograph or painted image, compromise their first nature, drawing it inescapably into the second by making it a cultural experi-ence.[55] Primal confrontations with nature, or what has been called the immeasurable, have been virtually lost: "L'avion a transformé la mer en lac, et seule la tempête peut nous rappeler qu'elle reste non mesurable."[56] Yet set any holder of frequent flyer miles on a single-handed yacht to sail around the world, and (however skilled a sailor) he or she will experience some palpable, albeit relative, manifestation of that "first" nature.

Indeed, the *idea* of wilderness is tenacious, irrespective of actualities. Wildernesses survive above all in the minds of people who want them to exist; wholly metaphysical as this may seem, the fact that we each contrive our own idea of wildness and wild places does not

FIGURE 34. Yosemite with car park below cliffs (photograph: Marc Treib).

mean that the idea of wilderness cannot be realized by different people in different ways. Each matches his or her idea to an appropriate or feasible actuality; David Robertson has explored the different ways in which earlier wilderness writers had been able to access this first nature, in the process also exploring the viability of the idea for himself and various colleagues and students at the University of California.[57] For somebody who only knows Brooklyn and Prospect Park, the Blue Ridge in Virginia could be a veritable wilderness; a person brought up in Montana will have different expectations and standards. So it was as early as the fourteenth century for Sir Gawain, venturing into the wilderness in search of the Green Knight:

> By a mountain next morning he makes his way
> Into a forest fastness, fearsome and wild;
> High hills on either hand, with hoar woods below,
> Oaks old and huge by the hundred together.
> The hazel and the hawthorn were all intertwined
> With rough raveled moss, that raggedly hung.
> With many birds unblithe upon bare twigs
> That peeped most piteously for pain of the cold.
> The good knight on Gringolet [his horse] glides
>   thereunder
> Through many a marsh and mire, a man all alone.[58]

Gawain's wilderness is defined in implicit contrast to the courtly world left behind him in his search for the Green Knight. One criterion of wilderness is its hostility, its "otherness," its ability to bewilder (as the etymology instructs). In the Himalayas, the Rockies, the Sahara, or the Australian outback, some western urbanites would still be bewildered, that is to say, disoriented, without sense of location or even purpose; there is a parcel of wood and wetlands on Nantucket where somebody recently got lost for days, unable to find a way out.

Many, many people at the end of the twentieth century have probably never moved out of a second nature. So first nature has largely existed for some time now only as an idea or a constructed facsimile. As we have seen, Olmsted incorporated within New York public parks areas that recalled picturesque or sublime territory outside the city; Las Vegas and Disney fabricate imagery of wild places that is clearly compelling or convincing to many of their visitors. For those who do not know or cannot reach the "real thing," perhaps for those who do not believe it still exists, these substitutes offer imaginary zones that should not be gainsaid.

Just as a highway or airplane, for those fortunate enough to afford the travel, physically connects them to their preferred "wilderness," so our very ideas of that sought-after "other" nature link it to the rest of our experiences. We come to terms with first nature and explain our encounters with wilderness by talking of wonder, awe, fear, or distaste. We see it as divine, the nature of the gods (in Cicero's terms); or we excoriate it as hostile territory and mask it off, as in some medieval representations; or we are more ambiguous and accommodate it philosophically, for instance, by labeling it the sublime. The switch from locating the sublime not in rhetorical productions but in landscapes [59] during the eighteenth century may be explained as part of an effort to make acceptable without diminishing the newly available experiences of wild European scenery. Tourists in first nature could translate their wonder,

awe, and fear into a shared commodity, that in its turn became part of their cultural second nature and was occasionally translated into designed landscapes.

There are many instances of this accommodation of some territorial "other" into familiar experiences. Oelschlaeger's own instance is the poetic narrative of Gilgamesh's battle with Humbaba, the mighty forest god, which translates "the relentless Sumerian encroachment on the ancient forests and the triumph of civilization over the wilderness." [60] But another, Petrarch's celebrated ascent of Mont Ventoux in 1336, anticipates developments within eighteenth-century sublime. [61] His letter describing this event, no less carefully constructed (despite its final profession of hasty improvisation) than Bonfadio's on the scenery of Lake Garda, stresses from the first the absorption of the experience of high mountains within the cultural traditions available to him.

His narrative implicitly presents the excursus into a hostile terrain [62] as taking him beyond habitual society and scenery: none of his friends is willing to join him, and peasants along the way in the valley discourage him from climbing the mountain. When he does, he leaves behind tokens of the normal world, the clothes and objects that would impede the climb. Yet Petrarch's affirmation that he wanted to expose himself to the mountain's primal nature, to "view the great height of it," is counterbalanced by the presence of his brother as well as by the famous gesture, once arrived on the summit, of consulting his copy of Saint Augustine's *Confessions.* Here he reads and feels reproached by the remark that men forget themselves in their love for the natural world. In retrospect, we see that the difficult and frustrating climb into a zone where "the nature of things does not depend on human wishes" (p. 174) has all along been accommodated to the worlds Petrarch customarily inhabits; its narration is constantly justified by spiritual and philosophical arguments, including citations of authority (writers like Ovid) and typological parallels—Mounts Olympus and Athos—as well as by Livy's account of Philip of Macedonia's climb of Mount Haemus. In more ways than one, then, Petrarch can only seem to gain access to first nature through a second—the encounter with the old shepherd is as carefully situated in the narrative as is the pastoral valley in the topography below the mountain.

Second nature. Despite eloquent commentary arguing that all our ideas of nature are wholly constructed or invented,[63] there is some point in distinguishing between different kinds of nature that people identify; even confusions between them are predicated on implicit distinctions. People who choose to see examples of landscape architecture like the Merritt Parkway in the late 1930s as uncomplicatedly "natural"[64] are declaring their sense of different treatments or versions of the natural world available to them. Even parkland can be taken to be other than designed: few of the people whom Geoffrey James encountered while photographing Olmsted parks thought that they were "really created," and more of them assumed they were "just a parcel of nature fenced off."[65] If that is the response to deliberately landscaped sites, then the confusion of second nature with the first is even more likely and understandable. There is nothing wrong with the "mistake" or self-deception, which people should be allowed to enjoy (they will anyway). But Cicero's account of a second nature does recall us to the essential fact that, like the third, it is brought into being by deliberate and physical human agency. It is only the "first" nature, implied by Cicero's *alteram naturam*, that can be unmediated, untouched, and primal, in reality or imagination.[66]

Between first and third natures, the second may be seen as a middle or intermediate mode. In most cases it probably intervened historically, for that is Bacon's point about the perfection of gardening and Bonfadio's about *terza natura*. It is also important to realize how many strategies and elements of second nature, developed as humans carved their agriculture and urban developments out of the first, were invoked in the later

place-making we call landscape architecture. Agrarian interventions and methods of cultivation were simply extended into horticulture and the layout of gardens; but so, too, at least as early as the Roman Empire, was urban imagery taken up and applied to garden walks, hippodromes, colonnades, exedras, and such like.[67]

Agriculture was a prime element of second nature for Cicero, as we can see from another of his writings on old age, *De senectute*.[68] In a rosy survey of the pleasures of farming, he expresses joy in both the "natural forces of the earth" and the human industry that cultivates them. The activities he celebrates—such as irrigation, planting, grafting, cattle raising, bee-keeping—and the resulting variety and textures of "grainfield, grassfield, vineyard and olive yard . . . kitchen-garden and orchard" yield produce that is "practically valuable" and "aesthetically pleasing." Farming also institutes a world of necessary buildings, enclosures, tracks, bridges, "orderly rows of trees . . . and groves." Everything, in short, that transformed what French eighteenth-century terminology called "terres vaines et vagues" into an agrarian second nature.

But we must include urban developments within the zone of second nature; these are where a majority of western men and women nowadays choose or are forced to dwell. Cities and towns have their own structures and infrastructures that parallel those of agriculture—places of government, of worship, of commerce, of leisure—along with the physical means of supporting them and connecting them to those who use them in the town and in the countryside. When William Penn carved Philadelphia out of the forests of Pennsylvania in the late seventeenth century, he seemed to invoke both urban and rural traditions of second nature: between the Delaware and Schuylkill Rivers was stretched the rectangular grid of streets, within which pattern were the plots, yards, and gardens of houses as well as the necessary repertoire of public buildings. There were also five squares, situated so that all citizens would have equal access to open green spaces.

FIGURE 35. Agricultural terracing on the Greek island of Patmos, 1990.

Philadelphia's foundation is a late instance of the emergence of a sophisticated second nature from a first (or what the early colonists deemed to be a first). More rudimentary reasons of survival dictated earlier and more primitive maneuvers of this sort: woods were cleared for building and for farmland; walls would have been erected to protect crops within fields or to keep penned animals from escaping; hillsides were terraced to grow crops.[69] These manifestations of a second nature are clearly the beginnings of an activity similar to the place-making that we call gardens. However, these agricultural sites (Figures 35, 36) have little scope and variety of internal organization; although deliberate,

they lack what we'd call design. The idea of productivity that we associate with fields or orchards has not been translated into a sense of these spaces as sites of consumption, where different ideas of possession and dwelling apply.[70] They have not yet advanced into what is here being termed "third nature," or what William Mason in the eighteenth century explained as "the soil, already tam'd, [being given] its finish'd grace."[71]

We largely live in a world of second nature, places where humans have made over the environment for the purposes of survival and habitation, where labor and productivity dominate, and where the traces of that work are everywhere visible. But there are some examples of second nature that are more slight and/or temporary even than fields and walls. They may not involve actual intervention upon the land, although they

FIGURE 36. Head of Langdale Valley, the English Lake District, 1960s.

certainly envisage some modification of it in the mind's eye. They all share a recognition of some space as special, as crucially different from surrounding first nature. It may even be marked off from it in some (often imperceptible) way, though without the complexity and complication of intervention that characterizes most landscape architecture. A few instances of this will help us approach the main topic, third nature.

Australian aborigines tell of ancestors who always carried a pole, which they set up at nightfall to mark the center of their temporary world; they thus identified an invisible but nonetheless crucial space within

which they could exist and feel secure during the night. But if the pole was accidentally broken, their world literally fell apart.[72] A comparable, yet more permanent gesture by which space is marked and protected is the standing stones known in the Breton language as place markers.[73] And the permanence of the stone has its organic equivalent in the tree that occupies a special place in Greek and Ottoman villages, marking the center and innermost space of community; this central tree is, of course, endlessly repeated in the smaller units of family compounds where subsidiary spaces are maintained. A final instance of this cultural control of territory, even though we cannot be certain of their full implications, are the geoglyphs or land markings of South America (Figure 37): far more than astro-

FIGURE 37. Nasca lines, Peru.

nomical (if that is what they are), these huge workings of the earth are a cultural and ideological colonization of first nature, marking out a space of second nature by which early civilizations could accommodate themselves to their environment.[74]

There are forms of second nature where the human intervention is still more residual and does not involve, in the first instance at least, even marking the land with pole, stone, or tree. Another aborigine perception of shape and space in the Australian landscape has been narrated in Bruce Chatwin's *The Songlines*:

> He went on to explain how each totemic ancestor, while travelling through the country, was thought to have scattered a trail of words and musical notes along the lines of his footprints, and how these Dreaming-tracks lay over the land as "ways" of communication between the most far-flung tribes.
>
> "A song," he said, "was both map and direction-finder."

Providing you knew the song, you could always find your way across country."

"And would a man on 'Walkabout' always be travelling down one of the Songlines?"

"In the old days, yes," he agreed. "Nowadays, they go by train or car."[75]

These songlines mark and define the land and its cultural spaces without utilizing anything so palpable, or as fragile, as a pole; unlike the use of the pole, songlines lay their "interlocking network of 'lines' or 'ways through'" permanently across the landscape—permanently, that is, while the songs are retained in aborigine memory ("if the songs are forgotten, the land itself will die").[76]

In an aggressively rationalist and pragmatic world, such recognition of what is essentially sacred space or sacred markings of otherwise hostile terrain may seem at best unavailable to us, if not at worst plain naiveté. It would be wrong to think so. It is worth registering at this point that there is a long history of isolating sites in first nature as significant, thereby reconstituting them as having a more cultural, controlled status. Some, like the aborigine territories, are extensive; others, like their campsites, can be finite and temporary. Each is made special and sacred, yet none enjoys the physical elaboration and complexity that we have come to associate with the third nature of gardens.

Mircea Eliade has shown that *homo religiosus* learned very early that some ground was marked out as sacred, and this required no activity on his part except a sympathetic reception of that very fact.[77] The Bible articulates famous examples of this hierography, including the recognition of sacred mystery in a specific place: Moses is told by God not to approach—"Put off thy shoes from off thy feet, for the place whereon thou standest is holy ground" (Exodus 3:5). And Jacob dreams that a ladder ascends into heaven from the place where he is sleeping and that God tells him, "The land whereon thou liest, to thee will I give it, and to thy seed" (Genesis 28:13).

The sense of sites as ineluctably special continues to be part of contemporary human experience. It is an instinct that does not belong exclusively to what we would call "religious" people. This may raise the question of whether such privileging of place transfigures a site into first or third nature—does it make it divine territory or something like a garden? It can presumably be either or both: if some deliberate and formal intervention is attempted (i.e., invoking forms not available on-site), then it certainly aspires to landscape architecture. A garden has the status for some people today of a sacred spot. The passions aroused by a dedication to the natural environment and/or by the activity of gardening suggest to how fundamental and "religious" an experience each of these activities gives access. Much modern place-making calls up a deeper sense of the noumenous than we generally care to acknowledge, and it brings to the recognition of something special in a place a far greater wealth of cultural resources than we have so far encountered in the aboriginal pole, the Ottoman tree, or even the geoglyphs and songlines.

v

Third nature. As this phrase was coined by Bonfadio and Taegio, it referred to villa gardens. It may usefully be extended to describe, as was implicit in Bonfadio's letter anyway, those human interventions that go beyond what is required by the necessities or practice of agriculture or urban settlement (i.e., Cicero's second nature). Several extra elements would be involved here: the specific intention (of the creator, but sometimes of the perceiver, visitor, or consumer, however we want to call him/her);[78] some relative elaboration of formal ingredients above functional needs;[79] some conjunction of metaphysical experience with physical forms, specifically some aesthetic endeavor—the wish or need to make a site beautiful.

Several of the gestures explored in the previous discussion of second nature contribute arguably to this profile: spaces created around the aboriginal pole or the Ottoman tree, geoglyphs, songlines, and other hierographies all move toward, without achieving, third nature. Landscape architecture can often be a special, if largely unregarded, case of hierography. The garden, especially, is prime territory for this kind of experience by its often complex materializing of sacred place and rituals. By deliberate and physical intervention on some specific site, a *genius loci* is either recognized or created (both recognition and creation involve a subject, though the former supposes an independent, a priori object).

Gardens may be created directly within the primal wilderness, an action that pilgrims and Puritans in the New World took as a metaphor when they claimed to establish the re-reformed church as a garden in the wilderness of a new land.[80] But more usually gardens are extrapolated from and elaborated out of the various forms of second nature, urban and agricultural. Consequently, as Francis Bacon noted, garden-making followed upon building: "When Ages grow to Civility and Elegancie, Men come to *Build Stately*, sooner than to *Garden Finely*: As if *Gardening* were the Greater Perfection."[81] This tardiness of "fine" gardening in the cultural process has many explanations. The first is obviously a preliminary need for shelter, the human instinct to establish that part of a habitat first. Then sufficient ground that can be spared from other life-sustaining functions needs to be available. It also takes more leisure and more technical skill to create, maintain, and use gardens. Given, too, that gardens are private or privileged enclaves set off against a public world ("public garden" always seems a contradiction in terms), then society has to develop a sufficient complexity for there to be desire and occasions for withdrawal from it into gardens.

Despite James C. Rose's mockery of "serious" books —like this!—that cite Bacon's observation,[82] it is undeniable that gardens *are* likely to be established as societies become more developed. Bonfadio's final overview of the territory he describes in his letter presents it as a history of civilization in miniature, with third nature at its climax. In Daniel Defoe's tendentious parable of civilization, though Robinson Crusoe never achieves anything he would call a garden, once he has established his house with its "cellar," enclosures fenced against the "wilderness," a "castle," as well as a "country-house" to go with his "sea-coast-house," he does create a "bower" in the "country" and discovers what he calls a "grotto" at the seaside.[83]

Garden territory necessitates a more concentrated effort of implementation and maintenance than do, say, orchards and vegetable gardens, which in their turn may require more involvement, activity, and perhaps even a sense of ordering than do fields. In Ming culture, the garden [*yuan*] stood in formal opposition to field [*tian*] above all in respect of its coherence; by contrast, agricultural land was scattered.[84] Examples of third nature display a concentration of effort and will, a cohesion, and an appeal to notions of beauty entertained either by their contemporaries or their succeeding visitors.

Anyone who has driven through the Val d'Orcia in southern Tuscany (Figure 38) will be struck by a beauty of organization that, while not wholly imposed, is inherent in the process of its cultivation and comes close to rendering these fields as elaborate and intense an experience as the finest garden.[85] Such a reaction to the Val d'Orcia will derive in part from its modern visitors' reading their expectations of gardens into its agrarian scenery; what ultimately prevents accepting the territory as a garden is presumably its large extent, its necessary lack of any holistic design, and the confidence of an overall intention at any point or points of its evolution.

Clearly, we must accept a sliding scale of cultural intervention in the natural world, a scale which moves from a residual second nature, where labor and productivity dominate, through a minimalist yet recognizable third nature, to full and sophisticated enclo-

FIGURE 38. View in the Val d'Orcia, southern Tuscany, 1998.

sures that we are used to calling "pleasure gardens" and that Robinson Crusoe, so pragmatic a survivor, never got round to allowing himself. There are many instances of the interpenetration or porousness of these two natures, perhaps significant of the cultural moment of their creation.[86] The early literature of gardening in the territories that became the United States also makes it clear that there was little time for the luxury of some gardening left behind in Europe: after agriculture, only kitchen and physic gardens feature prominently in the literature until M'Mahon's *American Gar-*

dener's Calendar of 1806, where "pleasure-grounds" are first given a prominent role.[87] Yet this did not mean that settlers had lost touch with the idea of a sliding scale of natures, where wilderness slipped into field and orchard into garden. John Cotton of Boston, expounding on the *Canticles* in 1642, explained, "All the world is a wildernesse, or at least a wilde field; only, the Church is God's garden or orchard."[88]

Nor does this late development of the American pleasure garden mean that beauty had not been previously identified in agricultural work. In the early publications on horticulture in the American colonies, there was little time or concern for what would only later be called ornament; yet some colonists insisted on the ornamental aspect of certain necessary agrarian functions—thus, the mulberry tree which "in addition to serving as food for the silkworm, was useful for its timber, as hedging, and 'worth planting for shade, ornament, and beauty.'"[89]

Nor should we assume that early examples of landscape architecture did not elicit aesthetic appreciation, even if the science of aesthetics was of a later invention. The Renaissance botanical garden (see Figures 58, 59, 61) would have been no less delightful and pleasurable to its visitors because it served a practical, scientific purpose.[90] Similarly, we know that the Mughal emperor Babur, whenever he talked of gardens, "made little distinction between ornamental and economic trees."[91] And in those great hunting preserves that Assyrian kings carved out of the desert—one of the earliest examples of a landscape garden, the word for which has joined English as *paradise*—it would be hard to adjudicate between their beauty (for they had decorations within them) and their function.[92] The parklands established by late Elizabethan and Jacobean gentry and aristocrats were clearly designed to be pleasing to the eye and mind as well as to serve various social and political functions.[93] Indeed, we have to recall that distinctions between beauty and utility, or between pleasure and profit, are largely of recent origin and did not impede earlier discussions of place-making where the terms may have overlapped or coincided.[94] The exchange works in both directions. A pleasure garden could be useful and productive, yielding herbs and simples, for instance, as well as flowers, which themselves served many practical functions such as perfuming interiors. Equally, much delight and pleasure were taken in the more useful kitchen and physic gardens.

The pleasure gardens' evolution out of sophisticated agrarian and urban contexts testifies to their generally accepted sequence in cultural history. Yet sometimes, whether or not they signal the *history* of cultural process, we encounter examples of third nature that have been established directly within the primal wilder-

ness. There are the hunting parks of ancient China in the Warring States Period that grew out of a tradition for sacred precincts. Or we have some eloquent images of gardens set like precious jewels in the inhospitable world of desert or mountainscape: there are oasis gardens, resolutely watered and kept green against the aridity of surrounding sand, or tiny walled enclosures betraying their presence in the red-brown Sinai Desert with the tell-tale green fingers of their cypresses (Figure 39). These last remind us of the Hebrew etymology of *gan* (garden), which shares roots with verbs for defense—hence the protected space of gardens—and for deliverance—with the implication of giving shade.[95] They also recall the Koran's contrast between the desert of its prophet and the deliverance of the faithful into the cool shade of paradise.[96]

In North America, too, there are striking examples of gardens set down directly in the "wilderness." Bacon's Castle, in Surry County, Virginia,[97] the earliest known colonial example in America, comprised an enclosed, tripartite garden set down uncompromisingly in the midst of what was then wild and hostile territory. Some fifty years later in the 1740s the stunning terraces of Middleton Place in South Carolina (Figure 40) were raised from the midst of swamps. As late as the 1920s, the Italianate fantasy of Vizcaya in Florida was established directly within the tropical forest (Figure 41).[98] A final set of examples of third nature establishing itself within the first is narrated by Kenneth Helphand, gardens created within such hostile environments as World War I trenches, internment camps, and West Bank settlements.[99]

The visual contrasts in all such examples, however, are misleading to the extent that the idea of their place-making had almost certainly evolved out of agrarian practice and experience elsewhere and was thence transferred into first nature. The Allen family at Bacon's Castle brought with them a European experience of gardens and a design format that was at least as old as the fourteenth century.[100] Gardens established within the primal wilderness will almost always be the prod-

FIGURE 39. St. Catherine's Monastery, Mt. Sinai (photograph: I. Ševčenko).

FIGURE 40. Aerial view of Middleton Place, South Carolina.

uct of a culture that has first developed them elsewhere from a second nature. The hermit saints, whose sojourn in the desert is the theme of Byzantine and Renaissance imagery (Figure 42), are each represented as enjoying some flowering garden shade, presumably a reminiscence or approximation of gardens in monastic communities (the reminiscence, of course, may be the painter's).[101] Vizcaya derived its garden concepts from a range of Italian and perhaps even Spanish-Moorish sources before inserting them into the Florida forest.

Similarly, the entirely different gardens that Charles K. Savage created from 1928 at Thuya Lodge on Mount Desert Island, Maine, found their inspiration elsewhere — turn-of-the-century herbaceous borders, cottage gardens, American Impressionist paintings — before finding their rather astonishing niche along the flank of Mount Eliot (Figure 43). His intervention is certainly announced by a series of terraces and rock staircases up which the visitor arrives and which had been established by an earlier owner of Thuya, Joseph Henry Curtis, a Boston landscape architect; but, once reached, however, the surprise and impact of this gar-

FIGURE 41. Aerial view of Vizcaya, Florida.

den oasis in the coastal woodland are striking. This effect is contrived equally by the garden's distinct contrast with the surroundings and the equally studied fashion by which these very surroundings—the rock and woodland—are allowed a presence within the enclosure of the designed space, spilling (so to speak) through the fence toward the regular and horticultural elements of the site.[102]

The more usual process of evolution, then, would be for gardens not only to emerge out of traditions and practices of second nature but also to lie contiguous to such agrarian zones. Nowhere is this evolution dis-

played more eloquently than in the series of paintings of villas owned by the Medici in the Tuscan countryside, executed by the late sixteenth-century Flemish artist Giusto Utens. These lunettes were commissioned to decorate the reception hall of one particular Medici villa at Artimino; they constitute a miniature history of the Medici control of their larger territory,[103] displaying the variety of cultural interventions made on different sites and over time in the countryside around Florence.

From Utens's depictions we can register how garden elements have evolved out of and alongside the cultural landscape of fields and hunting territory, like the walled orchard set apart from the groves of other fruit trees at Marignolle or Lappeggi (Figure 44) or the

FIGURE 42. Anonymous, *Death of S. Ephraim the Syrian*, icon, fifteenth century. Athens, Byzantine Museum.

fenced area of square flower beds privileged within the orchard at La Magia. What is striking here is how certain elements of an essentially agrarian layout have been treated in ways that give them added value—whether that value is privacy, protection, or aesthetic shaping by way of spacing and grouping. Utens implies all this by

the juxtaposition of their enclosures to the larger spaces of farming or by recording how a cistern at Marignolle is decorated with a jet of water or a fish tank at La Petraia is treated as a reflecting pool (Figure 45).

With the exception of the distant Pratolino, the closer these Medici properties were located to the cultural and urban center of Florence (Castello [see Figure 18], the Boboli Gardens, or La Petraia), the more elaborate became the elements and areas of third nature. All

FIGURE 43. Thuya Gardens, Mount Desert Island, Maine, 1997.

have connections with agrarian management and activity that are still sometimes imaged at the edges of the lunettes. In the case of La Petraia, however, when no agricultural terrain is shown, the descending terraces of the enclosed garden increase in design complexity as they move from rows of what look like espaliered fruit trees, through simple but geometrically figured parterres flanked by pavilions with open loggias, to the final level with a pair of double pergola circles enclosing more fruit trees, now set in quincuncial form.

Other villas adjudicate their place-making, especially the prominence given to garden artifice, according to the function of the property, which in turn depends on its location. Poggio a Caiano literally marginalizes its pleasure garden within an enclosure at the right, dedicating the remaining territory to simple squares of orchard, groves, or shrubs (Figure 46); yet this undemonstrative acknowledgment of rural business or *ne-*

gotium is contrasted with the elegant aspect of *otium* suggested by Sangallo's building. The whole complex nicely calculates its status as humanist country retreat. By contrast, at Il Trebbio, the most isolated of these Medici properties, Utens depicts only a residual pleasure ground. Its sloping and walled garden is separated from the larger farming and hunting territory; yet the privacies and seclusion of its tiny garden plot seem to have grown out of the utilities and necessities of the cultural landscape. Even the pergola-covered walk, the enclosure's only decoration (which still, incidentally, survives [Figure 47]), is an elegant extrapolation of an essential agricultural feature.

VI

As these considerations of what I have called the three natures suggest, the garden's place within them

FIGURE 44. Giusto Utens, *The Medici Villa of La Peggio* (the modern Lappeggi), tempera on canvas, 1599. Museo Firenze Com'era.

is complex. Its relationship as well as its complexities will be evoked constantly throughout this book. What is necessary here is only to insist that the third nature of gardens is best considered as existing in terms of the other two: not only do we recognize and better understand any one nature by its relationship with the other two, but the third, with which this book is principally concerned, is always engaged in a dialogue with the other two.[104]

As an example of this self-constructing relationship, we might look finally at a famous and beautiful painting by Giovanni Bellini of *Saint Francis in Ecstacy* (Figure 48). Here the three natures are intermingled yet distinctly registered and so work to define each other.[105] Bellini represents a "wilderness," an unmediated topography, hinted at throughout as the appropriate retreat for such saintly activity, especially the rude rocks that dominate the foreground and Saint Francis's exposure to the sky; however, inasmuch as the saint is depicted without his sandals, perhaps Bellini is alluding to an instance of hierography ("Put off your shoes . . . for the place . . . is holy ground"). Then there is the culti-

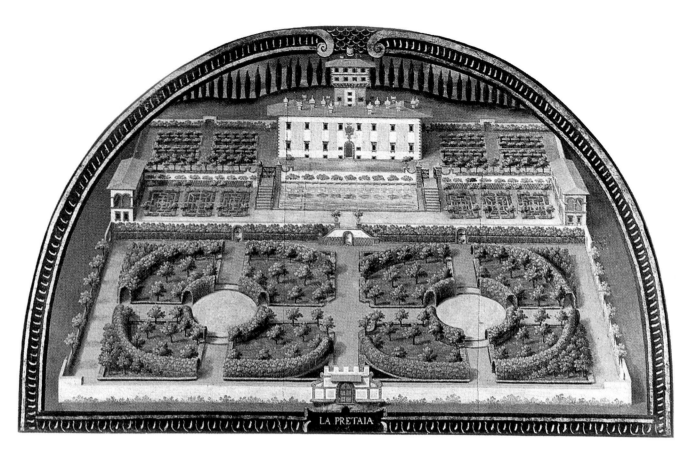

FIGURE 45. Giusto Utens, *The Medici Villa of La Petraia*, tempera on canvas, 1599. Museo Firenze Com'era.

vated landscape of farmstead, fields, and distant villa-castle (maybe a town), a territory aptly inhabited by a shepherd. Finally, there is the modest effort at creating a third nature which Saint Francis has evidently initiated in his little garden, with its drainage or water-collection channel, its raised flower bed, and a pergola with regular horizontal side pieces, a seat, and the arched enclosure it forms with the cave.

Bellini's painting is necessarily focused on symbolic or typological readings of its scenery, inhabitants, and effects;[106] these constitute its powerful and magical aura. But they are grounded on the artist's subtle grasp of different topographies and on his appreciation of different scales and effects of human intervention in the land.[107] So the pergola and trelliswork, certainly to be registered as symbolizing the cross,[108] also indicate much about the saint's place-making and its relation to the other natures. For many of his rudimentary garden forms allude to elements in the other natures: the water channel, to drainage ditches in the second nature and to streams in the first; a pergola and a bench, to the shade and place for rest that are everywhere found on the edges of woodland. A pergola, as at Il Trebbio, is perhaps one of the primary forms of garden-making in hot climates where shelter for humans, the exposure of fruit

FIGURE 46. Giusto Utens, *The Medici Villa of Poggio a Caiano*, tempera on canvas, 1599. Museo Firenze Com'era.

to the sun for ripening, and the decorative potential of its arch or tunnel are eloquent of the cultural transition from second to third natures. What Saint Francis, however, has not been allowed by Bellini is some form of enclosure for his residual garden, a gesture perhaps to the saint's surrender of himself to the wilderness.

FIGURE 47. Pergola overlooking the small walled garden at Il
Trebbio, Tuscany, photographed in 1970s.

FIGURE 48. Giovanni Bellini, *St. Francis in Ecstacy*, tempera and
oil on panel, c. 1480. The Frick Collection, New York.

CHAPTER 4

Representation

Learn of the green world what can be thy place
In scaled invention or true artistry.
  —Ezra Pound, *Canto* 81

The beautifying, not the beautified, is really the
beautiful.
  —Third Earl of Shaftesbury

As is the Gardener, so is the Garden.
  —Thomas Fuller

I've wanted to copy nature, but I haven't managed
to. . . . Nevertheless I was pleased with myself for
discovering that the sun, for example, cannot be
reproduced, but has to be represented by some other
means.
  —Paul Cézanne

I
_____

The deliberate move from the first and second
into third natures, whenever and wherever this occurred, involves a whole cluster of motifs and motives.
As we have seen, the garden is a resilient, central aspect
of human culture precisely because it is, in the words of
a scholar of Ming gardens, "a site of contested meanings," subject to the "pull of a number of discursive
fields."[1] Among these is one that is more than usually
neglected by modern theory and practice of landscape
architecture: namely, the garden's reference to what lies
beyond its boundaries, boundaries that (as we've seen)
peculiarly define it and yet do not insulate it from the
worlds in which and out of the materials of which it is
constructed.

A ubiquitous feature of garden-making in all cultures has been the inclusion of references within the
site to other places, events, and themes. I shall call this
re-presentation, the presentation over again in garden
terms of a whole range of other cultural and natural elements and occurrences. Knowledge of both—the garden formulations and their "referents"—enhances the
experience of each.

Representation emerges as a theme in the earliest
records of gardens. Chinese emperors re-created in the
imperial parks to the northwest of Peking the sights
of several regions that they had seen on their southern
tours, and Suzhou gardens replicated the northern sites
and sights of Peking.[2] But perhaps the earliest recorded
instance of representation is the so-called Hanging
Gardens of Babylon. However modern archaeology
figures their site, structure, and meaning, early (though
not contemporary) accounts of the Babylonian gardens
stress that they were invented to recall a particular geomorphological phenomenon, the mountains north of
the ancient city.[3] Down on the plains a distant mountain topography was represented through a series of
stepped terraces covered with greenery. These "Hanging Gardens" fueled memories of the distant mountainscape and yet stirred curiosity about their own status
and construction. This double response is significant.
Even as the Hanging Gardens triggered recollections
of faraway mountain sites, they asked to be considered
more attentively for their own sake as a construction
or representation. The here and now was given special
significance by its reference to the there and then.

The Babylonian gardens, partly because of their legendary status among the wonders of the world, have

FIGURE 49. Le Jardin Atlantique, Montparnasse, Paris, designed by Michel Pena and François Brun, 1997.

surely informed later ideas of the garden; they thus help us illustrate another aspect of representation. The Babylonian gardens are "quoted" by later designers, whether it is the hanging gardens of the Trump Tower on Fifth Avenue in New York or the wonderful fantasy of the Jardin Atlantique created above the departure and arrival platforms of the Gare Montparnasse in Paris (Figure 49; and see Figure 73). Since the latter so

literally repeat and recall the Babylonian achievement, hung as they are across the railroad void below, part of their effect and meaning is to represent our mental or mythic idea of gardens. They do this at the same time that they participate in the more specific representational exercise, similar to the Babylonian original, of representing a distant landscape, in this case the Atlantic coast with its cliffs, waves, weather, boardwalks, and seaside fun and games.

Another example will be useful before we look in more detail at what representation means in and to

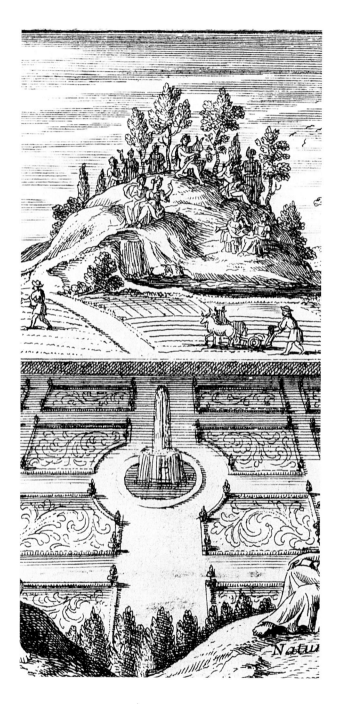

FIGURE 50. Detail of frontispiece, *Curiositez de la nature et de l'art* by l'Abbé de Vallemont, Paris, 1705 (see Figure 22.)

landscape architecture. There is a simple, strikingly diagrammatic instance of garden representation in the frontispiece to the Abbé de Vallemont's *Curiosities of Art and Nature*, discussed in the last chapter. In the center of the regular garden is a fountain (Figure 50), which is shown directly on axis with a natural spring that gushes from the hillside beyond the agricultural fields. This fountain is a formal version of the spring, a technologically sophisticated rendition, suitable for the center of such a garden, of a natural *source* in the wild countryside beyond. A related aspect of garden representation would have struck the original readers of the Abbé's work as they looked at his frontispiece: the workers in the field have their counterparts, though unseen, in the garden, for this latter space is but a more intensified zone of cultivation, especially when compared to the barren lands further off. Both the fountain, with its reference to the hillside spring, and the parallel activities of field and garden, would have signaled something self-evident to gardenists around the year 1700: that gardens were recapitulations of other natures, an understanding that was variously registered in their use of terms like *represent[ation]* or *epitome*.

II

Represent / representation has been a useful and versatile word; it continues to enjoy considerable prestige as a critical term of choice in the humanities.[4] It has an assured role in the toolkit of critics; it has acquired its own theoretical nimbus, earning in an encyclopedia like *Critical Terms for Literary Study* an entry by W. J. T. Mitchell, editor of the influential journal *Critical Inquiry*.[5] It even has its own journal, entitled *Representations*.

Yet the term *represent[ation]* contains inherent complexities and ambiguities.[6] Just how do British members of Parliament, for example, "represent" their constituency in the House of Commons? And if the Labour Government installed in 1997 were to introduce "proportional representation," would this change the scope and meaning of the word? Anyone reading the stimulating and lively issues of *Representations* since that journal's inception in 1983 will have to admit that the eponymous term permits an astonishing range of concerns that do not readily elucidate the word under the auspices of which they are gathered, nor does the title, *Representations*, immediately clarify their inclusion. Indeed, the journal was launched with no editorial explanation of purpose or scope.

Its very first article, however, was an essay by Svetlana Alpers that goes some way to explain its focus, or at least a focus on the word *representation* that can be useful for understanding garden art.[7] Alpers asked why Velázquez's painting *Las Meninas* had eluded full discussion by art historians. She argued that it had elicited only two kinds of critique: one seeking to confirm that what appeared on the canvas were indeed actualities of Velázquez's time and place—the people were named, their positions and relationships explained; another supplying an explanation or "plot" for what was happening. Rather than either of these approaches, Alpers wanted to ground questions of subject matter and meaning in what she called questions of representation. This she expressed as a "concern with picturing something," which meant stressing the manner and means rather than the subject matter of the painting. There was, in fact, nothing new about this concept: Aristotle had identified a tripartite form of representation that invited consideration of a work's subject matter, its manner, and its means, and Immanuel Kant generalized that "our representation of things . . . conforms . . . to our mode of representation."[8]

What is useful about Alpers's discussion for our purposes is her distinction between saying, "I see the world" and "The world is being seen"; between—to translate her terms into ours—"I see nature in the garden" to "The garden is showing us a nature." Beyond simply stylistic explanations of why Velázquez should paint *Las Meninas* in that particular way or beyond traditional discussions of the objects of his mimesis, Alpers wanted to exploit a gap between the painting itself and a recognition of its cultural determination. She found in the painting, or imposed upon it, a certain self-reflexivity, which in turn became her theme. Its imagery of events was seen as being represented, that is, presented over again by the artist. Representation makes visible, at one and the same time, references to itself, to the materials of its creation, and to the idea or fiction of painting (or place-making).

This is a theme that has also interested Michel Foucault. In *Les Mots et les choses* he celebrated what he nicely calls the "blank space that separates the presence of representation and the 're-' of its repetition."[9] I want to annex this interest for the study of landscape architecture, which, because it deals sufficiently with "natural" things, has perhaps fallen into the delusion that its representations are themselves straightforward or "natural." For Foucault, a picture or—as I would now have him say—a garden is both a thing represented and a thing representing. And when he says that "representations are not rooted in a world that gives them meaning," I take it that it is not enough to identify the historical thing represented or the circumstances of its representation such as time, place, or patronage, for "representations open of themselves onto a space that is their own, whose internal network gives rise to meaning." I detect there a fossil of the old idea that art is self-sufficient and self-referential (that "internal network"), that it is not to be explained by authorial intentions or other contextual considerations.[10] But onto that old stock has been grafted the new proposal that representations speak of themselves.

This self-consciousness and self-referral, which a critic like Foucault would locate in a picture, a garden, or any other sign, involves above all an answering self-consciousness on the part of viewers; they find an object, like a garden, and make it a sign by analyzing it and acknowledging that it derives meaning by virtue of that analysis. Gardens are particularly remarkable for the alertness and self-confidence of their visitors, who respond to the garden's deliberate presentation of some nature. Foucault clearly states that "language exists in the gap that representation creates for itself." Or, finally, "the picture [or garden] has no other content in fact than that which it represents, and yet that content is made visible only because it is represented by a representation." What I find useful there is the (muted) acknowledgment of representation's outward reference (to actual objects or even ideas) as well as of its self-reference.

This is not language calculated to endear itself to garden enthusiasts or to pragmatic professionals. Yet that in itself must not distract from the essential wisdom of the invitation to see creations of gardens and experiences of gardens as being, each in their own way, deliberate and self-conscious. When we link this with the garden's presentation, within itself and through its materials, of worlds outside, as illustrated by the Babylonian gardens or Vallemont's frontispiece, then the idea of representation is indeed a central concern for landscape architecture.

III

Foucault's position may be exemplified easily in landscape architecture with the work of Lancelot "Capability" Brown. His landscape scenery comprised set pieces (pictures) that were to be viewed from some specific location, like the window of a house or the platform of a temple, and views that unfolded along a drive or during a walk. The contents of these pictures are (in Foucault's terms) nothing less than what they represent: trees, hillsides, water, sky, and sometimes bridges or buildings introduced into the spaces. What is presumably harder to grasp is the contention that Foucault goes on to make, namely, that the contents are made visible only because they are represented (re-presented) in landscape forms. But hostile contemporaries of Brown clearly understood this concept *avant la lettre*.

Sir Joshua Reynolds was the most measured critic. With Brown obviously in mind, in 1786 he addressed the issue of artistic imitation and declared, "Garden-ing, as far as Gardening is an Art, or entitled to that appellation, is a deviation from nature; for if the true taste consists, as many hold, in banishing every appearance of Art, or any traces of the footsteps of man, it would then be no longer a Garden."[11] What Reynolds points to is that the very medium of Brownian landscape design tends to conceal its message.[12] Gardens must declare their art, which cannot be done if the modish taste of being wholly natural in the choice and disposition of materials is followed. In those circumstances no gap, in Foucault's terms, has been created between the objects represented (trees, waters, hills, etc.) and their presentation anew in some parkland. Reynolds's stricture would, of course, have been more accurately aimed at some of Brown's inept followers, for his own work seems—even from this distance—a very self-conscious affair. But it was nevertheless to the designs of Brown himself that a more antagonistic critic, Sir William Chambers, pointed when he said that Brown's landscapes "differ very little from common fields."[13]

But Chambers (maybe deliberately) missed the point. In the best of Brown's parklands, trees were helped to behave as ideal trees should; water and earth were made to curve and dip as their elements ideally prescribe, and even the sky was allowed the opportunity to appear as quintessentially sky. The real quality of Brownian design, what distinguished it from routine place-making, lay in the eloquent re-presentation of its materials, which thereby made their distinct properties visible and revealed their capabilities (hence Brown's nickname).[14] We may identify this achievement in other designers, too, like Roberto Burle Marx, whose re-presentation of botanical materials draws attention to them, makes them more visible, not simply by rescuing them from the Brazilian forests but by featuring them for us to see and appreciate.

Brown's contemporaries might have linked his careful re-presentation of nature with what they would have termed *la belle nature* and certainly not with the common fields. And further, this perfected nature was a specific, local version, an ineluctable English landscape: *la belle nature anglaise*. Brown's landscape representations, then, not only drew out the ideal forms and presences of natural materials (trees, water) and effects (the sky), but through that emphasis represented the larger world of English nature and culture. Jane Austen understood this perfectly when she let Emma exclaim of the landscape at Donwell Abbey that "it was a sweet view — sweet to the eye and the mind, English verdure, English culture, English comfort, seen under a sun bright, without being oppressive." Emma is granted the opportunity of understanding representation in a scene where it is well done.

Now Reynolds had clearly recognized the significance of all this, too, for the declared topic of the lecture in which he raised the issue of landscape gardening was imitation or mimesis, sometimes a synonym for, but always a specific issue in the wider field of, representation. And Brown knew it, too, though this has never been argued: his oft-quoted but little understood remark to Hannah More that "there I make a comma, & there, where a more decided turn is proper, I make a colon"[15] surely refers to his recognition that he was, as a landscape designer, engaged in a rhetorical art, an art designed to persuade its viewers of the idealized nature of English scenery. In those few brief words he registered how his own art paralleled that of rhetoric by virtue of its skills at representing a site, as a skilled writer uses all resources including grammar and punctuation to represent an argument.

IV

But if Foucault's observations on representation are readily exemplified by the work of Brown and the comments upon it of his contemporaries, Brown also stands for the moment when people began to lose any understanding of garden art in terms of representation. This loss was ironically endemic to his best work. Although the extent of his radical move is much exaggerated by modern historians, Brown tended to eliminate or at least downplay the role of such items as temples, statues, and inscriptions in designed landscapes. One effect of such "ornaments" was that they drew attention to their site, as Wallace Stevens's jar does to the Tennessee hillside where it is placed; another effect was to highlight the effort of representation, like the parterre fountain in Vallemont's frontispiece. Brown's designs chose to rely far less on these built features, for despite being an architect he clearly saw the distinctive opportunities of landscape forms and materials by themselves. Like Roberto Burle Marx later, Brown's work suggests that unlike architecture, where according to Karsten Harries it is "genuine ornament" that draws attention to its representational status,[16] the designed landscape does not need these devices to engage in representation. But when the naturalistic medium became all-important, when designs became indistinguishable from second nature or common fields, the notion that the landscape gardener's business was representation of a perfected nature slipped from sight. When far less talented designers than Brown were at work (see Figure 24), the idea of landscape as representation got even more wholly obscured, with disastrous results for both the practice and the theory of landscape architecture.

Brown's art constitutes, then, a watershed. Before him the idea that gardens somehow represented the natural world anew in forms devised, revised, and augmented by artifice was a commonplace. Thus Joseph Addison had noted in 1712 that Italian gardens consisted of "a large Extent of Ground covered over with an agreeable mixture of Garden and Forest, which represent every where an artificial Rudeness."[17] But by the last quarter of the century, as we have seen with Reynolds and Chambers, forest could only too readily be taken to be just forest. A new insistence upon and taste for naturalness had effectively collapsed the distance between medium and message. It is something of an irony that Brown's consummate artistry and ambition lost for gardens their claims to the status of a fine art, which the concept and practice of representation had earned them. Indeed, it was their very claim to repre-

FIGURE 51. Cornelis Elandts, map of the Ridderhofstad of Werve near Voorburg, c. 1665, Voorburg, Westelijk Wegenbouw Centrum.

sent, long a desideratum of the fine arts, that allowed garden art into the pantheon of the beaux arts during the eighteenth century. But in France, A. C. Quatremère de Quincey (1755–1849) refused the garden any status as an imitative art simply because by the time he was writing the materials of its medium were not sufficiently different from its objects. In seeming to yield up their traditional role of imitating nature, gardens became only what they represented—flowers, shrubs, trees, and so on.

It is worth reviewing more extensively the garden's earlier claims to represent, not for merely historical reasons but because this ambition needs clarification as it becomes once again an issue in current practice. So we must descend from the ridge of that Brownian watershed into the more detailed landscape of garden theory and practice in the two centuries or so before him.

During that period there were two modes of garden representation. They are distinct but not mutually exclusive. The first is localized, specific, and can be dangerously close to mere copying, imitation, or pastiche; this is easy enough to demonstrate from garden writings. The second eschews simple facsimile and represents the "principles and spirit" of its subject, offering "images not copies," or what we might want to call "fictions";[18] this is less susceptible to precise illustration.

We tend to withhold the term *representation* in the first instance, considering it "broader" than mimesis.[19] In the second, modern theory seeks to enlarge the scope of representation as much as possible, for, as Keith Moxey writes, it "has less to do with a perennial desire to obtain mimetic accuracy . . . and more with cultural projection, with the construction, presentation, and dissemination of cultural values."[20] Yet the two modes are not mutually exclusive. Mimetic items can play their part in larger representation endeavors: the garden fountain represents by formally imitating the natural spring in the hillside of Vallemont's frontispiece, but that fountain is also a significant element in that garden's representation of "cultural values." Con-

versely, while Bonfadio praised gardens on the shore of Lake Garda because they somehow epitomized a cultural history of human habitation, that would not have meant that individual items in those gardens did not also have some mimetic intention.

We are looking then at a sliding scale from mimesis or imitation to representation in its largest sense. The latter does not require specific iconographical programs, nor does imitation involve mere copying.[21] Another way of identifying this scale of representational effects and achievements would be to invoke another (this time, semiological) triad of icon, symbol, and index as different modes by which a garden or elements within it can make reference to larger worlds.[22] What is chosen for such reference, what is deemed apt or relevant for representation by whatever means in a garden, will depend on the interests, concerns, and even obsessions of a given period and culture. Finally, it is important to note that representation can gesture both to things that actually exist (grottoes to caves, for example; whole gardens to their creators) and to what exists only in the imagination (mythic gardens of Eden or the Hesperides). Representation in landscape architecture is particularly geared to invoke both what is actual, palpable in the material world, and what lives only in the wide spaces of the human imagination.

The claim that a garden's specific features represent elements outside was derived partly from the fashion by which so many garden features had grown out of or were extrapolated from agrarian activity. Every item in a garden had some direct or more obscure origin in the world of second or even first nature, elements of which they took further (hence their characterization as a "third" nature). Drawing attention to origins does not by itself, of course, constitute representation; but if (as seems clear) viewers are involved in the reception and understanding of representation, then their grasp of the schemata by which landscape architecture has at different periods formulated its representations will be crucial. The third nature, as that term implied for Bonfadio and Taegio, drew upon and enhanced the imagery and procedures of second nature; hence the grammar and syntax of that cultural landscape tended to yield a means of understanding how gardens had taken matters further. Only later when garden theory tried to argue that its schemata were derived from painting did it seem to suppress the continuities between agrarian and horticultural practices, at the same time also ignoring how some landscape models invoked in this appeal to painting were themselves clarified or rarified visions of second or even first nature.

v

The development of gardenist forms and techniques out of horticultural and agricultural practices is certainly an important (and perhaps unduly neglected) theme of garden studies.[23] Clearings in a forest or a flowery meadowland became lawn and grass sward.[24] Ornamental canals in Dutch gardens were an aesthetic extension of drainage ditches in the low-lying polders (Figure 51). Terraces were derived from hillsides shaped for agriculture (see Figure 35): this was clearly stated by the Dutch garden writer Pieter de la Court van der Voort, when he wrote in *Les Agrémens de la Campagne* that terraces had their origin in sloping mountains ("Les Terrasses firent leur origine des Montagnes panchées").[25] In similar fashion, fountains and hydraulic systems grew out of irrigation needs and techniques, or the elaboration within gardens of allées and bosquets (groves) developed from the forester's management of woodland and hunting territory (Figures 52 and 53).

John Evelyn acknowledged this development of garden forms from natural phenomena when he wrote in his manuscript "Elysium Britannicum" that "Grottoes are invented to reppresent Dens and caves"; he was probably copying Jacques Boyceau, who in his turn had declared that "les grotes sont faites pour representer les Antres Sauvages."[26] Both writers, however, were not simply identifying a garden mimesis; they were alluding to a larger representational theme, one that we have already encountered in Bonfadio's letter. Just as the

Italian writer contrasted the *signori* in their lakeside villas on Garda with the wild men of the mountains behind, so Evelyn and Boyceau are noting how garden grottoes mark the progress of civilization from the savage state. Yet neither Evelyn nor Boyceau would have stopped there: the thrust of garden art for them was its celebration of the superiority of human creation and art over the natural world. It should delight the eye and the mind with representations by which men and women demonstrated both their creative skills and their understanding of the natural and cultural worlds; to rework or recapitulate major themes from those worlds was to use art, science, and technology to display the scope of human reason and imagination.

The garden, then, performed or represented through its own materials and effects—as a dramatist and actors could through different means in the theater—the larger worlds outside. Mounts in medieval and early Renaissance gardens represented hills or mountains (Figure 54); in Ming gardens, rocks performed the same task.[27] What were called "wildernesses" in western design were gardenist versions of the wild wood or first nature; so, too, were labyrinths (Figure 55)—a highly wrought image of the outside world's confusion and perplexities, but to anyone who has actually got lost in one, also an extremely palpable enactment of disorientation. Labyrinths became less fashionable precisely as it became clear that the whole garden could assume the role of representing both the confusions of the larger world and its ultimate meaning.[28] Pergolas were like paths through woodland; sixteenth-century arbors and berceaux were walks through denser growth where clearings suddenly opened out, as later were the high hedges and cabinets in seventeenth-century gardens (see the arbors along the edges of the second and third sections of the Wilton garden, illustrated in Figure 32). Canals represented rivers—at Moor Park in Surrey, Sir William Temple made this palpable when he allowed the local river to run in two parallel forms, one abstracted as a straight canal, the other in its unmediated or natural lines (Figure 56). Similarly at Zorg-

FIGURE 52. Avenues in the garden of the Château Corbeil-Cerf,
Oise, 1992.

FIGURE 53. A regular plantation of trees alongside the parterres
at Champromain, Thiville, Eure-et-Loire, 1992.

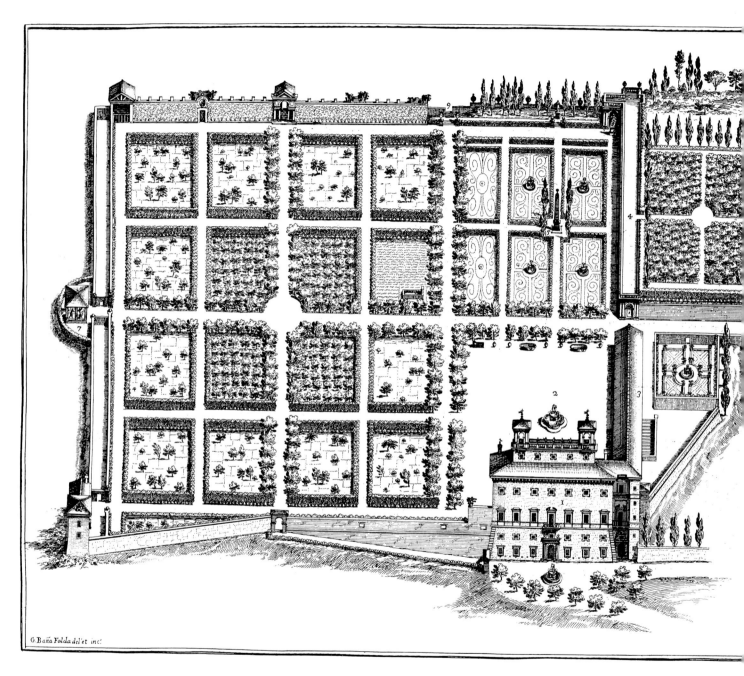

FIGURE 54. G. B. Falda's engraving of the mount in the Villa
Medici, Rome, 1670s.

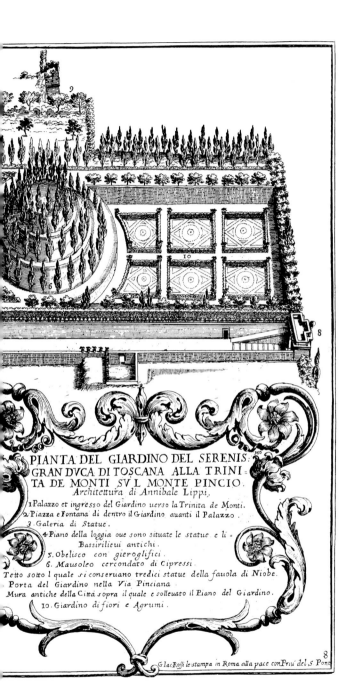

PIANTA DEL GIARDINO DEL SERENIS.
GRAN DVCA DI TOSCANA ALLA TRINI-
TA DE MONTI SVL MONTE PINCIO.
Architettura di Annibale Lippi.

1 Palazzo et ingresso del Giardino uerso la Trinita de Monti.
2. Piazza e Fontana di dentro il Giardino auanti il Palazzo.
3. Galeria di Statue.
4 Piano della loggia oue sono situate le statue e li
   Bassirilieui antichi.
5. Obelisco con gieroglifici.
6. Mausoleo cercondato di Cipressi.
Tetto sotto l quale si conseruano tredici statue della fauola di Niobe.
Porta del Giardino nella Via Pinciana
Mura antiche della Città sopra il quale e solleuato il Piano del Giardino.
10. Giardino di fiori e Agrumi.

G IacRossi le stampa in Roma alla pace con Priu del S Pont

vliet in the Netherlands, the river first ran in a straight channel alongside the gardens and then, still within sight of the gardens, was suddenly allowed to resume its natural form.[29] William Kent played games with this mode of representation when at Rousham, Oxfordshire, he created the serpentine rill as a formal parody of the River Cherwell meandering along the bottom of the gardens. The systematization of natural river forms similarly delighted Isamu Noguchi at Costa Mesa (see Figure 16) and FFNS, the Swedish firm that redesigned the church square of Partille some years before the California Scenario (Figure 57).

Waters seem to provide some of the more exciting and inventive moments of garden representation. Pools in Ming gardens were lakes and seas.[30] The Italian feature known as a *catena d'acqua* or water-chain is the formalized version of a stream cascading down a hillside—its representational function is obvious when it is experienced on the sloping sites of Villa Lante, the Villa Farnese at Caprarola, the Villa Torlonia at Frascati (Figure 58), Chatsworth, or Buscot House, Oxfordshire. Dramatic cascades, like the Fountain of Tivoli or the Fountain of the Organ at the Villa d'Este, are more obviously facsimiles of natural waterfalls.[31] Indeed, a visitor to Tivoli in the 1640s took one look at the Fountain in the villa gardens and set off in search of its "model," the Aniene River cascades in the town;[32] we shall need to return to his apparent dissatisfaction with garden representations.

VI

Since we are rarely concerned today with this aspect of landscape design, we tend to ignore the many places where these representational aims of garden art are described in earlier documents or enacted on the ground. Yet, as we shall see more fully in Chapter 7, late seventeenth-century gardenists were convinced of the scope of garden representation. And their concern leads us from its specific or local forms to what is ultimately

FIGURE 55. The Labyrinth at the Villa Donà delle Rose, Valsanzibio, Veneto, 1980s.

of more continuing interest. When John Worlidge argues that "gardens, orchards, partirres, avenues . . .
represent unto us epitomized, the form and idea of the
more ample and spacious pleasant fields, groves, and
other rustick objects,"[33] he moves the argument from
local or mimetic forms to larger concerns. These latter
are addressed directly by John Evelyn when he writes in
the preface to his *Acetaria* of "that Great and Universal
Plantation, Epitomiz'd in our Gardens";[34] he refers to
the representation of the macrocosm itself within the
smaller (epitomized) microcosm of the garden.

How does the garden do this? How may we experience or read gardens in that fashion or, at least, learn
how earlier visitors did so? In part, Evelyn and Worlidge's claims are based on a theoretical conviction that
all gardens follow the first, Eden, in endeavoring to
be complete. Certainly, individual gardens are often in
dialogue with an idea of the garden, an idea that is derived from a mental review of all possible forms, actual

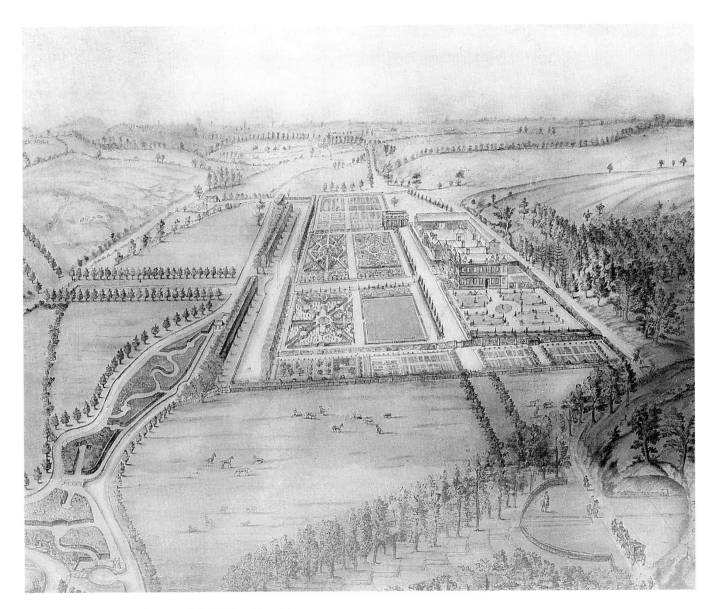

FIGURE 56. Anonymous, drawing of Sir William Temple's garden, Moor Park, Surrey, 1690s. Surrey History Centre, Woking.

FIGURE 57. Thorbjörn Andersson, Kyrktorget (the Church Square), Partille, Sweden, 1991 (photograph: Sven Westerlund, courtesy of the designer).

and legendary; in this mental image the original garden clearly features prominently. We might compare this acknowledgment of Eden via its explicit or implicit representation with a similar concern among some architects to imitate an ideal or ur-structure, whether Solomon's temple or the primitive hut.[35]

In practice, the seventeenth-century botanical garden came closest to achieving this representation of Eden; as John Prest has shown,[36] it was an attempt to gather together again in one place the scattered botanical riches of the whole world, a conspectus lost to us after the Fall. The circular form of the Hortus Botanicus at Padua was a reference to the globe, whose botanical resources were once again to be gathered together and represented there, and an image of the perfection of that achievement. Evelyn's rough design for a botanical garden in "Elysium Britannicum" (Figure 59) includes a full repertoire of microclimates, as we would call them, thus ensuring as complete a collection of plants as possible. A similar range of spaces constituted the Jardin du Roi, which Evelyn visited in Paris (Figure 60) and where he commented specifically on

FIGURE 58. The water cascade
at the Villa Torlonia (now
public gardens), Frascati, as
restored in 1998.

FIGURE 59. John Evelyn's plan for a botanical garden, from "Elysium Britannicum," folio 330, late seventeenth century. The British Library, London.

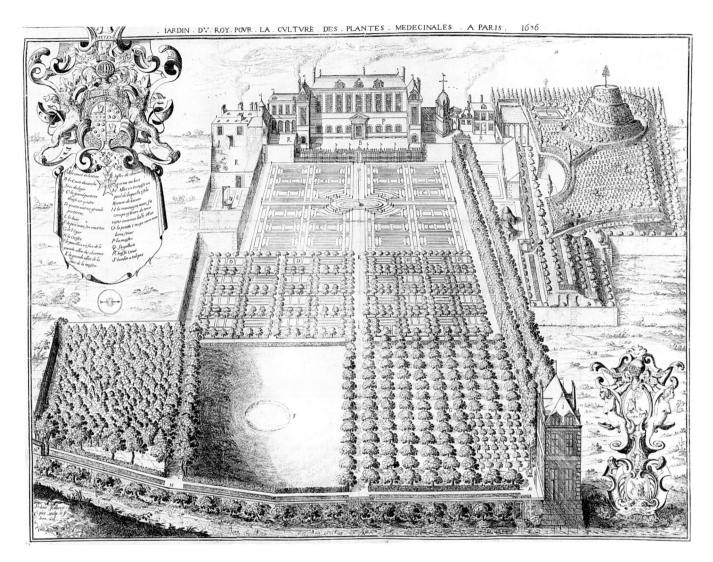

FIGURE 60. The King's botanical garden in Paris, drawn and engraved by Frederic Scalberge, 1636. Private collection.

its incorporation of "all sorts of varietys of grounds . . . hills, meadows, growne Wood, & Upland, both artificial and natural."[37] The title page of John Parkinson's *Theatrum Botanicum* (London, 1640) shows emblems of the four continents, the sources of this collection (or theater) of plants (Figure 61). Besides meaning a collection, *theatrum* for Parkinson also signals a stage—like the old Globe Theater—where, as its name implies, the whole world could be represented; so on Parkinson's title page is a platform where two actors perform—the first gardener, Adam, and the wisest of postlapsarian humans, Solomon, through whose modern science Adam's botanical world could be recovered.

FIGURE 61. Engraved title
page of John Parkinson, *The-*
atrum Botanicum: The Theater
of Plantes, London, 1640.
Dumbarton Oaks Research
Library and Collections.

FIGURE 62. From Salomon de Caus, *Les Raisons des forces mouvantes*, Paris, 1615. Private collection.

A botanical garden, like modern zoological gardens, aims at inclusiveness; hence its claims to represent the world are sufficiently evident. But the botanical garden for Evelyn or Worlidge was no different from other gardens. When Worlidge wrote in his *Art of Gardening* that Italian gardens were "the mirrors of the World, as well as [for] those ornaments as for the excellency of the Plants that are propogated in them,"[38] he meant that they reflected—or represented—a whole world of incidents. This was achieved in part by their collections of sculpture, which, as an unequivocally representative art form, brought into the garden images of famous heroes, historical and legendary, and by implication all the events in which they had made themselves famous. Hydraulic devices (Figure 62) went even further and contrived an illusion of animation and action for both human figures and such natural phenomena as "Raine-bowes, Stormes, raine Thunder and other artifical meteors" or the "motion and chirpings of Birds, Satyres and other (vocall) Creatures, after a wonderfull manner."[39]

Imitations in these microcosmic spaces were experienced in the same way as huge collections or amalgamations of history and myth. Upon first entering the Earl of Arundel's sculpture garden overlooking the Thames,

Sir Francis Bacon is reputed to have exclaimed, "Ah! the Resurrection." Christopher Arnold, later professor of history at Nuremberg, explained in 1651 that Arundel's (by then neglected) gardens still contained "rare Greek and Roman inscriptions, stones, marbles: the reading of which is actually like viewing Greece and Rome at once within the bounds of Great Britain."[40]

This way of seeing gardens and, we must therefore deduce, this motive for creating them gave priority to their presentation of "Histories and Scaenes"[41] that were derived from the world at large. In "Elysium Britannicum," Evelyn argues that "in our conceit A mount raised with the perfect dimensions of the Greater Aegyptian Pyramid . . . would reppresent to our imaginations one of the most sollemne and prodigious Monuments" (folio 140). But such "conceits," either individually or in the ensemble, authorized seeing gardens as expressions of their owner and his or her culture and worldview. Whether deliberately designed with this motif or not, gardens came to be read as expressions of their maker: "As is the Gardener, so is the Garden."[42] The Villa d'Este, to take one example, was specifically designed to represent the eminence and learning of its owner and patron, Cardinal Ippolito d'Este II: its conceit that the dragon which once guarded the golden apples in the legendary Garden of the Hesperides was now reinstalled as a fountain (Figure 63) in the new gardens at Tivoli was a tribute above all to the munificence and humanism of the cardinal.[43]

We know that all great European gardens of the seventeenth and eighteenth centuries—the Hortus Palatinus at Heidelberg, Vaux, Het Loo, Castle Howard, Stowe, Rousham, Worlitz—were developed as expressions of their owner's status and position in the world; we know, because the gardens made it their business to alert visitors to this fact. And because such gardens represented their creator's place in and his view of the world, they came in their turn to be read in that way by countless visitors. If that had not been the case, neither the Catholic armies that destroyed the Palatine garden at the start of the Thirty Years' War, nor Louis XIV, jealous of Fouquet, the creator and owner of Vaux-le-Vicomte, would have wasted their energies on eliminating and despoiling as much of these sites as they could. And what can be easily said of the elite gardens was probably true, though in more modest and less self-conscious ways, of many smaller examples or vernacular examples.[44] Dutch cartoonist Stefan Verwey makes this wonderfully clear in his contrast of two competing representations of the natural world in adjacent front gardens (Figure 64).

VII

Now representation is not a topic very congenial to landscape architecture, perhaps because of its tendency to look toward architecture which (much more than music) finds representation an especially difficult notion to take on board.[45] To the modern gardenist this discussion of representation may even be foreign or silly: foreign, because today's garden maker and garden visitor will rarely conceive of sites in this way;[46] silly, because if landscape architects do attempt to invoke such strategies, the results, in order to draw responses that are in effect unusual, will often be extravagant or even kitsch. The horses galloping across the "stream bed" of the plaza at Las Colinas, Texas, offer a particularly good example of weak mimeticism.[47] The insistent "meaningfulness" of Noguchi's California Scenario, along with the simple representationism of such elements as the water course or the desert ground, are arguably another instance.

Of course, such dubious representations are by no means new. The re-creation of the Matterhorn in miniature in a Victorian alpine garden seems particularly inept.[48] We are amused, too, by Andrew Marvell's description of a fortification garden, set out in flowers, at Lord Fairfax's estate of Nun Appleton, Yorkshire.[49] Cardinal Richelieu had a representation of the Niagara Falls in his gardens at Rueil. Even Capability Brown reputedly proposed a flower bed at Brocklesby,

FIGURE 63. Fountain of the Dragons in the Villa d'Este, Tivoli, 1971.

FIGURE 64. Stefan Verwey, cartoon, originally published in *De Volkskrant* newspaper, the Netherlands.

Lincolnshire, in the form of a flower,[50] and Repton laid out his rose garden at Ashridge in the shape of a rose,[51] a mimetic device that continues to be invoked particularly in the layout of this kind of garden (Figure 65).

Nor is skepticism with such effects new. It was precisely because representations were thought to be sloppy, ineffective, or plain silly that they were rejected in the past. That visitor to the Villa d'Este in the 1640s was plainly disenchanted with the garden representation of a natural waterfall when he could see the real thing for himself. In a letter to Samuel Hartlib in 1659, John Beale expressed scorn for what he called "narrow mimicall way[s]" of representation in gardens.[52] "Foppish great merchants" in the Ming period were pilloried for conspicuous consumption precisely because their gardens contained elements that did not fully represent them ("there are no hills and valleys in their breasts").[53] George Mason, beginning to lose a grip on the idea

of representation in the mid-eighteenth century, could not accept that old Persian paradises were "similitudes of forests" or that the area of Stowe known as Hawkwell Field could represent a farm.[54] And as late as the 1770s, William Gilpin, visiting General Conway's estate near Henley-on-Thames, found a "piece of *rock-scenery*, consisting of half a dozen large stones brought together. Nothing can be more absurd. They neither give any idea of what they were intended to represent; nor are they suited to the country, in which they are introduced."[55] Gilpin makes clear that he judges the rock-work for its mimetic force, including its aptness for that particular site: "To turn a level country into a mountainous one, or a smooth scene into a rocky one, is absurd." He also reminds us that this expectation of and popularity for *good* representation lasted long into the Brownian or naturalistic phase of landscape design.

It must also be acknowledged that this tendency

FIGURE 65. The Rose Garden, Wellington Botanical Gardens,
New Zealand, 1988.

toward representational strategies, however criticized,
has not been lost; in fact, it seems to grow stronger and
stronger. Given the Renaissance delight with aquatic
forms of representations, it is not surprising that these
continue to be prominent. If the Renaissance, invoking
classical precedent, used to image the source of a stream
with the statue of a river god pouring water from

an urn (Figure 66), we have our own versions of the
same event. The line of granite blocks at Parc André-
Citroën, Paris, from each of which issues an arc of
water (Figure 67), is more geologically literal, closer to
the spurt of a spring from below ground—except that
the effect is here repeated many times and the lines by
which the blocks have been mechanically quarried are
visible (thus drawing attention to the re-presentation).
Or that more witty, perhaps facetious, moment on the
Boulevard St. Germain in Paris (at its junction with

FIGURE 66. River god in the gardens of the Villa Lante, Bagnaia, 1970s.

the Rue de Rennes) where water gushes up through the sidewalk, forcing pavers into the air in imitation of a bursting main or like the unsettling prelude to some disaster movie.

Lawrence Halprin's wonderful fountains in Portland, Oregon, recall the mountainscapes to the east of that city (Figure 68). Another example of simple, effective representation of water effects, the Tanner Fountain by SWA outside the Harvard Science Center in Cambridge, Massachusetts (Figure 69), requires the design to recall, in almost iconic[56] simplicity, an analogous geological event in first nature. These are all essentially single items that draw upon traditional representational effects in sculpture, whether the mode is iconic, symbolic, or indexical or even a mix of them. But the move can be more extensive and still thoroughly explicit, as when Martha Schwartz and her colleagues set

FIGURE 67. Fountains along the side of the white garden, Parc André-Citroën, Paris, 1994.

out along the narrow site in Yorkville, Toronto, a whole series of replications of local Ontario topography and terrain (Figure 70), a process that involved moving a huge boulder into town from the countryside.

With our current concern for "nature" and the environment, it is not surprising that representations of geomorphology are prominent in the imagery of land-

scape architecture. Even a restored wetlands can be viewed as the re-presentation of a previously polluted or damaged site. But it is precisely in that modern, ecological instance that we confront once again what may be called the Brownian fallacy. By insisting on naturalistic design, landscape architects run the risk of effacing themselves and their art.

What needs to be rescued for landscape architecture from these various exercises in representation is the idea of creating sites that are fictions. David Leatherbarrow

FIGURE 68. Ira's Fountain, Portland, Oregon, designed by
Lawrence Halprin (photograph: Marc Treib, 1993).

has written in the same way about architecture, an even
more recalcitrant medium to link with representation:
"The sense of imitation I intend is not a copy or mechanical reproduction of a particular human event or
experience . . . ; instead, architecture imitates some
human possibility. As such a possibility must be imagined, architectural imitation is necessarily fictional. Because fictions lack perfect antecedents, their invention
is productive; they augment reality."[57]

The same must be insisted on for landscape architecture. Yet, as indeed in some literary fictions, replication
or imitation of the sort Leatherbarrow eschews can be
effective (there it is called realism or naturalism). It
happens to be a strength in the Tanner Fountain, which
needs to bring us close to a real geological moment of

FIGURE 69. Tanner Fountain, designed by SWA, Harvard Science Center, Cambridge, Mass. (photograph: Nancy Ševčenko, 1997).

water and mist rising between boulders, or at St. Germain des Prés, where the literalness of the gesture is a necessary part of the wit.

Three recent public parks in Paris also imply a renewed concern with, if not even compulsive return to, representation as fiction. Both Parc Bercy and Parc André-Citroën set out a repertoire of effects: at Bercy (Figure 71), it is images of different kinds of gardens, from the spare urban spaces at the west through the anthology of different parterres or growing areas in the center to the romantic landscape at the west. Each zone, but especially the last, has the slightly awkward self-consciousness of symbolic gesture. Parc Citroën, despite proclaiming that it was "ni français, ni anglais," nevertheless seemed to offer itself as a "theater"

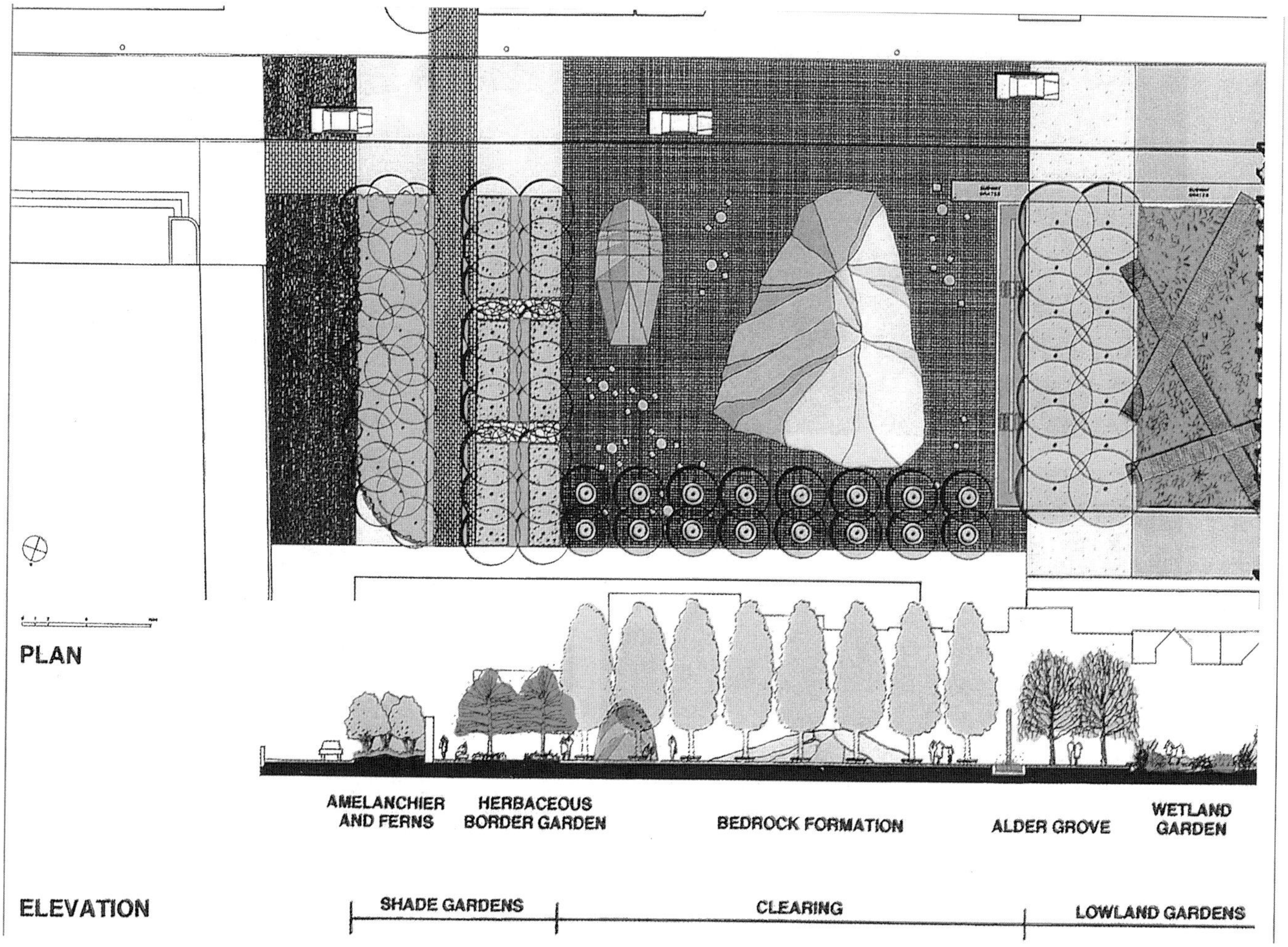

PLAN

ELEVATION

AMELANCHIER HERBACEOUS
AND FERNS   BORDER GARDEN   BEDROCK FORMATION   ALDER GROVE   WETLAND
GARDEN

SHADE GARDENS   CLEARING   LOWLAND GARDENS

FIGURE 70. Plan of the Yorkville park, Toronto, designed by
Ken Smith, Martha Schwartz, and David Meyer (photograph
courtesy of Martha Schwartz).

of styles, augmenting those already available by the
creation of something fresh (Figure 72); both its glass-
houses and the so-called garden of movement are also
designed to represent a conspectus of both cultivated
and wild wasteland plants.[58] The Jardin Atlantique
(Figure 73, and see Figure 49), already discussed as a
modern counterpart to the Hanging Gardens of Babylon, plays wonderful representational games that draw
attention to themselves, to the mental idea or fiction
of a garden, and to the more distant actualities of the

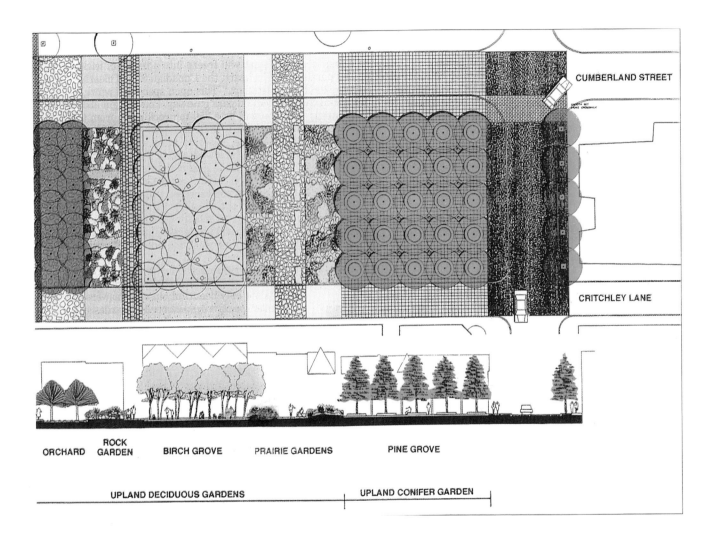

CUMBERLAND STREET

CRITCHLEY LANE

ORCHARD

ROCK
GARDEN

BIRCH GROVE

PRAIRIE GARDENS

PINE GROVE

UPLAND DECIDUOUS GARDENS

UPLAND CONIFER GARDEN

Brittany seaside, which passengers reach on trains that depart from the railway station beneath.

VIII

Representation, then, is a recurring and crucial strategy in place-making from Babylon to Bercy. It is not, however, always an easy or a comfortable element for either the designer or the visitor/consumer. The slippery term *representation* refers to a confusing range of activities and events from actual places to mental images, and by now it is fraught with a conceptual baggage that should make us wary of invoking it without whole chapters of orientation. As has been shown, garden representation functions in such a variety of modes—by replicating a catalog of natural items, or by miniaturizing, by copying, abstracting, or even recalling, even by standing for itself—that one may wonder whether one word can really cope adequately with all these modes and motives. Yet no other term has

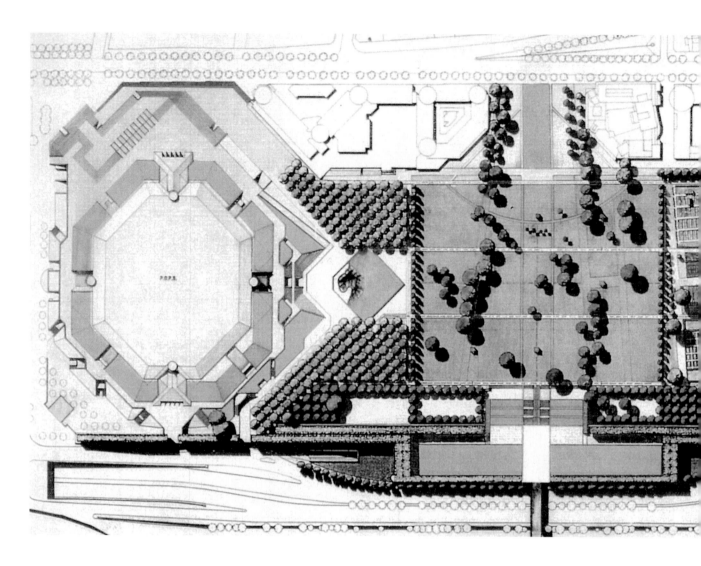

FIGURE 71. Plan of the Parc Bercy, Paris, designed by the late
Yan Lescaisne and Philippe Raguin (photograph courtesy of
Paris Department of Parks).

either adequate contemporary currency (however modish) or historical precedence (it is striking how often
seventeenth-century gardenists used it).

Neither philosophical, let alone semantic, objections
to notions of representation in garden art nor the
practical awkwardness involved in some manifestations
of it seem to prevent its continuing life and usefulness. The aspirations, for instance, of the seventeenth-
century botanical garden to represent the whole uni-

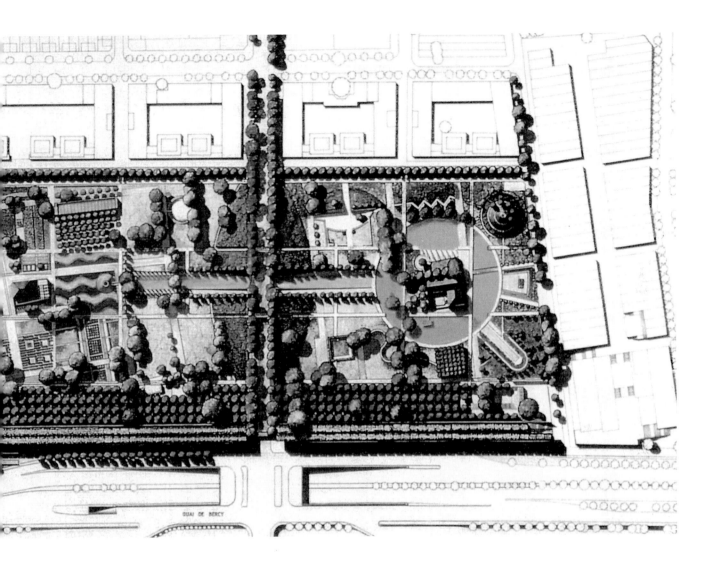

verse of plants, to restore Eden in all its prelapsarian plenitude, may have fallen victim to the extraordinary wealth of botanical specimens that poured into Europe from newly explored continents;[59] the mimetic ambition was defeated by the profusion of items it needed to represent. But such failures never pre-empted the development of more selectively representational gardens—American or alpine gardens, say, in the following centuries.

Representation in landscape architecture functions on a scale of effects and in a variety of modes. In the terms suggested by Leatherbarrow for architecture, there are fictions to suit all tastes: from pulp fiction to serious reading, and it is wholly right that this range should exist—from Disneylands through casino and mall landscaping to Parc La Villette. This scale necessarily ranges from mere facsimile to subtle and elusive recollection; yet even this latter, which takes the

FIGURE 72. Poster for the Parc
André-Citroën, Paris, 1980s.

FIGURE 73. Le Jardin Atlantique, Montparnasse, Paris, 1997.

FIGURE 74a. Ian Hamilton Finlay, the "flock of sheep" in Stockwood Park, Luton (photograph courtesy of Ian Hamilton Finlay).

form of stimulating memory and associations, functions along a similar scale—from the recall of ancient Rome in the Elysian Fields at Stowe by the simple expedient of re-creating an antique temple, to the suggestive pastoral artifice of the Long Meadow in Prospect Park, the wilder scenery of the Hudson Valley in the Ramble of Central Park, and the assemblage of "seaside" events in the Jardin Atlantique.

Some contemporary place-makers invoke representational strategies almost satirically, as if to avail themselves of its scope while distancing themselves from its potential banalities (Martha Schwartz's bagel garden or the gilded frogs in Atlanta),[60] or to draw attention to historical precedents and their contemporary revisions. Finlay's installations, to be examined in more detail later, play with the historical traditions of representation: blocks of stone represent sheep in the pastoral scenario of Stockwood Park, Luton (Figure 74). At the Max Planck Institut outside Stuttgart (Figure 75), Finlay uses both words (themselves arbitrary representations of things like windflowers, wave, or sail) and abstract forms (concrete slabs as sails, concrete undulations as waves) to recall both the Institut's researches into the physical world and the immeasurable worlds of time and tide beyond the tamed nature of these German suburbs.

FIGURE 74b. Ian Hamilton Finlay, the inscription on one of the blocks (photograph by Werner J. Hannappel, courtesy of Ian Hamilton Finlay).

The garden (third nature) took its place in a scale of human inventions into the natural world; that place was in part signaled by the complexity and motives of garden design and in part by references that the garden made to other zones, the first and second natures. It is within that scheme of references that we should situate landscape architecture's representation; it is a spe-cific and direct appeal from designed elements to other phenomena, some cultural, some natural, but many of them mixed.

But underlying most claims for a garden as a repre-sentational art has been the expectation that, above all, a garden "imitated nature": for that reason, William Hanbury in 1770 categorically stated, "Nature must be imitated in all our works."[61] Once this by no means re-ferred only to natural scenery or natural materials like plants; it included all aspects of the world, including human nature, which was deemed to be the central

FIGURE 75. SCHIFF, de-
signed by Ian Hamilton Finlay with Ron Costley, marble,
1976. Max Planck Institut,
Stuttgart, photographed in
1991.

focus of all art:[62] thus Sir Philip Sidney's *Apologie for Poetrie* argued that art creates "things either better than nature bringeth forth, or quite anew, formes such as never were." Yet by the end of the eighteenth century the term had dwindled into meaning simply a botanical and/or scenic nature in which humans and their cultural effects were not included. Garden makers saw the natural phenomena of a site as not just the raw materials of their art's mimetic effort but its effects as well: as Alexandre Laborde put it in 1808, garden art was "la science de produire, dans un lieu quelconque, l'aspect le plus agréable que le site soit susceptible de représenter."[63]

The danger of such an appeal to "nature" is, of course, that it challenges the usefulness or efficacy of any human mediation. The influential eighteenth-century poem by the Abbé Delille continues to speak for many landscape architects in its contempt for "imitating man":

> Then Nature's bold effects were soon restor'd;
> But if no threat'ning mass thy fields afford,
> Nature's proud rival Art presumes in vain
> To rear a faithless copy on a plain.[64]

So we are again brought round to the Brownian dilemma: that the necessary medium of nature must not be allowed wholly to subdue the evidence that it is itself being imitated.

This challenge is made particularly clear with Brown or with modern so-called ecological design. But it is posed throughout the history of landscape architecture, which is full of examples of both aggressive and self-effacing art. It is also full of confusions between the appeal to mimesis (imitation, copy, facsimile) and that mimesis which Aristotle originally glossed as a fiction, a re-presentation that unveils, uncovers, and reveals.[65] History also testifies to the variety of "natures" that have been chosen for representation: the English translation of Dézaillier d'Argenville's *Theory and Practice of Gardening* thought terraces, "exactly level and well supported," would look as "disposed so by nature."[66] Not many years later Robert Castell championed "a close Imitation of Nature" now characterized by irregularity that betrays "no Appearance of that Skill which is made use of . . . Rocks, Cascades, and Trees, bearing their natural Forms."[67]

When A. J. Downing in 1841 asked, "In what manner is nature to be imitated in Landscape gardening?" he was struggling with precisely the extent to which it would be permissible in the eastern United States at that period to insist on the representational strategies of his professional activity.[68] But it is a perennial topic, a question endlessly adjudicated according to the cultural moment at which it is posed. This can be better appreciated by examining three further aspects of the subject: a particularly crucial moment in theory and practice (Chapter 7); another kind of representation—namely, the imagery of landscape architecture held up in verbal and visual arts (Chapter 6); and, first, the role of word and image in place-making (Chapter 5).

CHAPTER 5

Word and Image in the Garden

Seeing is forgetting the name of the thing one sees.
—Paul Valéry

This is the crux of the matter; crossing the spatiality of the narration with the temporality of the [landscape] architectural project.
—Paul Ricoeur

THE VERBAL AND VISUAL play two roles in landscape architecture. First, there is the actual part they play in the design and configuration of gardens, which this chapter considers. Second, there is their dual role in our experience, reception, or thinking of gardens, which if we wish to articulate it needs words or images; this forms the topic of Chapter 6, which approaches the idea of the garden—mental representations of it—through visual and verbal images of it in art and in writing (outside the design treatise or horticultural manual).

But the two roles are linked, at times almost indistinguishably. Words—in the form of inscriptions, names of garden elements, even iconographical programs or stories—have guided the design of gardens and are also to be found inscribed in them. In visiting gardens, those verbal "supplements" to their organic and inorganic materiality can guide or even dictate how we experience sites; the knowledgeable garden visitor may even anticipate those verbal prompts. In that way the design and the experience of a garden share verbal elements. Equally, pictorial structures are a central element in place-making, and we discuss designs partly in terms of their visual scope. Visitors ideally need to identify and appreciate these, but they also ar-

rive with pictorial and visual preconceptions acquired from paintings, photography, films, and other gardens and landscapes. How the designer's intentions meet and mesh with (or miss) visitors' expectations is a fascinating theme, too little studied.

I

Let us return to Ian Hamilton Finlay's installation outside Stuttgart, at the Institut named after the distinguished physicist Max Planck. Its words and images are all abstract representations of things: on the one hand, there are linguistic abstractions like WINDFLOWER, VNDA, or SCHIFF, deliberately arbitrary in their appeal to three languages; on the other, we see physical abstractions that mostly take the form of concrete panels. One of these is corrugated, a breaking wave along whose length the Latin word VNDA enfolds itself from recognizable jumble into correct format, helped along by the compositor's conventional wavy signal to the printer to "transpose" letters (Figure 76). Another consists of two tall and rectangular slabs facing each other across a small pool of water, two sails: the calligraphic inscription in German, *Schiff*, is reversed so that we can only read it correctly—upon reflection—in the pool below (see Figure 75).

Retrospectively, we may then see the first, undulating panel also as a set of sails, while the panels that hang from the roof of the Institut on the hill turn that building into a tall sailing ship above the smaller "boat" in the valley. For some of the abstractions, their real-life referents are present, like the flowers blown by the wind beside the iron lettering of the English

FIGURE 76. VNDA, designed by Ian Hamilton Finlay with Ron Costley, concrete and stainless steel, 1976. Max Planck Institut, Stuttgart, photographed in 1991.

WINDFLOWER; for others, miniaturized referents like the pond and pool stand in for the sea, where wave (VNDA) and sail (SCHIFF) are usually found.

This installation, a series of insertions into the Institut campus (the whole of which, incidentally, is not under his aegis), is typical Finlay. The visitor's responses to these creations are interactive; they can open up not only the enigmas of symbolism and abstraction (upon which a Latin inscription on a plinth in the pond insists)[1] but also our sense of mystery and meaning in the physical world, which is what this research institute is all about. Finlay instigates dialogues between word and image, between the site and his insertions into it, and between the specific location and the larger physical world to which it refers or which it represents. Though we are likely in the first instance to be primarily absorbed by the words and by the concrete panels, the natural elements of the site matter just as much—specifically water and the ensemble of bushes, reeds, and trees that, stirred, signal the presence of the otherwise invisible wind. Indeed, the natural elements of the site are highlighted by Finlay's insertions into them (Figure 77). Nor is such a deliberate analysis as I have attempted here the only access; an adequate response to the site could be below the level of consciousness or formal articulation.

Finlay is undoubtedly a special case in modern landscape architecture. He is special not because he is different but because his radical invocation of basic devices from the history of place-making makes more of those traditions than most other designers. He therefore provides an exemplary opportunity to study the re-

FIGURE 77. Latin inscription on plinth in pond, designed by Ian Hamilton Finlay with Ron Costley, marble, 1976. Max Planck Institut, Stuttgart, photographed in 1991.

lation of word and image in the process both of garden-making and, by extension, of garden-dwelling.

It has been a consistent argument throughout this book that making and experiencing of place—the subject experiencing the site yet to be made and the subject visiting the landscape once made or initiated—are intimately allied. Nevertheless, it will serve the purposes of the next two inquiries better to keep them notionally apart.

II

The unveiling of the Franklin Delano Roosevelt Memorial in Washington, D.C., in the summer of 1997, with the public debate on the (non)depiction of Roosevelt's polio, overemphasized the visual at the expense of the verbal elements of Lawrence Halprin's design.

What is striking is the extent to which it relies on words (Figures 78, 79): FDR's words above all, but also words that dictate how we are to respond to the site, legends incised into the pavements, and captions, some combination of which sustains a narrative of his presidential career. And nobody thought this verbal element excessive, unlike the visual reticence about FDR's polio.[2]

Words do not necessarily have to function in landscape architecture as they do, say, in a newspaper; they can be part of a site's visual world, marks on the stones of history, as Halprin uses them sometimes in the FDR Memorial. Dieter Kienast turns letters of the famous Latin phrase "Et in Arcadia Ego" to practical use as the railing of a private woodland belvedere overlooking the Zurich countryside.[3] Or take the case of Finlay's Stuttgart inscription (see Figure 77; its text is transcribed in note 1): if we cannot understand the Latin,

FIGURE 78. The FDR Memorial, Washington, D.C., designed by Lawrence Halprin, 1997.

the incised words nevertheless lend a tonality, *gravitas*, or even noumenous quality to the scene. Words, in advance of supplying meaning, can thus be a visual sign of cultural suggestion in the same fashion as non-verbal items like topiary or statuary. Further, if we read inscriptions aloud, they contribute to the plenitude of sounds that make a site, just as a dizzily flashing visuality of electric words supplements the scenery of Las Vegas before we actually pick out their messages.[4] In

the case of the sentences incised on the FDR Memorial, Halprin might also want us to take them as visual symbols of the radio broadcasts that Roosevelt used to reach so many American households.

But the primary function of words on a landscape architectural site would be to communicate certain kinds of meaning, including hints of a narrative. The FDR Memorial cannot work fully without its visitors reading, and reading lots of words as bearers of information, as messages, to remind them of famous utterances, or for non-Americans (for whom FDR can be a less potent figure) to articulate his significance through his

FIGURE 79. The FDR Memorial, Washington, D.C., designed by
Lawrence Halprin, 1997.

own words ("I hate war"); both sorts of visitors are
also reminded of the sequence or storyline of FDR's
career. The wordage, then, plays a major role in help-
ing Halprin to represent the life and times of a great
American. The memorial's other materials—notably
rock and water—function in a far less explicit way in
the overall representation; indeed, there seems to be
some disjunction between the verbal elements and the
strong impact of the Carnelian South Dakota granite
and different flows of water. Sometimes the world of

place-making can become so logocentric and inscriptions are so clearly deemed an indisputable part of it
that a designer may create a significant, circumscribed
zone by the simple insertion of words into the larger,
usually natural scene, as Gilbert Boyer did on the Mont
Royal (Figure 80) in Montreal.[5]

Memorials are in business to recall and remind,[6] and
they are liable to do this best with verbal communications, from simple names and dates on gravestones (the
Vietnam Memorial in Washington, D.C., being a sublime extension of this mode) to plaques with brief historical summaries of past events and their significance
(the historical markers along American highways). This

FIGURE 80. Gilbert Boyer,
La montagne des jours, 1991,
one of five disks installed
on Mont Royal, Montreal,
along the Olmsted Road.
Public Art Collection, City
of Montreal (photograph by
André Clement, courtesy of
the artist).

usage relies on the rhetorical strategy known as *proso-popeia*, by which a lost voice is supposed to speak from the site to its privileged visitors.[7] Considered as memorial, the FDR site's use of words is nothing unusual; as landscape architecture, it is different in degree rather than kind from most examples.

Yet the mistrust of "literary" as well as "scenic" values in modern design is considerable. The "linguistic turn" of Robert Venturi et al.'s *Learning from Las Vegas* is not widely accepted, let alone enacted, even though the liberation of architecture (and of landscape architecture, by implication) from its mute forms has continued to be urged forcibly, and even though the verbalization of architecture continues to form a substantial part of professional criticism.[8] Nevertheless, between "recounted time" and "constructed space" a modernist barrier has arisen that is difficult to cross.[9]

Nonetheless, this refusal of some "prefabricated" literary idea or expression goes against the grain of much of landscape architecture's past accomplishments, as would the rejection of pictorial scenography. Given a garden's ambition to be a complete conspectus, a representation of *all* human concerns, its reliance on words as well as a sequence of images appeals to both halves of the human brain. Indeed, many examples of landscape architecture can be instanced to show how the verbal is invoked to augment the impact of the other senses: from the Latin that celebrates the Elector Palatine and his stupendous creation of the Hortus Palatinus on the hillside at Heidelberg, to the inscriptions that commemorate owners, designers, and gardeners at Dumbarton Oaks; from verses hung in Chinese gardens, to the words of Walt Whitman on the railings of Battery Park City Esplanade in New York. The examples are legion.

A primary function of such inscriptions is to engage readers simply or complexly in a site's relationship with its past. We tend to treat inscriptions as having originated sometime and somewhere else before and outside the site where we read them, and we judge them for their aptness, including their efficacy in directing our response to whatever it is in the world beyond the site that is represented. Words are by no means the only way of directing attention to that world—imagery, statues, can do the same—but clearly they are thought to do so with special economy or precision. And verbal supplements above all contrive for gardens and other designed sites the character of what the French call *lieux de mémoire*.[10] Gardens have a peculiar relationship with time—existing in time ("time shall make it grow"), they look forward; but they also carry with them traces of nostalgia, recollections of when they were initiated (whether that was yesterday or 350 years ago). Gardens have earned considerable visibility as places of memory in recent years,[11] both on account of fresh analyses of design intentions and of visitors' experience. A certain individual, society, or culture could choose garden forms (as we've seen) to represent its place and time, what we call its "take" on the world; so for contemporaries the site exists as a memory theater of a set of concerns and ideas beyond the immediate garden, while later generations are involved in a historical as well as a spatial recollection. The same is true when we rejuvenate a site where once a healthy ecological system had flourished and announce its recovered past with images and text.

What is designed to prompt the memory in one culture or society may not, of course, function effectively for later visitors, who have to learn to "read" that particular time and place as it is now made available to them. Yet the original designers cannot guarantee let alone control subsequent readings, where new visitors—and rightly—bring to the experience their own "take" on the world.[12] Gardens survive from the past, therefore, in part because they furnish new generations with sufficient stimulation for eye and mind; some of those stimulations, as inscriptions, place-names, stories, history, will be performed through words.

Words in landscape architecture can be explicit, as in Battery Park or in the identifications and short biographies inscribed on William Kent's Temple of British Worthies at Stowe (Figure 81). Such verbal supplements to the architectural forms and the reshaped togography and plant materials (see Figure 4) are introduced because the designer or owner/patron wishes to increase our attention or prompt our recollections. The former motive also explains the most pragmatic of wordage—directional signs, botanical labels,[13] injunctions on how to behave—NO BALL GAMES, or PLEASE KEEP OFF THE GRASS being minimal modern versions of the more complicated "garden law," or *Lex hortorum*, which it was the Roman and Renaissance custom to post at entrances.[14]

Some words, however, will be only implied: for example, nowhere is the Temple of British Worthies so named on-site at Stowe; nor at Rousham, Oxfordshire, does Kent's other memorable architectural invention, the Praeneste Terrace (Figure 82), get called within the garden by the name known from private papers to have been used about it. Yet both appellations are necessary clues to the full meaning of these designs. The lack of any sign in the Elysian Fields of Stowe indicating that the Temple of British Worthies was so called may be explained by the fact that none was thought necessary in the 1730s because its significance could have been explained by family members. Or maybe it was withheld as part of an interactive garden experience where part of the fun was to solve puzzles. The Chinese, too, delight in inferring but never directly stating the meaning of gardens. It was also considered probable that any visitor to Stowe, needing to know enough Virgil to appreciate a telling *omission* from a Latin quotation on the Temple, would also be able to work out its name and its dialogue with other structures within the Elysian Fields. Once Stowe began to acquire a certain fame, it is significant that its various buildings and sectors were first made available to this larger and potentially less informed public through a poem written by one of the inner circle of initiates, then through a series of commercially produced guides.[15] The Praeneste Terrace at Rousham, which received neither this public attention nor tourist visitation, has never enjoyed the significance that its proper name would earn for it.[16]

FIGURE 81. The Temple of British Worthies, Stowe, designed by William Kent in the late 1730s, detail.

Sometimes this matters less than others. Places like Prospect Park in Brooklyn and Central Park in Manhattan have signs that announce the names of different sectors—the Ramble, Haarlem Meer, the Ravine, Nethermead, and so on. These are public parks where it cannot be assumed that all visitors know where they

FIGURE 82. The Praeneste Terrace at Rousham, Oxfordshire, designed by William Kent, 1739 (photograph: Marianne Majerus).

are at any given moment. Yet the names bear far less significant freightage than those in the private enclaves of Stowe or Rousham or, say, the Parterre de Latone at Versailles. Dumbarton Oaks in Washington, D.C., first created as a private garden, but now regularly opened to the public, does not label its sectors with the names given them over the years by their creators; instead, a plan handed to visitors identifies them. It might be argued that this naming of parts does not endow these gardens with any extra significance, even though it may enhance the experience of sharing a visit ("Ah, now we're in the Rose Garden," or "Meet you at the Ellipse").

The naming of gardens seems to be taken more seriously in China. Whereas in Europe sites tend to be named after their owner or the topographical location, the Chinese consider the naming of gardens, or parts of them, an even more arduous task than the physical making, because more is at stake than the formal arrangement of rocks and trees. It was Cao Xuegin, in the eighteenth-century novel *Story of the Stone*, who wrote that "those prospects and pavilions—even the rocks and trees and flowers will seem somehow incomplete without that touch of poetry which only the written word can lend a scene."[17] The group of characters who are visiting the recently established garden in that novel vie with each other to "complete" its different scenes with suitable inscriptions. And in many cases the verbal supplements that are eventually deemed apt would be inscribed on-site through the display of the relevant characters (at once verbal and visual in Chinese). Western gardens generally rely far less on such local indicators of meaning or hints for a proper response; however, the naming of whole gardens —at least in the United States (Naumkeag, Vizcaya, Asticou, Dumbarton Oaks, Monticello)—has often a more "poetic" resonance than their European counterparts, where ownership and location play a more important role in nomenclature.

The use made of verbal insertions or clues will depend on the visitors. Indeed, that a garden needs to call a response out of its visitors at all—an activity to be examined later—goes a long way to substantiate the claim that gardens fully exist only as a melding of an object (their physical ingredients) and a subject (the receiving, perceiving visitor). Private enclaves— as Stowe or Dumbarton Oaks once were—presumably were shown to visitors by informed insiders (even the owners) whose words could direct attention or who could interpret verbal elements within the design. Louis XIV devised several versions of a guidebook to the gardens at Versailles in part because his personal control over visitors' itinerary and their consequent responses would otherwise have been inadequate.[18] Modern visitors to sites of some importance can usually furnish themselves with a guidebook that sets out their route for them, verbalizing significant elements; if such a portable guide is not available, or even if it is, abbreviated versions of its directions are likely to be posted throughout the site. Today Louis XIV would probably have recorded his guidance on an audiocassette.

One function of verbal elements, often insisted upon by garden historians, is to promote and shape a story, narrative, or iconographical program about the site. Since humans are creatures that tell stories, what Stephen Jay Gould has called *Homo narrator*,[19] this is quite plausible. The work of Canadian artist Gilbert Boyer (see note 5) certainly provokes and relies on that storytelling instinct, as we seek to extrapolate narratives from his verbal insertions into sites. Equally, verbal prompts at the Villa d'Este (combined with visual ones) are supposed to lead us to recall how Hercules stole the golden apples from the mythical Garden of the Hesperides, having slain the dragon that guarded them, and brought them here to Cardinal Ercole d'Este's garden, to be watched over by newly installed (stone) dragons (see Figure 63).

John Raymond, visiting Italian gardens during the seventeenth century, remarked how "marbles [i.e., antique sculpture and inscriptions] speak Roman history more palpably than any author."[20] He alludes both to Roman historical writings and to the "speech" of individual items in a garden, a remark which infers different modes of verbal communication. At the Villa d'Este, situated on the classical ground of Tivoli, Raymond would have sought out ways of getting the garden imagery to provoke in him recollections of historical narrative read earlier and elsewhere, which could thereby be given immediate and palpable form. But other sites in other locations—a botanical garden, for instance—might trigger different expectations, different stories, and different ways of telling them. On some of Boyer's sites, there is little local history that would be obvious without his invented incidents and announcements.

We need to step back for a moment and examine the different kinds of verbal supplements or attachments that landscape architecture benefits from, needs, or elicits. Paul Ricoeur has set out some parallels between kinds of narrative and a variety of architectural impulses, analogs we might borrow for our own purposes of understanding how narratives are attached to place-making. He cites the human instinct for ordinary, conversational accounts or narratives, where action is rudimentarily organized in words and is seen in its symbolic order or evaluated in terms of ethical and social rules; this he compares to the simpler building functions that organize inhabitation. In terms of humans' most residual gestures toward place-making, this means enclosure of spaces for specific purposes (various microclimates, keeping animals out), assignment of different purposes within spaces (to medicinal herbs, to vegetables, to fruit growing), establishment of entrances and exits, of paths and gateways. All of these would be linked to rudimentary, conversational narratives ("I go down this path," "We grow apples in this orchard," "He irrigates this patch").

It is during the next stage, a movement out of this second nature, as Cicero termed it, into a third nature of garden or landscape architecture (comparable perhaps to the move from building to architecture), that narrative becomes more complex, more various, and also paradoxically more independent of the site. On the level of design, the landscape architect now works to synthesize segments of his site: transitions are perceived and either eliminated or enhanced, formal means of linking sectors are elaborated, and a whole begins to emerge from a sum of parts. The narrative equivalents of this stage take us from conversation, casual verbal formulations as we move around the site, into more self-conscious and literary recountings; words or narratives can now move away from the pragmatic things of the garden and attend to larger issues, either announcing how separate parts are related within the designed whole or connecting what is within to a world of myriad concerns that lie outside the enclosure. At this stage narrative emanates from the garden, but it is not necessarily implicated in it nor co-extensive with it; above all, it depends on the visitors' receptivity to items placed before them and to their previous experience. Raymond was prepared to listen for the "speech" of antique statuary, and he presumably knew his "Roman history" as other visitors, say, might know their botany.

But narratives that recount time past do so in the present, which with landscape architecture is intimately linked to the configurations of the site that functions both as setting and presumably as prompt for the narrative to be recounted. Further, the "reader" is thrust into prominence; the narrative of a place relies on the verbal skills of its visitor, who has to infer or "translate" from the given materials, which can never (*qua* narrative) be as complete as they would be, for instance, on the pages of a novel. As a consequence of that extra responsibility, the preferences of the visitor/narrator come into play—does he or she prefer sequence and sense of an ending or fragments and the diachronic? does he or she seek some relevance of the narrative to the context in which it is read, or does that person desire some wonderful escape, some magical freedom from the actual place of narration? In short, the site *qua* site may play a greater or a lesser role.

A landscaped site has, I believe, one important, if generally unremarked, impact on any narrative it promotes. When we come upon a site that draws attention to some internal coherence in its design, we also know that its spaces have evolved in time: time has gone into the process of making them, time will affect their growth and development; further, they have almost certainly been created within other spaces (or natures) that have themselves been shaped over time. Thus the temporal needs of whatever narrative that site might provoke ("Once upon a time . . .") will be matched sympathetically by the contributions of time to the space where the narrative will be (re)told.[21]

There is nothing in a garden's structure that will guarantee a story is read, let alone read correctly, however insistent are its verbal prompts. For one thing, true narrative depends on a determined sequence of events, yet the routes around most sites are sufficiently numerous and flexible that all but the most authoritarian direction of visitors, like Louis XIV's, will fail to ensure an apt sequence.[22] All gardens are in this sense hopelessly postmodernist! What seems a much more plausible explanation of garden narrative is that visitors put together a story or plot retrospectively from scattered hints during their explorations of a garden—the hints may have been planned, designed, or the visitor may project them; once a story has been deciphered or otherwise invented, or indeed was known beforehand, visitors can follow a route that either makes this narrative more palpable and effective or lets them pick up segments of the story at certain points along the route and piece them together in the alternative spaces of the mind. At Tivoli, for instance, I could notice the Fountain of the Dragons (see Figure 63) once I had descended the terraces below the palace, then I would somehow be reminded of the cardinal's given name (Hercules in Italian), remember that oranges, set out in terracotta pots during the summer along the upper level, were thought to be the golden apples of the Hesperidean, and so put together from bits and pieces of recollection the intended narrative about one of the labors of the legendary Hercules and its relevance to this site. I would still have to match visual as well as verbal clues, including inscriptions, with my prior

knowledge of such events. An ecologically restored site also tells of an original biotopic process, which narrative the knowledgeable and alert visitor can recover in the footsteps of its landscape architect. But neither of these narratives is similar in its construction or unfolding to a literary one.

However, we cannot insist that gardens require verbal supplements, let alone depend wholly upon them.[23] Indeed, there will be many whose firm belief is that a garden is a garden is a garden; or, to cite another American who more carefully explored the border between abstraction and real, between symbolization or narrative and the actual:

The eye's plain version is a thing apart . . .

　　　　　　pure reality, untouched
By trope or deviation . . .
Straight to the transfixing object, to the object

At the exactest point at which it is itself,
Transfixing by being purely what it is,
A view of New Haven, say, through the certain eye.

Wallace Stevens explores how a poem could represent objects without obvious mediation, how it could deliver the "vulgate of experience."[24] By analogy, there is garden experience that "transfixes" without visual trope or verbal deviation and much more easily than Stevens's poetry, which is obliged to use words. This celebration of the thing itself is resolutely opposed to landscape architecture's exploitation by agendas, meanings, narratives, programs, above all when those are established a priori. If we do promote word over image in the garden and, borrowing from Tom Wolfe's jaundiced diatribe against modern art, *The Painted Word*, "first . . . get the Word, and then . . . see [the garden],"[25] we are liable to lose touch with a whole range of garden experience.

All sorts of garden images that are not glossed in the first place by words may acquire significance or meaning, sometimes logically, sometimes by happenstance.

In another context Erwin Panofsky writes of how "spiritual meaning is attached to a concrete, material sign and intrinsically given to this sign."[26] We tend to translate these meanings into words, even though it is never required. Even if landscapes are all about "letting nature speak for herself,"[27] humans still tend to translate "her languages" into their own, as environmental writing constantly illustrates.[28] It is, of course, sheer logocentricity to assume that the language by which we translate encounters in a garden (or elsewhere for that matter) need to be verbal; they can be registered in feelings or, colloquially, "gut reactions"; the forms of landscape architecture may delight visual sensibilities; a particular sound or smell may send a *frisson* of pleasure through a visitor. Though rudimentary in their narrative structures, a gesture (shrug or caress) can tell a tale. Dance and mime, far more complex in their vocabulary and syntax, also narrate. Nonetheless, as we shall see in the next section, all that range of experience is more often than not translated into linguistic expression, and human responses to the garden are no exception. Perhaps it is because humans want to share the affects and effects of their experience that they tell others about them. *Homo narrator* cannot exist without listeners any more than without words.

Beyond the need or urge to identify, explicate, educate, and generally guide or control the garden visitor within its spaces and to ensure that he or she is put in touch with the site's immediate concerns, verbal supplements are a means of gesturing beyond those fairly precise events to matters that are not on the face of it essential to the garden nor, indeed, often within the garden. The allusiveness of much Chinese naming of gardens functions in this way. As we've seen in the previous chapter, references beyond the garden constitute an important aspect of its larger mode of representation, which will have many motives. For instance: calling the series of red structures in Parc La Villette "follies" (Figure 83) is to link them at once with a whole tradition of garden buildings.[29] Or at Stourhead, Wiltshire, the actual or implied naming of such features as

the Pantheon (Figure 84) and Alfred's Tower initiates a wider, discursive meditation on the garden's representation of its place in a cultural history that goes well beyond the immediate context.[30] However tenuous or casual are the links that the garden forges between itself and things elsewhere, or however well visual resemblances to distant or mythic events work without verbal translation in garden representations, it is largely by words that the here and now of a site is linked with the there and then of its references.

III

But the visual comes before the verbal in landscape architecture. Indeed, an imaginative design will require that we see in wholly new ways, forgetting in the process (as Valéry said) the "name of the thing one sees." Visual imagery in garden design should be a much less contentious topic than the role of the verbal. Nobody could deny the visual components of a landscaped site, and there are many luscious coffee-table books around nowadays to insist upon this. One consequence, however, of this visual glut is to marginalize, not only the meanings and metaphysical concerns that some designers would still seek to convey, but the other sensual aspects of garden experience. We are concerned far less, if at all, with sounds, taste, and touch, though these are precisely the elements that many relish in gardens, and indeed these would constitute gardens for people who are blind.

Brought up on a diet of photographic elegance, modern garden makers and visitors are largely content to survive on an uncritical reiteration of pictorial or picturesque structuring. Professional designers, too, will be happy to have their built work featured in glossy images, even designing it for that purpose. Both professionals and non-professionals appeal to "scenery" and "pictures." Even when such static and predetermined visual references are strongly refused, their strenuous rejection betrays the uneasy legacy of pictorial taste in landscape architecture. This is a common enough habit

FIGURE 83. Parc La Villette, designed by Bernard Tschumi, photographed in 1995.

FIGURE 84. The Pantheon, Stourhead, Wiltshire (photograph: Katherine Gleason).

in experiencing landscape—like Annie Dillard, spreading "my fingers into a viewfinder; more often I peek through a tiny square or rectangle—a frame of shadow —formed by the tips of my fingers and thumbs held directly before my eyes."[31]

Designers, however, can be skeptical of such "scenic" effects. Perhaps they are more aware of the ambiguous boundaries of sites, edges that cannot function like picture frames or viewfinders to screen off unwanted and unattractive elements; or they appreciate zones of transition that are the very essence of garden space but which the camera does not narrate and the static image fails to signal.

Pastoral and arcadian images have been essentially scenic (i.e., pictorial as well as theatrical). Their formulae have enjoyed a tenacious control over landscape design, and, incidentally, not the least of the continuing appeals of both the pastoral and the picturesque is their intimate link with words that rehearse the narratives they suggest.[32] For the proponents of the English landscape garden, the leading models cited for this pictorial framing included Claude Lorrain's pastoral schemata, Nicolas Poussin's arcadian structures, and Salvator Rosa's melodramatic scenography of rock and wood. During the picturesque debates at the end of the eighteenth century, Humphry Repton, somewhat ironically, adduced a whole repertoire of painters on which various encounters with the real world could be modeled: "Our kitchens may be furnished after the designs of Teniers and Ostade, our stable after Woovermans, and we may learn to dance from Watteau and Zuccarelli." His other remarks on different picturesque models for what are, in effect, the three natures are more straightforward: "In forest scenery, we trace the sketches of Salvator Rosa and of Ridinger; in park scenery, we may realize the landscapes of Claude and Poussin; but, in garden scenery, we delight in the rich embellishments, the blended graces of Watteau, where nature is dressed, but not disfigured by art."[33]

But long after the time when Repton's gallery of artists could be counted on to inform landscape design,

the term *picturesque* is still invoked to discuss landscaped effects. Its range of meaning is ample, not to say vague. Beyond implying something simply visual, however, there always lurks within the usage a gesture to actual pictures and picturing. But pictorial tastes change, partly because the values that sustain them change.[34] In the late nineteenth century, the models by which gardens were designed shifted to include both watercolors of (supposedly) rural cottage gardens and the horticultural densities and textures of Impressionism.[35] More radical painterly models, though, were slow in affecting landscape design, and this despite radical challenges to conventional pictorialism by cubists, expressionists, or abstractionists, or by the ironies of René Magritte, the title and meaning of whose *Domaine of Arnheim* allude to Edgar Allan Poe's fable about picturesque landscaping.[36] There was a brief flurry of "cubist" gardens in France during the 1920s,[37] and such items as Thomas Church's swimming pool in the Donnell Garden (Figure 85) have been linked to the painted forms of Hans Arp or Joan Miró.[38] Now in the late 1990s, Peter Walker is appealing to painterly minimalism.[39] It is a rare designer, like Adriaan Geuze in the Netherlands, who genuinely refashions our picturesque viewing, invoking the geometries of Mondrian for the landscape of black mussel and white cockle shells he designed at the Oosterschelde Weir (Figure 86).[40]

It still remains to be asked why we would structure landscape designs in terms of other images, let alone painterly models. One answer is that when we enter a site we are looking for something that is composed or spaces that we recognize as structured from previous experience. These hints can be both verbal and visual, as is frequently the case with Ian Hamilton Finlay, who said of his own garden at Little Sparta, "Usually each little area gets a small artefact, which reigns like a kind of presiding deity or spirit of the place."[41] Finlay's emphasis is careful: he is not replicating or copying, say, the famous watercolor, *The Great Piece of Turf*, by Dürer, nor is he contriving a "vista"[42] that includes it. Rather, he is inserting an artifact—in this case it is

FIGURE 85. The swimming pool at the Donnell Garden by
Thomas Church, photographed in 1990.

FIGURE 86. Nature Reserve at Oosterschelde, designed by
Adriaan Geuze (photograph courtesy of WEST 8, Rotterdam).

visual and verbal (Figure 87)—into a carefully prepared context so as to focus the visitor's mind at a particular spot that is thereby given point or meaning ("spirit of the place").

While words can promote such a structured experience, even to the extent of establishing a whole narrative or iconography, visual organizations of spaces are probably more immediate as well as available at various distances. which inscriptions, for instance, are not. Much of Finlay's garden at Little Sparta consists of very tight, intense spaces, which ensure that we are placed close enough to read whatever inscriptions reign over each little area. Inscriptions in the Elysian Fields at Stowe may play a similar role in defining genius loci, but they come into play at very different points in our exploration of this part of the gardens.

The Elysian Fields, from whichever direction they are entered, resolve themselves into, or are quickly seen (logocentrists will say that they are "read") as a molded, wooded valley, with a stream conducted through it and with buildings and other objects of different shapes and sizes scattered along both banks. Its words (inscriptions and the names of its temples) play in the first instance a negligible role in our apprehension of the Elysian Fields. We can never have a view of the whole, so we register various spatial events as we move through them. Although we may stop and take a finite and static glance at any point of the Elysian Fields, as we do when we fix an especially well formed part of it in the viewfinder of a camera, our apprehension or idea of the site is probably composed of an infinite number of impressions, registered while we are moving around. We are rarely conscious, unless wholly in thrall to still photography, of privileging any one fixed image over another. We experience it as endless transition. Indeed, even the political and cultural narrative of the Elysian Fields requires that we register at least two vistas at once (toward the Temple of Ancient Virtue on one side of the valley and the Temple of British Worthies on the opposite bank);[43] in practice, we can either position

ourselves so that both items are within our view, or we can recall one while looking at the other.

How we would record and represent this whole experience is another matter entirely from talking about it: one way would be via the sort of photo collage that David Hockney made famous in the 1980s (Figure 88). This device, though rarely used to real effect, is recently much in favor among design students who have learned to manipulate multiple color prints; the difficulty is that while this format articulates experience, it cannot readily set out how some visual effect is to be structured on the ground. In other words, how we have talked about or represented a landscape experience at Stowe is not necessarily how this section of the grounds would have been designed or, once designed, explained to contemporaries before its implementation.

We may have—in fact, we talk about having—a "picture" of some garden or part of it, even though we would be hard put to identify some specific spot where that picture materialized before us. What happens is that we put together a composite image, the visual equivalent of the verbal narrative discussed above; this is "a synthesis or 'mental fusion'"[44] of innumerable visual "takes," which will derive from the site whether or not the site has been composed to yield them in that way. Some of those "views" will prove to be important, central to the whole experience that eventually suggests itself; others will be discarded as irrelevant. And our synthesis will include that width of regard that eyesight enjoys while a human is perambulating, yet which most camera lenses cannot match. Incidentally but appositely, some of the most interesting photographs of gardens have been taken by Geoffrey James (Figure 89) with a camera that surveys an arc of territory, thus mimicking in part the roving eye of exploration.[45] When an actual photograph or painting of a site strikes us as "right," it will have managed to incorporate more of our experience of that place, nonvisual as well as visual, than other less successful images.

Apart from such residual spaces as roof terraces, bal-

FIGURE 87. "The Great Piece of Turf," Temple Pool, Little
Sparta (photograph: David Paterson, 1975, courtesy of Ian
Hamilton Finlay).

FIGURE 88. David Hockney, *Walking in the Zen Garden at the Ryoan-Ji Temple, Kyoto, Feb. 21, 1983*, photo collage (courtesy of the artist).

cony gardens, window boxes, or Wardian cases, gardens have always been designed to be walked through while looking—"an intertwining of vision and movement."[46] Movies could well serve as a prime visual model for such landscape experience and design (though with the caveat about focal range just noted), but they are rarely invoked. Because landscape architecture is still in thrall to the picturesque, still needing to deploy graphic imaging of sites as a professional tool, designers often cannot

divorce themselves from the older habit of thinking in terms of fixed vistas, views, pictures, or scenes. Thus Richard Morris in 1825 explained the illustrations to his essays on design with the remark that "a glance at this sketch, it is presumed, will determine the correctness of what has been advanced."[47] Clients, too, like to "see what it will look like" in composed scenes; digital images of movement through a proposed site do not (yet) seem an adequate substitute. Yet the success of a landscape design on the ground will be judged less by its provision of satisfactorily discrete views than by the sum of its parts as they are experienced from all directions.

We think of the English landscape and picturesque

garden as being the most indebted to pictorial format. When William Gilpin visited Stowe as a young man in 1747, long before he embarked on his popular and influential picturesque tours of Great Britain, he wrote a *Dialogue* about the gardens: in it he made one character exclaim in puzzlement about being confronted with a blank hedge and his companion reassure him that this was simply a device to rest the eyes before the next set piece.[48] Gardens were required to behave like perspectival paintings, best viewed from a specific point that could even be marked on the ground in front of them. Out of this kind of experience in gardens came the invention of "stations" for the picturesque tourist in the countryside at large, places where the best authorized view could be taken by a stationary tourist (note the passive voice). And we have seen already the range of painterly models that could be invoked by eighteenth-century connoisseurs to organize as well as to give added value to their landscape experiences. We continue to be bombarded with photographic images of famous gardens of all kinds that necessarily take their views from fixed and formal points. These sites/sights are not usually so impressive or so tedious in reality, for the simple reason that we have moved through and into them, earned our right to stand and relish the aptness of their placement, or been distracted by other sights; we look, too, with memories of what was also in our vision just a moment ago.

Little in the garden has escaped reformulation by the pictorial, especially in a modern age of readily available reproductive images. We might feel, for instance, that the layout of a vegetable garden at least owes nothing to such models, depending simply on the practical needs of growing, maintenance, and gathering; but the recent fascination with the *potager* and its imaging in color photography has provided even the grower of vegetables with pictorial structures to emulate.

The so-called formal garden from Renaissance to Baroque was no different from the later picturesque one in respect of its painterly debts, except that its vistas were modeled on a different kind of pictorial taste. Its structured spaces derived from strongly perspectival formulations of the visual world, and the "picturesque" expectations (*avant la lettre*) of its garden visitors derived from their familiarity with painting that was much in thrall to a geometrical understanding and presentation of space that had been replicated in gardens.[49]

This seems to confirm that an underlying motive for devising gardens in terms of visual images—by designers and then by visitors—is to structure expectation as we cross their thresholds, engage with the strange, even disconcerting territory within, and bring it into relationship with our other prior experience. And part of that expectation is aesthetic satisfaction. We do not look to landscape architecture to present us with disagreeable or visually unpleasant imagery; there is little point to designing an "ugly garden just in order to demonstrate that ugliness is part of our society."[50] Mind you, if one insists on a garden's obligation to represent its surrounding culture, "ugly" gardens may be necessary. The way out of that paradox is surely to invoke fresh ideas of what can be beautiful—something that Richard Haag achieved in his exemplary Gas Works Park, Seattle, between 1971 and 1988, and more recently Peter Latz and Bernard Lassus proposed in very different ways (Figures 90 and 91) for the reclamation of the old steelworks at Duisburg in the German Ruhr.[51]

We derive and refurbish our notions of beauty from many sources, but the visual arts (including movies or computer imagery of fractal geometry)[52] are a major influence. So the visual structuring and character of landscape architecture will continue to depend on painting and other visual arts as part of a desire to please, be attractive, and satisfy expectations. Scale, color, and arrangement of effects in place-making can derive from and appeal to our knowledge of these same factors in the visual arts. The riot of a herbaceous border and the "casual" fecundity of "cottage gardens" (much honored still at the Chelsea Flower Show) were inseparable from

FIGURE 89. Geoffrey James, photograph of the Villa Donà delle
Rose, Valsanzibio, 1984.

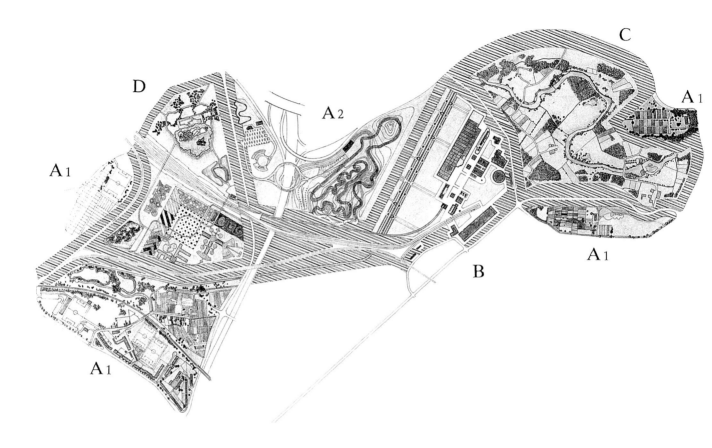

FIGURE 90. Bernard Lassus, design for the Park of Duisburg-Nord (photograph courtesy of the designer).

visions of these compositions in painting; flowers were grouped like splashes or dots of paint. A similar analogy, deriving garden design from painterly techniques, was advanced by Alexander Pope when he allowed as how "you may distance things by darkening them and by narrowing the plantation more and more towards the end, in the same manner as they do in painting."[53]

Garden-making has established some close affinities with visual arts (not least the long history of painting's depiction of designed landscapes, to which we shall now turn). As a consequence, pictorial references became inescapable for the designer and visitor alike. What frustrates contemporary designers, I think, is that they cannot discover in the developments of twentieth-century art their own equivalents to the parallels that Pope or Victorian gardenists invoked. While it is true that much place-making does not seem to call on modernist art—exceptions like Burle Marx or Geuze only prove the rule—I think we need to acknowledge that designers have learned to draw richly and energetically on such visual strategies as collage for the presentation of their ideas of place-making.[54] It is the places themselves that still seem innocent of modernist art in their making and realization.

D

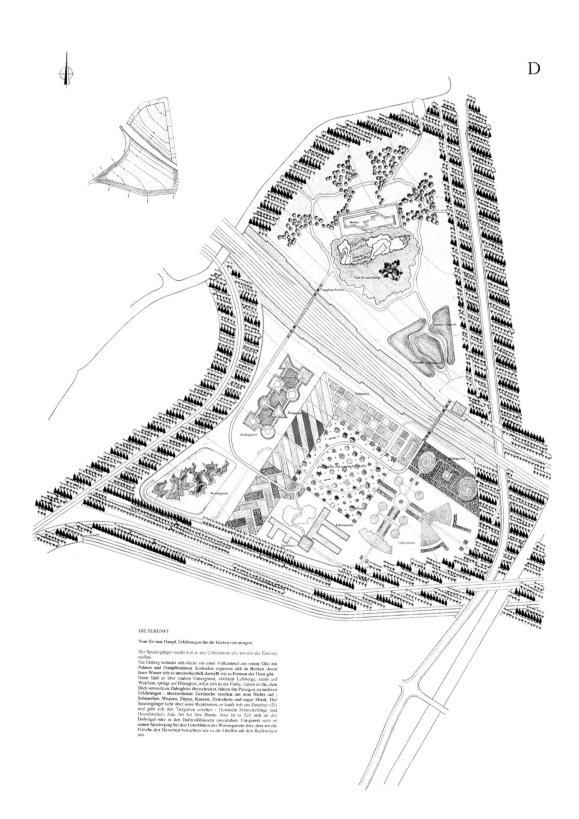

DIE ZUKUNFT

Vom Eis zum Dampf, Erfahrungen für die Gärten von morgen.

Der Spaziergänger taucht dort in das Unbekannte ein, wo sich die Extreme
treffen.
Ein Eisberg befindet sich direkt vor einer Vulkaninsel aus rotem Glas mit
Palmen und **Dampffontänen.** Kaskaden ergiessen sich in Becken deren
laues Wasser sich so unterschiedlich darstellt wie es Formen der Haut gibt.
Dann läuft er über rauhen Untergrund, erklettert Luftberge, rennt auf
Weichem, springt auf Flüssigkeit, wälzt sich in der Farbe. Indem er die, dem
Blick versteckten, Bahngleise überschreitet, führen ihn Passagen zu anderen
Erfahrungen : überraschende Geräusche tauchen aus dem Nichts auf ;
Schnarchen, Wispern, Zirpen, Kauzen, Zwitschern und sogar Musik. Der
Spaziergänger locht über seine Reaktionen, er kauft sich ein Emscher–Eis
und geht sich den Tiergarten ansehen : Hummeln Schmetterlinge und
Heuschrecken. Jede Art hat ihre Blume. Jetzt ist es Zeit sich an der
Duftorgel oder in den Dufttreibhäusern auszuruhen. Entspannt setzt er
seinen Spaziergang bei den Lotusblüten des Wassergartens fort, dort wo die
Frösche den Menschen betrachten wie es die Libellen mit den Bachstelzen
tun.

FIGURE 91. Cowperplatz
in the Park of Duisburg-
Nord, designed by Peter Latz
(photograph courtesy of the
designer).

CHAPTER 6

Gardens in Word and Image

Descriptions of gardens, like paintings of gardens, are generally hopelessly inadequate.
— Arthur Ponsonby

Inside the garden we can construct a country of our own.
— Robert Louis Stevenson

"WHAT IS 'writing about gardens,' and what are 'pictures of gardens'?" asks Craig Clunas.[1] These are not obvious questions. Gardens come fully into existence only when we become aware of them, when we start to give an account of them. In part at least they are "created" by the ways we talk about them, by the ways we image them, which in their turn derive as much from our ideas of gardens as from our experience of specific examples of landscape architecture.[2] Given the extraordinary range of human concerns that determine gardens and find expression in them,[3] it can only be useful to ask what aspects of landscape architecture are represented in image and word.

This chapter will not take an art historical or literary critical approach, nor can this be a thorough survey. I will ask, rather, in the interests of isolating topics about place-making, what these media reveal of recurring importance in the cultural esteem of gardens. To keep the discussion within manageable proportions, the focus will be strictly on what the practice of garden theory can learn from the ways in which made places have been represented visually and verbally.

I

First, images of gardens. They occur, most obviously, in paintings and drawings, but also in photography and film, where they have been deliberately selected either as a main subject or as the apt setting for one. Partly because of this element of deliberation, these will provide my main documentation.[4] But designed places also figure in such imagery as cartoons (see Figures 5 and 64) or advertisements, where their role is to tap people's undeclared assumptions about such spaces, which also need to be studied.

No period or major garden-making nation has been without garden pictures, but among western cultures both the Netherlands and England have seen preeminent talent in this field, as has China. By about 1720, country house portraiture in Britain had become what a modern scholar and champion of the genre calls "a phenomenon as nationally English as Perpendicular Gothic or Tudor Renaissance."[5] Because of that concentration of effort, along with what seems set to be a modern revival of the genre, British examples are liable to feature prominently in the following discussion.

Garden paintings have, of course, been frequently invoked for their documentary value in landscape history, especially to demonstrate formal and stylistic developments as well as to extrapolate information about planting.[6] These are not my concerns, partly because I have no wish to perpetuate tired discriminations about style, and partly because it is exactly the positivist assumption that garden paintings must describe actual layouts that I need to bypass. It is what the paintings may declare or even betray about the ideas and uses of gardens, not their value as records of historical sites, that is in question here.

In having recourse to both artistic and literary evidence, I am interested in the ways in which different media highlight aspects of garden art through adhering to, or sometimes by deliberately straining to evade, the "logic of their processes."[7] In the most basic terms, paintings and photographs treat of what Henri Cartier-Bresson called "decisive moments,"[8] while poetry can cope with narrative or sequence. Visual imagery celebrates the thing itself, and verbal, its connotations. But as Robert Burley, Lee Friedlander, and Geoffrey James, the trio of photographers who documented Olmsted's work for the Canadian Centre for Architecture book *Viewing Olmsted*, make clear, these conventional assumptions about the capacities of different media are readily challenged: the image can be a record of both time and experiences of landscape rather than of the landscape itself.[9]

One last point by way of preamble. In Chinese culture, garden depiction and garden description were very closely allied with garden-making, and the three arts, developing in parallel, frequently coincided.[10] If we look at Ch'ien Hsuan's thirteenth-century image of *Wang Hsi-chih Watching Geese* (Figure 92), we see a famous poet depicted in a garden pavilion, from which he is watching geese on a lake. The visual image records both what we may take to be a designed landscape and a historical figure who was famous for his garden interests and for his calligraphy (a visual and a verbal talent in China, as we can see from the upper left of the scene). Ch'ien Hsuan's painting makes it very hard to draw clear distinctions between the painting of places, place-making, and, by implication at least, writing about such places.

There have been comparable moments at other times and places in the history of garden painting, when the sister arts, as Horace Walpole called them,[11] collaborated to champion a fresh vision of landscape. At such

moments it can prove difficult to separate the contributions of those arts: for example, the graphic skills and syntax of art nouveau, art deco, cubist, or expressionist artists represented gardens on paper that would have been difficult to match with actual (especially horticultural) forms on the ground.[12] But it is usually possible to register differences between artists' representational skills and how the gardens so depicted might themselves be reformulated on the ground. It is in that gap that depictions of place-making can discover things which even the most assiduous of garden explorers, let alone garden writers and perhaps even designers, are liable to miss.

II

Eight primary topics emerge from depictions of landscape architectural work and may assist the practice of garden theory; some are more obvious than others.

1. *They help us understand place-making as a spatial art.* What garden paintings tell us of space may seem the least exciting of the eight topics (if only because it should be even more palpable in gardens themselves). But it is as if the painter, constricted to a single image and often to a single perspective, must work harder to suggest the spatial adventures that beckon from even the smallest sites. In a similar fashion, the painter is challenged by the double obligation to honor a garden's essential changefulness ("maturity is always immediately succeeded by decay")[13] while using his skill to transform this transience into a timeless and ideal moment.

There are essentially two painterly modes of conveying the spatial aspect of gardens. One is the bird's-eye view, which owes much to cartographic conventions and in which the sheer extent of ground depicted invites the sight to explore the spaces (see, for example, Figures 19, 20, and 51). Only since the advent of air travel (hot-air balloons in the first instance) have these

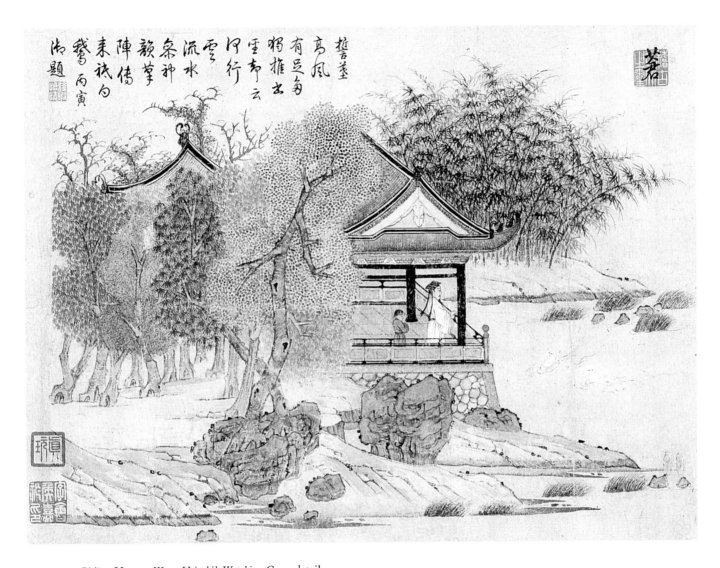

FIGURE 92. Ch'ien Hsuan, *Wang Hsi-chih Watching Geese*, detail, thirteenth century. Metropolitan Museum of Art, New York.

bird's-eye views been achievable in reality—what Paul Vera's book *Les Jardins* of 1919 saw as the viewpoint of the aviator.[14] Before that, they were ideal, imaginary perspectives, mental constructs, like maps. In the second mode of representing space, the viewer of the image is set down more or less on the ground without a map, perhaps intrigued by being abandoned where left and right are concealed, where the middle and far distance are less and less distinct, if not even blocked by some building or other landscape incident.

These rival graphic modes coincided for a time: the overall "map" of space would be surrounded by the close-up individual images (Figure 93; see also Figure 51), whereby the teasing frustrations of the series of local vistas could be plotted and the stages of a possible

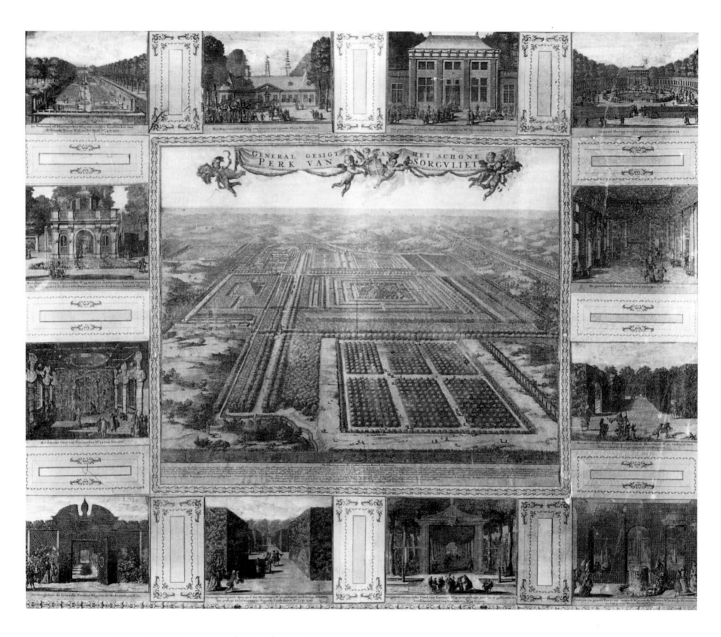

FIGURE 93. J. vande Avelen, engraved view of the gardens at
Zorgvliet, 1696.

circuit or narrative established. A modern adaptation of this device is collage, the bringing together of different sightings of the garden, perhaps in a series of photographic prints, as Hockney did (see Figure 88). It is sometimes said that the regular or "formal" garden is always imaged in the bird's-eye view, while the irregular or "picturesque" design is described in the low-level, grounded images. But many "formal" sites in the Netherlands were depicted in both modes, for while the whole layout still needed to be celebrated, a Dutch dedication to carefully detailed moments, whether spatial or horticultural, elicited many examples of close-up ground views.[15] But what is worth noting is that the double focus—as in Figure 94—occurs at precisely the moment when new forms of garden layout were emerging; this in its turn suggests that we need to reexamine our understanding of how so-called formal gardens were experienced. And it is to new ways of experiencing gardens that we should look for a better understanding of viewpoint in paintings that hover ambiguously between the bird's flight and the ground. This is the ideal perspective for honoring intricate parterre designs, the full effect of which is best viewed from above, while at the same time seeming to offer the promise of walking and discovering the botanical specimens and their patterned arrangement at close range.[16] Utens's portraits of Medici gardens (see Figures 18 and 44–46) are more like maps, recording formal patterns and divisions on the ground; yet, especially with hindsight, we may use them to understand better what exploring them would have entailed.

Among the pleasures of gardens is knowing their spaces and how we use them—in our minds, in plan, in view (actual or graphic), stationary on the ground at key points, moving, exploring, knowing the flow and sequence of their sectors, indeed deciding what divisions exist within them, seeing them whole or inspecting their intricate details separately and close up. This plenitude of experiencing space can only be hinted at by artists, some of whom nonetheless are skilled at sug-

gesting what spatial opportunities exist in very different sites, whether it is the late fifteenth-century illustrator of the *Romance of the Rose*, who shows different compartments divided by a trellis fence, the anonymous and somewhat naive painter of Mutton Davies's italianate place at Llanerch (Figure 95), or Jacob Thompson's watercolor of the seventeenth-century terraces at Drummond Castle now decked out in Victorian horticulture.[17]

Attentively read, these throw some intriguing light on spatial experience in gardens. The late medieval example shows two sectors divided by a fence and laid out in different ways (a flowery mead in one; gravel and raised beds in the other); but since the elegant archway linking them so dominates the scene, their connection seems to be of the essence. Further, since this arch is shown immediately above a closed gateway that gives access to the whole site, we are introduced emphatically to the prime experience of crossing thresholds into and within gardens—a liminal theme, of course, that the verbal text of the *Romance* clearly authorizes by its story of the lover's gradual penetration of the Rose Garden.

The low viewpoint of the terraces at Drummond Castle, like any modern photograph that looks up a garden slope (see Figure 47), tantalizingly conceals what the higher terraces would offer visitors as routes through its rich planting, which also obscures those opportunities. Llanerch, by contrast, maps the staircases, bridges, detours, and openings to be negotiated. The painting exploits its naive handling principally to set out a maplike invitation to explore, yet different zones are seen from slightly different perspectives. We look straight down onto the Neptune pool, an apt angle by which to appreciate the plan of its concentric terraces, while we look more obliquely at the descents beneath the house in a fashion that shows off their grottoes and espaliered walls; the grove or "wilderness" to the bottom right is only hinted at with the white bridge that leads to it. A modern artist like Anthony Green deliberately exploits these multiperspectives within the

FIGURE 94. Anonymous, *Roman de la Rose*, c. 1485, The British Library (Harley MS 4425, folio 12 verso).

Gardens in Word and Image **149**

FIGURE 95. Anonymous, *Llanerch, Denbighshire*, oil on canvas,
1662. Yale Center for British Art, Paul Mellon Collection.

FIGURE 96. Anthony Green, *The Enchanted Garden. 20th Wedding Anniversary, 1981*, oil on board, courtesy of the artist and Juda Rowan Gallery, London.

picture surface (Figure 96). The effect is not just to capture what is obviously a gardenist dedication to concentrated and dense planting in his Cambridgeshire garden (which he has painted well over two dozen times), but to suggest the rich and complex explorations and experiences of the site, including its magical, spiritual, and psychological associations.

The illustration of the *Romance of the Rose*, the painting of Llanerch, and Green's own garden imagery all suggest, further, how permeable are the interior divisions of gardens. This is in strong contrast to the way in which the boundaries of gardens are quite firmly delineated: indeed, all that medieval artists sometimes needed to do to suggest garden space was to depict a wattled enclosure.[18] Some interior divisions will be barely perceptible; others, tightly rendered, will lead visitors across thresholds insistent enough to alert them to that process of discovery—maybe invitingly open, maybe partly closed with half-gates or grills, maybe blocked but with solid, openable doors, or barred by flights of steps the height of which precludes long vistas.[19] And there are many ways of rendering these adventures of edges and transitions visually: a familiar moment in Chinese images is the sight of figures proceeding through the spaces, poised exactly at a moment of liminal scope, or some elevated perspective that sets out a sequence of visitable zones (Figure 97). By contrast, much English country house painting omits any visitor within its scenery, leaving the surrogate visitor, the painting's viewer, to take up the spatial invitations that the artist has positioned him to appreciate vicariously.

2. Much else follows from graphic depictions of garden space. *These images also document the difference between gardens and adjacent zones of human intervention, what we have designated the "three natures."* Some of the earliest surviving garden paintings, from classical Roman sites, document a fascination with understanding various kinds of intervention, human and divine, on the land.[20] In a famous example, Livia's garden room at Prima Porta, near Rome, painted walls surround us with a trompe l'oeil landscape of trees and flowers; we are meant to view this illusionary space as if from a cave or grotto, the roof of which is depicted along the top of its walls. From here we are meant to think that we look first over a garden perimeter—a low trellis, then a circumambulating grass walk, and finally a low wall—toward a densely planted and fecund orchard scene.

When later artists were hired to show off whole estates, often at key moments of change (redesign) by new owners, or departure and loss by others, it was part of their job to distinguish the constituent parts of the property. No English country-house owner could forget his estate as an economic, political, and social complex, which innumerable portraits of estates collected and discussed by John Harris reveal: at Denham Place, Buckinghamshire (Figure 98), its anonymous painter typically knows full well that the gardens are part of a larger agrarian estate, each part of which is rendered differently by him, as it is variously treated on the ground by gardeners, stewards, farmers, and tenants. A revival of interest in aerial views among such contemporary British garden and estate artists as Jonathan Myles-Lea, Jonathan Warrender, and Marcus May[21] brings the garden's special place within a larger territory once more into prominence.

Yet in many records of a complex and varied territory, the garden or third nature is singled out for special emphasis. Such is the wonderfully fresh panorama of Gisburne Park; Stonor Park with its deer park, kitchen gardens, and mansion displayed against the long sweep of wooded hillside; or James Canter's truly expansive view of the famous Deepdene seen across the roofs, fields, and town gardens of Dorking in the late eighteenth century.[22] The anonymous painter of Borg Scheltkema-Nijenstein (Groningen) fulfills those obligations (Figure 99), but the delicate, miniature-like rendering of the flower garden glimpsed between the barn and the mansion makes its effect largely by

FIGURE 97. Shen Zhou, *Spring Gathering*, handscroll, ink and color on paper, Ming before 1487. Freer Gallery of Art, purchase 34.1.

contrast with adjacent agricultural zones and woodland. Indeed, so precious was much Dutch garden space within land won for cultivation from the drained marshlands that it is often singled out as a privileged and elaborated territory of conspicuous pleasure and consumption.[23] The significance of gardens within a larger landscape seems occasionally to be such that they are graphically singled out, with a blithe disrespect for perspective and scale: such is Nathan Drake's Nun Monkton Priory, where an animated hunting scene across the foreground is no impediment to the sharply rendered garden with statues and summer house in the distance.[24] Similarly, though for different socioecological reasons, Chinese paintings of estates reveal a scale of landscape interventions, as our eye learns to detect small garden spaces among the extensive riverscapes and mountain scenery (Figure 100).

This insistence on a garden's setting within other territories survives the artist's transition into bourgeois society. Juxtapositions can be emphatic and confrontational, especially when public gardens are envisaged within another landscape—seaside gardens at Le Tréport for Achille Duchêne or for Claude Monet at Sainte-Adresse. But intensely private enclaves keep the outside at bay, either subtly suggested—Edouard Vuillard's flower garden at Vaucresson[25]—or announced only by its exclusion (Figure 101). Impressionism particularly valued dense enclaves of horticultural technology, allowing barely a hint of what lies beyond. What these private worlds of impressionism also image is the garden as domestic space, leisure made palpable, materialized, given its appropriate forum; always a site of leisure, *otium*, or gardening as pastime, the garden of the bourgeois is now distinctly and self-consciously

a space set apart from the workspace, dedicated to the invention and sampling of a new commodity called leisure; children are guaranteed their portion of this new luxury in areas where they play on their own.[26]

3. This attention to different intensities of intervention in the world stems in part from what visual artists can make especially their own: *the celebration of formal effects, whether natural or artificial.* Artists are necessarily alert to formal matters—the shapes of steps, fountains, seats, and the contrary play of natural growth and beauty. Some images wholly surrender to what the artist can make of these effects—like Jean-Paul Agosti's *Carré Zen, ou la vibration du feuillage* or any number of works by Gustav Klimt, like his *Farm Garden with Sunflowers.*[27] The aerial view is especially organized to signal slightly different formal contrasts, setting the sharper edges of geometry within the looser territory of woodland and fieldscape. But even views taken from

closer to the ground, like Rex Whistler's Lavington Park, enjoy the purely formal play of flat lawns, broad gravel paths, and wide terrace set against a fieldscape that the painted surface turns into another planar expanse.[28]

But the essential game of landscape architectural forms, as the topiary makers knew and played to the hilt, is the deliberate mix and dialogue between hard and soft materials: sharp edges of steps or balustrades and stone sculpted into urns or obelisks, alongside cascading vines or the emergence of ground cover between pavers. Not surprisingly (since he depicts the gardens of Sir George Sitwell, whose essay on garden-making is one of the prime literary meditations on its topic), Richard Wyndham's 1930s painting of Renishaw Hall composes a studied symphony of shapes out of the reflecting pool, urns, pyramidal yews, statuary, lines of steps, and balustrades hidden or subsumed by a vegetable hedge (Figure 102). So, too, does James Hart

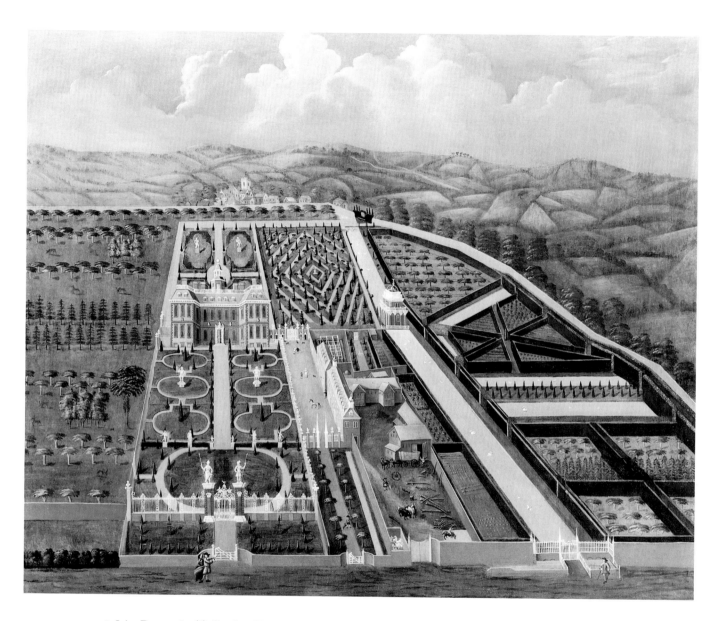

FIGURE 98. John Drapentier (?), *Denham Place, Buckinghamshire*, oil on canvas, c. 1705. Yale Center for British Art, Paul Mellon Collection.

FIGURE 99. Anonymous, *Borg Scheltkema-Nijenstein*, 1650–60.
Groninger Museum, Groningen.

FIGURE 100. Tang Yifen, handscroll, nineteenth century. The
British Library, London.

FIGURE 101. Pierre Auguste
Renoir, *The Garden in the
rue Cortot, Montmartre*, 1876.
The Carnegie Museum of
Art, Pittsburgh.

FIGURE 102. Richard Wyndham, *Renishaw Hall*, oil on canvas,
c. 1933. Collection of Francis Sitwell, Esq.

Dyke's view inside the garden designed by Brenda
Colvin at Steeple Manor, where the volumes of bushes,
gables, and pillars are played off against the intricate,
shifting texture of flower and vegetation, which are all
seen at dusk with strong shadows thrown across the
grass.[29]

Perhaps we learn from visual artists even more than
from direct garden experience to relish the effects of
light; committed to the depiction of one moment, yet
by its skillful choice and the effects which that instant
can be shown to generate within the given spaces and
plantings, paintings bring out the fundamental fashion in which all good design relishes and manipulates
the local potentialities of light, making in one hour or
in one day a whole anthology of impressions. This appeal to weather, to climate, and to the play of light
across surfaces and masses at different times of day
is essentially a modern experience of gardens that has
its beginnings in the eighteenth century, as both literature and visual arts attest.[30] Earlier garden visitors
must surely have attended to light and shadow as an
unavoidable element of the physical scene or relished
how the sky was enlivened by clouds; but the change-

ableness of weather and the essential character of light in garden experience become the themes of painting and literature only by the late eighteenth century. John Constable speaks for this new concern: "a beautiful calm autumnal setting sun is glowing upon the gardens of the Rectory." To the man who complained that a painting was merely an architectural subject, Constable retorted that on the contrary it was "a picture of a summer morning, including a house."[31]

4. *Paintings occasionally reveal to what extent gardens are places of work, involving arts of maintenance as well as of design and so intermingling pleasure with profit, aesthetics with pragmatics—a theme that the coffee-table garden book tends to eschew.* The images that celebrate the formal effects of mass and detail, stone and plant, in varying lights will have implicitly acknowledged that gardens are more than just "found" worlds. For the production of all these effects in the place depicted, whether actual or imaginary, would have been the result of hard work. The contribution of the gardener is made especially significant in what we are liable to call "formal" gardens, where the presence of laborers recall the effort required to maintain the forms and patterns that, though they may derive from the natural materials themselves, are still abstracted and reified by human agency. But there are other, especially nineteenth-century and modern, paintings which immerse us in the fecund tangle of garden planting; here the dialogue between human and plant order is reversed, either to celebrate the ultimate victory of the vegetable world (the abandoned or ruined garden) or to hint at the mysterious efficacy of human control over even the most resolute fecundity of things.

Sometimes the painter will wish to see his site as preternatural, magical, and therefore as not easily explicable, above all at the level of maintenance: a miraculous burgeoning of color, shape, and space. But at other times, due acknowledgment is rendered to those whose labor creates and sustains the magic: gardeners.

Though I am constantly surprised how little these people feature in art and, above all, in modern illustrated books of fine landscape design, there are some images where their role is truly acknowledged. I'm not talking of the token worker leaning upon his scythe, the picturesquely abandoned barrow and tools in the middle distance; nor the armies of agricultural workers deployed in many estate portraits that, as we've seen, survey the workings of a whole property. Rather, the series of paintings by Balthasar Nebot of Hartwell House springs to mind as the most generous acknowledgment of the army of men, women, and youths who constantly trimmed its hedges and shrubberies (Figure 103). A view of the front of Tottenham Park by Andreas Rysbrack shows a pair of busy gardeners and the huge stone roller that keeps its lawn smooth; John Setterington's set of views of Ledston Hall also honor the heavy roller pulled by the solitary gardener between the compartments of the walled garden.[32] Dutch artists were notable for their recognition of gardeners at work—in mythological terms this meant the depiction of Vertumnus and Pomona in garden settings, or the famous scene of busy workers by the elder Pieter Brueghel, the great moving of pots in a riverside garden by David Teniers the Younger, or the wheelbarrow pushed across the very foreground of Frans Decker's view inside the Haarlem Proveniershof.[33] Flowers need as much attention as lawns or bowling greens, and the gardener at work on flowerbeds makes an occasional appearance also in English art, notably in those paintings dedicated to famous flower gardens—William Mason's flower garden at Nuneham Courtenay, painted by Paul Sandby (Figure 104), or the wonderful series of views by Thomas Robins.[34] Camille Pissarro captures the intense concentration of a woman weeding, and Georges Seurat's old gardener, packing garden refuse into a basket, combines weariness with patience.[35] Despite what could be simply an artist's delight in formal rhythms of pots or spatial arrangements inside greenhouses, images

FIGURE 103. Balthasar Nebot, *Hartwell House, Buckingham-shire*, oil on canvas, 1738. Buckinghamshire County Museum, Aylesbury.

FIGURE 104. William Mason's Flower Garden at Nuneham
Courtenay, from Paul Sandby's *The Virtuoso's Museum* (London,
1778). Edinburgh University Library.

of these horticultural forcing-houses also testify to the continual labor of producing a garden.[36]

5. *Paintings also reveal how gardens have functioned as theaters: not just periodically as places for performances (lieux de théâtre) but as sites of role-playing.* Another perspective that paintings open upon garden use and experience is the display of them as stages, as theaters. This involves more than just the inclusion of theatrical spaces within gardens, as I have discussed elsewhere[37]—the exedras, the platforms viewed from quasi-auditoria, even the inclusion of actual green theaters in the design. Simply the platform of a terrace, framed by pyramid yews, in Wyndham's Renishaw Hall (see Figure 102), invites theatrical scenarios, dramatic possibilities, that the Sitwell family must certainly have entertained.

But paintings reveal something more about the theatrical potential of gardens: that role-play spills out beyond actual dramatic performances, beyond the physical forms of *caveae* or *auditoria*, to the whole garden. This is above all true when a society indulges in elaborate protocols during garden ceremonies or visits. It has become a cliché of cultural history that great seventeenth-century gardens—Versailles is perhaps unique rather than typical—were devised and exploited precisely to display the authority and status of their owners, though often with a subtlety and intricacy of imagery that tends to disguise the brute power play involved. But what painters' records of Versailles under Louis XIV also show (see Figure 107), as later in the eighteenth century do Bernardo Bellotto's portraits of other aristocratic European societies in gardens around Vienna and Munich,[38] is how hard it is to distinguish between set pieces of theatrical performance and court life generally. Gardens offered themselves as spaces where stage and auditorium, theater and world, were constantly interchanged, where socially imposed roles could be played out before an understanding if critical audience, and where social artifice was "naturalized"

amid the garden's greenery in ways that it could never exactly be within doors.

This theatrical aspect of great gardens gradually passed to lesser aristocracy and later still to the bourgeoisie, suggesting the garden's special place as a theater for exploring social protocols. Some of the imagery commissioned to celebrate such showpieces as Lord Burlington's new gardens at Chiswick House (Figure 105) seem to insist on the social dramas and theatrical opportunities of its spaces. But the most interesting aspect of this whole topic is its extension into a whole range of bourgeois gardens. The broad terraces and later the wide lawns of country mansions were invitations to promenade and display everything from new clothes to new acquaintances, as in Richard Wilson's view at Moor Park, Hertfordshire, or in Angelo Inganni's anthology of social events in one Lombardy villa garden (Figure 106).[39] Victorian society, as testified by painting and writing alike, could never have scripted and dramatized its essential ideologies without also having developed gardens as their appropriate stages.

Alternatively, the transgressive social roles that the advent of public gardens as well as the greater privacy of small bourgeois gardens elicited make for some striking images, like Monet's portrait of his wife, Camille, seated on a park bench, talking to an unidentified man.[40] The hothouses or winter gardens of nineteenth-century mansions seem to have permitted if not encouraged the flouting of social decorum, as witness another suggestive painting by Manet of a couple deeply engaged in conversation inside a conservatory; but the privacy that these conservatories afforded was the opportunity for solitariness as well as less licit socializing, and artists' depiction of their lush and often exotic scenery sustains their aptness as stages for some unconventional playacting.[41]

6. *One aspect of role-playing in gardens that paintings also evidence is the blurring of private and public worlds.* This is a theme which has already made itself clear,

FIGURE 105. Jacques Rigaud, the great obelisk at the southwest
entrance to the gardens at Chiswick House, drawing, c. 1733–34.
Devonshire Collection, Chatsworth. By permission of the
Trustees of the Chatsworth Settlement.

but it becomes more evident in the genre of conversation pictures, valued especially in the Netherlands
and England; these frequently have landscape settings
(see Figure 111). Even the more mundane, less self-
conscious presentation of garden owners or visitors in
the apparently everyday world of the garden, like Julian
Barrow's picture of James Lees-Milne reading in the
garden that his wife, Alvilde, designed at Essex House,
Badmington,[42] announces the blurred edge between
private and public for which the garden world is a particularly apt setting. By the late eighteenth century,
gardens had lent themselves to a new concern for privacy, to such an extent that today we tend to think of
gardens as essentially private places where we feel able,
as we say, to "be ourselves" (by contrast, "public garden" seems something of a contradiction in terms). Yet
even while celebrating that seclusion, the painter constantly recalls us to the obligations of privacy, maybe
to the obligations of ownership, the responsibilities of
creating, maintaining, or even just visiting a garden,
and to the self-conscious requirements of apt garden
behavior (a notice in the small Market Street plaza in
Bangor, Maine, admonishes, "No Inappropriate Behavior"). Equally, images of public open space—whether
large areas like the Bois de Boulogne or the smaller
Parisian squares—suggest that even here their visitors

FIGURE 106. Angelo Inganni, *The Gardens of the Villa Richiedej at Gussago*, 1859, oil on canvas, Musei Civici, Brescia.

also seek privacy, somewhat against the grain of those civic arenas.

What fascinates in this class of imagery is the artists' keen apprehension of how the garden invites, even requires or compels its owners or its visitors to "per-form," to entertain a new self or to exploit the full potentialities of an old one. The very decision to depict owners and/or their guests in a garden, whether or not they are deliberately posing for the artist, is an invitation to show them behaving self-consciously or with that extra verve or spirit that comes from registering a special place and moment. We talk casually of garden "settings" or "scenes"; the etymological connection to

FIGURE 107. Jean Cotelle,
Bosquet du Théâtre d'Eau,
gouache on vellum, 1693.
Musée du Château de Ver-
sailles (photograph: Bernard).

the theater is no accident, and it transpires before and after the verbal supplement.

7. *Paintings of landscaped sites lend themselves to registering their magical, preternatural, even sacred meaning.* Garden perspectives may be metaphysical as well as physical. Artists often invite us to view sites as sacred, magical, or in some way special ("Bits and pieces of the moon. The real world is left aside").[43] Certain cultures identified gardens as sacred—Egyptian gardens associated with tombs, Western medieval *horti conclusi* associated with the Virgin Mary—and once we identify those associations we can appreciate the gardens' particular quality. Or the artist will invoke some visual trope—the presence of deities or mythological personages in gardens conveyed through their sculptural representations or by their material descent *ex machina* (Jean Cotelle uses both devices in his Versailles paintings [Figure 107]); the Dutch were especially fond of picturing garden deities like Pomona and Vertumnus, but often naturalized them as contemporary garden users or workers—which in essence they were, so familiar had their implied presence in gardens become.[44] Other tropes can be human levitation in Anthony Green (see Figure 96), the presence of romance heroes and heroines in Mughal gardens, or surrealist juxtapositions and *lacunae* in Carel Willink's fantasies of old sites. The total absence of human figures already noted in many English garden scenes—the anonymous Newburgh Priory, again, or Rex Whistler's Lavington Hall—contrive a peculiarly preternatural effect, as do the miniscule figures engulfed in Felix Kelly's ghostly, even sinister, views at Normanby and Henbury Hall.[45]

The most consistently pictured idea of a garden's special or magical zone probably involves the meeting of lovers, their amorous and erotic play. The range—social, ethical, horticultural—of this topic implies the capaciousness of the garden as a setting for this fundamental human activity. Men accosting or spying on women bathing in garden pools is a Mughal motif

(Figure 108) as well as one associated with painted versions of the Susannah story from the Bible. But mutually arranged encounters—Tristan and Isolde in the fifteenth-century Leiden manuscript with a brief suggestion of the setting; Krishna and Rahda in a much more lovingly shown bower of blossoms[46]—see the garden as an ideal and safe haven for such intercourse. The erotic play of other visions—French eighteenth-century images of courtship and amorous play in lush, slightly decadent park landscapes, a woman high on the swing between broken branches—contrasts with the more social pleasures of conjugal affection that increasingly dominated the painted world of bourgeois garden existence in the nineteenth century onward.

We need some vital and, of course, visual clues to trigger our recognition of the garden's magical status. On the face of it, Pompeian wall paintings of garden scenes or garden items (fountains, urns, trellis, visiting birds) may seem, however miraculously preserved from the eruption of Vesuvius, straightforward representations of actual gardens that once lay outside the houses; but their loving and playful realism, bringing exterior scenery indoors, hints at the Roman's deep respect for the magic, even sacredness, of *horti*.[47] The utter emptiness in Carl Willink's paintings alerts us to their fantasy; Samuel Palmer's well-known Shoreham garden has its preternaturally flowering tree; in Henri Rousseau's jungle gardens (their imagery derived from his visits to the Parisian Jardin des Plantes) the happy innocence of beast and the surrounding botanical *joie de vivre* are what nudge the viewer. Matisse's flagrant juxtaposition of a familiar red room with a green world seen through its window (*After the Meal*) sets the latter off as a special and not immediately accessible area, which is what magical gardens ought to be. Sometimes this works merely at the level of fantasy—when household pets or other small animals are the sole occupants of a garden and its scale suddenly changes,[48] or when Mutton Davies dreams of Italy in the Welsh countryside (see Figure 95) and the hint for us to appreci-

FIGURE 108. Anonymous,
*Tender Rendez-vous in a Gar-
den*, Isfahan School, c. 1600,
Bibliothèque Nationale,
Paris.

ate this is simply the startling exoticism of the garden within the workaday Welsh countryside.

Some images, which also register the plenitude and complexity of a garden world, make their fantastical claims for the sites depicted through a visual extravagance and exaggeration: Hans Bol's castle landscape, Essais van de Velde's garden parties, and many Dutch depictions of bumptious or sumptuous gatherings in outdoor settings impart a special aura to the site simply by the zest of its visitors and that of the painter's invention—this they share with the wholly different world of Thomas Rowlandson's Vauxhall Gardens.[49] Gardens have always been special sites for festive gatherings and parties, and the depiction of a varied crowd of merry-makers as well as of the full repertoire of an intricately designed site is a technical challenge that many painters cannot refuse—whether it is fully achieved, as in David Vinckboons's many images of estate festivities, or merely hinted, as in Pirro Ligorio's ink sketch of a party at a Roman villa.[50]

One means that artists use to show off the special or magical qualities of designed sites is, as we have seen, to display them as zones distinct from other forms of cultural or wild landscapes. The Mughal emperor, Babur, is shown (see Figure 13) laying out his gardens, over and beyond the walls of which are either empty voids of sky or a rugged white mountainscape. Another resonant and inventive image is Lucas van Valckenborch's *Spring Picnic with Elegant Company* (Figure 109), where a whole series of garden spaces is juxtaposed to cityscapes, castles, riverscape, hunting forests, and the flowery mead where the eponymous picnic takes place. It seems to take as much time to scan this panoramic scene as it would to explore it all on foot; whether imaginary or grounded substantially in fact, the painting contains many ideas of what the garden can be: an island set out as a labyrinth, pure form in the midst of watery flux; pleasure grounds centered on a fountain and surrounded by arbors; flower and possibly vegetable gardens, neatly subdivided. But none of this repertoire would be as meaningful if it were not set into a world formed by other less excessive and less aesthetic modes of control (bridges, roads, cities, harbors) and by other experiences of scenery, like the flowery mead or hunting avenues cut through woodland.

Yet we do not necessarily need a panoramic context to see gardens as special. Stanley Spencer's painting of cottage gardens at Burghclere (Figure 110), though giving a glimpse of fields and woods beyond, creates its sense of a magical and special zone by the density of the planting—and, of course, by the fantastic topiary—along with the boundary of wild hazel and brambles beside the road that signal, along with the white gate, the edge of concentrated cultivation and care.

8. *Finally, given the sometimes dazzlingly replete garden worlds that artists have given us, we learn more about the ambition of gardens to construct a complete conspectus of human ambitions and desires.* As the word *theater* in its meaning of a "complete collection" should remind us, gardens can be places of fullness and plenitude beyond all others. The huge bird's-eye views of Baroque gardens were an obvious way to make that point, as was anything as panoramic and expansive as Lucas van Valckenborch's picnic landscape. Sometimes artists will delight in depicting the wealth of animal life,[51] sometimes the dizzy whirl of society—the genre of the fête champêtre was a constant excuse for one of the supreme activities of private gardens and later public parks. But even the garden painting that focuses—perhaps obliquely—on just one segment of its site can intimate resources not fully disclosed. Those gatherings of Dutch gardening families—the van Mollens,[52] Agneta Block and her children (Figure 111)—offer perhaps the most complete painterly view of gardens: presenting to the viewer the *artificialia* and *naturalia* of their garden cabinets, always tantalizingly hinted at behind them; implying theatrical settings and attitudes; allowing magical glimpses into private human worlds opened now to our more public gaze; the bounty of nature given equal weight with other arts; the pragmatic blending happily with the intellectual.

FIGURE 109. Lucas van Valckenborch, *Spring Picnic with Elegant Company*, c. 1535–97, oil on canvas, Kunsthistorisches Museum, Vienna.

III

Writers in the garden often reiterate what painters have shown; sometimes they can do this better, sometimes less successfully. Garden poetry is certainly abundant, if not yet well worked as a repository of garden ideas, and its scope is as wide and varied as visual art.[53] But it would be beside the point to review the same topics in writing as in painting. Words do not cope well if at all with celebrating the formal effects of gardens, the mix of vegetation and built items, the passage of light, and the visual effects of seasons. (This does not mean that these effects are not raised in poetry, as when William Carlos Williams describes the bed of tulips pressing against the iron railing.) Nor do poets neglect the associations and sentiments attached to such formal matters. Writing may be less able to set out and explain the resonances of the three natures or how the treatment and handling of the third is different from other zones, although the modern poet is quick to note the unexpected insertion of "a long garden between a railway and a road" or the intensity of activity in railway allotments.[54] Poetry may vouch, too, for a garden's plenitude; yet conveying a sense of the site as a theater or conspectus of the world is not one of its conspicuous strengths, though again it gestures toward "the garden of the world" on the slightest of excuses.[55]

However, other aspects of the garden already discovered in the painter's repertoire receive more adequate treatment. There is a useful emphasis on work or what Wallace Stevens terms "the law of hoes and rakes,"[56] the physical struggle to maintain even horticultural order, which is a dominant note in especially contemporary poems on gardens (poets are nowadays their own gardeners). Spatial discoveries are particularly apt for verbal narration. While painters can suggest the spaces of a garden that await negotiation, may even suggest the routes by which actual visitors might proceed or even show us such visits in process, it will be the writer who is far better placed to record the garden

FIGURE 110. Stanley Spencer, *Cottages at Burghclere*, c. 1929, oil on canvas, Fitzwilliam Museum, Cambridge.

promenade. Writing as widely different as Madame de Scudéry's *La Promenade de Versailles* (1669) and Raymond Roussel's *Locus Solus* (1914) re-create people's process through a site, which is at the center of all landscape experience yet so hard to recapture outside the experience itself.

Time through which a garden grows, the times of day and season that change its aspect, the time it takes to explore—these processes are particularly congenial to the poetic medium if not always to the spirit. Andrew Marvell famously celebrates the escapism of the garden, only to reach at the end of his walk the skillful gardener's floral dial that utilizes the sun's passage (or in an alternative interpretation the diurnal or seasonal flowering of plants) to compute the time that he had sought to evade. The processes of growth, of movement, and of mental association are all forms of transition to which, more than spatial juxtapositions, poetry bears witness: so are views outside from a house or shed or views within complex landscapes, where more than meets the eye is held in the wide angle of the mind's resources. But, above all, poetry can convey those men-

taxonomy of "meaning" into which pleasure is admitted almost as an afterthought.[57] His undeclared but convincing premise, it seems, is that significances or meanings are not—so to say—optional extras but endemic to the whole design, creation, and experience of place-making. I suggest that it is to writers that designers might turn, not just to confirm the variety and range of "meanings" in garden experience but better to apprehend how "the mind, from pleasures less, / Withdraws into its happiness." Loaded as Marvell makes that—the lesser pleasures of the material environment are pitted against intellectual happiness—it still acknowledges how an unavoidable aspect of place-making is how the site stimulates the mind and the imagination. Surely designers could learn much from how writers present such stimulation. It is through writing that we are accorded access to the metamorphosis of simple environment into milieu (space into place), to the human subject's entering, literally and spiritually, into an objective site and to the consequences of that experience.[58]

Poets inevitably tend to privilege their own medium, and the poetical garden, readily sustained by rhetorical gesture and claim, is capable of even more tropes than the painted one. Anthony Hecht has written one of the best modern poems about gardens, and his appreciation of the Villa d'Este no doubt derives from his implicit analogy between the making of poetry and place-making itself:

> For thus it was designed:
> Controlled disorder at the heart
> Of everything, the paradox, the old
> Oxymoronic itch to set the formal structures
> Within a natural context, where the tension lectures
> Us on our mortal state, and by controlled
> Disorder, labors to keep art
> From being too refined.[59]

A different view of poetry's relationship to the garden, closer to part of Marvell's mischievous claim for

tal vistas that leave the garden to fix on distant events or memories yet are emphatically triggered, however briefly this is implied, by the immediate setting.

The word comes into its own when it can explore, explain, and share the associations, feelings, and ideas that designed sites promote—Marvell's "green thought in a green shade." And the distinctive contribution of poetry is that it avoids the awkward maneuvers by which "significance" or "meaning" get attached to landscape architecture. Marc Treib has sought to clarify this vexed but essential topic, but his analysis seems to me flawed by a reliance on creaky mechanisms of association and their explanation, as well as by a too rigid

FIGURE 111. Jan Weenix, *Agneta Block, Her Husband Sybrand de Flines and Her Children in Her Garden of Vijverhof on the River Vecht*, before 1697, Amsterdam Historisch Museum.

mental pleasures, is offered by W. H. Auden's "Their Betters." Wittily, wickedly, he manipulates the garden in favor of its verbal supplement, which only he can provide. We have here a virtual refusal of the garden's significance, the opposite of Hecht's easy transitions from place-making to poetry and back. Sitting in a deck chair and listening "to all the noises that my garden made," Auden translates into words what "vegetables and birds" have been denied and what is vouchsafed only to their "lonely betters," humans. Auden's logocentricity brushes aside the garden world in its fullness: he simply chooses to ignore the rift between that world and words available (even to a poet), a rift that Heidegger more readily confronts.[60] We are indeed, as Auden insists, "better" for our verbal skills than the materials and nonhuman inhabitants of the garden—we can lie, mark time, fall in love, laugh and weep eloquently, and discourse on concepts like loneliness and superiority. Yet that very linguistic facility is liable to cut us off, not just from a world of forms, smells, colors, spaces that have no obvious verbal equivalents (nor need of them), but also from an instinctive apprehension of the natural world that Auden condescendingly allows to the robin and the pollinating bee. Our "loneliness" is an inadequate acknowledgment of that isolation.

Auden makes us aware of a garden's resources simply by denying them and celebrating his verbal skills, which attend to other matters. Yet poets, ambitious by profession, do not necessarily ignore what is difficult of verbal access: in Kew Gardens D. M. Black wants "to sing an excess which is not so simply explainable."[61] It is surprising how much the corpus of poetry about gardens, if we read it attentively, has reached beyond its formal limits to explain the not so simply explainable, to stress nonverbal elements of garden design and experience, and to do so, of course, in ways other than wordless paintings. This is difficult to indicate briefly, but it includes an almost perverse attempt to treat of shapes ("intricate mesh of trees, / Sagging beneath a lavender snow / Of wisteria, wired by creepers"), tex-

tures ("the minted flesh of leaves / against the garden wall"), smells (Thom Gunn sniffing "at the bergamot / the fruit-sage smell"), or sounds that are beyond the recall of even a Tennysonian onomatopoeia ("The broad ambrosial aisles of lofty lime / Made noise with bees and breeze from end to end").[62] We need to notice how meaning and significance reside even in these sensual glances.

There is much to be gathered from poetical perspectives on gardens, writing that because it has other obligations is blithely indifferent to what painters show or what pragmatic treatises have to recount. When Vita Sackville-West studies garden catalogs (another literature of the garden) during the winter months, she acknowledges that the

> wisdom of perfection
> Never was ours in fact though ours in faith,
> And since we live in fabric of delusion
> Faith may well serve a turn in place of fact.[63]

This has, certainly, a horticultural point; it is also about the garden as prototypical dwelling place. William Cowper goes a bit further, saying he "can fib without lying, and represent [his own gardens] better than they are."[64] His "better" does not point simply to subject matter—to the fact that Cowper prefers writing about crisp gravel paths and a fecund greenhouse rather than noxious weeds (other poets take up that theme). His concern is about the garden as a place of inhabitation, a space made over and made better by human concerns as well as by the spade.

But a focus wholly upon poetry would miss the opportunities that the garden has afforded to other kinds of writing, to novelists certainly, but especially to that band of nonfiction garden writers, hard to categorize, who seem increasingly to dominate the publishing landscape today. It is a phenomenon that is worth considerable scrutiny.

The novel, the narrative par excellence of social life, has endlessly set its stories, or selected scenes from them, in gardens,[65] not simply as an occasion for pretty descriptive prose, but to appeal, usually tacitly, to a reader's shared apprehensions of the meanings of a garden. "Distinctly they heard again from the garden the raucous voices of the boys."[66] What might seem just a passing glance in John Banville's novel *Ghosts* gains in resonance if we think of changing the site of the juvenile play. Gardens are special territories of children's explorations, hopes and fears, mysteries and rites of passage, sometimes forever forbidden, sometimes penetrated with trepidation.[67] It may be Alice unable to get into the "loveliest garden you ever saw"; or the heroine of Frances Hodgson Burnett's *Secret Garden*, whose access to the locked and hidden garden involves the scary negotiation of a series of social and territorial thresholds; or most subtly of all there is Marcel Proust's young Jean Santeuil, in the unfinished novel of that name. For Jean the myriad world of a garden turns fleeting moments into duration; ordinary and external life is made coincident with the extraordinary and the intimate; in gardens his quotidien self acquires its first poetry, and without being aware of it Jean lays down for his adult life a fund of memories.[68]

The garden does not lose its appeal for narrators of adult life, perhaps because it never quite loses its intimations of childhood and childhood's alternate states of innocence and first experience. Samuel Richardson and Jane Austen are both particularly economical with their garden scenes—rarely describing in any detail, yet counting surely on a rich cluster of knowledge and associations to establish the nuances of character in action. At key moments of *Pamela* and *Clarissa*, the cycles of Richardson's heroines' trials, tribulations, personal triumphs, and social successes or sexual harassment are variously plotted along and against the heroines' and the readers' ideas of the garden. It is not simply that the gardens can mirror situations or moral positions by characters' implied responses; ambiguous and paradoxical themselves, gardens are also places where both social convention and its unlooked-for or secretly plotted

transgression are equally at home. Austen invokes a wider range of designed landscapes than Richardson: the privacy and loneliness of the shrubbery walk for Fanny Price in *Mansfield Park*, Elizabeth Bennet's apprehension of variety in designed parkland that maintained a careful balance between intervention and naturalism, or the false design tastes by which persons like Mrs. Norris will betray their moral ineptitude.

The use of the garden as indicator of character, moral position, or social nuance becomes a familiar mechanism for the novelist, as in the often cited description of Sir Charles Grandison's estate in the 1753 novel by Richardson.[69] But the obviousness of the motif should not blind us to the testimony this offers to the idea that gardens represent their makers and their culture "selon les lieux et le désir du seigneur," as Olivier de Serres wrote in 1600.[70] Lampedusa's tale of the vanishing of an old Sicilian order in *The Leopard* often takes its hero, Don Fabrizio, into decaying garden worlds like Donnafugata, where he encounters the "anonymous busts of broken-nosed goddesses" along the laurel walks and, at the fountain of Neptune and Amphrite, "gazed, remembered, regretted." The garden as *lieu de mémoire*, however, is not solely a nostalgic hinterland of recollection; albeit an extravagant example, Roussel's *Locus Solus* explores at length a surreal landscape of memory, allusion, and fantasy, a vision of the garden as memory-theater par excellence.

Two famous novels, Rousseau's *Julie, ou la Nouvelle Héloïse* (1761) and Goethe's *Die Wahlverwandtschaften* (Elective affinities) of 1809, both use landscape architecture prominently as settings and as metaphors.[71] What tells us more about gardens than either how people behave in them or how they are constituted as symbols, however, is the way in which characters are allowed to adjudicate the dialogue between nature and culture. Always a vital issue if not a cliché in gardens, it is extremely rare to find it sufficiently explored. But a writer can articulate this intricate exchange, as Rousseau does in his famous account of the visit of Julie, her husband, M. de Wolmar, and her former tutor and lover, Saint-Preux, to her enclosed *"verger"* called the Elysée.[72] Saint-Preux's narrative invokes both objects seen and the responses he has to them (despite his writing that he was more concerned with objects than their impressions—"J'étais plus empressé de voir les objets que d'examiner leurs impressions") and finally melds them in a wholly fresh understanding.

To start with, Rousseau can set out how impressions of the Elysée come one upon the other, influenced in part by remarks that other people contribute. What Saint-Preux is told will be a "verger" or orchard strikes him at first as an impressive wilderness, comparable to his images of the South Seas; when he is made to understand how contrived it is, he sees it as a "prétendu verger," and then once he has fully entered into the processes by which the place was made he acknowledges a "verger metamorphosé." His increasingly complex sense of the place is composed of all these impressions rather than simply the last one entertained; "curiosity" sustains his enquiry. The "espèce de mystère" he experiences as he approaches and enters the enclosure is never lost, only augmented and complicated both by the knowledge that the whole place is contrived and by his slow grasp of the methods of contrivance used by Julie and her husband. These include the contrivance of encouraging natural growth and what today we would call habitat formation; but they also involve the felicitous redeployment of old Baroque water systems from nearby terraces to create wetlands, streams, and pools within the enclosed Elysée. There is also a deliberate mixing of wild and cultivated species (garden plants "semblaient croître naturellement avec les autres [from meadows]"). The strong, even superlative reactions at the start ("le plus sauvage, le plus solitaire") are never dismissed; instead, a realization of just how that character has been effected is won both by firsthand experience and by listening to explanations of horticultural process. The climax of the visit is focused on the "volière" or bird sanctuary, presumably a delib-

erate invocation both of the Roman Varro's description of his own architectural aviary and of frequent attempts by later designers to re-create it from the Latin's verbal description. Julie's volière turns out to be a miracle of ecological nurture.

This can only be an abbreviated rehearsal of an extremely complex passage, but it can perhaps suggest how apparently simple garden experience (like garden design in the first instance) is composed of subtle and even paradoxical responses. We are not always aware of, but more often just intuit, this complexity; yet it constitutes the plenitude of such places, and it takes an accomplished writer to bring them to consciousness. Furthermore, the way that Julie uses her garden to represent social virtues, at once deliberate and instinctive, is shown to be also an expectation that it will in its turn affect cultural attitudes. The final sense of the narrator's visit to the Elysée is of the naturalness of culture, the hard work that conceals effort and (what had been adumbrated at the start) the intricate meanings of pleasure and utility (this latter being, in effect, what augments the potential of pleasurable retreat). Furthermore, this mysterious place gains in meaning through a contrast, stated and implied, between it and other zones of Julie's estate. Rousseau's celebration of "retreat," in short, does not involve what John Milton had once disparaged as "cloistered virtue"; rather, it coincides with what Ian Hamilton Finlay would say of garden retreats, that they were in fact often "attacks."[73]

Novels may offer one of the richest accounts of the part gardens can play in the practical, social, aesthetic, and spiritual economies of human life. But, outside the novel, there is a range of prose that is exceptionally difficult to categorize other than rather blandly as "garden writing." It seems to be particularly efflorescent in the late twentieth century, a by-product in part of the enormous growth in garden activity in the western world: we have garden centers, garden nurseries, garden clubs, and garden writing.

The origins of this now prolific genre go back a long

way, perhaps (at least in England) to such seventeenth-century examples as Sir Francis Bacon's essay "Of gardens," Sir Thomas Browne's arcane meditations on *The Gardens of Cyrus*, or Sir William Temple's *Upon the Gardens of Epicurus, or of Gardening in the Year 1685*. These are works that may linger on practical matters, may concern themselves in passing with design or planting, but always use the immediate gardening world as the occasion and the alibi for their larger meditations. The flavor and the thrust of such writings may be gathered from a few sentences of a letter that John Evelyn wrote to Browne in 1657 to explain how "Caves, Grotts, Mounts, and irregular ornaments of Gardens do contribute to contemplative and philosophicall Enthusiasms. . . . For these expedients do influence the soule and spirits of man, and prepare them for converse with good Angells; besides which, they contribute to the lesse abstracted pleasures."[74] Such "hortulan pleasures" and "hortulan saints," as they are called in the same letter, have often produced writing that has yielded material for understanding the mentality of a given culture's approach to place-making. But it is also worth taking it out of its immediate context and reading it for its identification of topics in place-making irrespective of their time and place.

This kind of literature acquired a new lease on life to keep pace with the middle-class discovery of gardens and gardening after the mid-nineteenth century, tempting some distinguished if unexpected writers including the Czech Karel Capek, who published some poetical reflections on the garden year in Prague in 1929.[75] Publishers continue to provide many examples of the genre: Michael Pollan's *Second Nature* (1991) argues for a middle ground between lawn and wilderness, Susan Hill and Rory Stuart's *Reflections from a Garden* (1995) is an almost archetypical title in this field, and Jim Nollman's *Why We Garden: Cultivating a Sense of Place* (1994) is a more sober meditation on the relation of gardener to garden. An analogous French example of this kind of garden writing, taken almost at random,

is Marie Rouanet's *Tout Jardin est Eden* (1993), which is part horticultural, part ruminatory (hardly philosophical—they are, after all, reflections, *aperçus*, not conceptions). The list of such books seems as inexhaustible as must be readers' enthusiasm for them.

And then there are—among the most revealing and demanding of verbal perspectives on the garden—the texts which employ a landscaped site as part subject, part metaphor, part excuse for their reflections, which in their turn refocus ideas about that landscape: from Louis Aragon's invocation of Les Buttes-Chaumont (see Figure 127) in *Le Paysan de Paris*, first published in 1926, to Jorge Luis Borges' gardens and spatial images in his parabolic tales, to Hubert Damisch's essay, "L'Inconscient en ces jardins," with its surprising and fruitful bringing together of Freud's developing ideas on the fantastic with the establishment of American national parks like Yosemite.[76]

This "garden writing" affirms various notions of its subject; it connects the garden with a whole conspectus of human feelings, ambitions, desires, beliefs; it rarely argues a case, preferring instead to imply some intersection of gardens with other concerns. Yet Borges makes it almost impossible to think of bifurcating garden paths or of the continuity between labyrinth and desert in the same way again; his connections—like those which Damisch offers between the Freudian construction of the unconscious and the American invention of national park systems—suddenly become ideas that we realize have haunted the garden or the park all along.

If I were to single out one such piece of garden writing, it would be Sir George Sitwell's great essay, *On the Making of Gardens*, of 1909. Written in part to fulfill the claims of its title about the *making* of gardens, it nevertheless functions insidiously to take up an agenda beyond the pragmatic. Itself a "genuine period piece" from the 1890s, as the author's son Osbert noted,[77] it draws on the contemporary symbolist ethos that espoused and created the noumenal and the spiritual. Sir George mocks the "practical Man" who can see only firewood in the cypresses of Italian gardens and who is constitutionally incapable of passing "over the threshold of fact" to discover some manifestation of the "ideal," some "ancestral memories," some magic or dream (echoes here of Thomas Carlyle's attacks on positivism or Dickens's satire of Gradgrind in *Hard Times*). Yet we should pause before seeing all this as solely a "period piece" or an apt instance of that garden writing which James Elkins gently accuses of being "mild soporifics" and "conceptually scattered."[78] For Sitwell's concern is to relate "the garden magic of Italy" to the "domain of psychology," a prime concern of artists and intellectuals in the 1890s and represented in the United States by William James's *Principles of Psychology* (1891), which Sitwell often cites. For him, gardens aspire to the condition of music, another appeal—this time via Walter Pater—that Sitwell makes, and they are made to call out the deepest resources of the human psyche. Great gardens, the result of collaboration on many cultural and practical fronts, are *gesamtkunstwerken*, analogous to Wagner's music-dramas, another of Sitwell's favorite reference points. He uses every resource of prose to make those connections at once conceptually clear and instinctively felt.

It is garden writing of the finest order and vision. It uses ekphrasis—the verbal emulation of pictorial expression or visual experience—and often does so because no other "illustration" is available to its author.

Some examples of garden writing are accompanied by graphic illustration these days, but many (like Sitwell's) have not been, at least in any substantial way. But *On the Making of Gardens* does not rest content just with ekphrastic energy or vividness.[79] It delights, certainly, in a convincing re-creation by its own verbal medium of nonverbal experiences; but that is only an intermediary stage for the garden ekphrastist, whether Sitwell, Pliny the Younger, or Thomas Whately,[80] who aims his prose at the very essence of a site the experience of which is both highly particular, even unique, and fully generalized.

That this is also the most difficult kind of writing to bring off, navigating the quicksands of bathos, platitude, pretension, and portentiousness, is sadly obvious; the bookstores and magazines yield only too frequent evidence of such failures. We should not, however, dismiss such garden writing because of the enormous risks it must run in taking us to the edge of fresh perceptions or, rather, to recognitions of what we had felt but never so well expressed for ourselves.

The garden in word and image is often a virtual reality rather than empirical testimony of actual sites. Many further examples could be adduced (for example, from Japanese garden culture) of places made in the imagination. We need to attend to what they show and tell us if for no other reason than because virtual realities can be the measure of actual ones.

CHAPTER 7

Historical Excursus: Late Seventeenth-Century Garden Theory

Hortulan affaires doe require varietyes of novell &
conceited amoenityes.
—John Beale, 30 September 1659

HAVING COVERED A RANGE of topical themes in landscape architecture, it is time to stand back and examine one particular "moment" of garden theory when many of these topics were in play. This moment has been chosen because it coincided with one of the exciting times in English intellectual thought, a time of scientific and philosophical inquiry that was open, wide-ranging, collaborative, international, and interdisciplinary. Garden interests were a central part of this discourse, which may be seen to focus around the establishment of the Royal Society in London in 1661. The roots of the Royal Society stretch back into the earlier seventeenth century, having Sir Francis Bacon as one of its prime movers; its continuing efforts and researches maintained their momentum into the early years of the eighteenth century.[1] Though consisting most famously of a body of learned amateurs and *virtuosi* devoted to what we would continue today to term scientific inquiries, the larger meaning of science as knowledge guided their deliberations and drew into its orbit a host of lesser scholars.

We shall be concerned mainly with four individuals: Samuel Hartlib, John Beale, John Evelyn, and Stephen Switzer, of whom the latter two are names clearly associated with garden theory and practice. Hartlib, an extraordinary figure,[2] is honored in part for his energetic correspondence whereby he put amateurs and schol-

ars, like Beale and Evelyn, in touch with each other on the widest range of topics; my insistence that garden-making itself involves a vast range of human concerns is both mirrored in Hartlib's activities and, arguably, endorsed by them.

It is largely through the work of John Evelyn that the garden concerns of the Hartlibian circle were carried forward. As a fellow of the Royal Society and a member of its Georgical Committee concerned with the land, Evelyn enjoyed opportunities that were denied to Hartlib and Beale to focus on the theoretical and practical aspects of "hortulan affaires." He nevertheless shared their conviction that gardens and gardening exercised a "seacret & powerfull influence . . . to operat upon humane spirits towards virtue and sanctitie"[3] and that the gardener is "one of the most usefull members of Humane Societie."[4] He had traveled widely in Europe, seeing many examples of gardens there, as well as being acquainted with garden-making in England throughout his long life. He undertook a wide-ranging study of gardening, to be gathered into an opus magnum entitled the "Elysium Britannicum," into which he sought to put everything he could learn, discover, or take over from other researchers (as in Beale's case) about the practical and philosophical aspects of garden-making. He never succeeded in publishing his much revised, endlessly interleaved, and augmented manuscript, the physical condition of which has led to its neglect by all but a few garden specialists.[5] This sometimes daunting compendium contains hints of a remarkable theoretical essay on garden art.

Stephen Switzer finds a place at the end of this historical excursus for reasons that are here argued for the first time: that his publications gave widespread, if belated, circulation to some of the central concerns of the earlier gardenists. No attempt will be made to argue that he was actually acquainted with ideas that had emanated from the Hartlibian circle or that he was familiar with topics canvassed in Evelyn's vast unpublished manuscript; there is no evidence of such contacts or influence. Switzer's place in this "moment" of garden theory is designed rather to show how widespread were late seventeenth-century concepts of place-making that we have subsequently forgotten. Ironically, Switzer's significance in the history of the articulation of certain key garden topics has been obscured by the proleptic use that subsequent commentators have tried to make of his work.

Our overall concern with this group of writers, then, is to understand and celebrate a highpoint in theorizing about what we now call landscape architecture and to derive from it some fresh perspectives on topics that recur in our own day.[6]

I
_____

Our excursus begins on 30 September 1659, when John Beale wrote a letter about his garden researches, probably addressed to Samuel Hartlib. Hartlib eventually communicated it to John Evelyn, who in his turn wrote it, with a few crucial additions, into the "Elysium Britannicum."[7]

Beale's letter was largely concerned with how he would landscape a site in the Backbury Hills in Herefordshire. But the bottom line was clearly his commitment to what he termed "the definition of a Garden"; this concern was also to be addressed in the first chapter of his proposed book on the pleasure garden, entitled "Howe and why a Garden."[8] It was an issue of wide significance and interest. What exactly constituted the thrust of garden art? Should it evince

humans' control over nature? their skills or ingenuity at working with its resources? their interference in natural purposes for profit or pleasure? or their celebration of God's bounty? These were all themes in which mid-seventeenth-century England was much absorbed. Even if none of these ideas had actually been translated into garden layouts (which is not the case at all, though the history of design takes little cognizance of them), it would still be essential to register the theoretical energies unleashed during this period.

Beale's letter, in fact, was a product not just of his interest in a particular site but of his proposals communicated to Hartlib for books on "Physique" and "Pleasure" gardens, and of his own 1657 publication, *Herefordshire Orchards, a Pattern for All England*; this had itself first taken shape as two letters to Hartlib in May 1656, prompted by the third edition of *Samuel Hartlib His Legacie* (1655). Out of these exchanges and documents emerged a cluster of shared assumptions, which for brevity's sake may be abstracted as four principles (as Beale wrote to Hartlib on another occasion, "I must be abrupt").[9] These principles bear a striking affinity to ideas of gardens as a third nature that had long since been mooted by Bonfadio (as discussed in Chapter 3). There is no indication at all that the Hartlibian circle knew of Bonfadio's letter or even Taegio's treatise on the villa, where the idea of a third nature was also adumbrated; it should be noted, though, that an English translation of Cicero's treatise, in which the cultural landscape or second nature was discussed and which arguably determined Bonfadio's and Taegio's thinking, appeared in 1683.[10] Further, Evelyn's ambitious project for a compendium of garden theory and practice depended, as did Hartlib's project for an international sharing of research, on a wide knowledge of primary and secondary materials. What is interesting, however, is that new English discussions of the garden in the seventeenth century took up topics already established as essential to its adequate consideration.

1. *Gardens were to be seen as the culmination, histori-*

cally or culturally as well as topographically, of a series of human interventions in the natural world. Hartlib's *Legacie* addresses this cultural or historical development when he notes that the "Art of Gardening is but of few years standing in England, and therefore not deeply rooted, nor well understood." It was only about fifty years ago, he continues, that hortulan *"Ingenuities* first began to flourish in *England."* [11] Hartlib thus introduces the theme of what we might call the advancement or progress of gardening in England. This became a leitmotif, even obsession, during the eighteenth century, together with an equally consistent interest in how to adapt to English conditions (cultural as well as climatic) the traditions of gardening, husbandry, and agriculture that can be traced back at least to classical times. Thus it is that modern England is claimed as the site for the recovery of ancient gardening, a historical prototype that for Beale seems to meld Greek with biblical perfections. [12] The ideal garden, which his letter to Evelyn identifies as the Backbury Hills, exemplifies this progress of the arts, since as well as recalling ancient examples it represents its own accomplished Britishness. Hartlib said (though erroneously) [13] that the site was inhabited by "the old Britains, the silures," and Evelyn noted that it is in "our owne Country."

Just as garden design develops over time, deriving some of its essential forms from earlier agricultural needs and practices, so do they in space; this we have seen already. It is as if the view from the mansion over its gardens, orchards, pasture, and tillage visually and locally recapitulated the historical sequence of a garden's evolution (see Figures 19–22). Hartlib's *Discourse for Division or Setting Out of Land, as to the Best Form* (1653) addresses this topographical scale of intervention in a theoretical fashion as part of a more specialized plea for enclosure. In it he borrowed from a correspondent, Cressy Dymock, a draft scheme (Figure 112) for an ideal estate layout, reworking it for publication in an even more austere and rigorous geometry (Figure 113). [14] His verbal commentary explained how "your house stands in the middle of all your little world . . . enclosed with the gardens and orchyeards . . . & all bound together as with a girdle" (this referring presumably to a circle of utilitarian buildings). Then come great quadrants of corn lands and meadows—"& all that covered againe as so (faire largeth) a cloak of meadow and tillage to which you may count the corn pasturage the cape if you please or the sleeves to the coate." Finally, beyond the furthest circle lie the animal pastures. The "proper domains" of each element of the estate's ensemble, as the published plan announces, are arranged certainly for convenience and pragmatic purposes ("right and ample use of every [piece] of ground"). But the layout also implicitly proposes a hierarchy of spaces whereby nearer the mansion are those which demonstrate greater control than those further away, more intensity of labor and greater aesthetic delight—"refreshed with the beautye (& Odour) of the blossomes fruit and flowers." To this idea of scale and relationship of parts Hartlib/Dymock gesture with such phrases as "and outwards to my Tillage." [15] This anticipates the second principle enunciated in these writings.

2. *This hierarchy was physically represented on the ground in a scale of artifice that decreased as one moved further away from the mansion.* By the time of the Hartlibian inquiries into garden form, country estates throughout Europe had begun to show this hierarchy of culture/nature beginning at the platform of the mansion with the parterre and following an axial line of avenues out into the distant countryside (Figure 114). Beale frequently lists the constituent parts of small country estates as a sequence based on gradations in the scale of mineral/vegetable or cultural/natural mediation: "We do commonly devise a shadowy walk from our Gardens through our Orchards." [16] But he also pays attention to the formal means by which each zone is to be registered: his projected treatise on "A Garden of Pleasure" contains a section on "Whether the large trees of the Orchard should be admitted into the Garden: Or the Orchard necessarily divided from

ye garden,"[17] while the letter to Hartlib asks "what sort of Trees, or what approach of trees may be allowed for the ornamt of the flowery regions." Beale equally sees orchards themselves as part of a hierarchical scale of artifice—being "the richest, sweetest, and most embellish'd Grove."[18]

The sequence or triad of "natures" has three aspects —historical, topographical, and evaluative. It is a historical development in that wild terrain came to be selectively enclosed for crops, rivers would be dammed, and then gardens were established, drawing on agricultural forms and technology. This triad of natures was also expressed topographically on the ground, as in Cressy Dymock's ideal estate plan. Finally, the notion of three natures authorizes qualitative judgments: arguing either that the more human intervention into the original first nature was for the better—a value that eventually entered English with the term "improvement"; or insisting that God's first nature was, after all, the best.

3. It was not always possible, owing to topographical or financial exigencies, to make this hierarchy of cultural control over territory visible on the ground. It might have to be executed approximately or piecemeal, but its underlying principle was clear. Here we could recall the mid-seventeenth-century gardens of Wilton House (see Figure 32), where the apparent wish to accommodate the River Nadder without regularizing it into a canal forced the least ordered section of the garden, its "wilderness," to be established in the middle, where the river flowed, not at the furthest distance from the house. The hierarchy of control across a whole landscape, which the interior Wilton gardens represented in miniature, would likewise often have to compromise with local and topographical exigencies.

Thus we can contrast what we might call the ideal or drawing board solution of Dymock that Hartlib published in his *Discourses for Division* with the empirical possibility that Beale considered for Backbury Hills in Herefordshire. Dymock proposes an ideal structure,

without any local application (and when Hartlib tidies up Dymock's sketches for publication, he introduces even more abstraction into the layout). By contrast, in Herefordshire Beale is constrained by topographical and financial exigencies from imposing such a thoroughgoing scheme as Dymock envisaged.

It is in the first place owing to financial considerations rather than because he is dedicating himself to naturalistic purism, as some commentators assume,[19] that Beale rules out "Architecture," the most conspicuously artificial ingredient of third nature, from his proposed garden. This is abundantly clear from his statement that the garden could be created for £100 as long as that estimate could exclude both "the charges of Architecture, conteining Walls, Statues, Summer-houses, Cesternes &c." as well as "the charge of Plants and workmanship in setting the Plants." As it is unlikely that planting and labor would be wholly excluded in even the most beneficent and fecund of sites, the reason for the exclusion of hard elements is surely financial.[20] So I suggest that the proposals for regulating Backbury according to gradations on the nature/culture scale differ in degree, not in kind, from Dymock. But here we impinge on the fourth and final of the principles that are at stake in these writings.

4. The ultimate significance and purpose of such visible garden hierarchies of control was, through the contrived forms of garden art and husbandry, to educate humans in the appreciation of the ideal perfection of God's handiwork in the larger world of nature. A variant and less explicitly theological version of that perspective, enunciated by the third Earl of Shaftesbury in his unpublished *Second Characters*, is that garden art represents—presents over again in its own forms—the proper character of the natural world that will be the better appreciated once a garden's compact version of it has been understood.[21]

Beale touches on this topic of representation generally and specifically. He was by no means against features like "mounts" or "caves," which were accepted as straightforward, even mimetic, representations. But

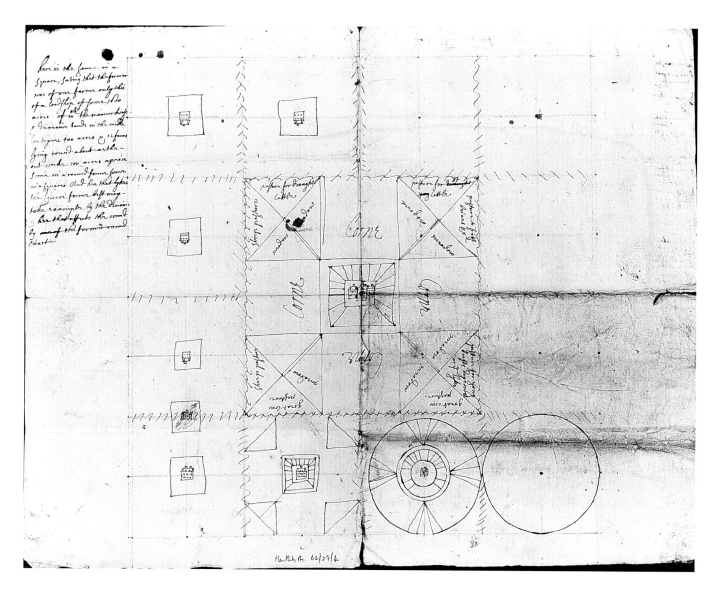

FIGURE 112a. Cressy Dymock, drawing of an ideal farm or estate,
Sheffield University Library (HP 62/29/4A).

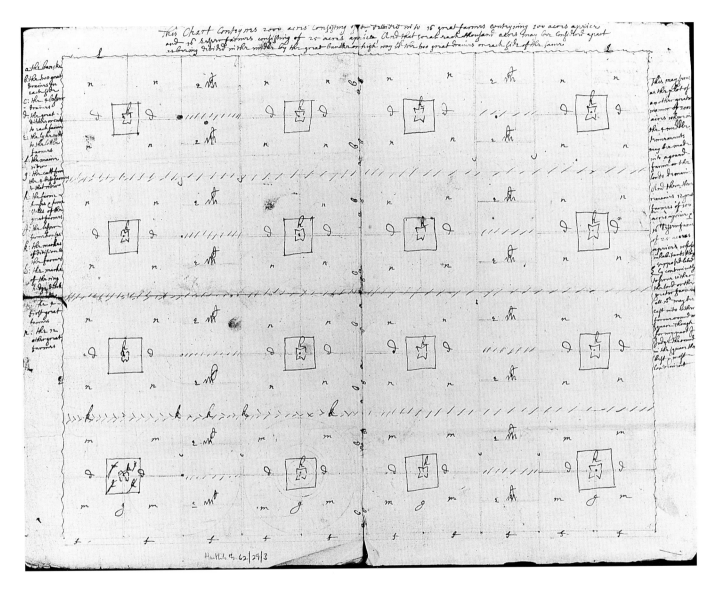

FIGURE 112b. Cressy Dymock, another plan for ideal farm or estate, Sheffield University Library (HP/62/29/3A).

This Chart conteins 2000 *Acres, confifting of or divided into* 16 *great Farms, conteining* 100 *Acres apiece, and* 16 *leffer Farms, confifting of* 25 *Acres apiece: And that fo as each t houfand Acres may be confidered apart, as being divided in the middle by the great Bank or high way, with the two great Drains on each fide of the fame.*

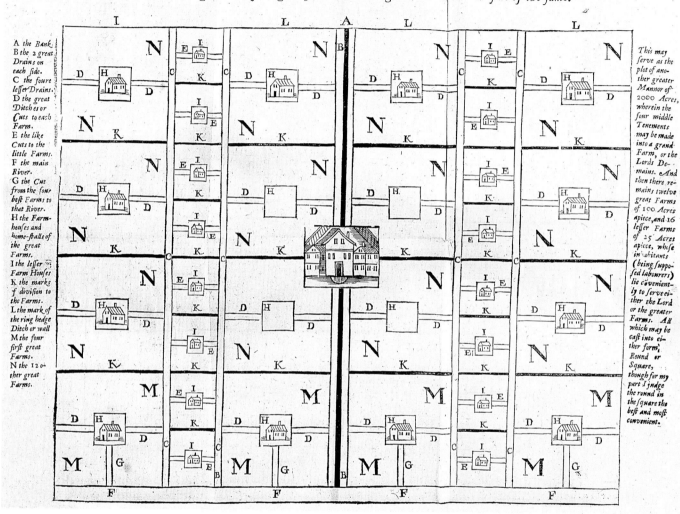

A *the Bank.*
B *the* 2 *great Drains on each fide.*
C *the foure leffer Drains.*
D *the great Ditches or Cuts to each Farm.*
E *the like Cuts to the little Farms.*
F *the main River.*
G *the Cut from the foure beft Farms to that River.*
H *the Farm-houfes and home-ftalls of the great Farms.*
I *the leffer Farms Houfes*
K *the marks of divifion to the Farms.*
L *the mark of the ring hedge Ditch or wall*
M *the four firft great Farms.*
N *the* 12 *other great Farms.*

This may ferve as the plot of another greater Mannor of 2000 *Acres, wherein the four middle Tenements may be made into a grand Farm, or the Lords De-mains. And then there re-mains twelve great Farms of* 100 *Acres apiece, and* 16 *leffer Farms of* 25 *Acres apiece, whofe inhabitants (being fuppo-fed labourers) lie convenient-ly to ferve ei-ther the Lord or the greater Farms. All which may be caft into ei-ther form, Round or Square, though for my part I judge the round in the fquare the beft and moft convenient.*

FIGURE 113a. Version of Figure 112a published in Samuel Hartlib,
A Discoverie for Division, 1653 (The Huntington Library).

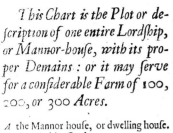

This Chart is the Plot or de-
fcription of one entire Lordfhip,
or Mannor-houfe, with its proper Demains: or it may ferve
for a confiderable Farm of 100,
200, or 300 Acres.

A the Mannor houfe, or dwelling houfe.
B the Kitchin Garden.
C the Orchyard.
D the Garden for choyce fruits or flow-
ers.
E the Garden for Phyficall plants, or
what you will.
F F the Dary and Landry.
G G the Sheep coats.
H H the two greateft of the home Clofes
to milk the Cows in, or to put a faddle
Nag in.
I I the Bake houfe and Brew houfe.
K the ftanding racks for Oxen, &c. and
the great Corn Barn.
L L Other Barns, Stables, Cow or Ox-
houfes, Swines ftyes.
M M the little houfes for all forts of
Poultry.
N N More ftanding Racks.
O O Coney-berries.
Q Q little Clofes for a ftoned Horfe, a
Mare, or Fole, &c.
R R Little Clofes for like purpofes.
S two little Paftures for fat Sheep.
T two Clofes for Pafture for Ewes,
Lambs, or weaker Sheep.
V two little Paftures for a fat Beef or two.
W two little Paftures for infected Cattle.
X two little Paftures for your own, or
your friends Saddle-horfe, that is for
prefent fervice.
Y two little Paftures for weaning Calves.

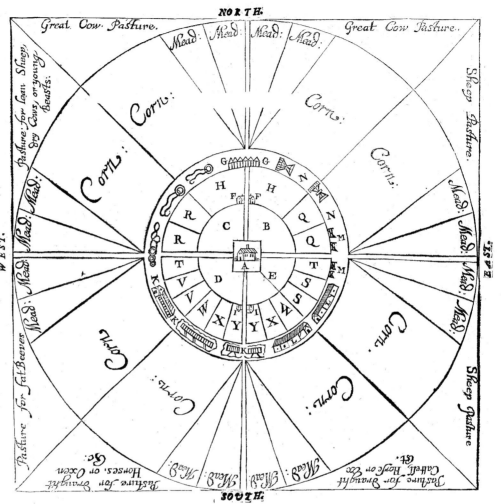

FIGURE 113b. Version of Figure 112b published in Samuel Hartlib,
A Discoverie for Division, 1653 (The Huntington Library).

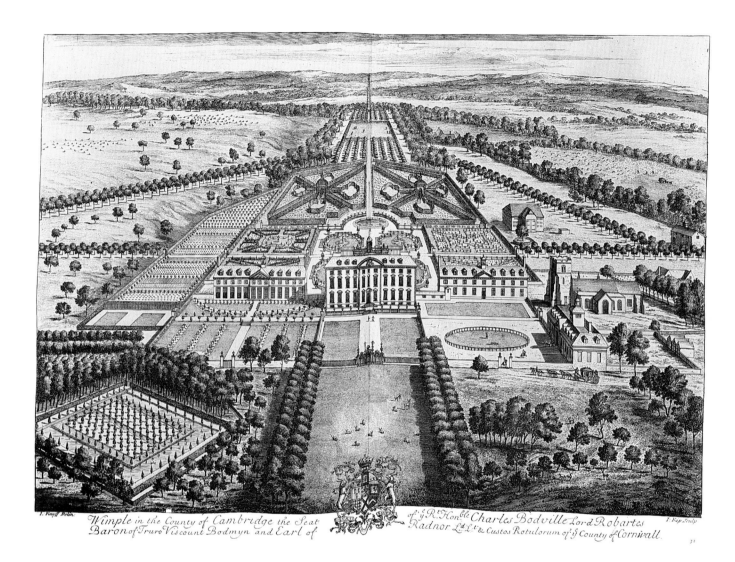

FIGURE 114. J. Kip after L. Knyff, engraved view of Wimpole,
Cambridgeshire, 1724–28. Dumbarton Oaks Research Library
and Collection.

when, as in Herefordshire, he has what Henry James might call "the real thing," he is far less satisfied with "poore mimical though sometimes chargeable mounts and wildernesses" in modern gardens.[22] His scorn for "our narrow, mimicall way" of garden design does not, in fact, mean the wholesale rejection of hortulan representation. If, for example, "a gap lies in the way between our Orchard and Coppice," he suggests that "we [may] fill up the vacancy with the artificial help of a Hopyard, *where a busy Wood gives the shape of a Wood*."[23] More explicitly he urges that "hortulane amoenityes [he had just instanced "Mounts, Prospects, Precipices, & Caves"] may sometimes bee soe representet to you."

Beale is concerned to put hortulan representation at the service of genius loci. One section of his proposed book on the pleasure garden was announced as "Adviseing Not to enforce the platforme to any particular phantsy, but to apply unto it the best shape, That will agree with the nature of the place."[24] He uses human knowledge, skill, and art to bring out the potential of the particular landscape, perfecting its own natural resources, its special *quidditas*, just as the gardener should manipulate the microclimates of his enclosures;[25] hence Beale's wish to improve the "beauty and taste" of flowers, using cultural resources to enlarge awareness of their "small beauty and taste." Beale's suggestion that Evelyn add a chapter on "Entertainments" is urged in its turn because they are "intended, as it were scenically, to shewe the riches, beauty, wondrs, plenty, & delight of a Garden"—in other words they reveal its best potential. Even though the Herefordshire site affords more extensive and various natural advantages to the gardener, he writes, than are available at Woodstock, Windsor, and Greenwich, there is still the need to "rectify and purify."

The Herefordshire site itself seems to imitate or represent gardens—a large, square, green plain on the summit of one hill "hath a perfect resemblance of an ancient flowre garden," just as the system of pathways that led to it from the house below becomes, in Beale's description, a version of garden paths and arbors, or

just as Evelyn's transcription of this passage in the "Elysium Britannicum" understands the natural stream by the house as a "rich and pure Fountaine" (fol. 56). It all amounts to what Evelyn, without ever himself visiting Backbury, calls "a sweet and naturall Garden"; an achievement, as he finally notes, "because Nature has already bin (as we may truly say) so Artificiall." If we still hanker after labeling this some naturalistic or picturesque landscape vision, Evelyn's final addition of a reference to Spenser's *Bower of Bliss* to his "source" in Beale's letter underlines the essential "Idea" (his word) of hortulan arrangements that have dictated Beale's and his descriptions.

We may put this another way by saying that it is only when Beale, Hartlib, and Evelyn have an idea of the garden as third nature that they can find its nascent forms in the second and first. As an ordering or formal rectification of a varied "natural" landscape, gardens required a knowledge and experience of the other, which were gathered in the light and appreciation of gardens. This will become, *mutatis mutandis*, the central thesis of Shaftesbury's discussion of how gardens encode and purify the characters of the natural world; thereby gardens become a school of moral vision. Hartlib and Beale saw husbandry not just as a matter of tilling and otherwise shaping the earth but as "true and real Learning and Natural Philosophy." The eighteenth-century garden writer Philip Miller clearly had learnt these lessons when he wrote in his account of wilderness that "evergreens . . . naturally grow in form of Pyramids, and there are others that grow in forms of cones, and some which spread and extend their Branches."[26]

II

These four concepts are taken further by Evelyn, who was both more widely versed in garden design and more capable of theoretical or contemplative analysis. It will also be useful to look to a few other writers for their glosses and supplements to these topics.

Evelyn was not perhaps by temperament a theorizer, at least if we judge him by the theoretical delirium of the modern academy. It is, indeed, with apparent relief at one point in the "Elysium" that he descends "now to the Particulars" from "Rules [that] may suffice for the Generall" (fol. 281). His *Sylva*, dedicated to the Council of the Royal Society of London for "Improving of Natural Knowledge," opposes "particulars" to "hard words," "speculation," and "Rhapsodies."[27] Of course, the whole spirit of the new science encouraged this loyal member of the Royal Society in a hostility to "Fantasms and fruitless Speculations." It was his constant business to denounce "spectres, Forms, Intentional Species, Vacuum, Occult Qualities, and other Inadaequate Notions."[28]

As a product of that scientific *mentalité* that we associate with the Royal Society, the "Elysium Britannicum" was necessarily dedicated to empirical inquiry, but it also clearly reflects Evelyn's own inclinations; his was a temperament sufficiently at ease with an accumulation of firsthand experience of gardens. His diary and correspondence, let alone the references and acknowledgments throughout the manuscript, show that he himself clearly lived by the advice that he gave to a young traveler in January 1657: "And I beseech you, forget not to informe yourselfe as diligently as may be, in things that belong to gardening."[29] That he missed no occasion on which to augment his fund of information is attested at every turn; he surely glances at himself in *Sculptura* when he writes of Giacomo Favi that "this curious person neglected nothing, but went on collecting. . . . There was nothing so small, and to appearance, trifling, which he did not cast his eyes upon."[30] He told John Beale in 1679 that the "particulars" he wished to insert into the garden manuscript were "daily increasing."[31] And yet he also recognized the need for some structure by which to order these particulars; thus he also remarked that the "inexhaustible subject (I mean horticulture) [is] not yet fully digested in my mind."

He glances here at the *paragone*—a word Evelyn himself employs (fol. 290) to mean comparison, but that also carried the sense of contest or rivalry—between, on the one hand, the "enormous . . . heap"[32] of details that constituted much of his work for the "Elysium" and, on the other hand, "the frame or Idea"[33] that would give them coherence. The slowness with which he constructed what we might call theoretical overviews, missing the wood for numbering of its trees, is surely one of the reasons by which we must explain his failure to complete the manuscript.

Evelyn claims that the "Elysium Britannicum" is the fruit of "solid and unsophisticated experiment" (fol. 199), that "unsophisticated" drawing its main force from a reference to the Greek sophists, notorious for privileging "rhetorical argument" over substance. There are innumerable occasions during the "Elysium Britannicum" when this predilection for *experiment* is made palpable: in the related senses of trying something out, relying on careful experience, as well as of concentrating on particulars.

He has a passion for lists: not simply lists of plants, which one would expect from a practical guide to gardening, but also lists that rhetorically relish the variety, the sheer abundance of examples: the minerals that may be used to create grottoes (fols. 135–36)—an anatomy of Alexander Pope's Twickenham grotto *avant la lettre*; mountains that have figured in biblical experience (fol. 147); persons—"*Patriarchs, Kings, and Heros*"—whose statues might be placed in gardens (fol. 154a). The visual equivalent of these rhetorical lists is his graphic rendering of massed garden tools on folios 50 and 51 (Figure 115). Even as he generalizes, for example, about soils or plants, he often escapes into "sundry peculiarities in which they differ from one another."[34] The "Elysium" is balanced sometimes awkwardly, sometimes agilely, between specific examples, or what were called "histories,"[35] and general ideas, or those things which Evelyn says are "to be discovered by the mind only."[36]

The mind's control or overview of experimental evidence was vital to Evelyn's gardenist purposes, espe-

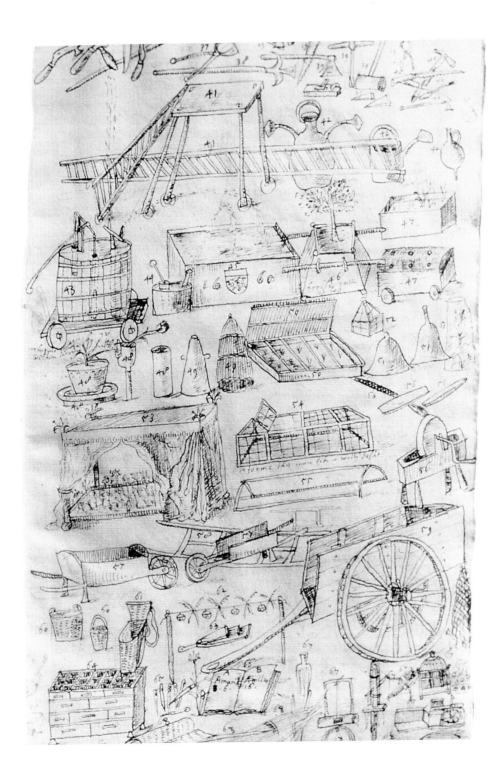

FIGURE 115. John Evelyn, drawing of garden tools from his "Elysium Britannicum," folio 51, late seventeenth century. The British Library, London.

cially if we recall either contemporary prejudice about the status of horticultural writing[37]—just as biased in the late twentieth century—or the conceptual and theoretical baggage with which the gardenist traveled in the seventeenth century. Among the most obvious of this cluster of associations, ideas, and even ideals, as the "Elysium" starts out by acknowledging, was the "memorie of that delicious place," Paradise, from which "our Fore-fathers" were exiled.[38] That this is not an idle conceit has been well documented by John Prest's book, *The Garden of Eden*.[39] Viewing the hortulan world in all its detail and variety through the lens of ideas or types was another commonplace of the age: thus Evelyn notes, again in the opening pages of the manuscript, that when people "would frame a Type of Heaven, because there is nothing in Nature more worthy and illustrious[,] they describe a Garden" (fol. 2).

Beyond such controlling ideas and types lay the urgent need for the subject of horticulture to be defined, to establish for itself an idea of the hortulan world so as not to be prevailed over by its empirical multitudinousness.[40] In this respect the "Elysium Britannicum" is exactly like a contemporary cabinet of curiosities, so crammed with *naturalia* and *artificialia* that it sometimes defied coherence.[41] Its first chapter, indeed, is headed "A Garden derived, and defined, with its distinctions and sorts."

When John Beale first wrote to Hartlib, who passed the letter to Evelyn, it was to express a similar concern for the "definition of a Garden." The desire to raise the intellectual stakes of garden discourse by theory, contemplation, and concept as well as by practical experiment was one way to persuade those who thought "this Arte [of gardening] an easy and insipid study" ("Elysium Britannicum," fol. 5). Elsewhere Evelyn insists that he "pretend[s] not here to write to Cabbage-planters; but to the best refined of our Nation who delight in Gardens, and aspire to the perfections of the Arte {& for Institution}" (fol. 10). His prospectus for the complete "Elysium Britannicum" sets out the range of materials that make up the subject of gardening and the knowledges that it requires ("Scientia pluribus disciplinis, et variis eruditionibus ornata": fol. 5); such an agenda required a controlling *idea*—a word he often uses.[42] So when he observes of gillyflowers that they are "impregnat with an *Idea* altogether celestiall and spiritual, which revives and cherishes them" (fol. 12), I would take that as an analogy for his theoretical concerns.

Evelyn's language is, as Michael Hunter has written, "highly literary";[43] but this does not mean just fine periods and fancy phrases. It announces the high status to which Evelyn wished to raise garden discourse; elevated style meant an elevated topic. He says that he wishes to "comprehend the nature of the Earth" (fol. 4) —"comprehend" meaning not only to understand but to take in the whole, to be comprehensive. He also writes of a "Royall & universall Plantation" (fol. 54) —"universall" also meaning, I think, comprehensive,[44] but extensive, complete, and perfect as well, an ideal garden that includes everything[45] or has universal application, a gardening work to end all gardening works ("These are forever": fol. 45). Such a large ambition inevitably presupposes some conceptual "frame or Idea."

So it seems to me that we lose a vital dimension of Evelyn's "Elysium Britannicum" if we neglect its necessary search for general principles, if we become hypnotized by the innumerable experiments and miss his own grapplings with theoretical and conceptual questions. He himself averred in *Silva* that "from a plentiful and well-furnish'd Magazine of true Experiments, they may in time advance to solemn and established Axioms, General Rules and Maximes; and a Structure may indeed lift up its head, such as may stand the shock of Time."[46] Perhaps the time has come again to structure such a conceptual framework for the new millennium. Evelyn's search for an adequate method, balancing generalization with sufficient detailed evidence, can be a model, so we must pursue it further. Then the final chapter here will try to build on his example.

III

On the progress of gardening from its antique beginnings until the modern and scientific age, Evelyn tries to be evenhanded in his adjudication of the contributions of ancients and moderns.[47] Yet the central ambition of the "Elysium Britannicum"—to "refine upon what has bin sayd" (fol. 199)—is an undertaking that is necessarily modern. Building on previous hortulan discourse—and the materials of Evelyn's wide-ranging historical readings provide him everywhere with firm foundations—he wanted to establish his own distinctly up-to-date idea of the garden. In articulating a theory of gardening that would nonetheless acknowledge and accommodate ancient practices, he was alive to the essential paradox that such a theory had to be modern; namely, that it had to take its perspective from as recent a time as possible simply to avail itself of all available data as well as to conduct its inquiry in the latest scientific spirit.[48] The "Artist Gardiner," he writes in the preface to *Acetaria*, takes many ages to be perfected.

However, gardening by its very nature occupied a special place in the ancient-modern *paragone*. Gardens were nothing if not alive, flourishing on the ground, and (in short) modern. While it might be possible to write a convincing pindaric ode or to reproduce the classical orders of architecture, it was impossible to create a facsimile of an ancient garden, not least because of the absence of adequate models. Evelyn's Surrey neighbor and garden enthusiast, Thomas Howard, earl of Arundel, had been a great collector of antiquities,[49] the sort of English virtuoso who would (in the words of an ironic Italian) have carted off the Colosseum had it been portable.[50] Yet whereas amphitheaters or Elgin Marbles can be dismantled and transported, ancient gardens, even if they still existed, could not. So when in 1692 Sir William Temple wrote (and Alexander Pope echoed him in the 1710s)[51] that the garden of Alcinous in Homer's *Odyssey* provided all the necessary rules for a fine garden, they were acknowledging im-

plicitly that ancient garden art could only be recovered by a double act of translation—from word into (mental) image, and from past into present. Nor was translation considered a diminution or declension; rather, it enabled foreign work to discover fresh life and language.[52] If the art of the garden was to flourish *anew* here and now in late seventeenth-century England—an elysium britannicum—then it had to reinvent ancient forms, which fresh inventions became in their turn modern. It was in that spirit that Evelyn redesigned the Albury garden for Arundel's grandson, as a memory theater of classical sites even as it was a new and unique English landscape (Figure 116)—"such a pausillipe is nowhere in England besides."[53]

An extra dimension of the ancient-modern contest or *paragone* was the so-called progress of the arts. This theme, alluded to obliquely at many points in the "Elysium Britannicum," would track the art of, say, gardens from classical times through their supposed medieval hibernation, to a reawakening in the Renaissance, and then across Europe until their final manifestation and apotheosis in England (if you were Swedish or French, then the finale came in Sweden or France; if Jefferson, then America). By virtue of his own literary translations (not just his garden designs) and those of his son (who Englished René Rapin's Latin poem on gardens), Evelyn was directly contributing to this transference, to the cultural movement of gardenist ideas northward to England, and to their improvement into English.

This point of view is wholly explicit in William Wotton's *Reflections upon Ancient and Modern Learning*, to the second edition of which in 1697 he adds a chapter "Of ancient and modern agriculture and gardening."[54] Wotton is less cagey than Evelyn, and he cites the latter's *Sylva* as containing things that the "Ancients were strangers to," saying that it is a book that "Out-does all that Theophrastus and Pliny have left us on that Subject" (p. 293). The ancients fell "far short of the Gardens and *Villa's* of the Princes and Great Men of the present Age" (p. 300); there is

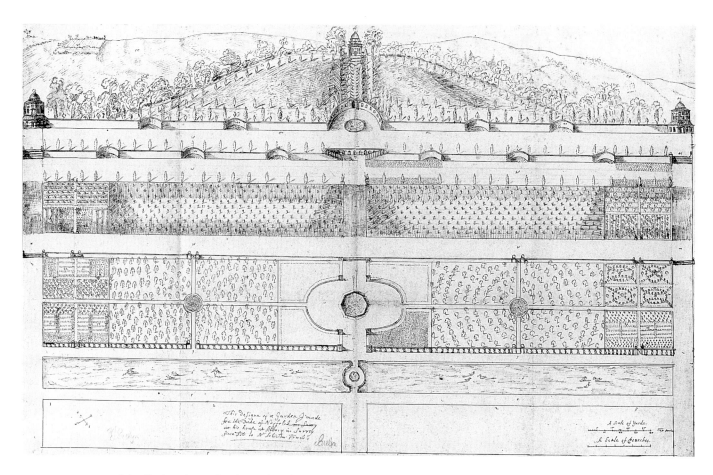

FIGURE 116. John Evelyn, design for the garden of Henry
Howard, Albury Park, Surrey, possibly 1667, Harry Ransom
Humanities Research Center, University of Texas, Austin.

far more variety in modern kitchen gardens, especially
with their greenhouse culture.[55] Moderns excel, too, in
the "great variety of plants remarkable for their beauty
or smell" and "large gravel-walks, surrounding spacious
grassplots, edged with beautiful borders" (pp. 304–5),
though he seems more dubious as to the diversifying of
colors, "sickly or luxurious Beauties which are so commonly to be met with in our Gardens." Nonetheless,
Wotton's general point is clear: the demonstrable superiority of modern over ancient gardening.

Evelyn seems more evasive and ambivalent. In a letter
to Wotton of 28 October 1696, Evelyn wrote that "the
gardening and husbandry of the ancients . . . had certainly nothing approaching the elegancy of the present
age."[56] He will note, too, how certain sundials achieved
"a moderne Elegancy" of construction, or how "This
dyall we have much reformed from that of Bettinus &
Schotti" (fols. 158, 194). In like spirit, he proposes sup-
planting pagan ornaments in gardens with Christian
and modern philosophical imagery: the "obscene Pria-
pus" and even the "lewd Strumpet," Flora, would thus
give way to a whole roster of "sacred stories" and "rep-
presentations of {great &} vertuous Examples" (fols.
153–55). His botanical sections implicitly declare, too, a

modern preeminence in quantity and quality. But beyond these few examples, he seems unwilling or unconcerned to champion contemporary achievements at the expense of old. This is, as we shall see, in striking contrast to Horace Walpole's claims for English gardening a century later. It is rare for Evelyn to come out and say, as in his address to the readers of *Sylva*, that he looks forward to a time when the deficiency of agriculture that Columella complained of "may attain its desired Remedy and Consummation in this [age] of Ours."[57] Yet throughout the leaves of the "Elysium Britannicum" there is another strategy at work to affirm, more subtly, the supremacy of modern over ancient garden art; it works by deploying what is, I believe, a radical version of another *paragone*—that between art and nature.

IV

In trying to come to terms with Evelyn's ideas here, we are hampered by a widespread predilection since the late eighteenth century for "natural" gardens and the corresponding assumption that Renaissance ones were somehow wholly artificial.[58] But it was perfectly clear to Evelyn that the garden was always a result of innumerable collaborations between art and nature, between, if you will, the plenitude and apparently random materials of the natural world and man's various modes of exercising control over it via science, technology, and design. Though recently writers have tried to make Evelyn a spokesman for natural gardening,[59] he gives, if carefully read, no hostages to that position. Succinctly put, Evelyn's double achievement was to see that in gardening (1) there was no nature without art, nor art without nature, and (2) the adjudication of those collaborations was always culturally determined, that is to say, they differed according to the time and place of their implementation.

It is hard to know whether Evelyn himself was fully aware of the extraordinary nature of his achievement in this most problematical area. And it would take more

space than is available to demonstrate in detail how those two perceptions—they never achieve the status of formal propositions—underlie countless passages in the "Elysium Britannicum." But at the risk of being excessively schematic, I can describe them briefly.

First and most obviously, Evelyn everywhere recognizes the *paragone* of art and nature: as he notes Sir Henry Wotton saying of the island of Rhodes filled with "as many Statues as living men," a garden too is a "poynt of fertility twixt Art & nature" (fol. 155). The long poem of Strada's quoted and translated in chapter XIII of the "Elysium" narrates one of those typical duels between a human artificer on the lute and the song of a nightingale; for Evelyn their mutual admiration and emulation are an emblem of the binary and productive relationship between art and nature. This is a leitmotif of the manuscript. In strikingly modern-sounding jargon he writes of how the "mediation of Art, supplie[s] in great measure, what nature, or a [garden owner's] lesse propitious fate, has denied him" (fol. 52). Or again, gardening is "that assisting Nature with the addition of Arte" (fol. 53); or, "if Nature prove not so propitious, as to serve our Garden spontaneously with that, without which it will soone become a Wildernesse: Arte must supplie our needes" (fol. 118a).

There is nothing extraordinary for the seventeenth century in these announcements of the joint participation of art and nature in garden-making. What is arguably new, however, are Evelyn's reflections on how and above all why the *ratio* of art and nature shifts in different situations. This brings me to the second, schematic point—that Evelyn always sees art and nature working in gardens toward representation. Within the garden, as *mutatis mutandis* in a painting or a dramatic performance, we see another world imitated, and when art reorganizes natural (and other) materials to that end we are able to see them freshly and significantly. Sometimes it will take more art to make some representations clear; sometimes less, even on occasions allowing unmediated elements of the physical world to represent themselves within the controlled environment of the garden, a proposal that Switzer would make more unambiguously.

As Chapter 4 explored, garden representation functions both at a local level and in larger ways. Evelyn's remark that "Grottoes are invented to reppresent Dens and Caves" (fol. 138) was cited as an example of the local level. By extension, the whole repertoire of garden forms contributes to representation, to presenting over again the world outside: this repertoire includes "Groves, parterrs, Viridaria, hills, mounts, fields, walks, statues, Grotts, Fountains, Streams & frequent Enclosures" (fols. 77 and 91), and these all have a representational function. Hydraulic equipment, the "Elysium" also explains, can "reppresent Raine-bowes, Stormes, raine Thunder and other artificial Meteors [i.e., fireworks] (fol. 132)," and its mechanisms can also re-create the "motion & chirpings of Birds, Satyres & other {vocal} Creatures, after a wonderfull manner" (fol. 187). It can even make fresh air ("artificiall Ventiducts" [fol. 144] being the prototype of air-conditioning). And Evelyn notes how alcoves imitate natural recesses and inlay work represents "flowers, birds, Landskips . . . in their natural colours" (fol. 143). Finally, sculpture augments the representational resources of gardens by showing action: "by this it is that we reppresent the figures of those {greate} Heros, & Genious's that have so well deserv'd of gardens" (fol. 149). This admission of action into garden representations, what elsewhere in respect of hydraulic devices are called "Histories and Sceanes" (fol. 138), contributes much to raising the status of gardening in the pantheon of fine arts, since the imitation of an action was the prime ambition of painting and literature in the seventeenth century.[60]

So far, so good and unexceptional, though we have largely lost touch with this notion of representation in gardens. But we need to understand why Evelyn can also attack puerile imitations in gardens or those that have no evident model in the natural world. Armies of topiary figures can be "lamely and wretchedly represented" (fol. 97), and when he allows that corals could be "counterfeitted" (fol. 137) in rockwork, the metaphor

of illegal, forged money (punishable by death) suggests some real qualms. In fountains the work should "be contrivd to resemble nature as much as possible" (fol. 128), and on that score "artificial elevations" of water or *jets d'eau*, for example, are less plausible (fol. 23). John Rea, too, in *Flora* similarly criticizes "ill done effects" in a garden.[61]

A curious feature of some of these discussions is Evelyn's statement that "they are also either Naturall or Artificial" (he is writing of grottoes).[62] On the one hand and straightforwardly, this implies that inventions and representations can apparently look either natural or conspicuously artificial; alternatively and, I think, predominately, the remark claims that even actual dens and caves—i.e., what we colloquially term natural ones—are in effect also forms of representation once they are incorporated within the contrived space of a landscape. If your land happens to include caves in its geomorphology, those can become—may be deemed—grottoes within the overall idea of the garden. That is precisely what Beale was arguing for, and what Evelyn accepted, in his account of Backbury Hill.

The point is not that Evelyn is a Capability Brown or Uvedale Price before his time. It is undeniable that Evelyn seizes virtually every opportunity to argue for "naturall and less uniforme" effects (fol. 138: here on caves again). Natural "Groves and Wildernesses," for instance, are to be preferred over artificial ones (fol. 90); so are natural falls of water (fol. 128) and real rockwork (fols. 134 and 137). But he is equally content to assert that in each of those instances where "in the originall disposure of the plott, we find them not already planted by Nature," they are nonetheless to be invented, "contrivd to resemble nature as much as possible." Genuine echoes, for example, are often unobtainable in gardens, so he provides a recipe (Figure 117) "to instruct you how to produce an Artificial Echo and by an innocent magick & without superstition, to raise up & deprehend that vocal & fugitive Nymph."[63]

One further element of the same kind that is difficult to accommodate within our usual aesthetic discrimina-

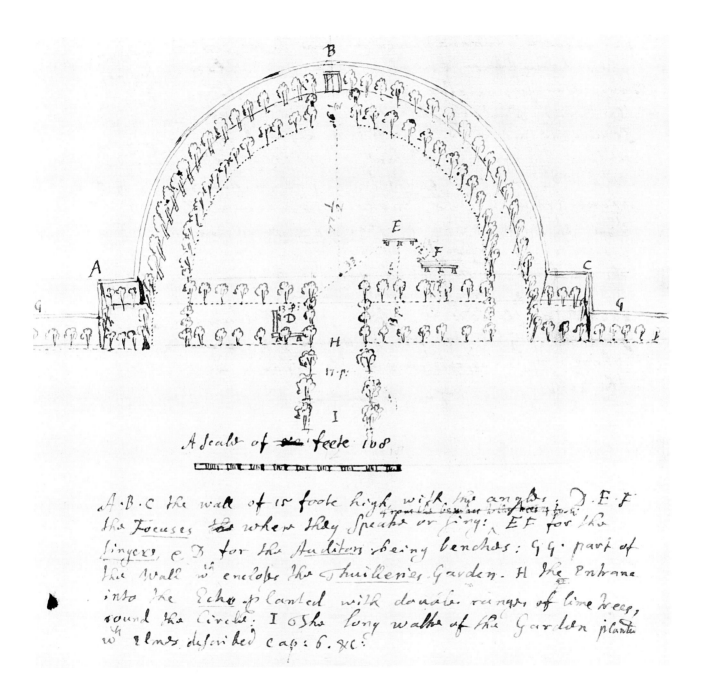

FIGURE 117. John Evelyn, design for an artificial echo, from "Elysium Britannicum," folio 171, late seventeenth century. The British Library, London.

FIGURE 118. Gabriel Perelle, engraved view of the trompe l'oeil perspective in the garden of M. Frieubet, Paris, from *Vues de belles maisons de France*, c. 1685. Dumbarton Oaks Research Library and Collections.

tions of gardens as *either* artificial *or* natural is Evelyn's enthusiasm for painted *trompe l'oeil* perspectives in French gardens (fols. 159–62); it seems to sit oddly with his advocacy elsewhere of natural effects. But perhaps the passage on the artificial echo helps here, too, since it says that a garden, "but for this onely[,] wanted nothing of perfection." In other words, since a garden aims

to be a perfect or universal world, it must be supplied with representations of whatever it lacks to complete its site—whether artificial echoes, imitation rockwork, or illusionary prospects (Figure 118). As observed already in Chapter 4, one aspect of a garden's representational ambitions was to epitomize the whole world within its own limited spaces: this was the raison d'être of the early botanical gardens, but the idea sustained many other garden designs. Evelyn argued in the "Elysium Britannicum" that the garden "hath of all other diversions the prerogative alone of gratifying *all* the senses virtuously" (fol. 167, my italics). The tripartite gardens at Wilton House (see Figure 32) represented in miniature a full range of human interventions in the land outside. It was equally true of eastern garden art: the Chinese emperor Ch'in Shih-huang "walled off a vast hunting preserve . . . [which] seems to have become a magical diagram, a symbol of the empire in miniature."[64]

But why should gardens need to be such universal plantations, filled if necessary with things "Desembld & imitated" (fol. 137)? Why should they "represent the beholder with a prospect of a noble and masculine majestie far surpassing those trifling bankes and busy knotts of our ordinary Gardens consisting of stiff and meane designe" (fol. 91)?

The point is that at its best and most perfect the garden engaged the whole world. In the preface to *Acetaria*, Evelyn writes of "that Great and Universal Plantation [i.e., the world], Epitomiz'd in our Gardens."[65] In *Systema Agriculturae* (1669) John Worlidge had also observed that "Gardens, orchards, partirres, avenues . . . represent unto us epitomized, the form and idea of the more ample and spacious pleasant fields, groves, and other rustick objects."[66] Gardens are an epitome of that world, not only in the sense that botanical gardens tried to recover the plenitude of the lost Eden, but in that they recall the attention of all gardenists to what the "Elysium" explains as "Now the Principle of all these Principles is nothing less then Nature herselfe" (fol. 6). Evelyn's father-in-law observed that he preferred "those arbors in which *all* trees are assisted to the *compleatest* perfection of growth, fruite, beauty."[67]

Here we reach the most interesting aspect of Evelyn's theoretical endeavor. The purpose of a garden's representation or epitome of "Nature herselfe" is to teach us about it, which is precisely why gardeners can be "most usefull members of Humane Societie." Some people will need to see nature mediated by art; others will have direct access to it. The majority of humankind will, as it always does, hover betwixt and between: for these, gardens were a sophisticated means of demonstrating both the mediation of art and the nature of the materials interpreted by its representations. The degree of artificial interference in and thus comprehension of the physical world will differ according to society, region, climate, and even individual gardeners. Each garden should be a fresh negotiation between the natural site and the arts of improvement and imitation available to its owner.

Evelyn's own response to the fractured state of his country (which he had left during the republican Interregnum) may well have been this move toward promoting the relative needs of different sites and different owners. Here was the opportunity to make Backbury Hill, with its supposedly ancient British history, different from John Evelyn's Sayes Court in Deptford, or from the Evelyn family home at Wotton in Surrey. Not only did the surrounding topography in each case provide a different second and even first nature for the third to imitate, thus affecting and effecting a garden's design; so, too, did the personal culture and social status of the owner of each site, which also figured in hortulan representation.

That even Beale, despite his enthusiasm for Backbury Hill, accepted this "relativist" or historicist position is evident from his subsequent admission to Evelyn that "you will not deeme mee so shallowe, as to dare seriously to compare our Herefordian Mountains with the Princelie & beautifull seates which doe surround the surcharging Metropolis."[68] But it is not only the specific and local realities, the ecology, of a site that will determine the mode of its place-making; it responds to or represents the intellectual-cum-spiritual needs of the owner. This is clear from the elliptical reference by Beale to Meric Casaubon's *Treatise on Enthusiasm* (2d ed., 1656), which implies that those who are above worldly cares will not need to exist in formal and princely gardens (i.e., within a wholly mediated nature). Yet Cusaubon's (and Beale's) apparent nervousness about these "madmen" and their "Ecstatie" among "rocks and mountains, and wild prospects" surely suggests why controlled nature in gardens was the apt route or the best "access to [solid] Truth" for the majority of humans.[69] The radical implications of the visionary's perspective were not exactly suitable for the generality of men and women; nor, incidentally, could their eccentric viewpoints be easily assimilated by those, like Evelyn or later Switzer, who wished to codify, that is to say, realize and universalize, garden ideas.

Much in Evelyn's work becomes clearer once we accept this conceptual and relativist framework. Painted perspectives, for example, provided gardens that naturally lacked them with relatively cheap and feasible "views" out into other territories, artificial axes that drew attention to the gradations of human meditation.[70] Similarly, Evelyn's otherwise odd insistence upon natural or artificial grottoes is more readily understood if we see artifice as a temporary, enabling, and educational device designed to return us to a proper understanding of natural ideas—so box hedges are "naturall & artificiall" (fols. 75 and 77); terraces, too, provide "naturall & artificiall *Perspectives* of the Gardens" (fols. 83–84); and "variety"—that crucial principle not only of garden art but of seventeenth-century aesthetics and theology as well[71]—is also "both naturall and artificiall." Thus it is that natural effects, which are not the product of design, are still paradoxically representations, for they recall or represent themselves with perfect propriety and economy.

"Art, though it contend with Nature; yet might by no meanes justle it out" (fol. 117), for the simple reason that gardening is all about appreciating nature, not art. Geometry is a tool for understanding the physical world, but not a prerequisite, as Sir Christopher Wren acknowledged when he wrote of "natural or geometricall Beauty."[72] In this light we can better appreciate Evelyn's enthusiastic welcoming of John Beale's description of a site in the Backbury Hills of Herefordshire, which he then wrote into folios 56–58 of the "Elysium Britannicum." But we can also under-

stand why Evelyn added to the Beale passage he transcribed a final summary of the refashioning that art might be called upon to give to a natural scene: "to render it *the uttmost accomplishments* [emphasis added], it might have likewise the addition of Walls, Architecture, Porticos, Terraces, Statues, obelisks, Potts, Cascades, Fountains, Basons, pavilions, Avaries, Coronary gardens, Vineyards, Walks and other Artificiall decorations."

A final point about Evelyn's and Beale's garden world: it practices, we might say, its garden theory, just as it theorizes its practice. It is in the light of that easy traffic between concept and actuality that we should read their exchanges about the Backbury Hill garden site. Beale had argued that it "hath a perfect resemblance of an ancient flower garden," yet he was prepared to intervene modestly to improve it. However, the idea of it and what he might do to augment the actual site seemed to coalesce. He could see its gardenist potential without the mediation of landscape architecture because—these are now Evelyn's words—"Nature has already bin (as we may truly say) so Artificiall." Evelyn continues by citing Edmund Spenser's lines on the Bower of Bliss as providing the essential idea of hortulan arrangements. So a "garden" is identified in Backbury Hill by Beale and Evelyn because they see it through the lens of their imagination, supplemented and endorsed by their knowledge of hortulan representations in other arts as well as on the ground. Evelyn, indeed, never went to the Herefordshire site, so he could see it only in his mind's eye. He welcomed Beale's account of Backbury Hill into the "Elysium" because it could stand for the idea of the garden toward which much else of his manuscript was moving. Not least, it was "no phantasticall *Utopia*, but a reall place" that offered experimentally what Beale's draft of a book on the pleasure garden explained theoretically: "in what points wee should disaffect the charges & cumber of Art, when the productions of Nature wil be more proper."[73]

V
_____

Stephen Switzer provides an interesting coda to this historical excursus. Much of the material cited here from the Hartlib and Evelyn circles was not published at the time; this does not, however, force one to argue that these ideas were not widely held during the final decades of the seventeenth century. There are hints that concepts of garden-making that Beale and Evelyn entertained were shared by John Worlidge, William Wotton, Sir William Temple, and the Earl of Shaftesbury, from whom Switzer could have derived his knowledge of the theoretical "moment" we have been describing. Switzer certainly compliments Evelyn in the one area where Evelyn had published, namely, arboriculture; significantly, Switzer emphasizes his predecessor's large role in enabling the progress or advancement of this aspect of gardening from classical times, through seventeenth-century French work, to contemporary British expertise. Evelyn is praised for "reanimating the Spirit of his Country-men" in georgic matters, like "another Virgil," while to his translation of de la Quintinie "is owing that Gard'ning can speak proper English."[74] Switzer inherited, too, the patriotic and scientific zeal of his predecessors. He acknowledged a man's obligation to "make what Advances he can in the Art he is brought up to, and in the Age he lives" (p. ix), and he saw the potential in indigenous "Natural Embellishments . . . as good Grass, Gravel, &c" (p. vii) for English garden-making to surpass continental examples.

Switzer adds a useful practical perspective to the "hortulan affaires" that were established before him. Although Evelyn and Shaftesbury made their own gardens, and Evelyn advised friends and neighbors on other sites, we have no clear idea how they translated ideas into practice or even derived their concepts from contemporary activities on the ground. Switzer, however, made his living as a professional nurseryman and designer, and even in his more theoretical moments he declares strong pragmatic instincts. When he plays down the incidence of his preferred mode of "Extensive Gard'ning" in England, he may in fact be exaggerating its novelty in order to promote his own practice of it: engravings and county histories contemporary with Switzer—like Robert Atkyns's *Ancient and Present State of Glocestershire* (1712) or John Harris's *History of Kent* (1718)—suggest that Switzer's "rural and extensive gard'ning" was firmly established in England by the time he was writing (Figure 119). His writings both confirm a tendency already apparent on many country estates and attempt to formulate its scope more conceptually.

As with Beale's celebration of the hillside garden in Herefordshire, Switzer's preference for "this Extensive way of Gard'ning, and of bringing the Pleasures and Produce of the Woods and Fields under the general Title of Hortus" (p. xxxviii) has been read as an anticipation of the English landscape garden later in the eighteenth century. It is far more logically and more usefully seen as a reformulation of earlier English developments and ideas. For Switzer shared the Hartlibian sense of intimate connections between gardening and agriculture and between the philosophical and aesthetic dimensions of place-making and the pragmatic activities of cultivation. Such connections were threatened if not severed during the century that followed: Edward Lisle's *Observations in Husbandry* of 1757, for instance, is focused wholly on practical hints for the conduct of the kitchen garden, the "orchard and fruit-garden," and has completely lost any sense that these belong to a series of gradations in garden art, as the Hartlibians believed. Switzer still chose to consider them together, affirming that "Agriculture (with which Gard'ning is inextricably wove)" (p. vi) or "unavoidably as well as pleasantly mix'd" (p. xl). He clearly shares the understanding of a gradation of spatial interventions on an estate—"Gardens, Meadows, Fields" (p. iii). His emphasis on this is—despite his claim that he is promoting

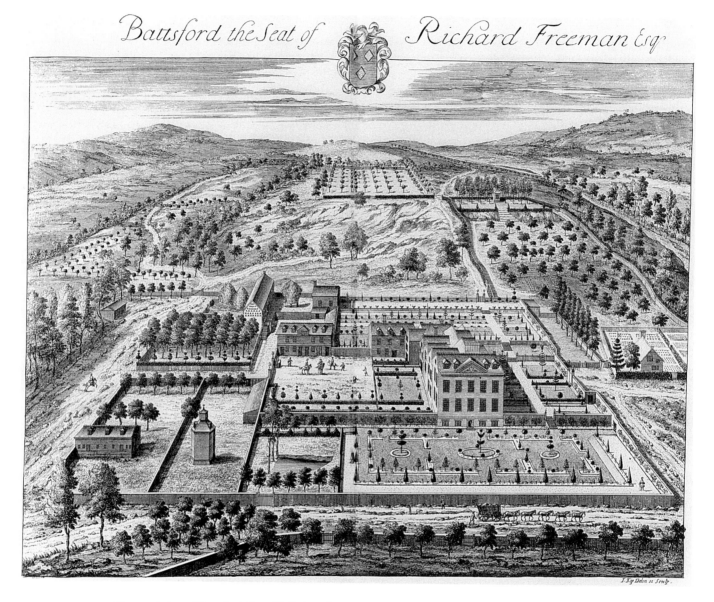

FIGURE 119. Engraved view of Battsford, from Sir Robert Atkyns, *The Ancient and Present State of Glocestershire* [*sic*], 1712. Private collection.

a largely fresh mode—consistent with both Hartlib's and Dymock's schemes for an entire estate, with Beale's celebration of natural gardening, with engravings like the frontispiece to Vallemont's *Curiosities*, or with contemporary country house portraiture.

Switzer urges "Enlargement" of the garden's views into "all the neighbouring Fields, Paddocks, &c [which] shall make an additional Beauty to the garden," while the "adjacent Country" would look as if it "were all a garden" (p. xxxvii). These links are effected through representational maneuvers, by translating elements from the agrarian landscape into the vocabulary of the garden. Springs may be brought "home" into the garden and used as fountains, cascades, and the like (p. xiv). "Eminences or Pits" should be left in the landscape rather than leveled, and the natural pattern of tree growth should be accepted (p. xxvii). Above all, woodlands can be created or stabilized (p. xxxvi) and thus transformed into an essential part of garden experience, perhaps by marking them with statuary. It is just such a move that won the day at Castle Howard, Yorkshire, where (with Switzer's involvement) the famed Wray Wood was spared a rigorously geometrical treatment and represented in its own full splendor. Switzer specifically claims, "'Tis there that Nature is *truly imitated*, if not excell'd, and from which the Ingenious may draw the best of their Schemes in natural and Rural Gardening: 'Tis there that she is by a kind of fortuitous Conduct pursued through all her most intricate Mazes, and taught ever to exceed her own self in the *Natura-Linear*, and much more Natural and Promiscuous Disposition of all her Beauties."[75]

Other designs by Switzer set out precisely a gradation of imitation, from gardens where "a more curious diligence" is expended[76] across agrarian land to wilder terrain. This is exemplified best in the well-known plan from volume 2 of *Ichnographia Rustica* for the Manor of Paston (Figure 120), especially when augmented by related drawings of the site in 1736 when the antiquarian William Stukely responded so sympathetically to its

rural and extensive design (Figures 121, 122): across the parterre of topiary pyramids, the grove or "wilderness" marks one declension of control over natural materials, the wide expanse of agricultural countryside, another. Switzer indeed insists that the countryside adjacent to a mansion and its garden should not be blocked off with high walls or the eye forced to see "woods misplaced" in the overall prospect or perspective.[77] It was a commonplace of the time: Worlidge's *Dictionarum Rusticum, Urbanicum, and Botanicum* of 1717 noted the need for straight lines leading the eye out into "delightful Prospect" that should not be blocked by "tall hedges"—hence the visitor will be led "insensibly . . . into new and unexpected Varieties."[78] Similarly, Timothy Nourse, in *Campania Foelix* (1700), argues that "beyond . . . the Territory of our Garden, let there be planted Walks of Trees to adorn the Landskip; Likewise a Bowling-Green and Poddock would be suitable . . . and thus at length the Prospect may terminate on Mountains, Woods, or such Views as the Scituation will admit of." Such scope and flexibility, determined by the specific site, is the basis of Nourse's claim for the superiority of English gardening over Versailles;[79] Switzer, too, would rebuke the "Grand Manier" of French gardening for lacking this close relationship with the rural fields and woods.

The focus on husbandry among the Hartlib circle had strong patriotic motives, having inherited from the sixteenth century traditions of urging national advantages of good agrarian practice.[80] Thus, Dymock makes frequent appeals to the "prosperitye . . . honor and plentye of this whole nation."[81] Anthony Lawrence, a coauthor of Beale's, explains that he writes in "Englands true interest," for "Hortulan Affaires are not the least of our Inland Commodities."[82] Evelyn's *Sylva* addressed, as its full title explains, the "Propergation of Timber in his Majesties Dominions." These traditions of identifying country (i.e., rural) matters with concerns of country (i.e., England) were applied in their turn to gardens, largely because the Hartlibians saw

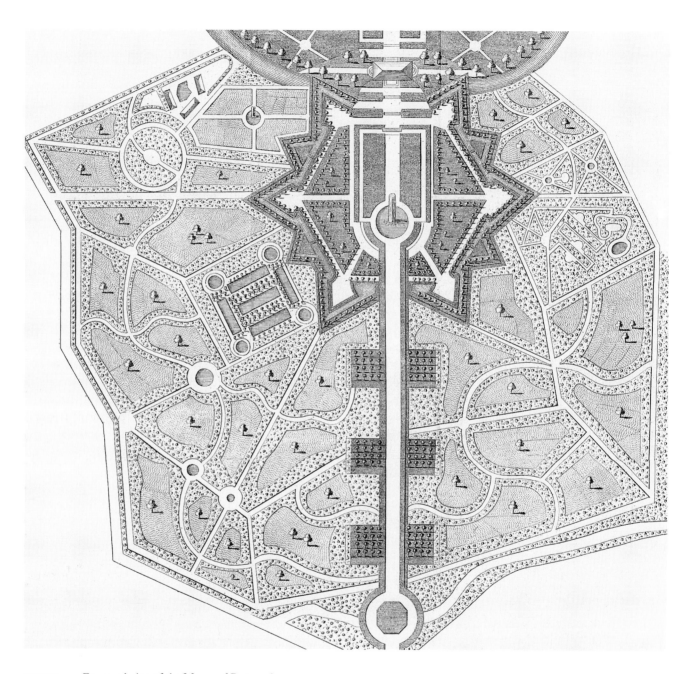

FIGURE 120. Engraved plan of the Manor of Paston, from
Stephen Switzer, *Ichnographia Rustica*, II, facing p. 115, Dumbarton Oaks Research Library and Collections.

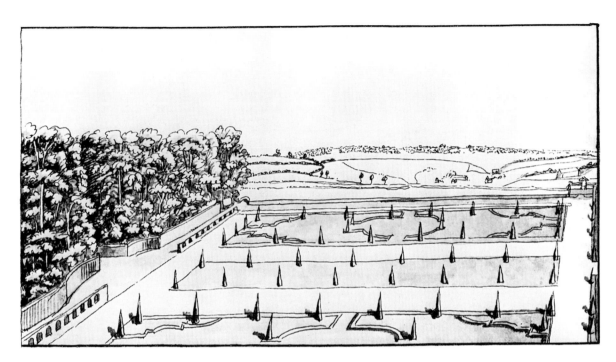

FIGURE 121. William Stukely, drawing of the parterre at Grimsthorpe, Lincolnshire. 1736. The Bodleian Library, Oxford (MS
Top Gen.d.14, folio 37v).

FIGURE 122. William Stukely, drawing of Grime's Walk at
Grimsthorpe, Lincolnshire, 1736. The Bodleian Library, Oxford
(MS Top Gen.d.14, folio 37r).

gardens or third nature as the proper refinement or extension of husbandry or second nature.[83]

The link between gardening and agriculture and their joint identification with the interests of England meant further that, when a garden re-presented or epitomized the world around it, it was in an important sense standing for England (just as England herself was compared to a garden). Moreover, the determination to celebrate modern English gardening over earlier and foreign models—the advancement or progress of horticulture and design—required that the English garden had to find its own conspicuous modes of procedure, suitable to climate, history, topography, social custom, and to that whole gamut of intellectual and ideological ideas we may conveniently label "culture." Given the social and political flux and upheavals of the seventeenth century, it is not surprising that so many different ideas of gardens were being canvassed[84] or that the Hartlibian circle enjoyed such a diversity of views about garden art. If the best gardens had to represent or epitomize England, the nation was not particularly unanimous about its preferred identity. But once that identity had been focused, once the nation had stabilized and prospered, it became easier to claim that its gardens were truly representative of a new and triumphant England. The beginnings of this move may be glimpsed in Switzer, but its culmination occurs fifty years later with Horace Walpole.

CHAPTER 8

Toward a New Historiography and New Practices

What we owe the future is not a new start, for we can only begin with what has happened.
—Wendell Berry

Field-room there is enough; Go on and prosper, ye illustrious Lovers of Gard'ning.
—Stephen Switzer

TO THEORIZE ABOUT GARDENS is justifiable for its own sake; moreover, it increases the pleasures of understanding. But, even as theory, its success may also be judged by its utility. There are two ways in which these chapters might be applied: to direct and shape a new history of gardens and landscape architecture, and to inspire and energize fresh developments in the practice of landscape architecture. The first is certainly, even desperately, needed; though this is not the occasion on which to write a new history, some guidelines will be in order. The second purpose of the practice of garden theory could be, at the very least, to initiate wide-ranging and properly informed debate among all those concerned with the future of landscape architecture—critics, teachers, professionals, and "consumers"—about its resources (and sources), its ambitions and visions. Proposing an agenda for such debates is also feasible here.

The two endeavors of this final chapter are linked to the extent that until we understand the history of the art of place-making—until we eschew all the clichés, tired formulae, and exhausted metaphors that determine our understanding of the past[1]—neither the present nor the future of that art will grow straight and healthy. The point is not that practitioners have to be qualified historians; it helps, certainly, if they understand the conceptual principles of a profession whose roots still draw nourishment from past achievements.[2] No, the point is that landscape architecture, locked into a false historiography, is unable to understand the principles of its own practice as an art of place-making.

I

During the historical excursus of the preceding chapter, we saw how Evelyn and Beale set themselves to understand diversity in garden modes. They were concerned with the historical dimensions of their explorations, though not in the interests of any forced teleology. They certainly seemed to subscribe to the dual notions of a progress of gardening and of the likelihood of a British supremacy therein, but they did not link these to one particular style. Garden modes transcended European political rivalries with surprising ease in the later seventeenth century. If I have correctly interpreted Evelyn, especially in the Hartlibian context, he advocated a diversity of garden modes according to time, place, and circumstance. This further involved an intimate link between garden design, horticulture, and agriculture on the ground and in the narratives of cultural history.

Stephen Switzer carried forward some of these ideas. His advocacy of "rural and extensive gardening" seems to have much in common with the scale of interventions, the "three" natures, that the Hartlibians espoused as well as with their agrarian projections. His professional practice would also have made him, one imagines, attentive to the differences of locality and social status. Yet perhaps this very same need to enhance his professional business meant that he came to promote English "rural gardening" over its continental counterparts; his writings already suggest far less enthusiasm for a diversity of garden modes than did Evelyn's or Beale's. Nor was Switzer alone at this time in seeming to slide toward a position where just one kind of gardening was to be honored: for example, John James dedicated his 1712 translation of Dézaillier d'Argenville's French treatise, *La Théorie et la pratique du jardinage* (1709), to James Johnston by writing: "we may hope to see, ere long, our English Pleasure-Gardens in greater Perfection, than any the most renowned, in France, or Italy, since our Woods and Groves, our Grass and Gravel, which are the great subjects of this Work, are allowed to surpass in Verdure and natural Beauty, whatever is to be found in those Countries."[3]

What James does in that argument, as Switzer does in some of his, is to premise an English gardening mode upon indigenous materials and climate; it is a version of the Hartlibian understanding that gardens represent their own locality, but one that begins to separate the medium from the message. It is not hard to see how this stance could slide into a whole-hearted promotion of the single mode of "Verdure and natural Beauty." And, sure enough, what James and Switzer had begun to suggest became thoroughly explicit in Horace Walpole's *History of the Modern Taste in Gardening*.[4] Now "informal" is pitted against "formal," and other nations, against the English. We are entertained to a wonderfully agile, often amusing, and horribly persuasive argument for the supremacy of one mode of gardening, one that is above all "natural," modern, English, and worthy to be acclaimed among the preeminent fine arts. Walpole's achievement has to be saluted all the more when it is realized that single-handedly he determined (or distorted) the writing of landscape architecture history to this day. One needs to look no further for evidence of his reach than the historical sketch

offered to readers of *The Meaning of Gardens*,[5] with its commentary on the "simplemindedness" of Renaissance humanism, the "anthropomorphic simplicity" of the French garden, and the "beginning of the modern view" with the blameless English garden ("hard to find fault with this Tradition").

There had been only a few other historical narratives before Walpole's.[6] Evelyn's historical survey lay unpublished in the "Elysium Britannicum." Switzer provided a chapter entitled "The History of Gard'ning, from its Original: with Memoirs of the greatest Virtuoso's, both Ancient and Modern" in *The Nobleman, Gentleman, and Gardener's Recreation* of 1715.[7] Richard Bradley reviewed the classical scene in *A Survey of the Ancient Husbandry and Gardening* (1725), and George Mason offered some historical observations in *An Essay on Design in Gardening* (1768). Walpole's *History* simply went further than any of them: he claimed from his very first sentence that gardening was "probably one of the first arts" and then linked it specifically with painting as a means of ensuring its place in the pantheon of beaux arts: "Poetry, Painting, and Gardening."[8] He also insisted, more than any writer before him, on the preeminence of the English achievement — in the process consigning a whole series of precedents to historical oblivion.

These two fundamental arguments of Walpole's essay were also the most paradoxical. The claim that gardening was an art sits uneasily with his attack on all the manifestations of "art" in designed landscape that had tainted and corrupted "sumptuous gardens . . . in all ages" (p. 6), such as embellishment, straight lines, patterns, symmetry, uniformity, and conceits (pp. 10-16). And the claims for British preeminence had to be based, given his rejection of precedents elsewhere, on a refusal to see gardens as representations of their local time and place (although Walpole had argued that every culture has "designed" the garden of Eden in its own image).

A casualty of the high claim for gardening as an art was its practical aspects, which had so engrossed the Hartlibians. If we compare their writings reviewed in the preceding chapter with such a basic work as Edward Lisle's *Observations in Husbandry* of 1757,[9] the alliance between practice and theory by midcentury is at best strained. Mason begins his essay by noting the uneasy relationship between aesthetics and the "mechanical Part" (i.e., grading), which is better left in the hands of professionals (p. 38). Walpole virtually puts aside all practical considerations in his essay. Here we can identify the beginnings of that divorce between active gardening and intellect that is so nicely symbolized during the 1910s in de la Fresnaye's panels and that continues to this day.

But the biggest casualty in Walpole's essay is history itself, especially any claims for interesting work in other civilizations or modes: the Hanging Gardens of Babylon, Pliny's villas, and Chinese landscaping, for instance, are all vilified, and only the most grudging praise is found for some, necessarily English, examples of pan-European garden design during the late seventeenth century. Walpole is simply not prepared to compromise his Whiggish narrative of garden progress with inconvenient facts.[10] Medieval deer parks—an early form of Switzer's "rural and extensive Gardening"—alone are credited with being a precedent for the English landscape garden.

Some aspects of this "History" had already been rehearsed by George Mason as well as by Thomas Whately's *Observations on Modern Gardening* (1770); but Walpole again makes the arguments more extreme and far more tendentious. Foreigners—so his story goes—had been misled since time immemorial into imposing themselves on nature. It was the English who discovered the only true mode of gardening, what a character in Tom Stoppard's *Arcadia* is made to describe as "nature as God intended."[11] Since this constituted the "most perfect perfection," it never needed to be altered (a not unreasonable argument, if you accepted the logic of all the rest). And it is famously to William Kent that Walpole gives the credit for having struck out "a great system from the twilight of imperfect essays" (p. 25).

This will be the system to be followed everywhere, as indeed Capability Brown is honored for doing at the time when Walpole is writing. Further, it was a system ripe for export, England's supreme gift to the natural environment elsewhere. And across Europe during the late eighteenth and early nineteenth centuries and along the eastern seaboard of the United States a little later, the so-called English landscape garden was celebrated on the ground and in treatises, usually with a grateful acknowledgment of how natural, modern, and "English" design provided salvation from the old despotic, geometrically designed gardens associated with the wicked French absolutism of the *ancien régime.*

Admittedly, Walpole cannot be held responsible for the excesses of theorists who came after him; indeed, he himself is recorded in 1771 as worrying that "English gardening gains ground prodigiously [in France]. . . . This new *anglomanie* will literally be *mad English.*"[12] But within the pages of the *History,* the lure of the *bon mot*—Kent "leaped the fence, and saw that all nature was a garden" (p. 25), or the equally seductive dismissal of regular gardening as "going up and down stairs in the open air" (p. 21)—has made Walpole's arguments irresistible; their single-handed contribution to the distortion of landscape architecture history is truly amazing.

This British historiography has not been the only one to generate bias, though it has been of international scope and influence, like the style it promoted. We could also look, for instance, at a parallel conduct of garden history in France. Le Nôtre is here the acknowledged *maître*—and rightly so, since he was a genius and a true artist of space; yet history is written around his eminence. The reluctance to accept alternative forms of design, even by Le Nôtre himself for, say, the Bosquet des Sources at the Grand Trianon (Figure 123),[13] has prevented the eighteenth century (let alone the nineteenth) from receiving proper attention. It is a rare French publication that chooses to celebrate the work of a later designer like Gabriel Thouin.[14] The same spirit of reverence for the inherently geometric tradition of Le Nôtre is presumably the reason why Ernest

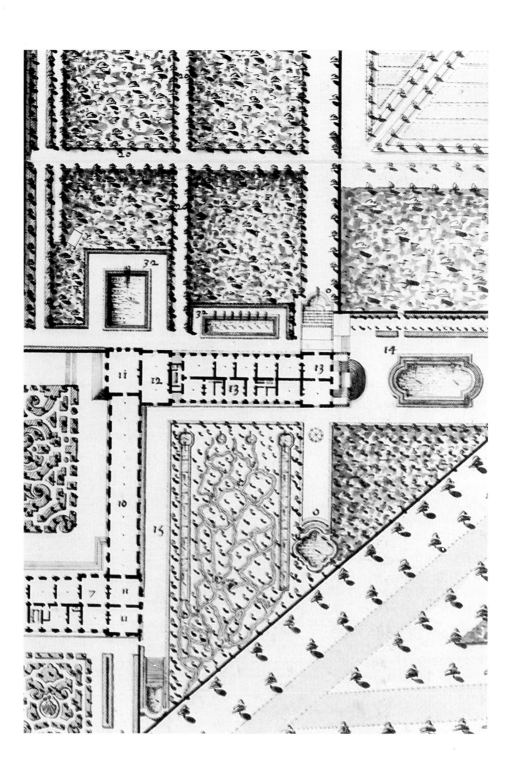

FIGURE 123. Grand Tri-
anon, Versailles, Bosquet des
Sources, designed by André
Le Nôtre. Nationalmuseum,
Stockholm (THC 22).

de Ganay's study of the so-called English or picturesque garden in France has never been published;[15] how early this French historiographical bias was initiated is shown by the amusing strategies through which the French, during the period that de Ganay treats, deflected contributions to garden design from across the English Channel by calling them "anglois-chinois." The Duc d'Harcourt even managed to omit all references to English gardens, dividing the world simply between the French and the Chinese.[16] And in the early years of the twentieth century, André Vera argued incessantly in print that the so-called picturesque garden style was no less than "an act of sabotage against the National Revolution."[17]

Some voices were raised, however, against both these (rival) histories, though subsequently we have paid them little attention. It must have taken rare presence of mind for anybody to challenge, especially the narrative hegemony of a progressive and naturalizing landscape architecture that came out of England. Yet from the late eighteenth century onward there were some theorists ready and willing to express skepticism of the prevailing historiography: Jean-Marie Morel and Alexandre, Comte de Laborde in France, C. C. L. Hirschfeld in northern Germany, Ercole Silva and Luigi Mabil among others in northern Italy, A. J. Downing somewhat later in North America—all tried in their different ways to resist a narrative that otherwise would have left them and their own territories in the uncomfortable position of merely mimicking a style that the British had evolved and established once and for all and of purveying a style that had little relevance to their own social, geographical, and climatic conditions. Yet when we recall the political state of their countries—France and America in revolution, the innumerable regimes of Germany and Italy still not centralized under one power—it is easier to understand how the expression of identity through place-making forced these writers to reconsider the available vocabularies of garden design. In this, they shared some of the same uncertainties and excitements as the Hartlibians during a period of English identity crisis.

These later European garden theorists have not as yet received their full due; in particular, Hirschfeld's *Theorie der Gartenkunst*, published in five volumes in Leipzig between 1779 and 1785, has largely been lost to sight, though it seems to have been read throughout Europe. Silva drew heavily on it for his *Dell'arte de' giardini inglesi* (1801 and 1813), and Luigi Mabil silently abridged it for publication as *Teoria dell'arti de' giardini* (1801).[18] Downing has eluded until recently our understanding of how he strove through different editions of his *Treatise* to find an authentically American theoretical framework for imported ideas of landscaping.[19] In their various ways these writers urged their readers to choose indifferently between modes of garden design and to use whichever was best suited to representing through the various forms of garden art the local or national culture and topography that gave landscaped sites their being. What also seems important is that in different ways they rescued for consideration some abiding topics of landscape architecture that the Walpolean discourse had suppressed: for the most part they did not see any ideological need to opt for either the "English" style or the "French." Laborde, in fact, chose to investigate garden design from earlier periods before that very opposition was set up. Hirschfeld argued for the reinvention of an iconography apt for new historical locations.

The Italian writers urged research in indigenous forms, precedents, mythologies, and plant materials. They identified and celebrated a variety of different interventions on the land, in Ippolito Pindemonte's terms—how "far combinare così i differenti spazi"; they firmly linked this different handling of spaces with the social, psychological, topographical, and climatic conditions of different parts of northern Italy.[20] This emphasis on local variations was also made by Morel, who saw four kinds of design related to different classes of owner. These theorists argued for representation (not

FIGURE 124. Robert Risko, vignette originally published in the *New Yorker* (4 August 1997), p. 60.

puerile imitation) in gardens, for which Laborde's remark may stand as the most subtle and flexible claim: "Le véritable art des jardins me paroit être *la science de produire, dans un lieu quelconque, l'aspect le plus agréable que le site soit suceptible de représenter.*"[21]

This varied group of independent thinkers, focusing on the conditions of garden-making in their own place and time, cannot be said to have exerted much influence on subsequent theory and history. The perspective that derived from Walpole remained unchallenged and virtually unchanged, with the French championship of Le Nôtrean garden art sounding a minor and local counterpoint. In garden writing generally, the nineteenth century was interpreted as a debate between "formal" and "informal," undistracted by any understanding about other ideas of the garden. Victorian practitioners get judged not in terms of their own cul-

ture but by whether or not they adequately fulfill the presumed ambitions of Capability Brown.[22] Even when an excellent alternative narrative was produced, namely, Alicia Margaret Tyssen-Amherst's *History of Gardening in England* of 1895, which downplayed the landscape phase in favor of earlier and later designs, it failed wholly to divert popular history from its well-worn tracks.

The gravitational pull of the Walpolean orthodoxy throughout the nineteenth century was augmented during the twentieth by the almost stupefying acclaim of "naturalness" in popular writing.[23] It continues to infect most of our narratives, often without their even being aware of the bias. Thus the revival of so-called formal gardening from 1900 or so onward is accommodated, if at all, as an interlude, a footnote in garden history, an "unnatural" turn that is easily attributed to the empty social whirl of Edwardian days and the dizzy twenties (Figure 124).

The inability of Walpolean history to account adequately for the course and variety of work in the nineteenth and twentieth centuries should of itself have called long since for some radical revision. But our narratives of garden history, like other popular fictions, still pit the goodies (natural, informal, modern) against the baddies (controlled, formal, old-fashioned): we fail to see that Prospect Park was just as contrived, just as factitious a mode of laying out grounds as Versailles had been (Figure 125); nor does it ever occur to any historian today that a restored wetlands is every bit as constructed, is just as much a culturated value, as was topiary.[24] The continuing absence of an adequate history of gardening is almost embarrassing.

But what would a fresh history of landscape architecture need to do? How would it position itself to take better account of the so-called progress of gardening? In other words, how would it renegotiate the English eighteenth-century assumption that garden art did "progress" (as opposed to constantly change)? How could a new historiography be a more useful guide to

FIGURE 125. "Nature at Work." Notice in Prospect Park, Brooklyn, New York, during restoration work, 1997.

contemporary practitioners, whose mistrust of history under the circumstances outlined here is, of course, wholly understandable. I offer six guidelines.

1. Fresh narratives must stop pitting formal against informal, Le Nôtre against Brown, gardens against landscape architecture, design against ecology, East against West. It will be hard working against conventional narratives: the Prince de Ligne admitted, "There is only one standard for good or bad taste, just as there is only one kind of music"; unfortunately, he continued, "For a long time, I used to think it improper for people to say: This is French, that is Italian. I would have liked them to say merely: It's good. I might make the same remark about gardens, but I realize there is a certain conven-

tion to be observed." This conventional view he then glosses as "Simplicity, nature, and disorder are the specialty of the English, whereas perspectives with straight lines and set pieces are the specialty of the French."[25] His is a fair enough version of most current narratives.

But different landscape architectural styles were the outward forms by which in some particular time and place the complex liaisons of nature and culture were set out in the course of making some place for habitation. A fresh history focused on that particular agenda would be invigorating.[26] But such a narrative would depend upon recognizing the importance of a representational mode of landscape architecture: for the "*what* of representation—subject matter—is most significant for what it reveals in having been chosen, and the *how*, the manner of treatment, reveals the syntheses and schemata."[27] Further, since representation always involves mental imagery,[28] how a person or society en-

FIGURE 126. Engraved view of the Chinese House, Le Désert de Retz, from Alexandre Louis J. de Laborde, *Descriptions des Nouveaux Jardins de la France*, 1806. Dumbarton Oaks Research Library and Collections.

visages designed space and, for example, expresses this in picture or poem will lead us to valuable ideas of the garden. The historian needs to reconsider these ideas or mental representations, not to go on attaching trite labels to them but to describe their cultural specificity as well as their acknowledgment of abiding values.

All design is "with nature," but all design is also "with culture"; indeed, sometimes the most "natu-ral" theory or practice, as Raymond Williams and John Barrell among others have argued,[29] has a cultural agenda at heart. Above all, it is impossible to say, with John Dryden, that "Nature is still the same in all Ages,"[30] when landscape architecture is specifically about how we identify a variety of natures according to our specific local circumstances and then represent them in the places we design for habitation. The "local" circumstances may, of course, involve perspectives taken from one culture into another, which need not be anything more than fantastic or mythic visions of past times or distant places: such is the significance of Chinese garden buildings within arcadian

FIGURE 127. The park of Les Buttes-Chaumont, Paris, engraving from William Robinson, *The Parks, Promenades and Gardens of Paris*, 1890 ed., plate xvi.

scenery (Figure 126), or of allusions to both classical mysteries and sublime horrors, geological as well as penal, that Barillet-Deschamps contrived for Les Buttes-Chaumont (Figure 127).[31] We need to explore these often complex representations rather than the styles in which they are articulated. That the modes we lazily call "formal" and "informal" are the direct products of cultural contexts is not a huge or surprising

claim these days, but it is more honored in the breach of historical analysis than the observance. All natures have been culturally constructed, and the garden historian must turn his/her attention to writing a history of those constructions particularly as they affect landscape architecture. This will also allow us to explore, not just how cultures express themselves through place-making, but how places, envisaged or made, determine social activity in their turn.

2. Some historical maneuvers—narrative assumptions, characterizations, and plot patterns—have become so unconscious that we must learn to challenge our in-

stinctive formulae.[32] One of these, the appeal to teleology, must be ruled out as a principle of narrative and especially as a principle of judgment.[33] Historians may explain Humphry Repton's design more clearly by seeing how he took over and responded to the earlier work of Capability Brown, and Brown himself may arguably be understood by how we see him in relation to his predecessor, William Kent; but we must not be fooled into accepting what is sometimes considered a related belief, that what comes later or what is more "natural" is better. Teleology may have been in the air of the late eighteenth century, but it cannot be the oxygen that drives our analysis. Repton's place in garden history has, for example, been distorted by his being written into the teleological progress of natural gardening, a story that finds it awkward to accommodate both his own gradual return to new forms of regular layout and the work of those, like J. C. Loudon and A. J. Downing, who took up these ideas after his death.[34] Indeed, the whole difficulty with the teleological bias of English historiography is how to continue the story, other than as the mapping of a battle of styles, after the supposed "end" in Capability Brown's "more perfect perfection." At least the French can evade teleological narratives by seeing a *recovery* during the nineteenth and twentieth centuries of the esteemed Le Nôtrean mode; but that in itself seems less than sufficient.

Part of a more nuanced account of modern place-making should be a greater discrimination in describing sites. There is a tendency to see every historical design in superlative terms, either wonderful or despicable, so it is rare to encounter an analysis where Versailles is judged less favorably as a design than Vaux-le-Vicomte.[35] Some critical nuance toward past practice would in its turn encourage more thoughtful appraisal of current designs—that is to say, finding time and energy to submit new work to thorough analysis and review on the basis of much more carefully worked out criteria and not being afraid of being what (negatively) is called "judgmental." The general dissemination of new designs in professional journals lacks this critical

dimension, inevitably when the designers themselves are part of the presentation of new work.

3. It follows, too, from the antiteleological argument that in our narrative quest we must look sideways, not always dead ahead toward the desired "end," but to smaller, non–"cutting-edge" design, and to other dynamics existing within a given culture of place-making: those between pleasure and profit,[36] between vernacular gardens and the lands of various contemporary elites,[37] between garden-making and other workings of the land like those of the farmer or smallholder.

The vanguard of fashion and taste in landscape architecture directs a valuable history, but it is never the whole story.[38] Thus, just when we would expect the Walpolean party line to be paramount in English practice during the late eighteenth and early nineteenth centuries, the continuing vogue for geometrical gardens should be registered, as Tom Williamson has argued;[39] so should the energies that were put into revising the Baroque parterre and wilderness into flower garden and shrubbery, as Mark Laird has also demonstrated.[40] But we need to go further than both Williamson and Laird have been willing to go and ask what deep cultural needs are signaled by this refusal of the natural garden (even on the part of Capability Brown himself).

4. The garden has always been a complex and central human activity, arguably a matrix of man's and woman's ambitions, instincts, and desires. "The garden," wrote Eugenio Battisti, "is invested with values that transcend its size, its destiny, and its temporal beauty."[41] The histories of it must therefore interrogate and narrate a cluster of concerns: how men and women represent themselves and their place in the world through the garden, and how gardens shape role-playing; how the garden becomes a special site of beliefs, myths, fictions, illusions, and the dialogue it maintains between those and the palpable, physical world of its phenomena; the design and use of exterior space for inhabitation, an art of *milieu* or *oecumen*,[42] and how that

changes from small to regional scale (at which point, for instance, the garden becomes a conceptual metaphor rather than a formal design model).

5. We must constitute garden history as independent of other histories and as its own distinct field of study. This independence is difficult to secure, given the professional, academic, and amateur claims on it.

Landscape architecture, the modern term used by professionals to characterize the activity of making gardens and other designed landscapes, was adopted by John Claudius Loudon in 1840.[43] It gestures awkwardly toward a dual or bifurcated activity that draws its energies from the older, more established, and theoretically grounded discipline of architecture and (given the derivation of the term *landscape*)[44] from the fine art of painting, which it was Walpole's concern to link with place-making for reasons of bolstering its prestige.

In the absence of any serious or sustained interest in the history and theory of its field from professionals or from the majority of programs within the academy that train them, the most energetic approaches to the study of landscape architecture have come primarily from academic historians of architecture and art. More recently, literary studies, geography, botanical history, sociology, anthropology, and cultural history—to name but a few disciplines—have each set its sights on the study of gardens. Now this interdisciplinarity is welcome: we need a diversity of approaches to engage with the diversity and richness of a garden's meanings. However, the garden has never been accorded its own status, sui generis, as a field independent of those disciplines that have generally supplied its students. Every colonizing approach—whether from art or architectural history, literature, biohistory, geography, or sociology—tends to treat the garden as an interesting element, but usually a marginal element, of that discipline.[45] Further, the politics of academe, including the pragmatics of establishing a career, do not readily encourage students to take up the full-time study of gardens. As an object of historical research and analysis,

gardens therefore remain, with rare exceptions, on the margins of professional academic life and are therefore themselves perceived to be marginal.

As "a site of contested meanings," Craig Clunas explains in his study of Chinese Ming examples, the garden is "subject to the pull of a number of discursive fields."[46] This in its turn requires what is loosely called interdisciplinarity, the ability to explore the various discourses drawn into the making and experiencing of gardens. In theory, this presupposes a truly herculean familiarity with a wide range of materials and methodologies; in practice, it may require much more collaborative work than is currently undertaken. Historians, too, will need to take a wide trawl through materials with no obvious connection to gardening. This is partly because the materials and documents that will sustain garden history are not always the obvious ones (legal documents, for instance) and partly because in order to understand why gardens occupy such a privileged place in human discourse we need to understand all aspects of our existence that might explain the garden's emergence, design, and use ("un abîme d'interrogations sur ce qui est la nature propre de l'humain").[47]

Since gardens have never been as marginal to human existence as they are when they appear on the map of academic study, we might look beyond formal scholarship to amateur considerations of them, in trade publishing books and magazines, the range and production of which seem inexhaustible. The pragmatic nature of their products tends to distract from any concern with the conceptual, misleading even those who might otherwise be interested into confusing gardening with gardens. However slight the theoretical concerns of such publications are, they often suggest themes ripe for deeper scrutiny; they identify, in their own way, essential elements of garden experience.

One fascinating aspect of their coverage, for instance, has been taken up in slightly different ways by art critic James Elkins and writer Martin R. Dean. Elkins inquired why gardens were "mild soporifics" and why garden writing so often turns away from the analytical toward the sentimental, the heterogeneous (i.e., un-focused?), and the "conceptually scattered" or incoherent, the kind of writing that chooses titles like *Green Enchantment: The Magic Spell of Gardens*.[48] Elkins implied that the language of garden writing, inasmuch as it rarely seems in touch with (self-constituted) garden scholarship, nevertheless rehearsed a wide and significant range of human concerns. He illustrated his argument with David Hockney's 1983 photo montage, *Walking in the Zen Garden* (see Figure 88), which, while by no means a conventional approach to gardens, suggested nonetheless a rigor of creative response.[49]

In a similar vein, Martin R. Dean, whose first novel was *Die verborgenen Gärten* (*Hidden Gardens*) of 1982, has asked what functions a garden might have today beyond "a keep-fit trail or a dog toilet." But his compelling answer is one altogether liable to defeat due academic process. He writes that gardens provoke "an interest in things without obvious interest." His visits to Parisian gardens while writing that first novel discovered for him a pleasure

> in becoming aware of seeing and experiencing something without a specific purpose and which stimulated flashbacks of memory and a panoramic sequence of thoughts and associations. People out for a walk were transplanted from the main streets into other times and spaces—without violence and by a purely synaesthetic art of seduction. Gardens are much like the imaginary landscape of a metropolis. They link thoughts to preconscious conditions while you walk, and reflect actual thought processes on a pre-rational level in their tendency to grow densely and run wild at the wayside.[50]

The "imaginary landscape" of gardens that Dean points us toward is one that, as was argued earlier, can be accessed usefully from literary works and painterly images. It also pervades much good nonscholarly writing about the garden—notably Sitwell's *On the Making of Gardens*, also discussed in Chapter 6—to such an extent that we cannot ignore this strain of "reverie" or "curious drifting," which Elkins and Dean are right to

identify and other garden historians and theorists are slow to acknowledge.[51]

The study of gardens needs to rely on many diverse approaches and disciplines; however—another paradox of the garden—it must maintain its independence from all of them. Its closest affinities are probably with social history and the history of mentality;[52] these approaches, partly because they are concerned as much with the process as the products of experience, might help to determine the shape of future garden histories, without hijacking the materials to their own destinations.

6. A major *desideratum* is a history of the reception or consumption of gardens, where social and mental experiences coincide. Here the collective responses to place-making in word and image will need to be systematically ransacked. There is a virtual dimension to the designed landscape, for, despite its palpable objectivity, it needs an addressee, as it were, a spectator, visitor, or inhabitant, somebody to feel, to receive, to sense its existence and its qualities.[53] To use or to inhabit a landscape should be regarded as a response to its design, and to study such responses or "conscious engagement"[54] will bring us to a better understanding of design history. So we need to track how people have responded to sites in word and image; the wealth of such material which writers and artists have provided is considerable, if largely untapped.[55] It is our only evidence of earlier landscape experiences—sometimes even the only record of now lost landscapes. But we should also expend more energy in systematically recording the experiences of contemporary visitors to both new and old designed landscapes.

Especially since one of the essential features of a landscape architectural site is its fragility, its changefulness, even the unpredictability of natural elements notionally brought under the control of a designer, one way in which to capture this evanescent character is to plot succeeding responses to it and to understand by what different processes visitors of different kinds have accessed the garden experience under different conditions.[56] This historical activity has been wittily dramatized, with fruitful lessons for the historian, in Tom Stoppard's *Arcadia*:[57] here two groups of people nearly two hundred years apart respond to the parkland of an imaginary country house. And as Stoppard's play also implies, the reception history of designed landscapes that I propose here will be forced to address the *longue durée* of place-making and place-visiting rather than focus only on specific moments. This in its turn will permit the new history to reformulate what hitherto has been read simply as a battle of styles or as a sequence of garden biographies in the nineteenth and twentieth centuries. Nor will this reception history be concerned—rather, it will actually be freed from the obligation—to ask whether a "reading" or experience of a garden is a correct one. We should seek to know how such-and-such a "reading" process occurred, how it was conducted, and under what circumstances, rather than to ask whether it squares with our own ideas and values.[58] Another way of explaining this strategy is to say that we should link a reception history to notions of semiosis, which shifts attention from the text of a semiotic message (such as a site) to the interpretative process whereby the listener or reader or viewer interprets it.[59] This explains why the way people have read, written, and imaged sites, as Chapter 6 suggested, is a fundamental study; it also necessitates a constant adjustment of our ideas of the garden as we study further instances of the reception of specific designed examples—but also as we contemplate fresh instances of their being remade.

III

The present, let alone future, practice of landscape architecture is problematical in an altogether different way than historical inquiry, which as Stoppard's *Arcadia* makes clear is not in any case unambiguous. Yet the two are fruitfully entangled to the extent that if we can jump-start a new historiography, practitioners, freed then from the constraints of an old and useless set of narrative paradigms and metaphors, may discover some directions and inspiration for their own work.[60] If the theories or "contemplations" pursued in these chapters are of any value, they should at the very least establish an agenda for ongoing discussion. The agenda that I propose has eight items, offered here with some suggestions for the scope of ensuing conversations; doubtless there are further lessons to be drawn.

1. First, we have to be clear that there are all sorts of place-making, and there have been since at least the Greeks.[61] Just as writing ranges from shopping lists to sonnets, so place-making comprises everything from front yards to golf courses, from urban parks with handicap access and full sporting amenities to academic and corporate campuses, from provision of adequate, controlled habitat for timber rattlesnakes in subdivision development to the invention of memorial landscapes, from the recovery of blighted industrial zones to the creation *ab nuovo* of new town landscapes, botanical trails, and inner-city gardens.[62] And just as some skills useful for sonnet writing will scarcely be called upon for the creation of shopping lists (while the latter in their turn require some logistical talent or penchant for improvisation when implemented), so in place-making the repertoire of concepts, skills, and invention will vary considerably according to the type of place to be created. In fact, this means recognizing in landscape architecture the same scale of activity as is accepted for architecture when it is distinguished from building. There are all kinds of building, not all of it architecture. So there are many kinds of place-making, not all of a landscape architecture, especially when it is inspired by the idea of the garden.

I have tended to invoke the terms *place-making, landscape architecture, garden art*, and other such analogic terms indifferently throughout this book. That was deliberate, although it may have been confusing for some readers. Just as there can be no architecture without building (though buildings without architecture certainly exist), so there cannot be landscape architecture or gardens without place-making as a basic endeavor, although, like building, this last can exist without being taken to any higher level. My aim throughout has been to execute a double maneuver: on the one hand, to return to the broadest set of principles in place-making, where nomenclature is less crucial than acknowledgment of the range and ultimate comparability of all strategies by which humans organize exterior spaces for their dwelling; and on the other, to rescue the idea of the garden as the distinguishing feature of all fine landscape architecture irrespective of whether gardens per se are what are actually established.[63]

That the garden is the ideal mode of all place-making has strong historical support. The modern profession of landscape architecture grew originally from those who for centuries had made gardens and who gradually were required to switch their skills from designing private enclaves to creating public spaces. Public spaces rightly necessitated different approaches to design, not least the scale at which they were projected and the extent of their visitation. But the mode of making gardens continued to supply, and continues to supply, much of the inspiration and invention in these larger sites. The usefulness of Bonfadio's idea of three natures is precisely that, without obviously being aware of such modern developments, he saw garden-making as the prime mode of place-making. History, for him, showed that humans intervened in their immediate environment with different intensities and objectives, and in the richness of their invention gardens were at the opposite end of that spectrum from the dwellings of those who lived in the wild mountains. Finally, as we have also seen set out by the Hartlibians and Shaftesbury in the seventeenth century, men and women could learn to appreciate the outside world, natural and cultural, by seeing it first epitomized and even "perfected" within gardens. The idea of the garden was, so to speak, a portable one and not necessarily to be abandoned when its designated site was left for the larger worlds of towns, villages, and farms or even the uncultivated wastes.

2. There are rivals to the garden as the ideal mode of place-making. The very range of place-making strategies—as Evelyn and Beale also reminded us—should help landscape architecture determine its own best procedures or those best suited to a specific project; but the need for some model or even rationale of place-making is also compelling. Landscape architecture has betrayed considerable uncertainties about what models or rationales would suit the performance of its various endeavors, often selecting one at the expense of the possible range: seeing everything in terms of planning and problem solving, say, or at the other extreme, appealing to the current art scene, most notably and seductively to land art.[64]

Interesting and often breathtaking as some creations by land artists have been (not least in directing our attention to their sublime setting), it is misleading to equate their work with place-making. Places are made to dwell in, to be in the middle of (hence, *milieu*), while special places (*hauts lieux*) like landscaped sites focus for their intended inhabitants a cluster of significances. Even those land art objects that can be "entered" —Robert Smithson's "Spiral Jetty," Michael Heizer's "Double Negative"—scarcely fulfill that requirement. More examples of land art, rather than designing a site, focus our attention by means of a single insertion into a landscape not otherwise physically altered.[65]

This activity has seemed to many, rightly, to be analogous to the parable of Wallace Stevens's "Anecdote of a Jar." Because this poem is also much cited by landscape architecture students,[66] as if it spoke for their own field, it has set up an erroneous analogy between land art and landscape architecture. A brief glance at the poem will show this: the poet narrates how he set a jar on a Tennessee hillside:

The wilderness rose up to it,
And spawled around, no longer wild.
The jar was round upon the ground
. . . .

FIGURE 128. The hillsides at Pitigliano, Tuscany.

It took dominion everywhere.
The jar was gray and bare.
It did not give of bird or bush,
Like nothing else in Tennessee.

The jar does not permanently alter the physical topography. It is indeed, we might say, ecologically wholesome, which is perhaps why it has become a fashionable metaphor for landscape architects (another unconscious lure for them is perhaps Stevens's nostalgia for a tradition, for Keats's Grecian urn as precedent for the vernacular American jar). The introduction of the jar onto the dreary hillside makes us see our familiar landscape with fresh eyes, which is also the aim of landscape architecture. But jar and Tennessee have no intrinsic reason to be juxtaposed, and it sets a bad example of extraneous intrusions into a site. Compare it with some earlier designs that have a certain affinity with contemporary land art — in central Italy the carved hillside and valley of Pitigliano (Figure 128) and Bomarzo (Figure 129) from the later sixteenth century[67] — and we can see that these Italian places are made less by insertions than by reconfiguring the very materials of the site, carving the indigenous rocks into figures of

FIGURE 129. In the Sacro Bosco, Bomarzo, near Viterbo.

gods, beasts, cornucopia, and seats. Their being drawn, so to speak, out of the existing landscape makes us freshly aware of its scope, shape, and "feel" and sets up some new spaces over which each of these objects exerts sway and through which we reinhabit the site physically and imaginatively. In contrast, the work of some land artists seems no better (and no worse) than graffiti inscribed on subways and downtown buildings.

Not that land artists (in the various manifestations of that activity)[68] do not have lessons for landscape architects. Above all, land artists can often return them to a fuller appreciation of the twin resources of all place-making—the earth in all its elemental and sometimes daunting materiality and the available vocabulary of abstract forms. Richard Long draws attention to the fragility of human marks upon the land; even though, given the fragility of some of the land, his work may probably survive longer than is usually claimed, it draws attention to the infinitesimally insignificant gestures that we make—even if they are as grandiloquent as Michael Heizer's "Double Negative"—in face of the enormity of space and its materials. More sympathetically than Long, Andy Goldsworthy draws us closer to the constant process and evolution, the changefulness, at the very heart of all landscape architecture; this is most obvious with his ice sculptures, but the entropy of seemingly more robust organic materials is also extremely eloquent. Other explorations by visual artists whom we could associate with land art celebrate the wonderful geometry of the natural world,[69] a phenomenal world of abstract wonder, which those who decry the "formal" gardens of the Renaissance and Baroque need to ponder. At its best, then, land art recalls the range of possibilities that are involved in place-making as well as some of the key issues, even if its more sculptural moves provide a too limited model for intervention. The lesson is, once again, that landscape architecture needs to seek its inspiration and its paradigms from within its own resources and traditions.

3. Keeping in mind the analogy with writing, we should register that landscape architecture addresses both factual and fictional issues. Francis Bacon, to quote now a remark less hackneyed than his saw about the garden's "greater perfection," distinguished between the "interpretation of nature" and "anticipations of nature."[70] Bacon unsurprisingly valued the first, being the deductions that science makes from empirical and theoretical considerations of what nature has done, over the second, where the human mind projects and invents. Such a distinction recalls the frequent and unnecessary confrontations today between scientific and humanistic understanding in landscape architecture. Bacon saw the anticipations of nature leading directly to error and distortion, but the terms of his displeasure may fuel our enthusiasm for what he rejects: "Idols of the Theater; because in my judgement all the received systems are but so many stage plays, representing worlds of their own creation after an unreal and scenic fashion."

We have seen how the garden can be a stage for the inventions and plays of human nature; this nature may be less quantifiable than Bacon's preferred territory of enquiry, but especially as we are now heirs to more accomplished probing and scrutiny of the human psyche than was the early seventeenth century, we can acknowledge its "unreal" and "scenic" productions as being among the realities that lend themselves to *interpretation*. For it must also be admitted, as André Breton put it, that "scientific knowledge of nature would be valuable only if contact with nature were reestablished by poetic—I dare say mythical—methods."[71] Today we might prefer to say that scientific knowledge of nature would be "more valuable," but Breton's point is otherwise well taken: humans need to do more than understand intellectually the workings of ecology, and need to gain access also to a symbolic or spiritual level of meaning. Sir George Sitwell has reminded us that gardens represent and are the product of that "blundering ghost-haunted miracle, the human mind," in all its fullness. Thus haunted by undeniable spirits, the environment can become landscape.[72]

The garden's hospitality to and expression of fiction as well as fact (to adapt Bacon's dualism) must be acknowledged in all place-making. The more we can learn, systematically and scientifically, about how people respond to places in this double regard, especially those special places that the French term *hauts lieux*,[73] the better we can learn to design with due regard to both factual (scientific, ecological) truth and imaginative truth. This will mean much more than studying pedestrian movements, ratios of male/female or senior citizen/child use, noise and light intensities, and so on; those inquiries will establish a firm basis for place-making, but not guarantee anything more in those instances where more is desired or preferable.

Due regard to the fictions of a place to be (re)made involves accessing human experience of place, including memory. Peter Jacobs's "Vision Statement for Landscape Architecture," privately circulated in 1990, begins, "Landscape contains the memory of natural process and human endeavour . . ." Deborah Karasov was quoted as saying that landscape architecture "is a social art, insofar as it must create for us experiences that have some meaning, that accord with our memories, thoughts, and needs."[74] These are both, in one way, simple and obvious points to make. Yet it is not as easy as it sounds to identify and comprehend those memories, thoughts, and needs; they lurk as much behind awkward and oblique expression (including silence) as they find expression in distinct and clarion tones. We find them in formulations that are fragile or frustrating in their capacity to capture the process of human interaction or mediation of place. Here the finest garden-writing has a fundamental role to play, if only we can learn to distinguish it. Often it seems to be the dross that gets published or attracts attention and the marvelously insightful writing that hides its light. How many landscape architects in any country have read Rudolf Borchardt's book on the passionate gardener, with its appeal for the garden as the human's best home, a complex totality of education, formation, and culture?[75]

4. Place-making of high quality involves, as has constantly been insisted, the meeting, the conscious engagement and interchange, of object and subject. We cannot focus exclusively or solipsistically on the human subject, despite or perhaps because of his/her endlessly fertile diversity; but what can be said objectively about the other part of the equation, the territorial object itself? Even if genius loci does not objectively exist or lend itself to scientific quantification, being in part a projection of the human subject upon a site, we may still understand the phrase as pointing to the phenomenal and cultural singularity of place.[76] It is this that landscape architecture tries to address and bring out for others to appreciate. The question then becomes one of inventing a place (object) that many as yet unidentified subjects (visitors) can connect with. Put differently, how can the landscape architect construe (i.e., inventively analyze prior to making) and then construct (make) places that will yield a full repertoire of possibilities, especially to visiting subjects whose identity cannot be known in advance?

This last is especially problematical in public work, as in modern art generally. In 1939 Clement Greenberg asked what would happen if, in an increasingly diversified world, "the writer or artist [we can add: landscape architect] is no longer able to estimate the response of his audience to the symbols and references with which he works."[77] The landscape architect's client—municipality, corporation, or other "entity"—is readily identifiable, though usually in the form of a committee; the ultimate clients or users are less likely to be so clearly defined or envisaged except in the broadest and most general terms. Designing or catering for such an amorphous audience leads therefore to addressing its lowest common denominator of receptivity. Yet this concern has probably distracted landscape architects too much from a primary commitment to the place and its potentialities (can we imagine an artist not painting what s/he wants?); this alternative focus, while it will not eliminate the problem, will undoubtedly enrich the process of its solution.

Put it schematically: in historical terms a person or culture (A) has communicated various meanings (B1) to a contemporary audience (C1) through the medium of a piece of landscape architecture (D). B1 continues to be viable and meaningful to later visitors (C2, C3, etc.), but these visitors may also find in that original D fresh versions of or alternatives to B (B2, B3, etc.), especially as the site itself will inevitably change or be redesigned (D+, D−, or even D2, D3, etc.). The original owner and designer (A) now has no control over these later evolutions of meaning. The lesson in this for contemporary practitioners (latter-day As) is that, rather than trying to anticipate the range of reactions to their design either at the time of its creation or subsequently (worrying about how much B the Cs will get hold of), they should try to exploit the potential of meanings in D itself, which has to be the vehicle of these expressions and communications anyway.

5. What we have learned from revisiting some of the central topics of landscape architecture mostly converge in ideas of place and the stages and scope of its making and remaking. Mary Miss has referred to the "information of the place," which sounds rather factual; but if the information is approached in the spirit of Clifford Geertz's famous definition of "thick description,"

FIGURE 130. Bernard Lassus, design for Le Jardin de l'Antérieur.

it could yield more resonant significance.[78] Information or ideas of place, then, range from the most prosaic to the extremely poetic, the full scale of which needs to be kept constantly in mind lest design slips through inertia toward the dull compromise of a midpoint where functionality is cosmetically enhanced with "poetry."

There are several aspects of place to be considered especially as they relate to its remaking. The understanding of the relationship of the designated space to its surrounding territory is essential; it is a relationship that can be either visual or mental, physical or metaphysical, or all of them together. In its turn this can be made palpable in the design through visual means—creating sightlines, carefully determining the approaches so that the very process of discovery becomes part of the experience of having arrived, or through some allusions to the unseen but necessary context. Such allusions may enter the domain of the poetic. When Bernard Lassus was invited to design a parkland for the new town of L'Isle d'Abreau in 1975, he proposed a Garden of the Past (Jardin de l'Antérieur: Figure 130); eerie sounds and submerged images of drowned villages would have emanated from the ponds on the outskirts of the brand-new development, an innocent magic to conjure a lost world for its latter-day inhabitants who did not suspect its existence until it was "invented" for them.[79]

Defining for a work of third nature how it may re-

FIGURE 131. Arc Seawall, Gloucester, Massachusetts, designed by Priscilla Randall (photograph by David Kellogg, courtesy of Randall and Rich).

late to the other natures has several important consequences: above all, it suggests the possibilities of where to intervene on the scale of art:nature. This cannot be an arbitrary decision, nor wholly a formal one, since the dialogue between art and nature alludes to the very context of the place—whether its geomorphogical, social, cultural, or political character or, where relevant, the character of the client (personal or institutional) and the anticipated users. Solutions are not always going to be logical or uncomplicated. A rocky Massachusetts promontory is a place to acknowledge the forces of nature and, where possible, to keep the Atlantic Ocean at bay; but the landscape architect Priscilla Randall was determined "to make nature obvious," and the triple bastions of her Richard Serra-like *Arc Seawall* help the sea to dramatize or represent itself and they also allow

a patio within the walls to serve as a belvedere for the observation of oceanic behavior (Figure 131).[80] But in addition to making nature obvious, the design forcibly underlines the art and intrusion of human colonization. No doubt, a multimillion dollar retreat may draw attention to itself, even if it is mostly passing yachtsmen who will most appreciate *Arc Seawall* (being barely visible from within the property); even so, the conspicuous effrontery of this latter-day King Canute in his face-off with first nature has been suitably dramatized, though with what satiric subtext is unclear.

6. Places tell stories to those who will listen, and listeners are helped by the landscape architect who translates stories so that they are clearer, more absorbing, perhaps more critical. No place lacks history, be it geological or cultural; each history will contain something unique, some element that makes its story locally significant and *sui generis*. This particular history has to be involved in the remaking of that place. (However, the

slight interest in the history of design by so many students of landscape architecture argues, sadly, for their
likely failure to be interested in history at all, including
the history of a site). Some of the earliest expressions
of advice to the practitioner on addressing this specific history of a locality come in Alberti's architectural
treatise. He distinguishes, just as we have just done,
between locality and area (for him the site of building);
this area will contain, necessarily or by deliberation, a
concentration of the qualities and effects of the larger
locality. Among the ways in which Alberti notes how
the history of locality may be drawn out in an area are
by focusing on key items of vegetation or by adding
sculpture.[81]

Paolo Bürgi, a Swiss landscape architect, was asked
to remake a forest where industrial damage had left
an ugly scar, but he did so by leaving a tangible reminder of that event in a recognizably different circle
of trees (Figure 132). In a similar fashion, Herman
Prigann created the Ring der Erinnerung (Circle of
Remembrance) in the forests along the old East/West
German border; its composition of dead wood for the
walls, its line of fence posts from the former border installation, even its five boulders inscribed with "flora,"
"fauna," "acqua," "aer," and "terra," will all eventually
disintegrate, for "entropy and evolution are processes
of life inseparably intertwined." Yet the changes, besides being a natural process that is endemic to the
landscape, also function symbolically for the cultural
process that will, it is hoped, eventually heal the breach
between people. So the site will lose its identity within
the forest as this episode in European history fades
from at least popular consciousness.[82]

The representation by landscape architecture of what
Evelyn, writing of fountains and other hydraulic devices, called "Histories and scenes" need not necessarily
result in such explicit narratives as the galloping horses
of Las Colinas (Figure 133) or the more abstracted
imagery of the California Scenario (Figure 134; and see
Figure 16). Yet whether or not the weak mimeticism of

those two examples wins universal approval, I suspect
that they can reliably engage a range of visitors in listening to the story of a site, as Halprin's FDR Memorial is also proving. Perhaps the techniques of storytelling in both their archetypal structures (e.g., fairy tales)
and their modernist variations (say, *Ulysses*) need to be
studied more carefully for whatever analogous strategies they can yield landscape architects. Narrative has
just a few basic structures that repeat in story after
story; but the hold of a good story derives equally from
its local and contingent elaboration of that basic archetype. More attention to the rich locality of place, in
both Alberti's sense and ours, could satisfy one of the
deep-seated desires of *Homo narrator*.[83]

A more recent creation of Bernard Lassus in 1992 for
the rest area at Nîmes-Caissargues combined the poetic
invention of his earlier Jardin de l'Antérieur with the
narrative contingencies of an actual, historical locality.
What might strike motorists driving the *autoroute* from
Spain to Italy as just some random Euro stopping place
turns out to play so inventively with a specific sense of
place—notably the nearby city of Nîmes—that even its
citizens drive out there to see for themselves where they
live. On a huge site of thirty-five hectares (Figure 135),
recovered from the quarrying that went to make the
autoroute itself, the highway bisects a huge formal green
carpet, with parallel lines of trees as in a seventeenth-
century garden by Le Nôtre, but punctuated erratically
with cypresses (we are, after all, in the south). Or perhaps it is the highway that is cut in two by this dramatic
feature, where the now-distracted occupants of vehicles
left behind in the parking lots among olive groves can
take a distant view of the city of Nîmes and discover
a series of architectural quotations from it. There is
a columnar facade from the nineteenth-century city
theater, rejected by Sir Norman Foster when he redesigned the site and donated by the mayor of Nîmes;
it has a ghostly air of displacement, a Roman temple
front in the wrong time and place. But then outlined in
steel is the silhouette of a genuine Roman feature, the

Tour Magne, one of the famous sites of the city below. A model of the same tower sits within the open belvedere or "folly," and so are initiated reflections on the game with scale that the whole site plays (Figure 136). Taking a rest stop, arbitrarily perhaps, during that long haul from Spain and Italy, drivers discover a locality reinterpreted for the modern fast-track traveler: a real but distant Nimes on the horizon, to be compared by the eye and the mind with fragments of its past abstracted or epitomized (a model of the whole city is planned for the site, too). And all this along an eloquently French promenade, a slice of gardenscape that disputes the topography with a modern highway made from the ground across which it stretches.

7. This attention to what stories places tell and how they tell them—each site having its own variation on a basic plot, geological or cultural—will actively work against the worst enemy of fine design, homogenization. But it takes time, much "research," and more than anything else much leisurely absorption of ambience, genius loci, or whatever term signals that deep and informed sense of place, no less tangible for all its elusiveness, that the great travel writers have sought like the Holy Grail. Yet the globalization of landscape architecture works wickedly against these skills; famous landscape architects are called to work anywhere in the world, without ever being allowed (it seems) adequate time to grasp the full implications of the locality where their firm is currently engaged. The current obsession of landscape architecture—to achieve (however belatedly) full membership in the modernist club of twentieth-century design—is also an enemy of the representation of locality; for a modernist agenda aspires to an international vocabulary that turns its back on the national, let alone the regional or the local. Landscape architecture is by its very nature a local art. Even botanical gardens, like Padua or Kew, make their collections or imagery derived from far-flung places relevant to local conditions (natural and cultural).

The depressing encounter these days with chains of

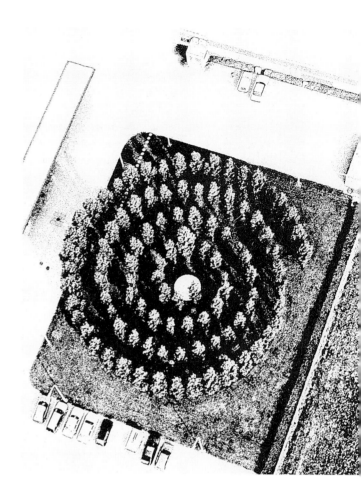

FIGURE 132. Paolo Bürgi, The Green Spiral, Ticino, 1985; drawing and site (courtesy of the designer).

fast food or clothing around the corner of any town in the world makes even more vital the insistence on locality in place-making, places to which we can escape from global hamburgers and the united colors of urban outfits. It would be a start perhaps if the local imperatives of climate, geomorphology, plant and other materials, as well as social habits, were not only observed but emphasized (keeping well this side of postmodernist bricolage).

Besides the European theorists reviewed briefly above, some modern gardenists have also raised their

FIGURE 133. Las Colinas, Texas, designed by SWA (photograph:
Marc Treib).

FIGURE 134. Isamu Noguchi, California Scenario (photograph: Marc Treib).

voices against the homogenization of a given style, against which they have urged the necessity of local forms. The German Willy Lange and the Irish William Robinson each pleaded for a diversity of gardens to match the diversity of landscapes in their countries:

> It is only by respecting the site itself and letting the plan grow out of it that we can get gardens free from monotony, and suggestive also, as they should often be, of the country in which they occur. Why should we not in these islands of ours, where there are so many different kinds of landscape and characteristics of soil and climate, have gardens in harmony, as it were, with their surroundings. (Robinson, inveighing against the "idea of the bastard Italian garden")

> The garden is always an enclosed part of the landscape in which it is situated. From the landscape we take motifs of design and through it will reach a diversity of gardens, just as we have a diversity of natural landscape characteristics. (Lange)[84]

Similarly, Danish designer C. Th. Sørensen discusses the relationship of locality to international styles in his

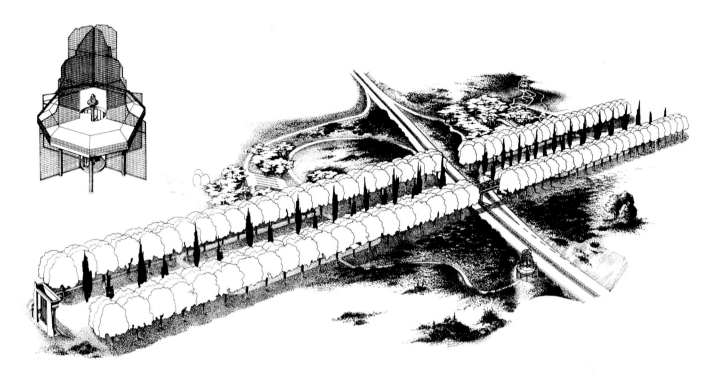

FIGURE 135. Bernard Lassus, view of the Nîmes-Caissargues *autoroute* rest area, Provence, with a drawing of one of the belvederes, 1992 (photograph courtesy of the designer).

short book on the origins of garden art. Like Evelyn and Beale, he chose to emphasize the relativity of various garden styles, the relative possibilities of different sites and clients. Sørensen links four of his five types of garden (all, that is, except the earliest and most residual of growing spaces) to geographical and cultural conditions of water management, since he considers irrigation or artificial watering as "perhaps the decisive factor in the development of gardening as an art."[85] Although it is too brief and oversimplified an account of garden history, it is remarkable and welcome precisely for its refusal to see history as either teleological or (despite his apologetic use of *stylized*) a battle of styles; he even reads the English garden as not essen-

tially different from either the French, Italian, or Spanish. These national foci are too broad for his analytical purposes, themselves too liable to generalized blur, especially when the modes are realized outside their "country of origin"; but Sørensen is right to premise his schematic history on local aquatic and hydraulic conditions and the knowledge of them by local artists.

Yet another approach to locality can be seen in a third Lassus design, this time at Rochefort-sur-Mer in the west of France. In this naval yard, Louis XIV's fleet was built and outfitted from the truly colossal Corderie Royale or rope-making factory that, now restored, dominates the site (Figure 137). Here French ships returning from the West Indies and the Americas were loaded with exotic plants. Here the town's intendant, Michel Begon, gave his name to the begonia, and the Marquis R. M. de la Galissonière, who sailed from Rochefort to become governor of Canada, imported

FIGURE 136. Theatre façade and belvedere designed by Bernard Lassus, at the Nimes-Caissargues *autoroute* rest area, Provence (photograph courtesy of the designer).

the first magnolia. But the River Charante, which was the lifeblood and the raison d'être of the town, silted up, the sea receded, and by the early twentieth century the rope factory had closed. Lassus has brought the site back to life—hence its name, Le Jardin des Retours— returning it to its true place in the urban and fluvial topography and rediscovering for its visitors a way to return them to its historical past.

The site is linked to the town via an immense ramp (see Figure 137) planted with Virginia tulip trees, one of the many references—along with palm trees—to the importation or return of plants in the holds of ships. The link to the river is achieved by cutting *percées*, another loan from classical French gardening, through which some increased river traffic catches glimpses of Blondel's fabulous building and the strollers on land

FIGURE 137. The Corderie Royale and ramp leading to the former
public gardens, at Le Jardin des Retours, Rochefort-sur-Mer,
designed by Bernard Lassus from 1987.

peek at the boats of the sailing club. History is returned to the present through an active rigging area re-
created on top of a World War II bunker and by a labyrinth (another garden quotation) of naval battles, where
models and interactive computers let visitors of all ages
replay great French maritime encounters (Figure 138).
Above all, the exoticism of certain plants has been re-
instated, and a begonia collection, purchased by the

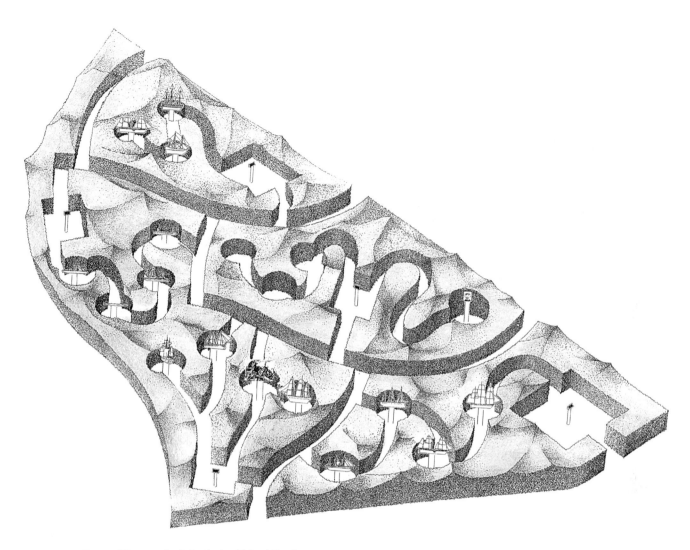

FIGURE 138. Bernard Lassus, the Labyrinth of Naval Battles at
Le Jardin des Retours, Rochefort-sur-Mer.

town, will make an experimental breeding station of
the place that first named this species of plant. Lassus's
strategy for linking the site to its locality, insisting on
its distinct character and identity, was not at all what
Robinson or Lange had in mind, but it adds to their
essentially horticultural interest a sense of theater, an
ability to play with scale and reference to time and
place, and some accomplished (and incidentally, time-

consuming) historical researches. Rochefort's recovery
of a sense of locality is understandably if paradoxically
earning it international acclaim.

8. Finally, as has been reiterated throughout, landscape
architecture is a representative art in the many ways in
which that term has been invoked. It re-presents forms
and motifs from other natures; it epitomizes the nature
and culture of locality, nation, owner, user; it realizes
some idea of the particular site, bringing out some of

its history. This bears upon another etymology of representation: less re-petition than a thing, *res*, made present.[86] Thus, from Jacques Boyceau to André Vera, "nature" is "shaped into intelligible forms" or found to be "so full of good and beautiful things only as much as they are shown off."[87] Landscape architecture also represents the process of its own creation, being necessarily self-conscious because it will (to a greater or lesser extent) need to make its visitors and users conscious of their interactivity with the place it has made. It finds ways of giving physical form to mental representations of special places, giving to a site what Thomas Whately, in writing of landscaped parks, called the "marks of distinction borrowed from a garden."[88]

"What raises architecture above mere building,"

writes Karsten Harries, "is representation";[89] we can adapt that claim for the purposes of suggesting how landscape architecture rises upon place-making. But such "self-reference," creating the fiction of a garden, a park, a memorial, whatever, requires some deliberate attention to what this book has called theory, to the contemplation of things before and after and even *as* they are built. In effect, such theory cannot avoid being balanced by practice. But in current circumstances, when theoretical motivation is at such a low ebb or strains beyond its own territory to emulate the excessive theorization of architectural discourse, an excess of contemplation that is properly focused on the traditions of landscape architecture itself might now be in order. We must learn to practice garden theory.

Conclusion: The Tune of the Garden

IN TOM STOPPARD'S PLAY *Arcadia*, a modern character, Valentine, tries to calculate the pattern of the grouse population over several decades on a Derbyshire country estate. To do so, he enters data into his computer from the mansion's old game books. He explains this research as the attempt to seize and identify a tune emerging from all the noise, the happenstance, and daily details of particular shoots and their participants.[1] These "noises" are many and in themselves fascinating, but they tend to obliterate the tune.

Stoppard's Valentine offers an apt analogy for the practice of garden theory. What we now call landscape architecture has appeared in all shapes and sizes, in virtually every period and culture, sometimes not even in forms we would now either recognize or esteem. These made places have been represented in many ways in verbal and visual art; they have also been the object of an astonishing number of interpretations, which themselves depend on a considerable wealth of different kinds of evidence. So much for the noise, among which W. H. Auden included all the sensual distractions of the garden.

Yet the serious study of place-making requires that its students, like the mathematician Valentine, occasionally transcend this noisy diversity of material to identify a tune, to isolate certain distinctive features of the object of their inquiries—what we call concepts or theories. The intriguing details of many particular sites and their archival leavings in place and time cannot wholly distract us from determining what Leon Battista Alberti, beginning his own inquiry into the distinctive properties of building in the fifteenth century, called "some integral property" of his subject: its tune.

John Evelyn has been something of an exemplary figure for this inquiry, not least because he seems to have understood the competing demands of "tunes" and "noises." We saw how he wavered—or drew a fine line—between empirical studies and abstract formulae, oscillating between practice and theory. On the one hand, he knew that theoretical formulations survived through their universal validity: to be "of incomparable use," as the "Elysium Britannicum" puts it, they had nevertheless to be "fit at all seasons" (fol. 86). On the other hand, that temporal relativity acknowledges something crucial in landscape architecture, which he described, now in *Acetaria*, as "the Hortulan Provision of the Golden Age fitted [to] all Places, Times and Persons."[2] In short, even in the search for theoretical positions, no gardener can afford to neglect the difference of territory, seasons, climate, or culture. Evelyn is no exception, and the leaves of his manuscript are studded with observations like "yet is the Autumne a more proper Season for . . ." (fol. 63). His concern for variations in climate, region, and season seems especially acute: "It will therefore be of high importance that our Gardner both observe & prepare for them [the fower Seasons] because the due knowledge of them will instruct him how he is to entertaine them" (fol. 19). So, too, with the "variety of *climates*" (fol. 6), and "what every region can, or cannot beare" (fol. 13): this is especially crucial, of course, when what is in question is making the modern British elysium preeminent above others both ancient and modern. Here the challenge of a northern climate augments English achievements: as William Wotton tried to argue it—since it is more difficult to husband the earth in Great Britain than in

Sicily, so modern achievements may "justly come into Competition with any ancient Performances."[3] Today the modern designer must equally observe the requirements of his or her time and place.

Flexibility and adaptability on the part of the gardener, however, did not distract Evelyn from seeking to define or achieve a "universal" garden (fol. 3), by which I take him to mean an adequate idea or tune of the garden. It seems obvious, however, that his constant dedication to seasonal, regional, and topographical difference, supported as it was by his experimental aptitude, effectively prevented Evelyn from pursuing theory more energetically.[4] It did not prevent him from nourishing an ambition of "building up a Body of real, and substantial Philosophy, which should never succomb to time, but with the ruines of Nature and the world it self." This would be a structure of general rules that "may indeed lift up its head, such as stand the shock of Time."[5]

We too need, every bit as much as Evelyn did in the seventeenth century, an idea of the garden so as not to be overwhelmed by the hundreds of opinions and options canvassed today (*tot homines, quot sententiae*, as he might have put it—as many opinions as there are people to have them). Moreover, such an *idea* would enable us to establish criteria by which we could make judgments about contemporary design, by which we could distinguish not only between different kinds of place-making but also (dare one say?) between the good, the bad, and the indifferent in each of those kinds. If we examined the role of theory in some of the great historical moments of place-making, whether formally articulated by designers or only implied within their actual designs, we would be in a better position to evolve and practice our own theory.

We can also learn from Evelyn's shrewd sense of the garden as aiming to represent a particular person's and/or a specific culture's historical perception of their relationship with the physical world in its fullest complexity. It would guide us in our thinking about restoration and conservation of historical gardens, making us more properly sceptical about our ability to recover past *mentalité* to such an extent that a facsimile of its gardens is worthwhile. We also want, as Evelyn and Walpole surely did, modern gardens that address our own concerns. Above all, we need to rediscover for our own time the relationship of the thoroughly mediated garden and of the designed landscape to the larger world of environmental purity. For, in the last resort, as we continue inevitably to make places for ourselves, the "presence & assistance of Art," as Evelyn put it,[6] is always "called to interpose" or intervene in the various worlds of nature.

NOTES

PREFACE

1. See Germain Seligman, *Roger de la Fresnaye, with a Catalogue Raisonné* (Greenwich, Conn., 1969), p. 166.

2. "Conceptual" is invoked by the profession—as in G. W. Reid's *From Concept to Form in Landscape Design* (New York, 1993)—but only to signal the designer's initial idea for a specific project.

3. It is, in fact, a long-standing complaint. Erasmus Darwin complained that agriculture and gardening were "without a true theory to connect them": *Phytologia; or the Philosophy of Agriculture and Gardening* (London, 1800), p. vii, while Lord Kames noted in 1762 that gardening "abound[s] in practical instruction necessary to the mechanic" who would "in vain . . . rummage them for rational principles to improve our taste": Henry Home (Lord Kames), *Elements of Criticism* (London, 1993), 2:430. See also the first note to Chapter 1 for some indications of the modern extent of this reaction.

4. The Loeb edition of Vitruvius (pp. 20-21) translates the Latin *ratiocinatione* as "theory," what we might still term ratiocination or thought. Or I might cite my colleague, James Corner, arguing that a theory of landscape architecture must allow for and absorb the "multiple skills and talents [of an] artisanal practice": "A Discourse on Theory I: Sounding the Depths—Origins, Theory, and Representation," *LJ*, 9 (1990): 61. See also Marco Frascari, "Maidens 'Theory' and 'Practice' at the Sides of Lady Architecture," *Assemblage*, 7 (1988): 15-27.

5. Indra Kagis McEwen, *Socrates' Ancestor: An Essay on Architectural Beginnings* (Cambridge, Mass., 1994), esp. pp. 2 and 4.

6. See ibid., p. 42.

7. Aristotle, *Metaphysics*, 982b12 (cited by McEwen, *Socrates' Ancestor*, p. 125).

8. Wendy Steiner has similarly argued in *The Scandal of Pleasure* (Chicago, 1995) for the essential and important role of pleasure in experience of the arts. So has Marc Treib, "Must Landscapes Mean? Approaches to Significance in Recent Landscape Architecture," *LJ*, 14, no. 1 (1995): 46-62.

9. My two lectures at the Collège de France were published as *L'Art du jardin et son histoire* (Paris, 1996).

CHAPTER 1. "FIRST PRINCIPLES" OR "RUDIMENTS"

1. Among such laments see John A. Jakle, *The Visual Elements of Landscape*, p. 166. See also Stephen R. Krog, "The Language of Modern," *Landscape Architecture*, 75, no. 2 (March-April 1985): 56-59; Allen Carlson, "On the Theoretical Vacuum in Landscape Architecture," *LJ*, 12, no. 1 (1993): 51-59, and the litany of similar regrets by the designers interviewed in Udo Weilacher, *Between Landscape Architecture and Land Art*. See also, for much earlier laments along these lines, the two citations in Preface, note 3.

2. Loudon's usage occurs in the title given to his edition of the writings of Humphry Repton; it had been used earlier in 1828 by C. L. Meason to describe depictions of architecture in landscape paintings (I owe this latter reference to Hugh Honour and John Fleming).

3. I refer to its derivation from the Dutch *landschap*, a painted representation of some territory, which is discussed below in Chapter 8, note 44.

4. I add "exterior" in deference to David Leatherbarrow, who reminded me that architects, too, make places (citing "Come over to my place").

5. I borrow the term *milieu* from Augustin Berque: see his *Médiance* as well as the more succinct summary of these ideas at the start of his *Les Raisons du paysage*, pp. 11-38. He has recently extended his arguments in *Etre Humains sur la terre* (Paris, 1996), where his preferred term now seems to be *écoumène* rather than *milieu*.

6. Of Australia George Seddon has written that "gardeners are, in fact, one of the most important groups of land managers in this country, since between us we manage more than 50 per cent of all urban land in Australia": *Landprints* (Cambridge, 1997), p. 183.

7. See Hanno-Walter Kruft's huge survey of the history of architectural theory, *Geschicht der Architekurtheorie* (Munich, 1986), or Alste Horn-Oncken, *Über das Schickliche: Studien zur Geschichte der Architekturtheorie* (Göttingen, 1967), p. 70. The first of those, which incidentally includes an attempt to "cover" garden theory (chapter 20, "Concepts of the garden"), has now received an English translation by R. Taylor et al., *A History of Architectural Theory* (Princeton, N.J., 1994). In English see David Leatherbarrow, *The Roots of Architectural Invention* (Cambridge, 1993).

8. See below, thesis two.

9. See Leon Battista Alberti, *On the Art of Building in Ten Books*, trans. Joseph Rykwert, Neil Leach, and Robert Tavernor (Cambridge, Mass., 1988), esp. pp. 9-23.

10. I shall focus later on the role of garden-making within that of landscape architecture. For now I shall tend to use them interchangeably, though fully aware that professionals would not, quite rightly, equate them. However, it will be part of my argument eventually that gardens constitute a special, even privileged, mode of

place-making, which activity is therefore best energized with the "idea" of the garden.

11. Rapin was only translated from Latin into French in 1773. English versions, however, had been made by John Evelyn the younger in 1672 and by James Gardiner in 1706; this latter went through four editions by 1795, by which time William Mason had adapted the genre to the new English garden. Mason's *English Garden* has a complicated publishing history, beginning in 1772; a revised edition, with notes by Mason's clerical colleague, William Burgh, was reprinted by Garland (New York, 1982); it also modeled itself on the four-book structure of Virgil's *Georgics*.

12. Among the significant treatises may be numbered those by the Mollets (see note 14) and Jacques Boyceau, *Traité du jardinage* (Paris, 1638) in France; Jan van der Groen, *Den Nederlantsen Hovenier* (Amsterdam, 1669) in the Low Countries and Johann Peschel, *Garten Ordnung* (Leipzig, 1597) and Pieter Lauremberg, . . . *Horticultura, Libris II* (Frankfurt, [?]1631) in the German-speaking countries.

13. There is as yet no translation of Boyceau's important work; only a partial translation of André Mollet's *Le Jardin du plaisir*, namely, *The Garden of Pleasure* (London, 1670). Palissy's recipe appeared as *A Delectable Garden* in a translation by Helen Morgenthau Fox (Peekskill, N.Y., 1931). On Palissy, see Frank Lestringant's edition of the *Recette véritable* (Paris, 1996) and Leonard N. Amico, *Bernard Palissy* (New York, 1997).

14. Claude Mollet, *Théâtre des plans et jardinages* (Paris, 1652), and André Mollet, *Le Jardin du plaisir* (Stockholm, 1651).

15. This hugely important work, transcribed by John Ingram, will at last be published by University of Pennsylvania Press in the Penn Studies in Landscape Architecture. Meanwhile, see the essay by Frances Harris on the surviving sections of this magnum opus, "The Manuscripts of John Evelyn's 'Elysium Britannicum,'" *Garden History*, 25, no. 2 (1997): 131–37.

16. As evidenced by their titles: e.g., Hugh Johnson, *The Principles of Gardening: A Guide to the Art, History, Science, and Practice of Gardening* (New York, 1979).

17. And as noted by Oleg Grabar, in the context of reviewing books on Islamic architecture in the *TLS* (18 August 1995), the "documentary values [of such popular publications] are often enormous, but [their] intellectual merits are, with some exceptions, relatively low." What he says ambiguously of Islamic architectural books may also be repeated for the vast array of garden publications: they "challenge the eye rather than the mind. . . . Since we are all tourists in, and lovers of, someone else's world, it is a perfectly legitimate and appropriate approach; it arouses the senses and sometimes even leads to thought."

18. G. A. Agricola, *A Philosophical Treatise of Husbandry and Gardening*, revised and with a preface by Richard Bradley (London, 1721), folio a1 verso (from the preface of the French translator).

19. Though nothing comparable to the volumes listed in note 7, a few English-language publications attest to the growing focus on theoretical concerns: Charles W. Moore et al., *The Poetics of Gardens* (Cambridge, Mass., 1988); *The Meaning of Gardens*, ed. Mark Francis and Randolph T. Hester, Jr. (Cambridge, Mass., 1990); Mara Miller, *The Garden as an Art* (Albany, N.Y., 1993); parts of George Seddon, *Landprints* (1997); Simon Pugh, *Garden—Nature—Language* (Manchester, 1988); Stephanie Ross, *What Gardens Mean* (Chicago, 1998). There are also various journals and magazines devoted with varying degrees of conceptual rigor to matters of garden design: for instance, the June 1996 issue of *Landscape Design* (no. 251), published by the Landscape Institute in the United Kingdom, devoted an issue to garden design.

The bibliography for especially French and Italian works is much longer, though these publications tend to be focused on larger issues of landscape within which the garden occupies only a sector. See principally works written or edited by Bernard Lassus and Augustin Berque, including Berque's collection *Cinq Propositions pour une théorie du paysage* (Seyssel, 1994), Alain Roger's anthology, *La Théorie du paysage en France (1974–1994)* (Seyssel, 1995), and his *Court Traité du paysage* (Paris, 1997), remembering that this large French interest in *paysage* extends beyond the designed into the cultural landscape. In Italian, where the focus has perhaps been more concentrated on designed landscape per se, see works by Massimo Venturi Ferriolo, Rosario Assunto's *Ontologia e teleologia del giardino* (Milan, 1988), and Marcello Fagiolo's *Natura e artificio* (Rome, 1979).

20. See the introduction to Leatherbarrow's *The Roots of Architectural Invention*, pp. 1–6. A comparable point to Leatherbarrow's "topics" is that by Hans-Georg Gadamer: "The classical is what is preserved precisely because it signifies and interprets itself; i.e., that which speaks in such a way that it is not a statement about what is past, but says something to the present as if it were said specially to it," *Truth and Method* (New York, 1985), p. 257. See also note 37 below.

21. For Evelyn's list of contents for the projected "Elysium Britannicum," see *The Genius of the Place*, ed. John Dixon Hunt and Peter Willis (Cambridge, Mass., 1988), pp. 67–69; for another attempt to establish an ideal, because inclusive, conspectus of necessary topics, see the outlines by John Beale for two gardening books reprinted in *Culture and Cultivation in Early Modern England: Writing and the Land*, ed. Michael Leslie and Timothy Raylor (Leicester, 1992), appendix 3.

22. I am thinking here of works by Mara Miller or Stephanie Ross or Simon Pugh cited already in note 19.

23. Many specialists of Japanese and Chinese gardens explain them in terms that seem to make them alien and exotic. But garden-making is no more mysterious in Asia than it is in the West; it may seem strange until we have mastered the cultural conventions by which it was directed.

24. Cf. the similar complaint about architectural theory made by

Marco Frascari, "A Heroic and Admirable Machine: The Theater of the Architecture of Carlo Scarpa, *Architetto Veneto*," *Poetics Today*, 10 (1989): 103 and note 1.

25. See above note 5. I have modified Berque's discussions slightly when applying them to the *making* of landscape architecture, which he does not choose to differentiate from the experiencing of landscape [*paysage*] in its various forms, whether painting, poetry, or gardens.

26. Literary critics may detect here a parallel with Coleridge's views of the imagination in contradistinction to the fancy (derived in their turn from German philosophy). See Coleridge's *Biographia Literaria*, chapter 13; such an echo of Romantic theory is certainly accidental in Berque's analysis, but I think that it may in fact prove useful when we seek criteria for judging good landscape (works of the imagination)—which will achieve a finer, more complete blending of object and subject. As an illustration of this, consider this remark by Chen Jiru (1558-1639): "When one's enthusiasm is exhausted, one's talent would be exhausted; when one's talent is no more, the elegance of the landscape also ceases to exist": quoted Stanislaus Fung, "Here and There in *Yuan Ye*," p. 8.

27. I owe this formulation to Michael Tanner, *Nietzsche* (Oxford, 1996), and to the review of his book by Nicholas Martin in the *TLS*.

28. In Pope's *Epistle to the Right Honourable Richard Earl of Burlington* (1731). Augustin Berque has also addressed the issue of genius loci in *Etre Humains*, pp. 185-87, as has George Seddon in *Landprints*.

29. That the art of the garden is constituted of nature and art is unlikely to be disputed. More arguable is the admission of inorganic materials from the physical world into the category of "nature." But it allows such a creation as Isamu Noguchi's marble court for the Beinecke Library at Yale to be considered a garden.

30. Everybody keeps on asking me, "What about the bowerbird?" The architect and garden designer Harold Ainsworth Peto (1854-1933) first drew attention to this bird, which builds "a meadow of moss before its conical hut or nest and decorates this 'garden' with fruits and flowers of pretty colour" (see Peto's *The Boke of Iford*, with a historical introduction by Robin Whalley [Marlborough, 1993], pp. 31-32). But the bowerbird, to my knowledge, doesn't write poetry about designing landscapes or paint pictures of gardens; he or she is no competition for the uniqueness of human involvement in this activity.

31. This is the case, I think, for both Berque's and Roger's analyses already cited (see notes 26 and 19), although they do not make anything of this implied model.

32. Genesis 2:9.

33. Jefferson to Hamilton, July 1806, *The Portable Jefferson* (New York, 1977), p. 503.

34. Thus Ian McHarg can enjoy the paradox that the "most beautiful gardens I have ever seen are pristine coral reefs in the South Pacific." See "Nature is more than a garden," in *The Meaning of Gardens*, ed. Mark Francis and Randolph T. Hester, Jr., p. 34.

35. In this respect see Wolfgang Iser, *Prospecting: From Reader Response to Literary Anthropology* (Baltimore, 1989), chapter 13, from whom I borrow the formulation used in this paragraph.

36. I owe the formulation of this phrase to Michel Conan: for Berque, see note 5.

37. Jackson, "Nearer than Eden," *The Necessity for Ruins and Other Topics* (Amherst, Mass., 1980), p. 20. Jackson's notion of an archetype seems close to what David Leatherbarrow terms a "topic": see note 20.

CHAPTER 2. WHAT ON EARTH IS A GARDEN?

1. See the poem, of which that is the [in]famous first line, by T. E. Brown in my *Oxford Book of Garden Verse* (1992), p. 190.

2. Ibid., pp. 321-22. Though it seemed apt to conclude the Oxford anthology with this open-ended and finally self-defining proposition, the different circumstances of this study require some greater contemplative rigor!

3. Ernst de Ganay, *Coup d'œil sur les jardins de France* (Brussels, 1993), p. 131, though the remark is actually made in the context of refusing to make comparisons between different gardens.

4. Ludwig Wittgenstein, *Philosophical Investigations I*, secs. 65-66: in German the last part reads "ein kompliziertes Netz von Ähnlichkeiten, die einander übergreifen und kreuzen. Ähnlichkeiten im Grossen und Kleinen."

5. I have derived a few of these from *The Meaning of Gardens*, p. 5. Generally speaking, that book's range of types is less ontological and is more predicated on people's use of and attitude toward garden space.

6. See John Brinckerhoff Jackson, "Nearer than Eden," *The Necessity for Ruins and Other Topics* (Amherst, Mass., 1980), p. 21.

7. Theodore Redpath, *Ludwig Wittgenstein: A Student's Memoir* (London, 1990), pp. 88-89, where Redpath recounts how the philosopher was offended by the width of the author's garden path! Incidentally, Wittgenstein had worked as a gardener's assistant in a monastery near Vienna in 1926 (ibid., p. 44n).

8. Giulio Carlo Argan defining landscape architecture in the *Encyclopedia of World Art* (London, 1963) 8:1066.

9. See Mara Miller, *The Garden as an Art* (Albany, N.Y., 1993).

10. Xenophon, *Oeconomicus*, 4:13, 21.

11. See the special issue of *Word & Image*, 14 (1998), dedicated in part to the landscape architectural motifs in this extraordinary work.

12. See my *Garden and Grove: The Italian Renaissance Garden in the English Imagination, 1600-1750* (new & rev. ed., Philadelphia, 1996).

13. *The Illustrated Dictionary of Gardening*, ed. George Nicolson (London, 1884), 1:43.

14. Willy Lange, "Ein Garten ist ein umzauntes Stuck Land zum Zweck der Pflanzenzucht," *Die Gartenkunst*, 7, no. 7 (1905): 114. For a commentary on Lange's ideas of the natural garden, which make this definition so tendentious, see Joachim Wolschke-Bulmahn, "The 'Wild Garden' and the 'Nature Garden'—Aspects of the Garden Ideology of William Robinson and Willy Lange," *JGH*, 12 (1992): 183–206.

15. However, what is offered here is not proposed as an alternative to the Florence Charter; it merely uses that document as a springboard for its own definition and concerns. See ICOMOS 1964–1984 (Paris, 1984), pp. 95–100; the text of the charter is also reproduced in *The History of Garden Design: The Western Tradition from the Renaissance to the Present Day*, ed. Monique Mosser and Georges Teyssot (London, 1991), p. 526. I have offered elsewhere a definition of the work of landscape architects: see "Garden" in *The Dictionary of Art* (New York, 1996), 12:61–65.

16. Miller, *The Garden as an Art*, pp. 6–16. "Philosophical" in her case involves both the aesthetic concerns announced in her title and such quibbles as that with the dictionary's "piece of ground," for instance, because it excludes the hanging gardens of Babylon (yet they were pieces of ground suspended, like modern roof gardens), or the rejection of the notion of "cultivation of plants" *tout pur* from a definition because moss in Japanese moss gardens is not cultivated; but it is certainly cared for.

17. This, however, Miller erroneously attributes to I. M. Pei. Nor is it clear why the Beinecke courtyard does not fit her definition, since its marble is "natural object."

18. This applies equally to Mara Miller and to another philosopher who published on the garden while I was making the final revisions to this book: Stephanie Ross's *What Gardens Mean*. Both authors strike me as being more concerned with engaging in argumentative quibbles than with understanding garden art. Although Ross rightly argues for the garden as a cultural creation sui generis, she nonetheless undermines her own instincts by laboring to assimilate the garden's procedures to those of other arts (e.g., "a garden can function like a poem"; "functioning like a painting . . . is clearly one among gardens' powers" [pp. 107, 120]). Ross does address issues of representation (see below Chapter 4).

19. Repton, *Fragments on Landscape Gardening and Architecture* (London, 1816), pp. 146, 141–42.

20. Anne van Erp-Houtepen worked on her *scriptie*, or master's dissertation, with me at the University of Leiden in the mid-1980s, and I continue to be grateful to her for the insights that her work gave me. Part of her work was published as "The Etymological Origin of the Garden," *JGH* 6 (1986): 227–31.

21. Xenophon, *Œconomicus*, 4:2–23. The word *paradise* first appears in Middle English in 1175: see Elizabeth B. Moynihan, *Paradise as a Garden: In Persia and Mughal India* (New York, 1979), p. 1.

22. It is a matter of nice theological dispute whether Paradise was

walled before the Fall. As Alastair Fowler has kindly advised me, there is no wall shown in the Flemish tapestry series of the Fall in the Accademia, Florence, nor in the illustration of the Creation in the 1485 German Bible of Johann Reinhard of Groningen. However, Milton's *Paradise Lost* seems to confront Satan with a perimeter wall *before* his Temptation of Eve—"One gate there only was . . . which when the arch-felon saw / Due entrance he disdained, and in contempt, / At one slight bound high over leaped all bound / Of hill or highest wall" (4:178–82). Gates have to be set in walls or hedges; that is clear enough. But the slight vagueness of "*all* bound / Of hill *or* highest wall" suggests some hesitation on the poet's part, as if he were saying that Satan leaped whatever boundary would have been there.

23. Quoted Craig Clunas, *Fruitful Sites* (London, 1996), p. 107.

24. See Moore et al., *The Poetics of the Garden*, p. 198, as for the full quotation later; for plans see pp. 200–202.

25. Among his many other essays on this garden see Wilhelm Diedenhofen's "'Belvedere,' or the Principle of Seeing and Looking in the Gardens of Johan Maurits van Nassau-Siegen," in *The Dutch Garden in the Seventeenth Century*, ed. John Dixon Hunt (Washington, D.C., 1990), pp. 49–80.

26. See particularly the discussion of third nature in the following chapter.

27. William Chambers, writing in all probability with some personal, politically inspired malice, *A Dissertation on Oriental Gardening* (London, 1772), p. v.

28. See Weiss, *Mirrors of Infinity: The French Formal Garden and Seventeenth-Century Aesthetics* (New York, 1995).

29. The perception is that of Bernard Lassus, "Le Paysage comme organization d'un reférent sensible," *Le Débat*, p. 94. See also Ganay, who refers, this time disparagingly, to the "mobilier vegetal," *Coup d'œil*, p. 25. Thomas Whately, *Observations on Modern Gardening* (London, 1770), pp. 136–37, addresses the same issue of how the parterre or immediate garden mediates between the mansion and the landscape beyond.

30. See the narrative of the aboriginal pole, retold below in Chapter 3.

31. See Diedenhofen, "'Belvedere,'" figures 5 (plan), 7, and 13.

32. James L. Wescoat, Jr., "Picturing an Early Mughal Garden," *Asian Art*, 2, no. 4 (1989): 59–79, from which the following remark is also taken. His article should also be read for its discussion of the hazards of interpreting visual imagery of historical gardens.

33. Pope, *Epistle to Burlington* (1733), in *The Genius of the Place*, p. 212.

34. This point has been made emphatically by Tom Williamson in both publications cited in the bibliography.

35. W. C. Pendleton, *History of Tazewell County and Southwest Virginia, 1748–1920* (Richmond, Va., 1920), pp. 169–70. I am grateful to Calder Loth for drawing my attention to this topographical feature and for referring me to Pendleton's account.

36. Malinowski, *Coral Gardens and Their Magic* (London, 1935), 1: xix.
37. Thomas Mann, *Death in Venice* (Harmondsworth, 1955), p. 62. For some consideration of the role of privacy in these unique urban sites, see my article "The Garden in the City of Venice: Epitome of State and Site," *Studies in the History of Gardens and Designed Landscapes*, 19 (1999): 46–61.
38. I stand by this distinction, although David Leatherbarrow's new, as yet unpublished, book, *Building Premises*, which he has kindly allowed me to read in draft, explores notions of building and horizon that would certainly call for refinement of my contrast here.
39. Ross, *What Gardens Mean*, p. 171.
40. See Isamu Noguchi, *The Isamu Noguchi Garden Museum* (New York, 1987). And for Wallace Stevens's "Anecdote of a Jar," see Chapter 8 below.
41. For "A California Scenario," see Lyall, *Designing the Modern Landscape* (London, 1991), pp. 162–63 and 184–89, and Weilacher, *Between Landscape Architecture and Land Art*, pp. 50–51.
42. Perhaps by a process of emulation, the surrounding urban spaces of Costa Mesa have recently spawned a whole variety of new green spaces and gardens, including work by Peter Walker, in the years since Noguchi created "A California Scenario."
43. There are, of course, many paradises to which allusion can be made: "the paradise garden at the beginning of time; the paradise garden at the end of time; the garden reserved for the faithful on the day of judgement; the garden stocked with every form of fulfillment that can be imagined; the earthly paradise that rivals those of Eden and the resurrection; and the earthly gardens that are signs for people of understanding." Thus, James Wescoat, "Picturing an Early Mughal Garden," citing Louis Gardet, "Djanna," *Encyclopedia of Islam*, new ed. (Leiden, 1965), and John MacDonald, "Paradise," *Islamic Studies*, 5 (1966): 331–83.

CHAPTER 3. THE IDEA OF A GARDEN AND THE THREE NATURES

1. I make this point about western attitudes toward garden space in light of similar remarks about the same transformation of Ming sites from orchards to luxury gardens in Craig Clunas, *Fruitful Sites* (London, 1996), p. 80 and seriatim.
2. See Leonard Amico, *Bernard Palissy* (New York, 1996).
3. I was first introduced to this phrase by Alessandro Tagliolini, who later set it out in his *Storia del giardino italiano* (Florence, 1988), pp. 26–28, though without exploring its significance. For a commentary in English and some further reading on this important moment of garden theory, see Claudia Lazzaro, *The Italian Renaissance Garden* (New Haven, 1990). Bernard Lassus also invoked the idea for his collection of conference papers, *Hypothèse pour une troisième nature* (Paris, 1992).

4. This is available in the modern edition of Bonfadio's *Le Lettere*, ed. Aulo Greco (Rome, 1978), pp. 93–98; translations are my own. But I also wish to acknowledge the translation by Rebecca Williamson prepared for my seminar on Renaissance gardens at the University of Pennsylvania, spring semester 1995. I have adapted for the present discussion my essay, "Paragone in Paradise: Translating the Garden," *Comparative Criticism*, 18 (1996): 55–70.
5. Pliny the Younger, book 5, epistle 6. It is available in many versions, but see an eighteenth-century translation printed as appendix 2 in Pierre de la Ruffinière du Prey, *The Villas of Pliny: From Antiquity to Posterity* (Chicago, 1994).
6. This is, incidentally, an extremely important formulation of landscape experience, especially when—as much later in the picturesque phase—so much emphasis was placed on surprise. What was then needed was an explanation of how one could continue to be surprised or involved on subsequent visits to a site. Bonfadio's plausible suggestion is that this occurs throughout the activity by which primary experience is translated into contemplation or "consideration" and then tested again against the site itself on subsequent visits.
7. Taegio, *La villa* (Milan, 1559), p. 66: "The industry of an accomplished gardener, incorporating art with nature, makes of the two together a third nature." For discussions of Taegio, see Bruno Basile, *L'Elisio Effimero: Scrittori in giardino* (Bologna, 1993), chapter 3; Gabriella Anedi, "Il giardino descritto," in *Il giardino depinto* (Milan, 1995), pp. 25–29; and Iris Lautenbach, "The Gardens of the Milanese *Villeggiatura*," in *The Italian Garden*, ed. John Dixon Hunt (Cambridge, 1996), pp. 152–59.
8. Editions of Cicero's *De natura deorum* had appeared in Venice, 1508; Paris, 1511; Leipzig, 1520, and Basel, 1534. An English translation appeared in London in 1683 as *Cicero's Three Books Touching the Nature of the Gods*.
9. Cicero, *De natura deorum* 2.152, my own translation. For a commentary on this crucial passage see C. J. Glacken, *Traces on the Rhodian Shore: Nature and Culture in Western Thought from Ancient Times to the End of the Eighteenth Century* (Berkeley, 1967), pp. 144–49. An introduction to Cicero's book as a whole is available in the Penguin Classics edition (London, 1972).
10. A comparable later exercise in classical "translation" is discussed by Douglas D. C. Chambers, "The Translation of Antiquity: Virgil, Pliny, and the Landscape Garden," *University of Toronto Quarterly*, 60 (1991): 354–73.
11. This is also the term that Simon Schama uses in his approach to a similar aspect of landscape in the third part of *Landscape and Memory* (New York, 1995).
12. I have drawn in this section on a series of essays I wrote during the last ten years, where I explored versions of the idea of the "three natures" set out here. Little has been lifted directly from them for this book, but I am very grateful for the opportunity to have tried out ideas in essay form. In chronological order they were a talk

given to the International IFLA Congress in The Hague, published as "Landscape, the Three Natures, and Landscape Architecture," in *Artivisual Landscapes* (Amsterdam, 1992), pp. 13–18; "Il giardino come territorio delle nature," in *Pensare il giardino*, ed. Paola Capone, Paola Lanzara, and Massimo Venturi Ferriolo (Milan, 1992), pp. 35–39; "The Idea of the Garden, and the Three Natures," in *Zum Naturbegriff der Gegenwart*, ed. Joachim Wilke (Stuttgart-Bad Cannstatt, 1994), 1:305–25; and "Why Garden History?" in *Gartenkunstgeschichte: Festschrift für Dieter Hennebo zum 70. Geburtstag* (Hanover, 1994).

13. See Schama's narrative of these cultural handles on wilderness in his discussion of the Yosemite Valley in *Landscape and Memory*, pp. 7–9; his quotations from John Muir make an interesting comparison with the remarks of Bonfadio examined above.

14. See my study of this problem in respect to French gardens for the French Ministry of the Environment, published as "Des Jardins de France," in *Trois Regards sur le paysage français* (Seyssel, 1993), pp. 215–61. The Japanese concept of *shakkei* (originally called *ikidori*) or borrowed scenery equally requires, for its full appreciation, views beyond the garden proper. On borrowed scenery in the Chinese context, see Stanislaus Fung, "Here and There in *Yuan Ye*," *Studies in the History of Gardens and Designed Landscapes*, 19 (1999): 36–45.

15. See D. Fairchild Ruggles, "The Mirador in Abbasid and Hispano-Umayyad Garden Typology," *Muqarnas: An Annual on Islamic Art and Architecture*, ed. Oleg Grabar (Leiden, 1990), pp. 73–82.

16. See Thierry Mariage, *The World of André Le Nôtre*, trans. Graham Larkin (Philadelphia, 1998), esp. pp. 42ff. My examples are taken from this discussion, but I am also grateful for extra information from Graham Larkin. Claude de Chastillon's *Topographie* was issued in Paris in various editions in 1641, 1648, and 1655.

17. I discussed this fully in an essay, "Il giardino europeo barocco: Più barocco del barocco," in *Il giardino delle muse: Arti e artifici nel barocco europeo*, ed. Maria Adriana Giusti and Alessandro Tagliolini (Florence, 1993), pp. 5–17.

18. Leonard Meager, *The English Gardener* (London, 1670), p. 214.

19. Moses Cook, *The Manner of Raising, Ordering, and Improving Forest and Fruit-Trees* (London, 1679), p. 137.

20. John Evelyn, *Silva*, 4th ed. [London, 1706] (the spelling first changed in this edition from *Sylva*), p. 304 (printed as 204); "Elysium," fol. 169. In his notes for *Sylva*, Evelyn copies André Mollet's remark, "The middle Alley should go out of the Garden Walk, out of sight into the Park," quoted in Douglas Chambers, "'Wild Pastorall Encounter': John Evelyn, John Beale, and the Renegotiation of Pastoral in the Mid-Seventeenth Century," in *Culture and Cultivation* (Leicester, 1992), p. 174.

21. Stephen Switzer, *Ichnographia Rustica* (London, 1718), pp. xxx, xxxvii. Thomas Hamilton also wrote of this general pattern that it had "a Center, Straight Walks from it, Ending on as good Views

as could be had." See Hamilton, *Forest Trees: Some Directions About Raising Forest Trees*, ed. M. L. Anderson (London, 1953), p. 58.

22. Wotton, *Elements of Architecture* (London, 1697), pp. 4–5, a passage Evelyn singles out for praise in his "Elysium Britannicum," fol. 55.

23. David Leatherbarrow, "Character, Geometry, and Perspective: The Third Earl of Shaftesbury's Principles of Garden Design," *JGH*, 4 (1984): esp. pp. 345–46. This topic will be taken up more fully in Chapter 7.

24. Shaftesbury, *Second Characteristics, or the Language of Forms*, ed. Benjamin Rand (London, 1914), respectively, pp. 163 and 14. It is because gardens offer such perspectives, literal and philosophical, that Shaftesbury and others like him considered garden art a moral activity. An interesting parallel to this idea that a garden teaches better understanding of a larger territory was put forward by Friedrich Fröbel, whose *kindergarten* gardens were devised so as to introduce children to the limited "totality" of the vegetable world before exposing them to agrarian materials: see Susan Herrington, "The Garden in Fröbel's Kindergarten," *Studies in the History of Gardens and Designed Landscapes*, 18 (1998): 5.

25. From Shaftesbury's own directions to his gardeners at Wimborne St. Giles, quoted by Leatherbarrow, "Character," p. 356.

26. I discuss this briefly in *The Figure in the Landscape*, pp. 201–4 with illustrations of that discussion.

27. For Bateman, see John Harris, "A Pioneer in Gardening: Dickie Bateman Re-Assessed," *Apollo*, October 1993, pp. 227–33. And for Walpole, see *Visits to Country Seats* (reprinted New York, 1982), p. 44.

28. The nationalistic bias of garden history continues even when new initiatives claim to reject it. Thus the new Parisian park named after André Citroën announced itself as "ni français, ni anglais" (see Figure 72), as if that helped to formulate a valid and strenuous new concept. I take up the need for and the possible shape of a fresh history of landscape architecture in Chapter 8. See also the chapter "Topical Questions in Architecture" in David Leatherbarrow's *The Roots of Architectural Invention* for arguments in favor of topical rather than stylistic discussion. As he says, the latter can come later.

29. See Mark Laird, *The Flowering of the Landscape Garden* (Philadelphia, 1999).

30. See the survey of eighteenth-century gardens by Tom Williamson and Anthea Taigel, *JGH*, 11, nos. 1–2 (1991), with similar arguments repeated in Williamson's *Polite Landscapes* (Baltimore, 1995).

31. All quotations from the short section on "Design in Gardening" in William Hanbury, *A Complete Body of Planting and Gardening* (London, 1770), 1:67–71.

32. Uvedale Price, *Essays on the Picturesque* (London, 1810), 2:148. Laird, *Flowering*, has shown that Brown did indeed do much of what Price credits him with.

33. Thomas Whately, *Observations on Modern Gardening*, p. 256;

see also pp. 137 and 180 where he analyzes the declensions of control across different terrains.

34. Ibid., p. 227.

35. Ibid., pp. 192–93 and 185.

36. Derived no doubt from Addison's similar triad of landscape experiences, William Chambers nevertheless associates them with different handling of ground; his discussion differs slightly in *Designs of Chinese Buildings* (1757) from his *Dissertation on Oriental Gardening* (1772).

37. Nigel Everett, *The Tory View of Landscape* (New Haven, 1994), pp. 116–22, contains a fresh analysis of the picturesque theorists, to which I am much indebted here.

38. These are endlessly reproduced, so I forebear to give further currency to the biased notion of picturesque developments which Everett has so usefully challenged. They are reproduced, among other places, in *The Genius of the Place*, figure 96.

39. William Gilpin, *Three Essays*, p. 45.

40. Quoted in Everett, *Tory View*, p. 185.

41. Other remarks connect the leveling of Brownian designs with the contemporary tendency for "the several ranks of men [to] slide into each other imperceptively." This passage from 1767 is quoted in full by Tom Williamson in *Polite Landscapes*, p. 113.

42. Quoted Everett, *Tory View*, p. 135.

43. Ibid., p. 163.

44. Ibid., p. 181.

45. Ibid., p. 173.

46. This relativism—that gardens did not have to be only regular, geometric, or what today we awkwardly call "formal"—is rarely considered in garden histories. But see Chapter 6 below for some discussion.

47. Hanbury, *Complete Body*, 1:68.

48. *Gardener's Magazine* 4 (1828): 89.

49. It is striking that in both parks Olmsted and Vaux signal one kind of landscape design and experience by its relationship to the others. The regular is represented in Central Park by the Mall and in Prospect Park by the concert garden; each has its pastoral spaces, lawns, and valleys; the Ramble in Central Park and the Ravine in Prospect Park represent the wild.

50. The literature is correspondingly vast: I have by no means read exhaustively, but I have benefited from reading particularly Max Oelschlaeger, *The Idea of Wilderness: From Prehistory to the Age of Ecology* (New Haven, 1991); George H. Williams, *Wilderness and Paradise in Christian Thought* (New York, 1962); and Hans Peter Duerr, *Dreamtime: Concerning the Boundary Between Wilderness and Civilization*, trans. Felicitas Goodman (Oxford, 1985).

51. According to the Blue Guide, *Greece* (6th ed., 1995), Mount Olympus was only successfully climbed by a French naval officer in 1780. Thereafter bandits who infested the region prevented any attempt upon the mountain until 1913 when two Swiss artists as-

cended to the traditional abode of the gods. The range was only mapped in 1921. Either gods or bandits, therefore, effectively kept this to all intents and purposes a realm of first nature until the twentieth century.

52. George H. Williams, *Wilderness and Paradise in Christian Thought*, p. 5; I am grateful to the Rev. Llewellyn P. Smith for this reference.

53. Oelschlaeger, *Idea*, pp. 11 and 29 specifically, though generally throughout his first chapter. Since I write explicitly from the perspective of gardens and place-making, it is difficult to share Oelschlaeger's own enthusiasm for an unhumanized world; but his emphasis on the *historical* construction of the idea of wilderness is well taken, as is his critique of fanatical ecology.

54. Seddon, *Landprints*, pp. 195–96, objecting to arguments advanced by, among others, Oelschlaeger, for the Judeo-Christian "domination" of nature.

55. The songlines by which the original Australian peoples negotiated their "wilderness," because impalpable, leave the wilderness less compromised for others.

56. Bernard Lassus, "Pour une poétique du paysage: Théorie des failles," in *Maitres et protecteurs da la nature*, ed. Alain Roger and François Guery (Paris, 1990), p. 241; now gathered into the translated collection of his writings published in the PSLA, *The Landscape Approach* (Philadelphia, 1998). Lassus's instance of the ocean is a historical revision of an older idea of the wild; a cultural revision might be the Icelander's and the European's very different concepts of the forest.

57. See David Robertson, *Real Matter* (Salt Lake City, 1997).

58. *Sir Gawain and the Green Knight*, trans. Marie Borroff (New York, 1967), p. 16 (lines 740 ff.)

59. See Samuel Holt Monk, *The Sublime: A Study of Critical Theories in Eighteenth-Century England* (1935; reprint, New York, 1960).

60. *Myths from Mesopotamia*, trans. Stephanie Dalley (Oxford, 1989), pp. 59–63, quoted in Oelschlaeger, *Idea of Wilderness*, p. 39.

61. From "Familiarum Rerum Libri," IV,1: see Francesco Petrarca, *Le Familiari*, ed. Ugo Dotti, I/1, pp. 362–77, for the Latin text and an Italian translation; for a French translation and some useful commentary see Petrarch, *L'Ascension du Mont Ventoux*, with introduction by Pierre Dubrunquez (Editions Séquences, n.p., 1990); for an English version see *Rerum familiarum libri I–VIII*, trans. Aldo S. Bernardo (Albany, N.Y., 1975), pp. 172–80. Further references are to these versions. See also Schama, *Landscape and Memory*, pp. 419–21, where the passage is offered as an example of the "tension between physical and metaphysical exertion" rather than as an adjudication of firsthand experience—real or feigned—of landscape.

62. What the French text rather freely renders as "notre désir de passer outre" (p. 31) for the Latin "crescebat ex prohibitione cupiditas" (p. 367).

63. Raymond Williams, *The Country and the City*, new ed. (London, 1985), and John Barrell, *The Dark Side of the Landscape* (Cambridge, 1980).

64. See Andrew H. Malcolm, "How a Parkway Became a Ribbon of Living Beauty," *New York Times* (5 February 1991).

65. *Viewing Olmsted* (Montreal, 1997), p. 100.

66. Geographers similarly distinguish between the biophysical environment (first nature, in my terms) and the historical, culturated landscape (second): see generally the stimulating collection of essays, *The Iconography of Landscape*, ed. Denis Cosgrove and Stephen Daniels (Cambridge, 1988). Hebrew also distinguishes between "sown" and "unsown"; see George Williams, *Wilderness and Paradise*, p. 12.

67. For the rural input, see some suggestive readings by Barbara Stauffacher Solomon, *Green Architecture and the Agrarian Garden* (New York, 1988); for the influence of urban upon villa layouts see Nicholas Purcell, "Town in Country and Country in Town," *Ancient Roman Villa Gardens*, pp. 187-203.

68. Cicero, *On Old Age and on Friendship*, trans. Frank O. Copley (Ann Arbor, 1967), sections 51-60.

69. On terracing see Régis Ambroise, Pierre Frapa, and Sébastien Giorgis, *Paysages de terrasses* (Aix-en-Provence, 1989), and David Bourdon, *Designing the Earth: The Human Impulse to Shape Nature* (New York, 1995).

70. On some interesting parallels in the Chinese Ming period see Clunas, *Fruitful Sites*, pp. 71, 91, 164, and 171.

71. William Mason, *The English Garden*, with commentary and notes by William Burgh (York, 1783), book I, lines 106-13.

72. See Moore et al., *Poetics of Gardens*, p. 30. Such, too, is the significance of the familiar image of the campfire lit by cowboys each evening in the wild.

73. See Aubrey Burl, *Megalithic Brittany* (London, 1985), with a further reading list.

74. See Helaine Silverman, "Beyond the Pampa: The Geoglyphs in the Valleys of Nazca," *National Geographic Research* 6 (1990): 435-56, esp. 453-54. Recent British research in Peru, reported in *The Independent* (29 December 1990), p. 7, puts the lines of Nasca between 200 B.C. and A.D. 600. See also Nigel Pennick and Paul Devereux, *Lines on the Landscape: Leys and Other Linear Enigmas* (London, 1989), and Bourdon, *Designing the Earth*. Contemporary land art, as Bourdon argues, returns in some fashion to these ancient forms, joining the later arts of sculpture and garden design with that of "primitive" markings: on land art see also Weilacher.

75. Bruce Chatwin, *The Songlines* (Harmondsworth, 1988), p. 13; for elaboration on this passage see also pp. 14, 108, 281, and 283.

76. Ibid., pp. 56 and 52.

77. Mircea Eliade, *Le Sacré et le profane* (Paris, 1965), from which the examples that follow are taken. Besides other works by Eliade, see a hefty collection of essays on this theme, *Luoghi sacri e spazi della santità*, ed. Sofia Boesch Gajano and Lucetta Scaraffia (Turin, 1990).

78. This qualification is to guard against the unnecessary exclusion of vernacular examples where the intentions of their creators are neither so explicit nor so articulate as those of professional landscape architects, yet which visitors will wish to acknowledge as prime examples of third nature.

79. See Mara Miller, *The Garden as an Art*, p. 15.

80. George Williams, *Wilderness and Paradise*, p. 99.

81. From Bacon's 1625 essay, "Of Gardens," reprinted in *The Genius of the Place*, p. 51.

82. "[O]ne thing you can depend on in a really 'serious' garden books [*sic*!] is that, somewhere along the way, it will sneak in that quotation from Francis Bacon." James C. Rose, *Gardens Make Me Laugh* (1965; new ed., Baltimore, 1990), p. 1.

83. Daniel Defoe, *Robinson Crusoe* (Harmondsworth, 1965), pp. 78, 157, 185, 92, 115, 184.

84. See Clunas, *Fruitful Sites*, p. 197.

85. An observation I owe to Nancy Ševčenko. The Val d'Orcia reinforces the point that Shaftesbury argued: once we have learned from garden art to appreciate the world outside, it too can seem similarly wonderful.

86. Anthony Littlewood notices the blurred edges of what I am calling second and third nature in descriptions of Byzantine gardens. See his "Gardens of Byzantium," *JGH*, 12 (1992): 126-53. In the eighteenth century Joseph Spence created a similar mingling of natures at his small property at Byfleet. See R. W. King's series of essays on "Joseph Spence of Byfleet," in *Garden History*.

87. See Brenda Bullion, "Early American Farming and Gardening Literature," *JGH*, 12 (1992): 29-51.

88. John Cotton, *A Brief Exposition . . . Upon the whole Book of Canticles* (London, 1642), p. 382; cited by Williams in *Wilderness and Paradise*, p. 106.

89. Bullion, "Early American Farming," p. 31, quoting Jared Eliot on the mulberry. Eliot also thought rows of mulberries regularly planted along country roads make "a very beautiful appearance" and contributed to people's pleasure.

90. See John Prest, *The Garden of Eden* (London, 1981) and M. A. Visentini, *L'Orto botanico di Padova* (Milan, 1984).

91. James L. Wescoat Jr., "Picturing an Early Mughal Garden," *Asian Art*, 2, no. 4 (1989): 72.

92. See J. K. Anderson, *Hunting in the Ancient World* (Berkeley, 1991).

93. See Michael Leslie, "An English Landscape Garden Before 'the English Landscape Garden,'" *JGH*, 13 (1993): 3-15, esp. p. 11.

94. Richard Surflet, trans., *Maison Rustique, or the Countrie Farm* (1600), does distinguish between areas of the garden set aside for pleasure and others earmarked for "the profit of the lord of the manor" (p. 38). That is not to argue that the prospect of profit did

not arouse as much pleasure as a flower garden and that we have lost touch with such coincidences of response.

95. See *The Meaning of Gardens*, p. 38, for this etymology. See *Meaning* also for some striking images: pp. 23 (for the oasis garden) and 39 (for the Sinai enclave in color). A slightly different enclave, but still small and fenced against intrusion, is the alpine valley garden depicted on p. 105.

96. Moore et al., *Poetics of Gardens*, p. 9. On etymology see the discussion in Chapter 2.

97. See Nicholas Lucchetti, "Archaeological Excavations at Bacon's Castle, Surry County, Virginia," in *Earth Patterns: Essays in Landscape Archaeology* (Charlottesville, Va., 1990), pp. 23–42, and Rudy J. Favretti, "Bacon's Castle and the Castle Garden," *Discovery* (1988): 11–15.

98. The owner of Vizcaya considered the charm of its location to be "the jungle effect," which he wanted preserved to the utmost around his gardens. I am grateful to Rebecca Davidson for this remark, which comes from a letter in the Vizcaya archives. See Davidson's "Past as Present: Villa Vizcaya and the 'Italian Garden' in America," *JGH*, 12 (1992): pp. 1–28.

99. Kenneth Helphand, "Defiant Gardens," *JGH*, 17 (1997): 101–21.

100. Many seventeenth-century engravings show this tripartite division. A garden's divisions into three is not, however, to be confused with the "three" natures elaborated here, though there may be some connections via analogy. The tripartite scheme of Moor Park, Hertfordshire, praised by Sir William Temple, clearly was aimed at echoing the larger scale of control that stretched beyond the designed spaces (see Hunt and Willis, *The Genius of the Place*, pp. 97–98).

101. See Ellen Callmann, "A Quattrocento Jigsaw Puzzle," *Burlington Magazine*, 99 (1957): 149–55. On the instinct for hermit life and its rewards, see Peter France, *Hermits* (London, 1996).

102. There is little literature available on this attractive and impressive design (well maintained, too); it does not even appear in William C. Mulligan's *Complete [sic] Guide to North American Gardens*, vol. 1, *The Northeast* (Boston, 1991). But see a brief entry in Marina Harrison and Lucy D. Rosenfeld, *Garden Walks* (New York, 1997), pp. 57–59, who nevertheless give a wholly inadequate impression by labeling it "formal."

103. These are much reproduced, but see, most usefully, Daniela Mignani, *Le Ville Medicee di Giusto Utens* (Florence, 1980), where they are all well illustrated.

104. See below in Chapter 4 where the gardens' references to the other natures via representation and allusion are discussed in more detail.

105. See Millard Meiss, *Giovanni Bellini's St. Francis in the Frick Collection* (Princeton, N.J., 1964). Meiss notes that its "landscape is composed of three quite distinct parts," but then describes these in conventional and formal terms ("cool blue-green foreground," etc.). See also John V. Fleming, *From Bonaventura to Bellini: An Essay in Franciscan Exegesis* (Princeton, N.J., 1982). While not concerned to read the landscape in terms of its intricate mingling of the spaces and ideas of the three natures, Fleming places emphasis (p. 81) on the power of Bellini's "synthetic imagination."

106. Such focus occupies much of Fleming's commentary: see, for instance, p. 160: "Only in local and topographic terms—if then insistently—is the desert La Verna. The Franciscan desert is the uncharted spiritual wilderness of the Pentateuch and the Psalms, of Cassian and the Carmelites, the desert of the religious life. Bellini's eremetic images, and particularly his desert fauna, are commonplace emblems of the monastic tradition."

107. Something that we would expect from an inhabitant of the Veneto, where considerations of land use had been much pondered and refined: for this see Denis Cosgrove, *The Palladian Landscape* (University Park, Pa., 1993).

108. Fleming, *From Bonaventura*, p. 89.

CHAPTER 4. REPRESENTATION

1. Craig Clunas, *Fruitful Sites* (London, 1996), pp. 102 and 177.

2. See ibid., pp. 60 and 62.

3. On the Hanging Gardens see Peter Clayton and Martin Price, eds., *The Seven Wonders of the Ancient World* (London, 1988), pp. 42–46; also Jan Pieper, "Die Natur der Hängenden Gärten: The Nature of Hanging Gardens," *Daedalus* 23 (1987): 94–109.

4. In this chapter I draw mainly on two of my previously published essays: "Imitation, Representation, and the Study of Garden Art," in *The Art of Interpreting*, ed. Susan C. Scott, Papers in Art History from the Pennsylvania State University 9 (1995): 199–215, and "La Représentation dans l'art du jardin," in *Hypothèse pour une troisième nature*, ed. Bernard Lassus (Paris, 1992), pp. 65–79. Stephanie Ross addresses the subject of representation in *What Gardens Mean*, but only as part of her exploration of analogies between the arts.

5. *Critical Terms for Literary Studies*, ed. Frank Lentricchia and Thomas McLaughlin (Chicago, 1990), pp. 11–22. See also the entry on "Representation" by David Summers in *Critical Terms in Art History*, ed. Robert S. Nelson and Richard Shiff (Chicago, 1996), pp. 3–16.

6. Summers is useful on the difficulties of the term. A taxonomy of the meanings and perspectives that the term has acquired is unnecessary here, but its range may be gathered from such a triad as Richard Wollheim, *Painting as an Art* (Princeton, 1987), which explains representation as seeing in a garden, say, an image of a whole elsewhere; Nelson Goodman, *The Languages of Art* (Indianapolis, 1976), who thinks anything can represent anything provided there is agreement about it; or Kendall Walton, *Mimesis as Make-Believe*

7. Svetlana Alpers, "Interpretation Without Representation, or the Viewing of *Las Meninas*," *Representations*, 1 (1983): 1–42.

8. See Mitchell in *Critical Terms for Literary Study*, p. 13, and Summers, *Critical Terms in Art History*, p. 12.

9. Quoted from the English translation of Foucault, *The Order of Things* (London, 1970), pp. xv–xxiv and 58–67.

10. In this respect see the famous essay by Monroe C. Beardsley and W. K. Wimsatt, Jr., "The Intentional Fallacy," *Sewanee Review*, 54 (1946): 468–88.

11. This is taken from Reynolds's thirteenth discourse to students of the Royal Academy.

12. A useful comparison, based on a similar argument, could be drawn from Louis Marin, *Détruire la Peinture* (Paris, 1979), p. 61: the "invisibility" of a painting's surface, or our missing its painterly texture, is a condition both of the visibility of the world represented and of our [mis]apprehension of it as "real" or "natural."

13. William Chambers, introduction to *A Dissertation on Oriental Gardening* (London, 1772). It must be acknowledged that Chambers was also motivated by some personal and political animus toward Brown.

14. The same point is made to distinguish building from architecture by Karsten Harries, *The Ethical Function of Architecture* (Cambridge, Mass., 1997), e.g., pp. 118, 121, and 123.

15. Quoted, e.g., by Dorothy Stroud, *Capability Brown*, rev. ed. (London, 1957), p. 198.

16. See Karsten Harries, *Ethical Function*, p. 128.

17. Joseph Addison, *Spectator*, no. 414 (25 June 1712).

18. The first is Quatremère de Quincy's, writing about architectural imitation, quoted by Sylvia Lavin, *Quatremère de Quincy and the Invention of a Modern Language of Architecture* (Cambridge, Mass., 1992), p. 104. The second is from Leatherbarrow, *The Roots of Architectural Invention*, pp. 89 and 215. Stephanie Ross, *What Gardens Mean*, p. 181, also sees the garden as "fictionally projecting a world [that] is neither true nor false."

19. This is Stephanie Ross's observation, *What Gardens Mean*, p. 199.

20. Keith Moxey, *The Practice of Theory: Poststructuralism, Cultural Politics, and Art History* (Ithaca, N.Y., 1994), p. 30.

21. Both claims are made, mistakenly in my view, by Stephanie Ross, *What Gardens Mean*, pp. 93 and 180.

22. See Summers, *Critical Terms*, p. 8.

23. However, in studies of Islamic landscape architecture and in the analysis of even the high art of André Le Nôtre, the debts of garden art to larger territorial management have been clearly identified. For the latter see work by Thierry Mariage and Chandra Mukerji; for the former see *Il giardino islamico*, ed. Attilio Petruccioli (Milan, 1994), and *Mughal Gardens*, ed. James L. Wescoat, Jr., and Joachim Wolschke-Bulmahn (Washington, D.C., 1996).

24. It was, of course, Thorstein Veblen's account of the origin of the lawn that it clarified or abstracted the common field or meadow: see *Theory of the Leisure Class* (1891; New York, 1981), pp. 134–35. See also David Ingersoll, "In the Garden of Even: Visual Grounds," *JGH*, 14 (1994): 55–62.

25. Sometimes considered the "first garden theorist of the Netherlands," van der Voort (1664–1739) was a Leiden cloth merchant and amateur who based his work on firsthand experience of his own country estate of Allemansgeest (today called Berbice) at Voorschoten. His work was published in Dutch (Amsterdam, 1763), in German, and in French (Paris, 1750), from which latter edition this quotation comes, p. 8.

26. Evelyn, "Elysium Britannicum," folio 138; Boyceau, *Traité du jardinage* (Paris, 1638), p. 80.

27. Clunas, *Fruitful Sites*, p. 172.

28. I owe this perception to John Hollander's "Instructions to the Landscaper," reprinted in my *Oxford Book of Garden Verse*, p. 287.

29. See figures 2 and 3 in Vanessa Bezemers-Sellers, "The Bentinck Garden at Sorgvliet," in *The Dutch Garden in the Seventeenth Century*, ed. John Dixon Hunt (Washington, D.C., 1990).

30. Clunas, *Fruitful Sites*, p. 172.

31. David Coffin, in *The Villa d'Este at Tivoli* (Princeton, N.J., 1960), quotes from the manuscript description of the Fountain of Tivoli at the Villa d'Este that "it represents the mountain and rivers of the countryside of Tivoli" (p. 85), while the water of the Fountain of Rome at the opposite end of the Hundred Fountains Walk "represents the sea" (p. 87).

32. John Raymond, *Il Mercurio Italico* (London, 1648), p. 170.

33. John Worlidge, *Systema Agriculturae* (London, 1669), D1v; Worlidge is, in fact, writing of town gardens.

34. John Evelyn, *Acetaria*, folio a4r.

35. See Harries, *Ethical Function*, pp. 111–14, and Joseph Rykwert, *On Adam's House in Paradise: The Idea of the Primitive Hut in Architectural History* (New York, 1972), p. 192.

36. John Prest, *The Garden of Eden* (London, 1981), to which excellent study I am much indebted in this section, drawing from him in particular the example of Parkinson's title page.

37. John Evelyn, *Diary*, ed. E. S. de Beer (Oxford, 1955), vol. 2.

38. John Worlidge, *Systema Horti-culturae* (London, 1677), p. 3.

39. Evelyn, "Elysium Britannicum," folios 132 and 187.

40. Thomas Tenison, *Baconiana* (London, 1679), p. 57; David Masson, *Life of Milton* (London, 1881), 4:350.

41. Evelyn, "Elysium Britannicum," folio 138, writing of hydraulic devices.

42. Thomas Fuller, *Gnomologia: Adages and Proverbs, Wise Sentences and Witty Sayings, Ancient and Modern, Foreign and British* (London, 1732), no. 701. A similar argument is advanced for Ming gardens: see Clunas, *Fruitful Sites*, pp. 69 and 200–202.

43. For this and much more on how the Villa d'Este glorified and

represented its owner, see Coffin, *Villa d'Este*, and Lazzaro, *The Italian Renaissance Garden*, chap. 9.

44. See those discussed in John Beardsley, *Gardens of Revelation: Environments by Visionary Artists* (New York, 1995).

45. However, see the much more sympathetic discussion of representation in architecture (especially in chap. 8) in Harries, *Ethical Function of Architecture*. See also Dalibor Vesely, "Architecture and the Conflict of Representation," *AA Files*, 8 (1985): 21-38. For an argument on behalf of music's representational scope, see Peter Kivy, *Sound and Semblance: Reflections of Musical Representation* (Princeton, 1984).

46. That owner-designers think differently is clear from such a work as Derek Jarman, *Derek Jarman's Garden* (London, 1995).

47. "Williams Square," *Landscape Architecture*, 75 (1985): 64-67; David Dillon, "Williams Square: Where Public Space Becomes Public Art," *Southern Accents*, 12, no. 6 (1989): 176B-J.

48. See Brent Elliott, *Victorian Gardens* (London, 1986), plate 77.

49. The relevant section of the poem is reprinted in the *Oxford Book of Garden Verse*, pp. 58-61.

50. See Mark Laird, *The Flowering of the Landscape Garden*.

51. See Repton, *The Landscape Gardening and Landscape Architecture of the Late Humphry Repton*, p. 530, for text and illustration.

52. See *Samuel Hartlib and Universal Reformation*, p. 360. For a fuller commentary on this remark, see below Chapter 6.

53. See Clunas, *Fruitful Sites*, p. 75.

54. George Mason, *Essay on Design* (London, 1758), p. 7.

55. Quoted by C. P. Barbier, *William Gilpin: His Drawings, Teaching, and the Theory of the Picturesque* (Oxford, 1963), p. 42.

56. I am invoking here the distinctions made by semioticians: icon, symbol, index. Mere mimesis—imitation like that at Las Collinas—pulls too strongly toward resemblance, or the iconic, whereas reformulated or abstracted imagery—Halprin's Portland fountains—is indexical. See Mitchell, *Critical Terms for Literary Study*, p. 14.

57. Leatherbarrow, *Roots*, p. 215. Cf. also Harries, *Ethical Function*, p. 120.

58. There is as yet little literature on the design of these: but for brief gazetteer details see Michel Racine, *Jardins de France* (Arles, 1997), pp. 198 (Bercy) and 201-2 (Citroën). For Citroën, see an illustrated report in *Topos*, 2 (1993): 76-79.

59. Again, I rely on Prest, *The Garden of Eden*.

60. See Martha Schwartz, *Transfiguration of the Commonplace* (Washington, D.C., and Cambridge, Mass., 1997).

61. William Hanbury, *A Complete Body of Planting and Gardening*, p. 70.

62. I discuss this theme at more length in *Gardens and the Picturesque* (Cambridge, Mass., 1992), pp. 106-22.

63. "The knowledge of producing in some place the most agreeable aspect that the site is capable of representing": Alexandre Laborde, *Descriptions des nouveaux jardins de la France et de ses anciens châteaux* (Paris, 1808), p. 51.

64. Abbé Delille, *The Garden; or, The Art of Laying Out Grounds*, translated by (?) Anthony Powell (London, 1789), 3:61. The attribution of the translation to Powell, gardener to George II and author of *The Royal Gardener . . .* (London, 1769), is based on the manuscript annotation of "par Wm [*sic*] Powell" on the title page of the copy at the Oak Spring Garden Library Foundation, Upperville, Virginia.

65. I owe this distinction to J. Hillis Miller, *The Linguistic Moment* (Princeton, 1985), p. 6.

66. Dézaillier d'Argenville, *Theory and Practice*, pp. 15-16.

67. Robert Castell, *The Villas of the Ancients Illustrated*, pp. 116-17.

68. See Judith Major, *To Live in the New World: A. J. Downing and American Landscape Gardening* (Cambridge, Mass., 1997).

CHAPTER 5. WORD AND IMAGE IN THE GARDEN

1. The Latin reads: HIC JACET PARVULUM QUODDAM EX AQUA LONGIORE EXCERPTUM—"Here lies a small excerpt of a [piece of] water from a larger one." It is also cited in Finlay's own garden at Little Sparta. The Max Planck version is illustrated as Figure 77 here.

2. See J. William Thompson, "Power of Place," *Landscape Architecture*, 87 (July 1997), pp. 63-71, 90; also Lawrence Halprin, *The Franklin Delano Roosevelt Memorial* (San Francisco, 1997).

3. See Udo Weilacher, *Between Landscape Architecture and Land Art*, p. 155 and (for another verbal railing) p. 149.

4. See, of course, the claims for wordage in Robert Venturi, Denise Scott Brown, and Steven Izenour, *Learning from Las Vegas: The Forgotten Symbolism of Architectural Form* (Cambridge, Mass., 1977).

5. See John Angeline, "Gardens Are for People: Gilbert Boyer and 'The Urban Project,'" *JGH*, 16 (1996): 298-309. And see Figure 82 below.

6. See *Places of Commemoration: Search for Identity and Landscape Design*, ed. Joachim Wolschke-Bulmahn (Washington, D.C., forthcoming).

7. Much used by the Romantics, especially Wordsworth: see Geoffrey Hartman's essays on inscriptions and genius loci in *Beyond Formalism: Literary Essays, 1958-70* (New Haven, 1970), and my own brief discussion of this rhetorical effect in "'Come into the Garden, Maud': Garden Art as a Privileged Mode of Commemoration and Identity" in *Places of Commemoration*, ed. Wolschke-Bulmahn.

8. Karsten Harries, for example, examines the linguistic turn sympathetically, but in the end rejects it as an effective means of creating architectural ethos: *Ethical Function*, esp. chaps. 1 and 5. See also Evelina Calvi, *Tempo e progetto: L'architettura come narrazione* (Milan, 1991).

9. This is the starting point for Paul Ricoeur's "Architecture and Narrative," from which I quote here: in *Identity and Difference* (Milan, 1996), p. 64. I owe much in the following discussion to

Ricoeur's stimulating essay, so I thank David Leatherbarrow and Marina Lathouri for drawing it to my attention.

10. See Pierre Nora, ed., *Les Lieux de mémoire*, 3 vols. (Paris, 1992). For a brief overview in English, see Nora's essay, "Between Memory and History: *Les Lieux de mémoire*," *Representations*, 26 (1989): 7–25.

11. See, notably Monique Mosser and Philippe Nys, eds., *Le Jardin, art, et lieu de mémoire* (Besançon, 1995), and Lucius Burckardt, "La memoria, come renderla visibile?" *Eden*, 2 (1993): 47–51.

12. It is this latter activity, discussed again and more fully in Chapter 8 below, that makes me nervous of Karsten Harries's insistence on the *intention* or *assertions* of verbal communication (*Ethical Function*, pp. 83, 88, and 89); for much of the verbal activity here located in gardens has neither of these deliberated motives, but is rather derived by the visitors from the experience of a site.

13. Sometimes moral injunction can be slipped in under the guise of pragmatic advice: the labels in an imaginary botanical garden described by Erasmus in *The Godly Feast* also have ethical injunctions: see *The Colloquies of Erasmus*, ed. Craig R. Thomson (Chicago, 1965), pp. 50–55, 76–78.

14. See David R. Coffin, "The *Lex Hortorum* and Access to Gardens of Latinum During the Renaissance," *JGH*, 12 (1982): 201–32.

15. See George Clarke, *Descriptions of Lord Cobham's Gardens at Stowe, 1699–1750*, Buckinghamshire Record Society, no. 26 (1990); Gilbert West's poem of 1731 (pp. 36–51) is still something of an insider's perspective and its verses often fail to name names, leaving this to be done by explanatory footnotes.

16. For Rousham, see my "Verbal versus Visual Meanings in Garden History: The Case of Rousham," in *Garden History: Issues, Approaches, Methods*, ed. John Dixon Hunt (Washington, D.C., 1992), esp. pp. 165–67.

17. Cao Xuegin, *The Story of the Stone*, trans. David Hawkes, 5 vols. (Harmondsworth, 1973), 1:324–25. See also Robert E. Harris, Jr., "Site Names and Their Meanings in the Garden of Solitary Enjoyment," *JGH*, 13 (1993): 199–212.

18. Louis XIV, *Manière de montrer les jardins de Versailles*, with an introduction and commentary by Simone Hoog (Paris, 1992).

19. Stephen Jay Gould, "So Near and So Far," *New York Review of Books* (20 October 1994), p. 26.

20. John Raymond, *Il Mercurio Italico: An Itinerary Contayning a Voyage, Made Through Italy, in the Yeare 1646, and 1647* (London, 1648), p. 78.

21. There is no opportunity here to explore what one might call the ekphrastic potential of gardens, but recent discussions of what have been defined as "verbal representations of a visual representation" are germane to this analysis. See the special issue of *Word & Image* (1999) devoted to ekphrasis. A consideration of this literature, especially of how ekphrasis "translates" another experience, would have benefited Stephanie Ross in *What Gardens Mean*, where consider-

able energies are devoted to examining the similarities of gardens to paintings and poems (chaps. 3–5). Ross's determination to see gardens as "just the same" as poems (pp. 55 and 59) and then as being able to ape painterly forms and subjects (pp. 100ff.) is overzealous, and this works especially against her better instinct to see gardens as being sui generis (p. 89).

22. There is an absurd predilection among gardenists to favor "circuits" around gardens where, supposedly, "a carefully ordered sequence of monuments, scenes, and vistas" is encountered: e.g., Stephanie Ross, *What Gardens Mean*, pp. 51 and 85. Are there, in fact, any sites where such a circuit is both prescribed and unavoidable, where casual and random exploration will not only be possible but will thereby frustrate narrative sequence?

23. Karsten Harries's analysis and final rejection of literary supplements in architecture is a useful analog here.

24. From Wallace Stevens's poem "An Ordinary Evening in New Haven."

25. Tom Wolfe, *The Painted Word* (New York, 1975), p. 60.

26. Quoted Erwin Panofsky, *Perspective as Symbolic Form* (New York, 1991), p. 41.

27. Hartmut Böhme, *Die Natur sprechen lassen*, an exhibition catalog for the Kulturstiftung Stormarn, *Projekt: Schürberg* (Hamburg, 1989).

28. This is one of the themes of *The Environmental Imagination*, Lawrence Buell's inquiry into environmental (or what he does not want to call nature) writing. It is a common motive of all environmentalists to tell us what nature means or "says."

29. See Patricia Deiters, *Een paviljoen in Arcadie: Geschiedenis van de Follie*, part of *Follies voor de Floriade* (Rotterdam, 1989).

30. The best analysis of this is Malcolm Kelsall, "The Iconography of Stourhead," *Journal of the Warburg and Courtauld Institutes*, 46 (1984): 133–43.

31. *Pilgrim at Tinker Creek* (New York, 1974), p. 83, quoted by Lawrence Buell, *The Environmental Imagination*, pp. 73–74.

32. See my discussions of this in *Gardens and the Picturesque*, especially chaps. 6 and 7.

33. Repton, *Landscape Gardening*, pp. 228 note and 365, respectively.

34. See, for instance, the fresh perspectives on the values of arcadian scenery offered by Jim Crace's novel *Arcadia* (London, 1992) or Tom Stoppard's play *Arcadia* (London, 1993).

35. See Anne Linden Helmreich, "Contested Grounds: Garden Painting and the Invention of National Identity in England, 1880–1914," Ph.D. diss., Northwestern University, 1994; and my own essay on Impressionist gardens and their influence in *Gardens and the Picturesque*, chap. 9.

36. *Collected Works of Edgar Allen Poe*, ed. T. O. Mabbott, III (Cambridge, Mass., 1978), pp. 1266–86—an early version of "The Domaine of Arnheim" (1847) was entitled "The Landscape Garden" (1842). Suzi Gablik, *Magritte* (Greenwich, Conn., 1970), figures 63 and 64.

37. See Dorothée Imbert, *The Modernist Garden in France* (New Haven, 1993).

38. Marc Treib, "Axioms for a Modern Landscape Architecture," in *Modern Landscape Architecture: A Critical Review*, ed. Marc Treib (Cambridge, Mass., 1993).

39. See Weilacher, *Between Landscape Architecture and Land Art*, p. 222. See also Peter Walker's own book, *Minimalist Gardens* (Washington, D.C., 1997).

40. See Weilacher, *Between Landscape Architecture and Land Art*, pp. 231 and 237. As far as I know, Geuze does not himself explicitly invoke Mondrian, who was (of course) also Dutch.

41. Ibid., p. 93.

42. Stephanie Ross, *What Gardens Mean*, p. 103.

43. On this see George Clarke, "Grecian Taste and Gothic Virtue: Lord Cobham's Gardening Programme and Its Iconography," *Apollo*, 97 (1973): 566–71, and my *Garden and Grove*, pp. 208–9.

44. Marc Treib, "Frame, Moment, and Sequence: The Photographic Book and the Designed Landscape," *JGH*, 15 (1995): 127, writing of different attitudes toward montage in early Russian filmmaking.

45. See bibliography for various volumes with photographic imagery by Geoffrey James.

46. Maurice Merleau-Ponty, "Eye and Mind," in *The Primacy of Perception and Other Essays*, ed. James M. Edie (Evanston, Ill., 1964), p. 162.

47. Richard Morris, *Essays* (London, 1825), p. 13; he also remarks that it is "of the utmost consequence that the entire design should be seen as with a painter's eye" (p. 21).

48. William Gilpin, *A Dialogue upon the Gardens . . . at Stowe*, introduced by John Dixon Hunt, Augustan Reprint Society, publ. no. 176 (Los Angeles, 1976), pp. 11–12.

49. See Michel Baridon's analysis of spatial expectations, "Les Mots, les images, et la mémoire des jardins," in *Le Jardin, art, et lieu de mémoire*, pp. 183–203; some of this same material is also available, and with reference to pictures, in his English essay, "The Scientific Imagination and the Baroque Garden," *JGH*, 18 (1998). Further, see Hamilton Hazlehurst's analysis of Le Nôtre's design in perspectival terms in *Gardens of Illusion: The Genius of André Le Nostre* (Nashville, 1980).

50. Sven-Ingvar Andersson, quoted in Weilacher, *Between Landscape Architecture and Land Art*, p. 165.

51. See *Richard Haag: Bloedel Reserve and Gas Works Park*, ed. William S. Saunders (New York and Cambridge, Mass., 1998). For Latz see Weilacher, *Between*, pp. 121–36; and *Landscape Transformed* (London, 1996), pp. 54–61; for Lassus see *The Landscape Approach* (Philadelphia, 1998).

52. See Charles Jencks, *The Architecture of the Jumping Universe* (London, 1995), esp. illustrations on pp. 51 and 54.

53. Joseph Spence, *Observations, Anecdotes, and Characters of Books and Men*, ed. James M. Osborn (Oxford, 1966), 1:253.

54. I am particularly conscious here of the graphic work of two Penn colleagues, James Corner and Anu Mathur: see James Corner and Alex S. MacLean, *Taking Measures Across the American Landscape* (New Haven, 1996), and Anuradha Mathur, "Recovering Ground: The Shifting Landscape of Dacca," in *Landscape Transformed* (London, 1996), notably the figures on pp. 84, 86–87.

CHAPTER 6. GARDENS IN WORD AND IMAGE

1. Craig Clunas, *Fruitful Sites*, p. 137.

2. See Michel Foucault, quoted by Clunas, *Fruitful Sites*, on "practices that systematically create the objects of which they speak."

3. If society is a "battlefield of representations," as T. J. Clark claims in *The Painting of Modern Life: Paris in the Art of Manet and His Followers* (Princeton, N.J., 1984), p. 6, then the garden is an important part of that topography, about which society's ideas and images will yield valuable insight. We might also recall here Clunas's remarks quoted above at the start of Chapter 4 on the garden as a "site of contested meanings," subject to the "pull of a number of discursive fields."

4. The following discussion is illustrated with a selection of images. But the range of reference that is needed cannot be readily accommodated by figures here. Therefore, the reader is advised that I have largely based my discussion on imagery that is available in a series of books and catalogs with an adequate range of examples. In order of publication, they are *Garten und Park*, catalog of exhibition in the Akademie der Bildenden Kunste (Vienna, 1964); John Harris, *The Artist and the Country House* (New Haven, 1979 and 1985); Bryan Holme, *The Enchanted Garden: Images of Delight* (London, 1982); Yves Perillon et al., *Images de Jardins Gardens Images [sic]* (Paris, 1987); Mac Griswold, *Pleasures of the Garden: Images from the Metropolitan Museum of Art* (New York, 1987); Anthony Huxley, *The Painted Garden: The Garden Through the Artist's Eye* (London, 1988); Virginia Tuttle Clayton, *Gardens on Paper: Prints and Drawings, 1200–1900*, an exhibition catalog from the National Gallery (Washington, D.C., 1990); *Il giardino depinto nella pittura lombarda dal seicento all'ottocento*, an exhibition catalog from the Villa Reale di Monza (Milan, 1995); John Harris, *The Artist and the Country House: From the Fifteenth Century to the Present Day*, an exhibition catalog for Sotheby's (London, 1995); Erik de Jong and Marleen Dominicus-Van Soest, eds., *Aardse Paradijzen*, the catalog of an exhibition of Dutch garden paintings from the fifteenth to eighteenth centuries (Haarlem, 1996).

5. Harris 1996, p. 6; see this exhibition catalog for some striking contemporary country house portraiture.

6. Laird has drawn extensively on visual materials to document his history of plants and planting, which is particularly useful in its avoidance of the stereotyped histories of the English garden: see *The Flowering of the Landscape Garden*. Anthony Huxley's concern

in *The Painted Garden* is also largely to identify, where possible, the plantings, but he is particularly mechanical with appeals to formal and informal history. See esp. pp. 10, 40, 60, 148, and—for some positivism—80 ("as it was"); see also Holme, *The Enchanted Garden*, p. 52.

7. Robert Burley et al., *Viewing Olmsted* (Montreal, 1996), p. 25.

8. Quoted in Marc Treib, "Frame, Moment and Sequence: The Photographic Book and the Designed Landscape," *JGH* 15 (1995): 133. Treib, however, goes on to write of that moment's "inherent deception" (p. 134).

9. See Phyllis Lambert's prologue to *Viewing Olmsted*, p. 7, and compare Geoffrey James's insistence upon the "mnemonic power" of photography, "a power to recall things, which painting doesn't have" (ibid., p. 100). On this theme see Treib, "Frame."

10. See Maggie Keswick, *The Chinese Garden* (New York, 1978).

11. *Satirical Poems by William Mason with Notes by Horace Walpole*, ed. Paget Toynbee (Oxford, 1926), p. 43.

12. This becomes clear if different images in Perillon's *Images de Jardins* are contrasted: those that offer "fine graphic" articulation of gardens as they might look when established (p. 130) versus those more conceptual renderings—collagic, surrealistic, digital (pp. 124–28).

13. Thomas Whately, *Observations on Modern Gardening* (London, 1770), p. 252.

14. See Dorothée Imbert, *The Modernist Garden in France*, fig. 5.7.

15. There are fascinating sequences of views of Heemstede, of a Dutch garden created near Moscow, and of a silk merchant's property near Haarlem, all illustrated in Jong and Dominicus-Van Soest, eds., *Aardse Paradijzen*, pp. 56, 103, and 104–5.

16. Giovanni Antonio Veneroni's portraits of Montalto Pavese are fine examples of this strategy (see *Il giardino depinto*, cat. 14–15 and 17), as are some anonymous views of wonderful English flower gardens (see Harris 1996, cat. 12 [unidentified house] and 21 [Newburgh Priory]). For Dutch instances at Spruytenburg or Huis ten Bosch, see *Aardse Paradijzen*, pp. 47 and 92.

17. Reproduced in Huxley, *Painted Garden*, p. 11.

18. Marilyn Stokested, "The Garden as Art," in *Mediaeval Gardens*, ed. Elisabeth Blair MacDougall (Washington, D.C., 1986), p. 182; see images in Clayton, *Gardens on Paper*, pp. 22 and 23.

19. See Huxley, *Painted Garden*, pp. 147 and 149. I do not think this effect is wholly linkable to the beaux arts tradition "with its canonical progression through contrasting space" (*Viewing Olmsted*, p. 11), for it is a longer-standing element of garden space.

20. For a recent survey of painted Roman gardens, see Ann L. Kuttner, "Looking Outside Inside: Ancient Roman Garden Rooms," *Studies in the History of Gardens and Designed Landscapes*, 19 (1999), 7–35. Livia's garden room is illustrated in Huxley, *Painted Garden*, p. 23.

21. See Harris 1996, cat. 124–26, 127 (inside the triptych), 130–31, 143–44.

22. Harris 1996, cat. 39, 86, and 74.

23. Jong and Dominicus-Van Soest, *Aardse Paradijzen*, pp. 128–29, among other examples.

24. Harris 1996, cat. 81.

25. See Perillon, *Images de Jardins*, p. 97, Griswold, *Pleasures of the Garden*, p. 115, and Huxley, *Painted Garden*, p. 107.

26. See my *Gardens and the Picturesque*, chap. 9; and for some literary equivalents see the essay by Michel Conan, "'*Puer aeternus*' in the Garden," *Studies in the History of Gardens and Designed Landscapes* 19 (1999): 86–101.

27. Respectively, *Images*, p. 117, and Huxley, *Painted Garden*, p. 109.

28. Harris 1996, cat. 18 and 117.

29. Ibid., cat. 115 and 133.

30. For this insight see Michel Baridon, "Les Mots, les images, et la mémoire des jardins," in *Le Jardin, art, et lieu de mémoire*, p. 192.

31. *John Constable's Correspondence*, ed. R. B. Beckett (Ipswich, 1962–68), 2:132 and 4:254.

32. Respectively, Harris 1979, cat. 194; Harris 1996, cat. 35 and 25; cat. 88 also features the roller, obviously a more painterly device than the later lawnmower.

33. Jong and Dominicus-Van Soest, *Aardse Paradijzen*, pp. 150, 139, and 114 (among many other examples in this catalog).

34. See John Harris, *Gardens of Delight: The Rococo English Landscape of Thomas Robins the Elder*, 2 vols. (London, 1978). Mark Laird's study of *The Flowering of the Landscape Garden* has drawn upon a considerable number of other images showing not only flower gardens but their gardeners as well. I have borrowed one example for Figure 25 here.

35. Griswold, *Pleasures of the Garden*, p. 135; Clayton, *Gardens on Paper*, cat. 94.

36. See Griswold, *Pleasures of the Garden*, p. 110; Huxley, *Painted Garden*, p. 123.

37. See Hunt, *Gardens and the Picturesque*, chap. 2.

38. See the relevant illustrations in Stefan Kozakiewicz, *Bernardo Bellotto*, 2 vols. (Greenwich, Conn., 1972).

39. Harris 1996, cat. 70; *Il giardino depinto*, cat. 76.

40. Monet's *The Bench*, c. 1873, illustrated in Joel Isaacson, *Claude Monet: Observation and Reflection* (Oxford, 1978), fig. 50.

41. *Il giardino depinto*, cat. 87, for a striking image of a lonely woman. The literary evidence for social transgression in conservatories is striking: see Michael Waters, "The Conservatory in Victorian Literature," *JGH*, 2 (1982): 273–84. For Manet's *In the Greenhouse*, 1879, see *A Day in the Country: Impressionism and the French Landscape*, ed. Andrea P. A. Belloli (New York, 1984), p. 213.

42. Harris 1996, cat. 139.

43. Michel Conan, writing in *Images de Jardins*, p. 17.

44. Jong and Dominicus-Van Soest, *Aardse Paradijzen*, pp. 143–47.

45. Harris 1996, cat. 117, 120–21, among many examples.

46. Jong and Dominicus-Van Soest, *Aardse Paradijzen*, cat. 84; Griswold, *Pleasures of the Garden*, p. 57.

47. Michel Conan, "Nature into Art: Gardens and Landscapes in the Everyday Life of Ancient Rome," *JGH*, 6 (1986): 348–56, esp. p. 354. See also Wilhelmina Jashemski, *The Gardens of Pompeii*, 2 vols. (New Rochelle, N.Y., 1979 and 1993).

48. Respectively, Huxley, *Painted Garden*, pp. 69 (Palmer) and 111 (Rousseau); Holme, *Enchanted Garden*, p. 94 (Matisse) and pp. 90–91 (Beatrix Potter), or Huxley, *Painted Garden*, p. 89 (*Cats playing in a garden*).

49. Jong and Dominicus-Van Soest, *Aardse Paradijzen*, pp. 23 and 132, among others; for Rowlandson, Ronald Paulson, *Rowlandson: A New Interpretation* (London, 1972), figure 14.

50. Clayton, *Gardens on Paper*, pp. 48 and 69.

51. Ibid., cat. 16 and 33.

52. Jong and Dominicus-Van Soest, *Aardse Paradijzen*, p. 197.

53. See my *Oxford Book of Garden Verse* (Oxford, 1993), from which some examples, mainly modern, will be taken. Other collections, devoted exclusively or in part to poetry, are Denis Wood, *Poets in the Garden* (London, 1978); Bernard and Renée Kayser, *L'Amour des jardins célebré par les écrivains* (Paris, 1986); *A Treasury of Garden Verse*, ed. Margaret Elphinstone (Edinburgh, 1990); *Cent Poètes côté jardin*, ed. Daniel Gelin (Paris, 1990); Roy Strong, *A Celebration of Gardens* (London, 1991); John Hollander, ed., *Garden Poems* (New York, 1996); Anne Marie Fröhlich, ed., *Garten: Texte aus der Weltliteratur* (Zurich, 1993); David Wheeler, ed., *The Penguin Book of Garden Writing* (New York, 1997).

54. Hunt, *Oxford Book of Garden Verse*, pp. 245 and 293.

55. Ibid., pp. 193, admittedly invoking the Caserta gardens, or 319, the myriad mosses of a Japanese garden.

56. Ibid., p. 217.

57. Treib, "Must Landscapes Mean? Approaches to Significance in Recent Landscape Architecture," *LJ*, 14, no. 1 (1995): 46–62.

58. The point is made by Augustin Berque, *Etre Humains*, pp. 99 and 101.

59. Hecht, "The Gardens of the Villa d'Este," in Hunt, *Oxford Book of Garden Verse*, p. 270.

60. Heidegger, "The Origin of the Work of Art," in *Poetry, Language, Thought* (New York, 1971), p. 49. Also quoted by Harries, *Ethical Function*, p. 159.

61. Hunt, *Oxford Book of Garden Verse*, p. 311.

62. Ibid., pp. 268, 310, 281, and 175.

63. Ibid., p. 232.

64. William Cowper, *Poetry and Prose*, selected by Brian Spiller (London, 1968), p. 795.

65. The resources of the novel have even been tapped by historians like Pierre and Denise Le Dantec for sections of their *Le Roman du jardin français* (Paris, 1987), a title that lost its challenging appeal to the novel as a record of gardens when it was Englished as *Reading the French Garden* (Cambridge, Mass., 1988).

66. John Banville, *Ghosts* (London, 1993), p. 110.

67. Humphrey Carpenter's classic study of nineteenth- and early twentieth-century children's fiction is, properly, entitled *Secret Gardens* (London, 1985). See also various garden poems about children: Hunt, *Oxford Book of Garden Verse*, pp. 273 and 293.

68. For Proust see Michel Conan, " 'Puer aeternus' in the Garden."

69. Reprinted in Hunt and Willis, *The Genius of the Place*, pp. 277–78.

70. Olivier de Serres, *Le Théâtre d'agriculture et mesnage des champs* (Arles, 1996), p. 736.

71. See, among other analyses, Eva Maria Neumeyer, "The Landscape Garden as a Symbol in Rousseau, Goethe, and Flaubert," *Journal of the History of Ideas*, 8 (1947): 187–97.

72. Rousseau, *Nouvelle Héloïse*, part 4, letter 11, written in the first person by the former lover. I have used the Garnier edition (Paris, 1960). On the significance of this and for further readings on Rousseau's garden, see Susan Taylor-Leduc, "Luxury in the Garden: *La Nouvelle Héloïse* Reconsidered," *Studies in the History of Gardens and Designed Landscapes*, 19 (1999): 74–85.

73. Finlay, *Nature over Again After Poussin* (Glasgow, 1980), p. 22.

74. *The Works of Sir Thomas Browne*, ed. Sir Geoffrey Keynes, 4 vols. (London, 1964), 4:275.

75. I've read it in French: Karel Capek, *L'Année du jardinier* (La Tour d'Aigues, 1997).

76. Hubert Damisch, *Skyline: La ville narcisse* (Paris, 1996), pp. 164–85.

77. See George, Sacheverell, Osbert, and Edith Sitwell, *Hortus Sitwellianus* (London, 1984), where the text (originally published in 1909 without illustration except for a wonderful art deco cover) is reprinted and occasionally illustrated. It is not a piece of writing that lends itself to economical quotation; the effect is accumulative.

78. See below Chapter 8.

79. See my essay, "Ekphrasis of Gardens," *Interfaces* (Université de Bourgogne), 5 (1994): 61–74, for a fuller typology of garden ekphrasis; also the special issue on ekphrasis of *Word & Image* has some relevant materials.

80. Whately's *Observations on Modern Gardening* (1770) was subtitled "Illustrated by descriptions," that is, verbal descriptions; only in a later edition of 1801 were engravings of gardens added. However, Whately's eighteen ekphrastic insertions (totaling 84 pages out of the total 257) do not simply perform the function of absent illustrations.

CHAPTER 7. HISTORICAL EXCURSUS: LATE SEVENTEENTH-CENTURY GARDEN THEORY

1. See Thomas Sprat, *History of the Royal Society of London* (1667). Modern commentary includes Charles Webster, *The Great Instauration: Science, Medicine, and Reform* (London, 1975) and Michael Hunter, *Science and Society in Restoration England* (Cambridge,

1981) and Michael Hunter, *Science and the Shape of Orthodoxy: Intellectual Change in Late Seventeenth-Century Britain* (Woodbridge, 1995), which incorporates his essay "John Evelyn in the 1650s: A Virtuoso in Quest of a Role," published subsequently in *John Evelyn's "Elysium Britannicum" and European Gardening*, ed. Therese O'Malley and Joachim Wolschke-Bulmahn (Washington, D.C., 1998). This volume offers a useful introduction to the whole garden world around John Evelyn.

2. See Michael Leslie et al., eds., *The Hartlib Papers on CD-ROM* (Ann Arbor, 1996).

3. Cited by Michael Hunter in *Evelyn's "Elysium,"* p. 104.

4. References in the text (here, fol. 4) are given by folio number. For the sake of easier reading I have silently incorporated Evelyn's corrections and insertions as transcribed by John Ingram, to whose work on this manuscript I am once again much indebted. Full indications of Evelyn's revisions, etc., will be incorporated in the edition by John Ingram to be published by the University of Pennsylvania Press in the PSLA series.

5. On this aspect of what elements of the "Elysium Britannicum" may have been issued, see Frances Harris, "The Manuscripts of John Evelyn's 'Elysium Britannicum,'" *Garden History* 25, no. 2 (1997): 131–37.

6. This chapter rescinds, combines, and revises three essays I have written over the past ten years and separately published: "Hortulan affairs," in *Samuel Hartlib and Universal Reformation: Studies in Intellectual Communication*, ed. Mark Greengrass, Michael Leslie and Timothy Raylor (Cambridge, 1994)—this volume should be consulted for further information and discussion of Hartlib himself; "Evelyn's Idea of the Garden: A Theory for All Seasons," in *John Evelyn . . . and European Gardening*, ed. O'Malley and Wolschke-Bulmahn (Washington, D.C., 1998), pp. 269–88; and "'Gard'ning Can Speak Proper English,'" in *Culture and Cultivation in Early Modern England: Writing and the Land*, ed. Michael Leslie and Timothy Raylor (Leicester, 1992), pp. 195–222.

7. A transcript of this letter (Sheffield Hartlib MS 87/22/1A) was published as an appendix to Greengrass et al., *Samuel Hartlib*; all further unidentified references in the text are to this source. The letter has previously been discussed by Peter Goodchild, "'No Phantasticall Utopia, but a Real Place': John Evelyn, John Beale, and Backbury Hill, Herefordshire," *Garden History* 19 (1991): 106–27.

8. Beale's outlines of his two proposed books on gardening (Sheffield Hartlib MS 26/6) are printed as appendixes to Leslie and Raylor, *Culture and Cultivation*.

9. Sheffield Hartlib MS 52/72b.

10. See Chapter 3, note 7.

11. Hartlib, *Legacie*, 1655 edition, p. 9. Since Hartlib makes few of the distinctions between kinds of gardening that are routine nowadays, these "ingenuities" are not giocchi d'acqua, terraces, and so on but "cabbages, colleflowers . . . at that time great rarities" (ibid.).

12. When Evelyn incorporates Beale's classical instance into "Elysium Britannicum," he augments it explicitly to include biblical resonances (fol. 56).

13. I am grateful to Michael Leslie for this fact—see "The Spiritual Husbandry of John Beale" in *Culture and Cultivation*, p. 164.

14. Hartlib, *Discourse for Division*, 1653, p. 10. Dymock had, as was usual in the Hartlib circle, communicated his ideas to Hartlib in an undated letter, now among the Hartlib papers at Sheffield, 62/29, and it is from this source that I take my quotations.

15. Ibid., p. 21. For another proposal for house, gardens, orchards, and working estate set out on similar principles to those of Dymock/Hartlib, see John Smith, *England's Improvement Reviv'd* (London, 1673). A recent attempt to extrapolate ground plans from Smith's descriptions makes the point graphically—see Peter Goodchild, "John Smith's Paradise and Theatre of Nature: The Plans," *Garden History* 25 (1997): 28–44, but esp. Figure 1.

16. Beale, *Herefordshire Orchards* (London, 1724), p. 28.

17. Leslie and Raylor, *Culture and Cultivation*, p. 230.

18. Ibid.

19. Goodchild's arguments in this vein are echoed by Timothy Mowl, "New Science, Old Order: The Gardens of the Great Rebellion," *JGH*, 13, nos. 1–2 (1993): 16–35.

20. When Evelyn transcribed Beale's passage into his "Elysium Britannicum," he added a passage precisely on the "addition" to Beale's landscape of various "Artificiall decorations" (see fols. 57–58). Beale would later acknowledge to Evelyn his relativist position, not wishing to regulate every garden in England by the Backbury model (see note 68).

21. See above Chapter 4, esp. note 4, and David Leatherbarrow's article on Shaftesbury.

22. I am referring to the witty and complex parable of art and nature in James's short story, "The Real Thing," published first in 1892. Beale refers to the accidents or "luckiness of situation" and the need to respect a "reall, & lofty hill" over an imitation mount (fol. 1B).

23. Beale, *Herefordshire Orchards*, p. 28: emphasis added.

24. Leslie and Raylor, *Culture and Cultivation*, p. 229.

25. Ibid., p. 227 ("To double the Sun rayes; Howe to lengthen our Autumne, And to praeoccupate our spring").

26. Philip Miller, *The Gardeners Dictionary*, vol. 2 (1739), see under "Wilderness."

27. Evelyn, *Sylva*, new 3d ed., 1679, fol. A2 verso.

28. Evelyn, *Acetaria* (1699), A3 recto. In his copy of the fourth edition of Evelyn's *Silva*, now at the Oak Spring Garden Library, Upperville, Virginia, Peter Collinson noted in a margin, "No credit to Monkish Stories" (p. 219).

29. *The Diary of John Evelyn . . . to Which Are Added a Selection from His Familiar Letters*, ed. William Bray, revised by Henry B. Wheatley, 4 vols. (1879), I:224–26, and E. S. de Beer, *Diary of John Evelyn* (Oxford, 1955), III:222 note.

30. Evelyn, *Sculptura*, A5 recto-b1 verso.

31. Arthur Ponsonby, *John Evelyn* (London, 1933), p. 269.

32. Evelyn, *Acetaria*, preface.

33. Hunter in *Evelyn's "Elysium,"* p. 8. In his address "To the Reader" of *Sylva*, Evelyn opposes "the Real Effects of the Experimental, Collecting, Examining, and Improving their scatter'd Phaenomena's" to the "Notional, and Formal way of delivering divers Systems and Bodies of Philosophy (falsely so call'd)": *Sylva*, 3d ed. (London, 1679), A1 verso.

34. "Elysium Britannicum," fol. 38, insertion. For example: he may acknowledge "the ultimate design etc" as when he writes: "The Earth does generally lye in beds, or couches *stratum super stratum*, in divers thicknesses; but for the most part, next to the surface, it is a foote thick, in some places deeper, more or lesse, which is ever the mould the most prolific, and naturaly endow'd for production of *Plants* as having bin temper'd and prepar'd by the activity, qualities, and operations of all those *principles* which we have before discoursed of; and so, from one degree to another, all the rest of the successive and subjacent beds." Yet at this point he cannot resist the urge to catalog varieties: "The usual sorts of mould are the pulla, alba, Topacea, rubrica, columbina" (fol. 23).

35. On the importance of case studies for English garden history see Michel Baridon, "Ruins as Mental Construct," *JGH* 5 (1985): 84–96.

36. "Elysium Britannicum," fol. 256, speaking of minute insects, in fact.

37. See what even his old friend, Thomas Henshaw, wrote of the translation of Nicolas de Bonnefons's *French Gardiner*, that it had taken Evelyn away from "Studies of a higher and nobler nature" (cited by Hunter in *Evelyn's "Elysium,"* p. 27).

38. "Elysium Britannicum," fol. 1. See also "as near as we can contrive [our Gardens] to the resemblance of that blessed abode [Paradise . . . of Gods own planting]," in *Kalendarium Hortense*, 7th ed. (London, 1683), p. 9.

39. Prest's subtitle is *The Botanic Garden and the Re-Creation of Paradise* (New Haven, 1981).

40. John Aubrey's garden investigations offer a comparable case, where he and indeed we may often forget his underlying concern to track the "Italian way of gardening" through countless local examples and memoranda (Bodleian Library, Aubrey MS 2, fol. 53 recto).

41. For discussions of the close connections and parallels between gardens and cabinets, see Erik de Jong, "Nature and Art: The Leiden Hortus as 'Musaeum,'" in *The Authentic Garden*, ed. L. Tjon Sie Fat and Erik de Jong (Leiden, 1991), pp. 37–60, and John Dixon Hunt, "'Curiosities to Adorn Cabinets and Gardens,'" in *The Origins of Museums* (Oxford, 1985), pp. 193–203.

42. See his remarks on Spenser, fol. 58; see also fols. 7 and 10. It is worth remarking that the references to Spenser and Sidney are added by Evelyn to the lengthy description sent him by John Beale.

43. As Hunter claims in *Evelyn's "Elysium,"* p. 104.

44. "[T]o the end that there may be nothing defective to accomplish this Argument & render it universal" (fol. 122).

45. See his remark, discussed below, that it is possible to create artificial echoes for gardens which, lacking real ones, are otherwise perfect (fol. 168).

46. "To the Reader," in *Silva*, 4th ed. (1706), **3 recto. The spelling of *Sylva* was changed to *Silva* in this edition.

47. On this larger theme, see Joseph Levine, "John Evelyn: Between the Ancients and the Moderns," in *John Evelyn's "Elysium Britannicum" and European Gardening*, ed. O'Malley and Wolschke-Bulmahn, pp. 57–78, and my own discussion there, pp. 274–76.

48. In this context it is worth recalling that Clarence J. Glacken, *Traces on the Rhodian Shore* (Berkeley, 1967), stresses the modernity of Evelyn's forestry ideas, which he says are "based on a philosophy of man's relation to his surroundings" (p. 490).

49. To which the "Elysium Britannicum" refers on fol. 154.

50. Edward Wright, *Some Observations Made in Travelling Through France, Italy . . .*, 2 vols. (1730), 1:vii.

51. See Pope's 1713 essay in *The Guardian*, reprinted in *The Genius of the Place: The English Landscape Garden, 1620–1820*, ed. John Dixon Hunt and Peter Willis (rev. ed., Cambridge, Mass., 1988), p. 206.

52. Evelyn clearly implies that his translations are also interpretations. See Geoffrey Keynes, *John Evelyn: A Study in Bibliophily, with a Bibliography of His Writings* (London, 1968), pp. 166 and 224, as well as Edmund Waller's prefatory poem to Evelyn's translation, *An Essay on the First Book of T. Lucretius* (1656).

53. Quoted by Douglas Chambers in "The Tomb in the Landscape: John Evelyn's Garden at Albury," *JGH*, 1 (1981): 37–54, and also John Dixon Hunt, *Garden and Grove: The Italian Renaissance Garden in the English Imagination, 1600–1750* (London, 1986), pp. 148–53. For Evelyn's recently discovered design for Albury, see Michael Charlesworth's note on this drawing in the appendix to *John Evelyn's "Elysium Britannicum" and European Gardening*, ed. O'Malley and Wolschke-Bulmahn, pp. 289–93.

54. William Wotton, *Reflections upon Ancient and Modern Learning*, 2d ed. (London, 1697), pp. 290–307.

55. Ibid., p. 303. See also Wotton's remark that the ancients did not know how to bring the "Sun under Rules (if I may use so bold an Expression) . . . which yet, by their Wall-Plantations, our Gardeners do every Day" (p. 305).

56. *Evelyn Letters*, 4:12.

57. *3 verso. And in the preface to *The English Vineyard*, added to the second edition of *The French Gardiner* (1669), Evelyn mocks French gardenists "new come over, who think we are as much oblig'd to follow their mode of gardening as we do of their garments" (A6 recto).

58. This predilection is ably diagnosed in the second edition of William Chambers's *Dissertation on Oriental Gardening* (London, 1772).

59. See Goodchild, "'No Phantastical Utopia,'" and Mowl, "New Science."

60. For a contemporary discussion of artistic imitation of an action, see John Dryden's "Parallel of Poetry and Painting," prefaced to his translation of Du Fresnoy's *De arte graphica* (London, 1695), in *The Works of John Dryden* (Berkeley, 1989), 20: 38-77. Beale's proposal for "Entertainments" in gardens (see note 73) was explained in terms of performances that enact or represent the best elements of gardens.

61. John Rea, *Flora* (London, 1665), p. 1.

62. See Evelyn's comparable observation of the diversity of ground, "both artificial and naturall" at the royal botanical gardens in Paris: see above Chapter 4, note 37. Boyceau's account of grottoes, from which Evelyn borrows (see Chapter 4, note 22), notes that they may either be carved in the "natural rock" or "expressly built" elsewhere (Boyceau, *Traité*, p. 80).

63. "Elysium Britannicum," fol. 168. That this was not simply a curiosity of the time or of Evelyn's is suggested by the allusion to the later construction of an echo on the grounds of David Meade in Kentucky—see James D. Kornwolf, "David Meade II: Pioneer of *le jardin anglais* in the United States, 1774-1829," *JGH*, 16 (1996): 265.

64. Maggie Keswick, *The Chinese Garden*, p. 34.

65. Evelyn, *Acetaria*, a4 recto.

66. John Worlidge, *Systema Agriculturae*, fol. D1 verso: he is, in fact, writing of town gardens.

67. Quoted by Douglas Chambers in "'Wild Pastorall Encounter': John Evelyn, John Beale, and the Renegotiation of Pastoral in the Mid-Seventeenth Century," in *Culture and Cultivation*, p. 174. Italics are mine.

68. Ibid., p. 165. No longer is Beale proposing that a Herefordshire scheme be the "pattern for all England," as the title of his 1657 publication had claimed.

69. Beale's references to Causaubon are somewhat approximate; see, in effect, Causaubon, pp. 61-62 and 68. That Beale was both glancing at and concealing his own "ecstacy" and prophetic dreams on Backbury Hill is clear from the letter quoted by Michael Leslie, *Culture and Cultivation*, pp. 165-66.

70. At the same time, painted images drew attention to representation in garden art with a more conventional example of this activity. In his "Elysium" (fol. 55) Evelyn praised Sir Henry Wotton's discussion of prospect or "royalty of the eye" that feeds "extent and variety" (cited in full above, Chapter 3). Evelyn himself, not surprisingly, owned a finely bound copy, designed for him by Abraham Bosse, of Jean Dubreuil, *La Perspective pratique*, 3 vols. (Paris, 1649-51), in which gardens are discussed in the first volume, published in 1642 and revised 1651.

71. H. V. S. Ogden, "The Principles of Variety and Contrast in Seventeenth-Century Aesthetics, and Milton's Poetry," *Journal of the History of Ideas* 10 (1949): 159-82.

72. From an "Appendix of Architecture . . ." in Christopher Wren, *Parentalia* (1750), p. 351. I am grateful to C. Allan Brown for drawing my attention to this passage.

73. The outlines of Beale's books (Sheffield Hartlib MS 25/6/1A-4B) are usefully printed in *Culture and Cultivation*, ed. Leslie and Raylor, pp. 226-30; the remark quoted, p. 229.

74. Stephen Switzer, *Ichnographia Rustica*, 3 vols. (London, 1718), 1:59. Switzer's work was first published in one volume as *The Nobleman, Gentleman, and Gardener's Recreation* (London, 1715).

75. Ibid., 1:87, emphasis added. See my discussion of this incident in *Gardens and the Picturesque*, pp. 33-37.

76. The words, in fact, of John Lawrence, *Gardening Improv'd* (London, 1718), but exemplified by Switzer's proposal for Paston Manor (Grimsthorpe).

77. Switzer, *Ichnographia Rustica*, pp. 1:xviii-xix.

78. Worlidge, *Dictionarum Rusticum, Urbanicum, and Botanicum*, 2d ed., "revised, corrected and improved," under "Garden," fols. G3 recto to G4 recto.

79. Timothy Nourse, *Campania Foelix* (London, 1700), in the section called "An Essay of a Country-House," pp. 322 and 299.

80. On this topic see Andrew McRae in both his Cambridge University Ph.D. thesis, parts of which I was able to read before its submission, and in his essay "Husbandry Manuals and the Language of Agrarian Improvement," in *Culture and Cultivation*, ed. Leslie and Raylor, pp. 35-62.

81. In Sheffield Hartlib MS 62/29, fol. 1A, Dymock says that his thoughts on the subject of better husbandry "I freely present to my Natyve Countrye."

82. Anthony Lawrence and John Beale, *Nurseries, Orchards, Profitable Gardens, and Vineyards Encouraged* (London, 1677), pp. 18 and 1, respectively.

83. Horticulture being, as the "Elysium Britannicum" put it (fol. 1), the "noblest part of Agriculture."

84. This point is well made by Timothy Mowl, "New Science." Its relevance to our own day and age is significant.

CHAPTER 8. TOWARD A NEW HISTORIOGRAPHY AND NEW PRACTICES

1. On the social and psychological influence of metaphor and on how metaphors rule our lives, see the readings listed by Lawrence Buell, *The Environmental Imagination* (Cambridge, Mass., 1995), p. 427, note 8.

2. An examination of picturesque traditions and their continuing if unconscious or uncritical life in current landscape architectural practice in New Zealand is a rare example of this understanding and might serve as a model for further explorations. See Jacky Bowring, "Institutionalizing the Picturesque," Ph.D. diss., Lincoln University, 1997.

3. Dézaillier d'Argenville, *The Theory and Practice of Gardening*, trans. John James (London, 1712), folio A2r.

4. Walpole probably wrote this essay during the 1750s and 1760s. Revised in 1770, it first appeared as part of his four-volume *Anecdotes of Painting in England* (printed 1771, published 1780 and in a second edition of 1782); it appeared as a bilingual English/French edition separately in 1785. The critical edition of Walpole's essay is *Horace Walpole, Gardenist: An Edition of Walpole's "The History of the Modern Taste in Gardening,"* ed. I. W. U. Chase (Princeton, N.J., 1943); but see also the Ursus Press edition, with an introduction by the present writer (New York, 1995).

5. *The Meaning of Gardens*, pp. 72–74.

6. I have discussed these in more detail in "Writing the English Garden: Horace Walpole and the Historiography of Landscape Architecture," *Interfaces*, 4 (1993): 163–80.

7. Switzer's single volume of *Nobleman* of 1715 was expanded into three in 1718, set in larger type and retitled *Ichnographia Rustica*; the text of Switzer's "History" is the same in both versions and I cite the later one here from vol. 1, pp. 1–97.

8. The phrase comes from Walpole's annotations to Mason: see *Satirical Poems by William Mason with Notes by Horace Walpole*, ed. Paget Toynbee (Oxford, 1926), p. 43. As noted above in note 4, Walpole's essay on garden history was originally part of his large survey of British painting, so it is perhaps inevitable that he would have emphasized their connections.

9. Lisle's *Observations in Husbandry* is a compilation of practical hints, often culled from earlier sources, on the conduct of the kitchen garden and the "orchard and fruit-garden." There is no sense that the latter belong to a series of gradations in garden art, as is implied constantly by Beale, Hartlib, and those writers on gardening and husbandry that I have examined, including Pierre Le Lorrain de Vallemont, *Curiosities of Nature and Art in Husbandry and Gardening* (London, 1707), pp. 3, 9, and 17.

10. See Quentin Skinner, "History and Ideology in the English Revolution," *Historical Journal*, 8 (1965): 151–78, especially his remark that "the most ideologically acceptable use of the historical information was also the least historically accurate" (pp. 176–77).

11. Stoppard, *Arcadia* (London, 1993), p. 12.

12. *Horace Walpole's Correspondence*, ed. W. S. Lewis et al., 48 vols. (New Haven, later Oxford, 1947 et seq.), 35:125–26.

13. See, for example, the entry on the Trianon in the *Oxford Companion to Gardens*, ed. Geoffrey Jellicoe et al. (Oxford, 1986), 588, or Christopher Thacker, *The History of Gardens* (London, 1979), 157.

14. A whole section of colored plates or "Cahier thématique" is devoted to Gabriel Thouin (1747–1829) in Michel Conan, *Dictionnaire historique de l'art des jardins* (Paris, 1997), between pp. 216 and 217; he further analyzes Thouin's work in a paper, "The Coming of Age of the Bourgeois Garden," read at the University of Pennsylvania symposium "Tradition and Innovation in French Garden Art," March 1998.

15. Ernest de Ganay's fully achieved, two-volume manuscript lies, unpublished and largely neglected, in the library of the Musée des Arts Décoratifs in Paris. It was consulted by Dora Wiebenson, *The Picturesque Garden in France* (Princeton, N.J., 1978).

16. See the Duc d'Harcourt's *Traité de la décoration des dehors, des jardins, et des parcs* (Paris, c. 1775). I am grateful to Ramla Ben-Aissa for this reference.

17. André Vera quoted by Dorothée Imbert, *The Modernist Garden in France* (New Haven, 1993), p. 53.

18. For Hirschfeld see Linda Parshall's article "C. C. L. Hirschfeld's Concept of the Garden in the German Enlightenment," *JGH* 13 (1993): 125–71, and her forthcoming translation and abridgement of Hirschfeld's five-volume *Theorie der Gartenkunst*, to be published by the University of Pennsylvania Press in the PSLA. Jean-Marie Morel's *Théorie des jardins* was published in Paris in one volume in 1776, with a second volume added in 1802; for advice on Morel, I am grateful to Joseph Disponzio. Laborde's *Descriptions des nouveaux jardins de la France* was issued in Paris in 1808; its letterpress essay on country life was issued separately in smaller format as *Discours sur la vie de la campagne* (Paris, 1808).

19. This is one of the major arguments and insights of Judith Major's *To Live in the New World* (1997).

20. I took this Italian segment of the post-Walpolian history somewhat further in a paper on "Translating the English Garden," read to a symposium at the British School of Rome on "Villas and Gardens, England and Italy," May 1998. Pindemonte's essay, "Dissertazione su i giardini inglesi e sul merito in ciò dell'Italia," was delivered as a lecture in 1792, then published in a collection of such lectures, *Operette di vari autori intorno ai giardini inglesi ossia moderni* (Verona, 1817), and eventually gathered into Pindemonte's *Prose e poesia campestri* (1823). A modern text is available in Bruno Basile, *L'Elisio Effimero*.

21. "The true art of gardening appears to me to be the means of producing, in whatever place you choose, the most pleasant aspect that the site is capable of representing": Laborde, *Descriptions*, p. 51, his italics.

22. For an Australian example of this, see George Seddon, *Landprints*, p. 91, and for a lengthier review of the dead weight of picturesque terminology on later New Zealand landscape architecture, see Bowring, "Institutionalizing the Picturesque."

23. Look, for instance, at the opening of Christopher Thacker's *History of Gardens*, widely read in many languages: "No doubt about it. The first gardens were not made, but discovered. A natural spot —a clearing in the forest, a valley opening up in a barren mountainside, an island in a remote lake. . . . No one tends this garden: it grows of its own accord" (p. 9).

24. What is so shocking, in a way, is that we have failed to listen to the rare voice raised in protest. A wonderful essay to which Michel Conan has drawn my attention in the collections at Dumbarton Oaks, an anonymous *Lettre sur les jardins anglois* (1775), wittily if

subtly argues for the altarity of styles. A similar essay—a mere sketch of an alternative history—is C. Th. Sørensen, *Havekunstens Oprindelse: The Origins of Garden Art* (Copenhagen, 1963), which I came across in the final stages of this book.

25. Charles-Joseph, Prince de Ligne, *Coup d'œil at Beloeil and a Great Number of European Gardens*, trans. Basil Gray (Berkeley, 1991), p. 72. This wonderful survey and meditation on gardens was first written in 1781, with subsequent versions until 1795.

26. There is no space here even to start that. But see my essay, "The Garden as Cultural Object," in *Denatured Visions: Landscape and Culture in the Twentieth Century*, ed. Stuart Wrede and William Howard Adams (New York, 1991).

27. Summers, in *Critical Terms in Art History* (Chicago, 1996), p. 13.

28. Ibid., p. 3.

29. Raymond Williams, "Nature," in his *Keywords: A Vocabulary of Culture and Society* (New York, 1976), but see also Williams, *The Country and the City* (new ed., London, 1985), and John Barrell, *The Dark Side of the Landscape* (Cambridge, 1980).

30. *The Works of John Dryden*, 20:57.

31. On Les Buttes-Chaumont, see Antoine Grumbach, "The Promenades of Paris," *Oppositions*, 10 (1977): 60–61.

32. It is not as if we haven't been told this before. Henry Vincent Hubbard and Theodora Kimball, *An Introduction to the Study of Landscape Design* (New York, 1917), wrote that "the two categories [formal, informal] have been the innocent cause of so much discussion and misapprehension" (pp. 33–34).

33. See Quentin Skinner, "Meaning and Understanding in the History of Ideas," *History and Theory*, 8 (1969): 3–53.

34. See my "Repton in Garden History," *JGH*, 17 (1997): 215–24.

35. As does Allen S. Weiss, *Mirrors of Infinity* (New York, 1995).

36. See the useful work on this in Craig Clunas, *Fruitful Sites* (London, 1995), esp. pp. 51 and 55.

37. See the forthcoming essay by Michel Conan in a Dumbarton Oaks volume on garden historiography, as well as his earlier argument in favor of the study of vernacular gardens, "The *Hortillonages*: Reflections on a Vanishing Gardeners' Culture," in *The Vernacular Garden*, ed. John Dixon Hunt and Joachim Wolschke-Bulmahn (Washington, D.C., 1993), 19–46. See also, among other recent studies of this essential dimension of garden making, Gert Gröning and Joachim Wolschke-Bulmahn, *Studien zur Frankfurter Geschichte . . . Ein Jahrhundert Kleingartenkultur in Frankfurt am Main* (Frankfurt am Main, 1995); *Cent Ans d'histoire des jardins ouvriers*, ed. Beatrice Cabedoce and Philippe Pierson (Grane, 1996); and Françoise Dubost, *Les Jardins ordinaires* (Paris, and Montreal, 1997; first published in 1984 as *Côté Jardins*).

38. In this respect compare Augustin Berque's questioning of modernism's attitudes toward landscape, *Etre Humains*, esp. pp. 17–26 and 46–55.

39. In a special double issue of *Journal of Garden History*, 11, nos. 1

and 2 (1991), and *Polite Landscapes* (Baltimore, 1995). See also Tom Williamson, *The Archaeology of the Landscape Park* (Oxford, 1988).

40. See Mark Laird, *The Flowering of the Landscape Garden: English Pleasure Grounds, 1720–1800*.

41. Letter to the author (16 September 1980) commenting on a draft editorial for the inaugural issue of the *JGH*, on whose advisory board Battisti had agreed to serve. Prior to the launch of the journal he had also sent a list of nine topics that he wanted to see explored. Some were very precise (hydraulics, computerized system of basic elements of design), but others, I now realize, were far-sighted projections of where garden study needed to go and have affinities with what I am belatedly trying to urge in this book. Battisti's topics included proper study of nineteenth-century gardens; the relation of gardening to farming ("rural economy and activity"); and documentary studies of gardens in literature, painting, movies and documentary films, advertising—with a view especially to studying "the symbolism of the garden, as an independent problem of the iconography of the garden, that is, the garden in itself, as an abstract model" (letter of 13 June 1980).

42. These terms I have derived from the French geographer, Augustin Berque: see his *Médiance: De Milieux en paysages* (Montpellier, 1990), and *Etre Humains*.

43. See Repton, *The Landscape Gardening and Landscape Architecture of the Late Humphry Repton*, trans. Loudon (London, 1840).

44. I refer to its derivation from the Dutch *landschap*, signifying a painted representation of some territory; but the involvement of painting as a model for especially landscape gardening, above all at the point when our current historiography was being determined, has also played its role in this dualistic labeling. See, for example, both William Shenstone's "I have used the word landscape gardener; because in pursuance to our present taste in gardening, every good painter of landscape appears to me the most proper designer" ("Unconnected Thoughts on Gardening," in *The Works*, 2 vols. [London, 1764], 2:129), and A. J. Downing's "Again and again has it been said, that Landscape Gardening and Painting are allied" (*A Treatise on the Theory and Practice of Landscape Gardening*, 4th ed. [New York, 1850], p. 72).

45. See, for instance, the wording used by David R. Coffin in introducing the studies that formed the first Dumbarton Oaks colloquium publication: "The literary historian of pastoral poetry, the scholar of landscape painting, and the architectural historian concerned with the villa realize that the garden is essential *to their interests*": *The Italian Garden* (Washington, D.C., 1972), p. viii, with emphasis added.

46. Clunas, *Fruitful Sites*, pp. 102 and (for the following phrase) 177.

47. Berque, *Etre Humains*, p. 12, signaling a chasm or abyss of inquiry into the particular nature of humans.

48. By Rosetta E. Clarkson (New York, 1940)—the example of this title is mine, not Elkins's, who is generally very sympathetic

to what a less careful analyst merely called a "squishy" reaction to garden matters: see Denis Wood, "*Culture naturale:* Some Words about Gardening," *LJ*, 11, no. 1 (1992): 58.

49. Elkins, "On the Conceptual Analysis of Gardens," *JGH*, 13 (1993): 189–98. An anxiety of excessive response has always lurked among gardenists: compare Elkins's remarks with Sir Henry Wotton's aside in *The Elements of Architecture* (London, 1624), that he will not describe his experience of some "incomparable [Italian] garden" because that would be "poetical" (pp. 109–10).

50. Martin R. Dean, "Nature as a Book—A Book as Nature," *JGH*, 17 (1997): 173. This passage recalls remarks by Louis Carrogis, called Carmontelle, about another Parisian garden, Monceau: in his 1779 publication he famously calls it a "pays d'illusions" where the visitor would encounter "tous les temps et tous les lieux" (p. 4).

51. The phrases are Elkins's: "On the Conceptual Analysis," p. 189. His essay remains a refreshingly clear and sharp diagnosis of the nature of gardens and what writing about gardens might address.

52. See in this respect the arguments of Michel Conan at the conclusion of "The Conundrum of Le Nôtre's *Labyrinthe*," in *Garden History: Issues, Approaches, Methods*, ed. John Dixon Hunt (Washington, D.C., 1992), 145–50.

53. Paul Ricoeur calls this "reader, the protagonist forgotten by structuralism," in "Architecture and Narrative," in *Identity and Difference* (Milan, 1996), p. 71; the following sentence in the text is also adapted from Ricoeur's argument.

54. The trajectory between subject and object Berque has called "l'engagement conscient": *Etre Humains*, p. 170.

55. We need perhaps a corpus of such analyses; the list could stretch from Petrarch's ascent of Mt. Ventoux to Berque's discussion of his sighting of Japan's Mt. Yotei (*Etre Humains*, pp. 145–46), and such landscape experiences should be compared carefully with those of designed landscapes. As early as 1976, George Seddon urged more "perceptual studies" of people's environments: reprinted in *Landprints*, p. 64.

56. I am thinking here especially of sites that were first private, then opened to public entry (Monceau, Stowe, Dumbarton Oaks). Reception study is not aimed, of course, at making the garden into a topos of the Berkeleian worldview, namely, that it exists only when perceived, but it might exist best through perception. However, a reception study of gardens should allow, more than reception theory generally does, for the problematization of the phenomenalism of "reading" a site.

57. I have discussed this at length in "A Breakthrough in Dahlia Studies: Tom Stoppard's *Arcadia*," *LJ*, 15 (1996): 58–64. See also Anja Müller, "Re-Presenting Representation: The Landscape Garden as Sight/Site of Difference in Tom Stoppard's *Arcadia*," in the special issue of *Word & Image* on ekphrasis.

58. This is also a way of insisting that garden history engage with the larger self-scrutiny in which history writing has engaged over the last fifty years. Currently, garden history seems totally innocent of the concerns of contemporary historiography, the literature on which is vast, exciting, and contentious. Garden historians might begin (where I myself started) with *Histories: French Constructions of the Past*, ed. Jacques Revel and Lynn Hunt (New York, 1995), and *A New Philosophy of History*, ed. Frank Ankersmit and Hans Keller (London, 1995).

59. See Michael O'Toole, *The Language of Displayed Art* (London, 1994), p. 215, commenting on a term emphasized by C. S. Peirce.

60. It is interesting that it was a practitioner, the Dane C. Th. Sørensen, who sketched the hints of an alternative historical narrative—see Sørensen's *Havekunstens Oprindelse*.

61. The list of types of garden extrapolated from the literature by Massimo Venturi Ferriolo is really remarkable: see "Homer's Garden," *JGH*, 9 (1989): 86–94, or the more extended version in his book, *Nel grembo della vita: Le origini dell'idea del giardino* (Milan, 1989).

62. The range of current practice is considerable and difficult to appreciate quickly without long exposure to professional journals, but see *Contemporary Trends in Landscape Architecture*, ed. Steven L. Cantor (New York, 1997), from which some of these items have been drawn.

63. For the Mughals, creators of fine gardens, we have been advised that the meaning of "garden" projects become more important for them than the label. See James L. Wescoat, Jr., "Gardens of Invention and Exile: The Precarious Context of Mughal Garden Design During the Reign of Humayun," *JGH*, 10 (1990): 114. For what is perhaps the return of an interest in the idea of the garden to landscape architecture, see Felice Frankel and Jory Johnson, *Modern Landscape Architecture: Redefining the Garden* (New York, 1991).

64. The temptation of land art for landscape architects has seemed intense, yet most practitioners whom Udo Weilacher interviewed in his book *Between Landscape Architecture and Land Art* resolutely rejected its lures.

65. There are many examples: Grizedale Forest in the English Lake District (see *The Grizedale Experience: Sculpture, Arts, and Theatre in a Lakeland Forest*, ed. Bill Grant and Paul Harris [Edinburgh, 1991]); the collections of the Parco di Celle at Pistoia (see the study by Marco Cei); and for a site in Pennsylvania see "Brooding Forest as Artist's Medium," *New York Times* (20 November 1997).

66. A special issue of *LJ*, 7, no. 2 (1988) on "Nature, Form, and Meaning," guest edited by Anne Whiston Spirn, reprinted Stevens's poem in full (p. 134).

67. See Lazzaro, *The Italian Renaissance Garden*, pp. 118–30, for both Pitigliano and Bomarzo.

68. See Weilacher's survey of the different movements, including Nature-Art, Environmental Art, "Individual Mythology," art in public spaces, "Securing of Evidence," etc., which superficially seem to have as much range as place-making itself.

69. See particularly Pat Murphy and William Neill, *By Nature's Design* (San Francisco, 1993).
70. I am indebted for Bacon's distinction to David Summers, who cites it in *Critical Terms for Art History*, p. 9.
71. André Breton, *Entretiens (1913–52)* (Paris, 1969), p. 251.
72. I have several times cited Augustin Berque on this essential distinction, but see also a similar claim by Bernard Lassus, quoted in *Landscape Research* 18, no. 1 (1993): 41.
73. Berque writes of those "high places," not always to be measured in meters, that "more than elsewhere, demonstrate the motivation that pushes the forms of landscape towards being," places in other words that heighten our existential being. See also Yves Bonnefoy's meditation on "Existe-t-il de 'Hauts' Lieux?" in *Entretiens sur la poésie* (Paris, 1990), pp. 352–59.
74. *AMACADEMY*, the newsletter of the American Academy in Rome (fall 1990): 15.
75. Alas, only available at present in its original German—*Der leidenschaftliche Gärten* (Zurich, 1951), in an abridged version; full text in his complete works (Stuttgart, 1987)—or an Italian translation by M. Roncioni, *Il giardiniere appassionato* (Milan, 1992).
76. Berque, who usefully defines genius loci as "the expression of the specificity" of a place (p. 185), registers the slipperiness of the topic when he also writes that "in itself" genius loci doesn't exist (p. 187). But see also my analysis above of Pope's famous invocation of the phrase in his "Epistle to Burlington."
77. Clement Greenberg, "Avant-Garde and Kitsch," *Partisan Review*, 6, no. 5 (1939): 34–35.
78. Deborah Nevins, "An Interview with Mary Miss," *Princeton Journal* 2 (1985): 102; Clifford Geertz, *The Interpretation of Cultures* (New York, 1973), chap. 1.
79. See *The Landscape Approach*. All other projects by Lassus cited in the remainder of this chapter are documented in this collection.
80. Alicia Rodriguez, "Letting Nature Have Its Way," *Landscape Architecture*, 87 (July 1997): 30–35.
81. See Alberti, *On the Art of Building in Ten Books*.
82. For Bürgi see his "Dimensionen der Erinnerung," *Topos* 2 (1993): 42–48; for Prigann, see Weilacher, *Between Landscape Architecture and Land Art*, pp. 174–75 and 185.

83. Berque, *Etre Humains*, pp. 203–4, where the author insists that even though "la nature est un fait, *mais aussi* récit de ce fait par Homo narrator."
84. William Robinson, *The English Flower Garden and Home Grounds*, 8th ed. (London, 1900), p. 30; Willy Lange, *Gartengestaltung der Neuzeit* (Leipzig, 1907), p. 13. Both are cited by Joachim Wolschke-Bulmahn, "The 'Wild Garden' and the 'Nature Garden'—Aspects of the Garden Ideology of William Robinson and Willy Lange," *JGH*, 12 (1992): 183–206. It is important to maintain an adequate separation between this essential insistence on the role of locality in design and the abuses to which it could be put: on these latter, see Wolschke-Bulmahn's "The Ideology of the Nature Garden: Nationalistic Trends in Garden Design in Germany During the Early Twentieth Century," *JGH*, 12 (1992): 73–80.
85. Sørensen, *Havekunstens Oprindelse*, pp. 8 and 34.
86. See Michele Weil, *Robert Challe Romancier* (Geneva, 1991), p. 75.
87. André Vera, *L'homme et le jardin* (Paris, 1950), p. 229; Boyceau, *Traité*, p. 35.
88. Whately, *Observations*, p. 227.
89. Harries, *Ethical Function*, p. 118.

CONCLUSION

1. Stoppard, *Arcadia*, pp. 46–47.
2. Evelyn, *Aceteria* (1706 edition), p. 202.
3. Wotton, *Reflections*, p. 296.
4. See Evelyn, *Silva*, 4th ed., p. 83: "If some of the following Discourses seem less constant, or (upon ocassion) repugnant to one another, they are to be consider'd as relating only to the several Gusts [i.e., tastes] and Guises of Persons and Countries."
5. Evelyn, *Sylva*, 3d ed. (1679), A2 verso. Cf. Evelyn's letter to Sir Thomas Browne where the society of "*Paradisi Cultores* . . . paradisean and hortulan saints" may happily "redeeeme the tyme." G. Keynes, ed., *The Works of Sir Thomas Browne* (London, 1964), IV, 275.
6. Evelyn, "Elysium Britannicum," fol. 118.

SELECT BIBLIOGRAPHY

The following bibliography gives the full references for all works on landscape architecture cited in the notes, where abbreviated details have often been used. The *Journal of Garden History* (since 1998 retitled *Studies in the History of Gardens and Designed Landscapes*) is abbreviated throughout as *JGH*, *Landscape Journal* as *LJ*, and the Penn Studies in Landscape Architecture series as PSLA.

Aardse Paradijzen. Ed. Erik de Jong and Marleen Dominicus-Van Soest. Haarlem, 1996. The catalogue of an exhibition of Dutch garden paintings from the fifteenth to eighteenth centuries.

Yves Abrioux. *Ian Hamilton Finlay: A Visual Primer*, with introductory notes and commentaries by Stephen Bann. First edition, 1985. Second revised and expanded edition, Cambridge, Mass., 1992.

G. A. Agricola. *A Philosophical Treatise of Husbandry and Gardening*. London, 1721.

Leon Battista Alberti. *On the Art of Building in Ten Books*. Trans. Joseph Rykwert, Neil Leach, and Robert Taverner. Cambridge, Mass., 1991.

Régis Amboise, Pierre Frapa, and Sébastien Giorgis. *Paysages de terrasses*. Aix en Provence, 1989.

Leonard Amico. *Bernard Palissy: In Search of Earthly Paradise*. New York, 1996.

Ancient Roman Villa Gardens. Ed. Elisabeth Blair MacDougall. Washington, D.C., 1987.

J. K. Anderson. *Hunting in the Ancient World*. Berkeley and Los Angeles, 1991.

Louis Aragon. *Le Paysan de Paris*. Paris, 1926.

Giulio Carlo Argan. "Landscape Architecture." *Encyclopedia of World Art*. London, 1963, 8:1066-70.

The Artist and the Country House from the Fifteenth Century to the Present Day. London, 1995. An exhibition catalogue by John Harris for Sotheby's.

Rosario Assunto. *Ontologia e teleologia del Giardino*. Milan, 1988.

The Authentic Garden. Ed. L. Tjon Sie Fat and Erik de Jong. Leiden, 1991.

C. F. Barbier. *William Gilpin: His Drawings, Teaching, and the Theory of the Picturesque*. Oxford, 1963.

Michel Baridon. *Les Jardins. Paysagistes—Jardiniers—Poètes*. Paris. 1998.

———. "Ruins as Mental Construct." *JGH*, 5 (1985), 84-96.

———. "The Scientific Imagination and the Baroque Garden." *JGH*, 18 (1998), 5-19.

John Barrell. *The Dark Side of the Landscape*. Cambridge, 1980.

Bruno Basile. *L'Elisio Effimero: Scrittori in giardino*. Bologna, 1993.

John Beale. *Herefordshire Orchards, a Pattern for All England*. London, 1724.

John Beardsley. *Gardens of Revelation: Environments by Visionary Artists*. New York, 1995.

Augustin Berque. *Médiance: De Milieux en paysages*. Montpellier, 1990.

———. *Les Raisons du paysage de la Chine antique aux environments de synthèse*. Paris, 1995.

———. *Etre Humains sur la Terre*. Paris, 1997.

Jacopo Bonfadio. *Le Lettere*. Ed. Aulo Greco. Rome, 1978.

Nicholas de Bonnefons. *The French Gardiner*. Trans. John Evelyn. London, 1658.

Yves Bonnefoy. "Existe-t-il de 'Hauts' Lieux?" *Entretiens sur la poésie*. Paris, 1990.

Jorge Luis Borges. "The Garden of the Forking Paths." In *Labyrinths*. Ed. D. A. Yates and J. E. Irby. New York, 1964.

———. "The Two Kings and Their Two Labyrinths." In *The Aleph and Other Stories*. Ed. N. T. di Giovanni. New York, 1970.

Rudolf Borchardt. *Der leidenschaftliche Gärten*. Abridged version. Zurich, 1951. Full text in his complete works, Stuttgart, 1987; *Il giardiniere appassionato*, trans. M. Roncioni, Milan, 1992.

David Bourdon. *Designing the Earth: The Human Impulse to Shape Nature*. New York, 1995.

Jacky Bowring. "Institutionalizing the Picturesque: The Discourse of the New Zealand Institute of Landscape Architects." Ph.D. diss., Lincoln University, Canterbury, New Zealand, 1997.

Jacques Boyceau. *Traité du jardinage*. Paris, 1638.

Lawrence Buell. *The Environmental Imagination*. Cambridge, Mass., 1995.

Brenda Bullion. "Early American Farming and Gardening Literature." *JGH*, 12 (1992), 29-51.

Paolo Bürgi. "Dimensionen der Erinnerung." *Topos*, 3 (1993), 42-48.

Ellen Callmann. "A Quattrocento Jigsaw Puzzle." *Burlington Magazine*, 99 (1957), 149-55.

Evelina Calvi. *Tempo e progetto: L'architettura come narrazione*. Milan, 1991.

Karel Capek. *L'Année du jardinier*. La Tour d'Aigues, 1997.

Allen Carlson. "On the Theoretical Vacuum in Landscape Architecture." *LJ*, 12, no. 1 (1993), 51-59.

Louis Carrogis, called Carmontelle. *Jardin de Monceau*. 1779.

Marco Cei. *Il Parco di Celle a Pistoia*. Florence, 1994.

Cent Ans d'histoire des jardins ouvriers. Ed. Beatrice Cabedoce and Philippe Pierson. Grane, 1996.

Cent Poètes côté jardin. Ed. Daniel Gelin. Paris, 1990.

Douglas D. C. Chambers. *The Planters of the English Landscape Gardener.* New Haven, 1993.

———. *Stony Ground: The Making of a Canadian Garden.* Toronto, 1996.

———. "The Tomb in the Landscape: John Evelyn's Garden at Albury." *JGH,* 1 (1981), 37–54.

———. "The Translation of Antiquity: Virgil, Pliny, and the Landscape Garden." *University of Toronto Quarterly,* 60 (1991), 354–73.

———. " 'Wild Pastorall Encounter': John Evelyn, John Beale and the Renegotiation of Pastoral in the Mid-Seventeenth Century." In *Culture and Cultivation* (q.v.).

William Chambers. *Designs of Chinese Buildings. . . .* London, 1757.

———. *A Dissertation on Oriental Gardening.* London, 1772.

Bruce Chatwin. *The Songlines.* London, 1988.

Cicero. *De natura deorum.* Venice, 1508; Paris, 1511; Leipzig, 1529, and Basel, 1534; and *Cicero's Three Books Touching the Nature of the Gods,* London, 1683.

Cinq Propositions pour une théorie du paysage. Ed. Augustin Berque. Seyssel, 1994.

Rosetta E. Clarkson. *Green Enchantment: The Magic Spell of Gardens.* New York, 1940.

Virginia Tuttle Clayton. *Gardens on Paper: Prints and Drawings, 1200–1900.* Exhibition catalogue for the National Gallery of Art, Washington, D.C., 1990.

Craig Clunas. *Fruitful Sites.* London, 1996.

David Coffin. *The Villa d'Este at Tivoli.* Princeton, N.J., 1960.

Michel Conan. *Dictionnaire historique de l'art des jardins,* Paris, 1997.

———. "Nature into Art: Gardens and Landscapes in the Everyday Life of Ancient Rome." *JGH,* 6 (1986), 348–56.

———. " 'Puer aeternus' in the Garden." *Studies in the History of Gardens and Designed Landscapes.* 19 (1999), 86–101.

Contemporary Trends in Landscape Architecture. Ed. Steven L. Cantor. New York, 1997.

Moses Cook. *The Manner of Raising, Ordering, and Improving Forest and Fruit-Trees.* London, 1679.

James Corner. "A Discourse on Theory, I: Sounding the Depths—Origins, Theory and Representation." *LJ,* 9 (1990), 61–78.

James Corner and Alex S. MacLean. *Taking Measures Across the American Landscape.* New Haven, 1996.

Denis Cosgrove. *The Palladian Landscape.* University Park, Pa., 1993.

Culture and Cultivation in Early Modern England: Writing and the Land. Ed. Michael Leslie and Timothy Raylor. Leicester, 1992.

Hubert Damisch. *Skyline: La Ville narcisse.* Paris, 1996.

Erasmus Darwin. *Phytologia; Or the Philosophy of Agriculture and Gardening.* London, 1800.

Rebecca Davidson. "Past as Present: Villa Vizcaya and the 'Italian Garden' in America." *JGH,* 12 (1992), 1–28.

Martin R. Dean. "Nature as a Book—A Book as Nature." *JGH,* 17 (1997), 171–75.

Abbé Delille. *The Garden; or, the Art of Laying out Grounds.* Trans. (?) Anthony Powell, London, 1789. There were many other translations of this poem.

Denatured Visions: Landscape and Culture in the Twentieth Century. Ed. Stuart Wrede and William Howard Adams. New York, 1991.

Antoine-Joseph Dézallier d'Argenville. *La Théorie et la pratique du jardinage.* Paris, 1709. Rev. eds. 1713 and 1747. English translation by John James, London, 1712.

The Dictionary of Art. New York, 1996, XII (vide "Garden").

A. J. Downing. *A Treatise on the Theory and Practice of Landscape Gardening.* 4th ed. New York, 1850.

Jean Dubreuil. *La Perspective pratique.* 3 vols. Paris, 1649–51.

Hans Peter Duerr. *Dreamtime: Concerning the Boundary Between Wilderness and Civilization.* Trans. Felicitas Goodman. Oxford, 1985.

Françoise Dubost. *Les Jardins ordinaires.* Paris and Montreal, 1997. First published in 1984 as *Côté Jardins.*

The Dutch Garden in the Seventeeth Century. Ed. John Dixon Hunt. Washington, D.C., 1990.

Mircea Eliade. *Le Sacré et le profane.* Paris, 1965.

James Elkins. "On the Conceptual Analysis of Gardens." *JGH,* 13 (1993), 189–98. A version of this essay is republished in his book, *Our Beautiful, Dry and Distant Texts: Art History as Writing* (University Park, Pa., 1997).

Brent Elliott. *Victorian Gardens.* London, 1986.

Anne van Erp-Houtepen. "The Etymological Origins of the Garden." *JGH,* 6 (1996), 227–31.

John Evelyn. *Acetaria, a Discourse of Sallets.* London, 1699.

———. *The Diary of John Evelyn.* Ed. E. S. de Beer. 5 vols. Oxford, 1955.

———. *Elysium Britannicum.* Transcribed and introduced by John Ingram. PSLA. Philadelphia, forthcoming.

———. *An Essay on the First Book of T. Lucretius Carus De rerum natura. . . .* London, 1656.

———. *Kalendarium Hortense, or the Gard'ners Almanac* (1664). Edition cited, 7th, London, 1683.

———. *Sylva.* London, 1664; *Silva* 4th ed., London, 1706.

Nigel Everett. *The Tory View of Landscape.* New Haven and London, 1994.

Rudy J. Favretti. "Bacon's Castle and the Castle Garden." *Discovery* (1988), 11–15.

Marcello Fagiolo. *Natura e Artificio.* Rome, 1979.

Massimo Venturi Ferriolo. "Homer's Garden." *JGH,* 9 (1989), 86–94.

————. *Nel grembo della vità: Le origini dell'idea del giardino.* Milan, 1989.

Ian Hamilton Finlay. *Nature over Again After Poussin.* Glasgow, 1980.

————. See also under Yves Abrioux.

John Fleming. *From Bonaventura to Bellini: An Essay in Franciscan Exegesis.* Princeton, N.J., 1982.

Peter France. *Hermits.* London, 1996.

Felice Frankel and Jory Johnson. *Modern Landscape Architecture: Redefining the Garden.* New York, 1991.

Marco Frascari. "A Heroic and Admirable Machine: The Theater of the Architecture of Carlo Scarpa, *Architetto Veneto.*" *Poetics Today,* 10 (1989), 103-26.

————. "Maidens 'Theory' and 'Practice' at the Sides of Lady Architecture." *Assemblage,* 7 (1988), 15-27.

Stanislaus Fung. "Here and There in *Yuan Ye.*" *Studies in the History of Gardens and Designed Landscapes,* 19 (1999), 36-45.

Ernst de Ganay. *Coup d'œil sur les jardins de France.* Brussels, 1993.

Garden History: Issues, Approaches, Methods. Ed. John Dixon Hunt. Washington, D.C., 1992.

Garden Poems. Ed. John Hollander. New York, 1996.

Garten und Park. Catalogue of exhibition in the Akademie der Bildenden Kunste. Vienna, 1964.

Garten: Texte aus der Weltliteratur. Ed. Anne Marie Fröhlich. Zurich, 1993.

The Genius of the Place: The English Landscape Garden, 1620-1820. Ed. John Dixon Hunt and Peter Willis. 2nd rev. ed. Cambridge, Mass., 1988.

Il giardino depinto nella pittura lombarda dal seicento all'ottocento. Exhibition catalogue at the Villa Reale di Monza. Milan, 1995.

Il giardino islamico: Architettura, natura, paeseggio. Ed. Attilio Petrucciolo. Milan, 1994.

William Gilpin. *A Dialogue upon the Gardens . . . at Stowe.* Ed. John Dixon Hunt, Augustan Reprint Society no. 176. Los Angeles, 1976.

————. *Three Essays.* London, 1792.

C. J. Glacken. *Traces on the Rhodian Shore: Nature and Culture in Western Thought from Ancient Times to the End of the Eighteenth Century.* Berkeley and Los Angeles, 1967.

Peter Goodchild. "'No Phantasticall Utopia, But a Real Place': John Evelyn, John Beale and Backbury Hill, Herefordshire." *Garden History,* 19 (1991), 106-27.

Mac Griswold. *Pleasures of the Garden: Images from the Metropolitan Museum of Art.* New York, 1987.

The Grizedale Experience: Sculpture, Arts and Theatre in a Lakeland Forest. Ed. Bill Grant and Paul Harris. Edinburgh, 1991.

Jan van der Groen. *Den Nederlantsen Hovenier.* Amsterdam, 1669.

Gert Gröning and Joachim Wolschke-Bulmahn. *Studien zur Frankfurter Geschichte . . . Ein Jahrhundert Kleingartenkultur in Frankfurt am Main.* Frankfurt am Main, 1995.

Antoine Grumbach. "The Promenades of Paris." *Oppositions,* 10 (1977), 60-61.

Richard Haag: Bloedel Reserve and Gas Works Park. Ed. William S. Saunders. New York and Cambridge, Mass., 1998.

Lawrence Halprin. *The Franklin Delano Roosevelt Memorial.* San Francisco, 1997.

Thomas Hamilton. *Forest Trees: Some Directions About Raising Forests.* Ed. M. Anderson. London, 1953.

William Hanbury. *A Complete Body of Planting and Gardening.* 2 vols. London, 1770.

Duc d'Harcourt. *Traité de la décoration des dehors, des jardins et des parcs.* Paris, c. 1775.

Karsten Harries. *The Ethical Function of Architecture.* Cambridge, Mass., 1997.

Frances Harris. "The Manuscripts of John Evelyn's 'Elysium Britannicum.'" *Garden History,* 25, no. 2 (1997), 131-37.

John Harris. *The Artist and the Country House.* New Haven, 1979 and 1985.

————. *The Artist and the Country House from the Fifteenth Century to the Present Day.* London, 1996.

————. *Gardens of Delight: The Rococo English Landscape of Thomas Robins the Elder.* 2 vols. London, 1978.

————. "A Pioneer in Gardening: Dickie Bateman Re-Assessed." *Apollo* (October 1993), 227-33.

Marina Harrison and Lucy D. Rosenfeld. *Garden Walks.* New York, 1997.

Samuel Hartlib. *A Discourse for Division or Setting out of Land, as to the Best Form.* London, 1653.

————. *Samuel Hartlib His Legacie.* London, 1655.

Samuel Hartlib and Universal Reformation: Studies in Intellectual Communication. Ed. Mark Greengrass, Michael Leslie, and Timothy Raylor. Cambridge, 1994.

The Hartlib Papers on CD-ROM. Ed. Michael Leslie et al. Ann Arbor, Mich., 1996.

F. Hamilton Hazlehurst. *Gardens of Illusion: The Genius of André Le Nostre.* Nashville, 1980.

Kenneth Helphand. "Defiant Gardens.'" *JGH,* 17 (1997), 101-21.

Susan Herrington. "The Garden in Fröbel's Kindergarten: Beyond the Metaphor." *Studies in the History of Gardens and Designed Landscapes,* 18 (1998), 46-61.

Susan Hill and Rory Stuart. *Reflections from a Garden.* London, 1995.

C. C. L. Hirschfeld. *Theorie der Gartenkunst.* 5 vols. Leipzig, 1779-85.

————. *Theorie der Gartenkunst.* Abridged version, translated and with an introduction by Linda Parshall. PSLA. Philadelphia, forthcoming.

The History of Garden Design: The Western Tradition from the Renaissance to the Present Day. Ed. Monique Mosser and Georges Teyssot. London, 1991.

Bryan Holme. *The Enchanted Garden: Images of Delight*. London, 1982.

Henry Home, Lord Kames. *Elements of Criticism*. 1762. 2 vols., London, 1993.

Alster Horn-Olcken. *Uber das Schickliche: Studien zur Geschichte der Architekturtheorie*. Gottingen, 1967.

Henry Vincent Hubbard and Theodora Kimball. *An Introduction to the Study of Landscape Design*. New York, 1917.

John Dixon Hunt. *L'Art du jardin et son histoire*. Paris, 1996.

———. "'Curiosities to Adorn Cabinets and Gardens.'" *The Origins of Museums: The Cabinet of Curiosities in Sixteenth and Seventeenth-Century Europe*. Ed. Oliver Impey and Arthur Mac-Gregor. Oxford, 1985.

———. "Garden." *The Dictionary of Art* (New York, 1996), vol. 12, 61–65.

———. *Garden and Grove: The Italian Renaissance Garden in the English Imagination, 1600–1750*. Rev. ed. Philadelphia, 1996.

———. "The Garden in the City of Venice: Epitome of State and Site." *Studies in the History of Gardens and Designed Landscapes*, 19 (1999), 46–61.

———. "The Garden as Cultural Object." In *Denatured Visions* (q.v.).

———. *Gardens and the Picturesque: Studies in the History of Landscape Architecture*. Cambridge, Mass., 1992.

———. "Il giardino come territorio delle nature." *Pensare il giardino*. Ed. Paola Capone, Paola Lanzara, and Massimo Venturi Ferriolo. Milan, 1992.

———. "Il giardino europeo barocco: Più barocco del barocco." *Il giardino delle muse: Arti e artifici nel barocco europeo*. Ed. Maria Adriana Giusti and Alessandro Tagliolini. Florence, 1993.

———. "Des Jardins de France." *Trois Regards sur le paysage français*. Seyssel, 1993.

———. "The Idea of the Garden and the Three Natures." *Zum naturbegriff der Gegenwart*. Ed. Joachim Wilke. 2 vols. Stuttgart-Bad Cannstatt, 1994.

———. "Imitation, Representation, and the Study of Garden Art." In *The Art of Interpreting*, ed. Susan C. Scott. Papers in Art History from the Pennsylvania State University, 9 (1995), 199–215.

———. "Landscape, the Three Natures and Landscape Architecture." *Artivisual Landscapes*. Amsterdam, 1992.

———. "Paragone in Paradise: Translating the Garden." *Comparative Criticism*, 18 (1996), 55–70.

———. "Writing the English Garden: Horace Walpole and the Historiography of Landscape Architecture." *Interfaces*, 4 (1993), 163–80.

———. "Why Garden History?" *Gartenkunstgeschichte: Festschrift für Dieter Hennebo zum 70. Geburtstag*. Hannover, 1994.

Michael Hunter. *Science and Society in Restoration England*. Cambridge, 1981.

———. *Science and the Shape of Orthodoxy: Intellectual Change in Late Seventeenth-Century Britain*. Woodbridge, 1995.

Anthony Huxley. *The Painted Garden: The Garden Through the Artist's Eye*. London, 1988.

The Iconography of Landscape. Ed. Denis Cosgrove and Stephen Daniels. Cambridge, 1988.

The Illustrated Dictionary of Gardening. Ed. George Nicholson. 4 vols. London, 1884–89.

Dorothée Imbert. *The Modernist Garden in France*. New Haven, 1993.

David Ingersoll. "In the Garden of Even: Visual Grounds." *JGH*, 14 (1994), 55–62.

The Italian Garden. Ed. David Coffin. Washington, D.C., 1972.

The Italian Garden: Art, Design and Culture. Ed. John Dixon Hunt. Cambridge, 1996.

J. B. Jackson. *The Necessity for Ruins and Other Topics*. Amherst, Mass., 1980.

John A. Jakle. *The Visual Elements of Landscape*. Amherst, Mass., 1987.

Geoffrey James. *Genius Loci*. Ottawa, 1986.

———. *Giardini Italiani*. Rome, 1985.

———. *The Italian Garden*. New York, 1991.

———. *Morbid Symptoms*. Princeton, N.J., 1986.

Le Jardin, art et lieu de mémoire. Ed. Monique Mosser and Philippe Nys. Besançon, 1995.

Derek Jarman. *Derek Jarman's Garden*. London, 1995.

Wilhelmina Jashemski. *The Gardens of Pompeii*. 2 vols. New Rochelle, N.Y., 1979 and 1993.

Charles Jencks. *The Architecture of the Jumping Universe*, London, 1995.

Thomas Jefferson. *The Portable Jefferson*. Ed. Merrill D. Peterson. New York, 1977.

Hugh Johnson. *The Principles of Gardening*. New York, 1979.

Bernard and Renée Kayser. *L'Amour des jardins célébré par les écrivains*. Paris, 1986.

Maggie Keswick. *The Chinese Garden: History, Art, and Architecture*. New York, 1978.

Geoffrey Keynes. *John Evelyn: A Study in Bibliophily, with a Bibliography of His Writings*. London, 1968.

R. W. King. Series of essays on "Joseph Spence of Byfleet." *Garden History*, 6, no. 3 (1978), 38–64; 7, no. 3 (1979), 29–48; 8, no. 2 (1980), 44–65; and 8, no. 3 (1980), 77–114.

James D. Kornwolf. "David Meade II: Pioneer of *le jardin anglais* in the United States, 1774–1829." *JGH*, 16 (1996), 254–74.

Stephen R. Krog. "The Language of Modern." *Landscape Architecture*, 75, no. 2 (1985), 56–59.

Hanno-Walter Kruft. *Geschicht der Architekurtheorie*. Munich, 1986. Trans. R. Taylor as *A History of Architectural Theory*, Princeton, N.J., 1994.

Ann Kuttner. "Looking Outside Inside: Ancient Roman Garden Rooms." *Studies in the History of Gardens and Designed Landscapes*, 19 (1999), 7–35.

Alexandre Louis J. de Laborde. *Descriptions des nouveaux jardins de la France*, Paris, 1808. Also published the same year without plates as *Discours sur la vie de la campagne*.

Mark Laird. *The Flowering of the Landscape Garden: English Pleasure Grounds, 1720–1800*. PSLA. Philadelphia, 1999.

Landscape Transformed (Academy Editions). London, 1996.

Willy Lange. *Gartengestaltung der Neuzeit*. Leipzig, 1907.

Bernard Lassus. *Hypothèses pour une troisième nature*. Paris, 1992.

———. *The Landscape Approach*. PSLA. Philadelphia, 1998.

———. "Le Paysage comme organisation d'un référent sensible." *Le Débat*, 65, issue on "Au-délà du Paysage moderne" (1991), 94–111.

———. "Pour une Poétique du paysage: Théorie des failles." In *Maîtres et protecteurs de la nature*, ed. Alain Roger and François Guery. Paris, 1990.

Pieter Lauremberg. *. . . Horticultura, Libris II*. Frankfurt, [?] 1631.

Sylvia Lavin. *Quatremère de Quincy and the Invention of a Modern Language of Architecture*. Cambridge, Mass., 1992.

John Lawrence. *Gardening Improv'd*. London, 1718.

Claudia Lazzaro. *The Italian Renaissance Garden*. New Haven and London, 1990.

David Leatherbarrow. "Character, Geometry and Perspective: The Third Earl of Shaftesbury's Principles of Garden Design." *JGH*, 4 (1984), 332–58.

———. *The Roots of Architectural Invention*. Cambridge, 1993.

Pierre and Denise Le Dantec. *Le Roman du jardin français*, Paris, 1987. Translated as *Reading the French Garden*, Cambridge, Mass., 1988.

Pierre Le Lorrain de Vallemont. *Curiosities of Nature and Art in Husbandry and Gardening* (Paris, 1705), London, 1707.

Michael Leslie. "An English Landscape Garden Before 'the English Landscape Garden'." *JGH*, 13 (1993), 3–15.

[Anon.] *Lettre sur les Jardins Anglois*. Paris, 1775.

Charles-Joseph, Prince de Ligne. *Coup d'œil at Beloeil and a Great Number of European Gardens*. Trans. and ed. Basil Gray. Berkeley and Los Angeles, 1991.

Edward Lisle. *Observations in Husbandry*. London, 1757.

Anthony Littlewood. "Gardens of Byzantium." *JGH*, 12 (1992), 126–53.

John Claudius Loudon. *See* Humphry Repton.

Luoghi sacri e spazi della santità. Ed. Sofia Boesch Gajano and Lucetta Scaraffia. Turin, 1990.

Nicholas Lucchetti. "Archaeological Excavations at Bacon's Castle, Surry County, Virginia." In *Earth Patterns: Essays in Landscape Archaeology*. Ed. William M. Kelso and Rachel Most. Charlottesville, Va., 1990.

Sutherland Lyall. *Designing the Modern Landscape*. London, 1991.

Luigi Mabil. *Teoria dell'arti de' giardini*. Bassano, 1801.

John Macdonald. "Paradise." *Islamic Studies*, 5 (1966), 331–83.

Indra Kagis McEwen. *Socrates' Ancestor: An Essay on Architectural Beginnings*. Cambridge, Mass., 1994.

Judith Major. *To Live in the New World: A. J. Downing and American Landscape Gardening*. Cambridge, Mass., 1997.

Andrew H. Malcolm. "How a Parkway Became a Ribbon of Living Beauty." *New York Times* (5 February 1991).

Bronislaw Malinowski. *Coral Gardens and Their Magic*. London, 1935.

Thierry Mariage. *The World of André Le Nôtre*. Trans. Graham Larkin. PSLA. Philadelphia, 1998.

George Mason. *Essay on Design*. London, 1758.

William Mason. *The English Garden*. 1772. Revised and edited with notes by W. Burgh, reprinted, New York, 1982.

Mediaeval Gardens. Ed. E. B. MacDougall. Washington, D.C., 1986.

Leonard Meager. *The English Gardener*. London, 1670.

The Meaning of Gardens. Ed. Mark Francis and Randolph T. Hester, Jr. Cambridge, Mass., 1990.

Millard Meiss. *Giovanni Bellini's St. Francis in the Frick Collection*. Princeton, N.J., 1964.

Daniela Mignani. *Le Ville Medicee di Giusto Utens*. Florence, 1980.

Mara Miller. *The Garden as an Art*. Albany, N.Y., 1993.

Philip Miller. *The Gardeners Dictionary*, 1731. 2 vols., London, 1739.

André Mollet. *Le Jardin du plaisir*. Stockholm, 1651. Partially translated as *The Garden of Pleasure*, London, 1670.

Claude Mollet. *Théâtre des plans et jardinages*. Paris, 1652.

Samuel Holt Monk. *The Sublime: A Study of Critical Theories in Eighteenth-Century England*. 1935. Reprint, New York, 1960.

Charles Moore, William J. Mitchell, and William Turnbull, Jr. *The Poetics of Gardens*. Cambridge, Mass., 1988.

Jean-Marie Morel. *Théorie des jardins*. Paris, 1776. 2 vols., Paris, 1802.

Timothy Mowl. "New Science, Old Order: The Gardens of the Great Rebellion." *JGH*, 13 (1993), 16–35.

Elizabeth Moynihan. *Paradise as a Garden: In Persia and Mughal India*. New York, 1979.

Mughal Gardens: Sources, Places, Representations, and Prospects. Ed. James L. Wescoat, Jr., and Joachim Wolschke-Bulmahn. Washington, D.C., 1996.

Chandra Mukerji. *Territorial Ambitions and the Gardens of Versailles*. Cambridge, Mass., 1997.

Pat Murphy and William Neill. *By Nature's Design*. San Francisco, 1993.

Myths from Mesopotamia. Trans. Stephanie Dalley. Oxford, 1989.

Eva Maris Neumeyer. "The Landscape Garden as a Symbol in Rousseau, Goethe and Flaubert." *Journal of the History of Ideas*, 8 (1947), 187–97.

Deborah Nevins. "An Interview with Mary Miss." *Princeton Journal*, 2 (1985), 96–104.

Isamu Noguchi. *The Isamu Noguchi Garden Museum*. New York, 1987.

Jim Nollman. *Why We Garden: Cultivating a Sense of Place*. New York, 1994.

Timothy Nourse. *Campania Foelix*. London, 1700. Reprint, New York, 1982.

Max Oelschlaeger. *The Idea of the Wilderness: From Prehistory to the Age of Ecology*. New Haven and London, 1991.

H. V. S. Ogden. "The Principles of Variety and Contrast in Seventeenth-Century Aesthetics, and Milton's Poetry." *Journal of the History of Ideas*, 10 (1949), 159–82.

Oxford Book of Garden Verse. Ed. John Dixon Hunt. Oxford, 1992.

Oxford Companion to Gardens. Ed. Geoffrey and Susan Jellicoe, Patrick Goode, and Michael Lancaster. Oxford, 1986.

Bernard Palissy. *Recette Véritable*. Ed. Frank Lestringant. Paris, 1996. Part translated by Helen Morgenthau Fox as *A Delectable Garden*, Peekskill, N.Y., 1931.

Linda Parshall. "C. C. L. Hirschfeld's Concept of the Garden in the German Enlightenment." *JGH*, 13 (1993), 125–71.

W. C. Pendleton. *History of Tazewell County and Southwest Virginia, 1748–1920*. Richmond, Va., 1920.

Penguin Book of Garden Writing. Ed. David Wheeler. New York and London, 1997.

Nigel Pennick and Paul Devereux. *Lines on the Landscape: Leys and Other Linear Enigmas*. London, 1989.

Yves Perillon et al. *Images de Jardins Gardens Images* [*sic*]. Paris, 1987.

Johann Peschel. *Garten Ordnung*. Leipzig, 1597.

Harold Ainsworth Peto. *The Boke of Iford*. Introduction by Robin Whalley. Marlborough, 1993.

Francesco Petrarca. *Le Familiari*. 3 vols. Ed. Ugo Dotti. Rome, 1991–94.

———. *L'Ascension du Mont Ventoux*. Editions Séquences, n.p., 1990. An English version of this account is available in *Rerum familiarum libri I–VIII*, trans. Aldo S. Bernardo. Albany, N.Y. 1975.

Jan Pieper. "Die Natur der Hängenden Gärten: The Nature of Hanging Gardens." *Daedalus*, 23 (1987), 94–109.

Ippolito Pindemonte. "Dissertazione su i giardini inglesi e sul merito in ciò dell'Italia." In *Operette di vari autori intorno ai giardini inglesi ossia moderni*. Verona, 1817.

Michael Pollan. *Second Nature: A Gardener's Education*. New York, 1991.

Alexander Pope. *An Epistle to Lord Burlington*. London, 1731.

John Prest. *The Garden of Eden: The Botanic Garden and the Recreation of Paradise*. London, 1981.

Uvedale Price. *Essays on the Picturesque*. 1794; 1796–98. Edition cited, 3 vols., London, 1810.

Simon Pugh. *Garden—Nature—Language*. Manchester, 1988.

Nicholas Purcell. "Town in Country and Country in Town." In *Ancient Roman Villa Gardens* (q.v.).

Michel Racine. *Jardins de France*. Arles, 1997.

René Rapin. *Hortorum Libri IV*. Paris, 1665. Translated into English by John Evelyn, Jr., London, 1672, and by James Gardiner, London, 1706.

John Rea. *Flora*. London, 1665.

G. W. Reid. *From Concept to Form in Landscape Design*. New York, 1993.

Humphry Repton. *The Landscape Gardening and Landscape Architecture of the Late Humphry Repton*. Ed. John Claudius Loudon. London, 1840.

Special issue on Humphry Repton. *JGH*, 16 (1996), 153–224.

Paul Ricoeur. "Architecture and Narrative." In *Identity and Difference: Integration and Plurality in Today's Forms*. Nineteenth Trienale di Milano, Milan, 1996.

David Robertson. *Real Matter*. Salt Lake City, 1997.

William Robinson. *The English Flower Garden and Home Grounds*. 1883. 8th ed., London, 1900.

Alicia Rodriguez. "Letting Nature Have Its Way." *Landscape Architecture*, 87 (July 1997), 30–35.

Alain Roger. *Court Traité du paysage*. Paris, 1997.

———, ed. *La Théorie du paysage en France, 1974–1994*. Seyssel, 1995.

James C. Rose. *Gardens Make Me Laugh*. New ed. Baltimore, 1990.

Stephanie Ross. *What Gardens Mean*. Chicago, 1998.

Marie Rouanet. *Tout Jardin est Eden*. Marseilles, 1993.

Pierre de la Ruffinière du Prey. *The Villas of Pliny, from Antiquity to Posterity*. Chicago, 1994.

D. Fairchild Ruggles. "The Mirador in Abbasid and Hispano Umayyand Garden Typology." *Muqaarnas: An Annual on Islamic Art and Architecture*. Ed. Oleg Grabar, 8, 1990.

Joseph Rykwert. *On Adam's House in Paradise: The Idea of the Primitive Hut in Architectural History*. New York, 1972.

Simon Schama. *Landscape and Memory*. New York, 1995.

Martha Schwartz. *Transfigurations of the Commonplace*. Washington, D.C., and Cambridge, Mass., 1997.

Madeleine de Scudéry. *La Promenade de Versailles*. 1669. Reprint, Geneva, 1979.

George Seddon. *Landprints: Reflections on Place and Landscape*. Cambridge, 1997.

Olivier de Serres. *Le Théâtre d'agriculture et mesnage des champs*. 1600. Arles, 1996.

Earl of Shaftesbury, Antony Ashley Cooper. *Second Characteristics or the Language of Forms*. Ed. B. Rand. London, 1914.

William Shenstone. "Unconnected Thoughts on Gardening." *The Works*. 2 vols. London, 1764.

Ercole Silva. *Dell'arte de' giardini inglesi*. Milan, 1801 and 1813.

George, Sacheverell, Osbert, and Edith Sitwell. *Hortus Sitwellianus*. London, 1984.

John Smith. *England's Improvement Reviv'd.* London, 1673.

Helaine Silverman. "Beyond the Pampa: The Geoglyphs in the Valleys of Nazca." *National Geographic Research,* 6 (1990), 435-56.

Barbara Stauffacher Solomon. *Green Architecture and the Agrarian Garden.* New York, 1988.

C. Th. Sørensen. *Havekunstens Oprindelse: The Origins of Garden Art.* Copenhagen, 1963.

Joseph Spence. *Observations, Anecdotes and Characters of Books and Men.* Ed. James M. Osborn. 2 vols. Oxford, 1966.

Tom Stoppard. *Arcadia.* London and Boston, 1993.

Roy Strong. *A Celebration of Gardens.* London, 1991.

Dorothy Stroud. *Capability Brown.* Rev. ed. London, 1957.

Richard Surflet. *Maison Rustique or the Countrie Farm.* London, 1600.

Stephen Switzer. *Ichnographia Rustica.* 3 vols. London, 1718. Rev. ed. 1745. Published initially in one volume, *The Nobleman, Gentleman, and Gardener's Recreation,* London, 1715.

Alessandro Tagliolini. *Storia del Giardino italiano.* Florence, 1988.

Bartolomeo Taegio. *La Villa.* Milan, 1559.

Susan Taylor-Leduc. "Luxury in the Garden: *La Nouvelle Héloïse* Reconsidered." *Studies in the History of Gardens and Designed Landscapes,* 19 (1999), 74-85.

Christopher Thacker. *The History of Gardens.* London, 1979.

A Treasury of Garden Verse. Ed. Margaret Elphinstone. Edinburgh, 1990.

Marc Treib. "Frame, Moment, and Sequence: The Photographic Book and the Designed Landscape." *JGH,* 15 (1995), 126-34.

———. "Must Landscapes Mean? Approaches to Significance in Recent Landscape Architecture." *LJ,* 14, no. 1 (1995), 46-62.

Paul Vera. *Les Jardins.* Paris, 1919.

———. *L'Homme et le jardin.* Paris, 1950.

The Vernacular Garden. Ed. John Dixon Hunt and Joachim Wolschke-Bulmahn. Washington, D.C., 1993.

Dalibor Vesely. "Architecture and the Conflict of Representation." *AA Files,* 8 (1985), 21-38.

Viewing Olmsted. Ed. with an introduction by Phyllis Lambert. Montreal, 1996.

M. A. Visentini. *L'Orto botanico di Padova.* Milan, 1984.

Marcus V. Pollio Vitruvius. *De architectura/On architecture.* Trans. Frank Granger. 2 vols. Cambridge, Mass., 1996.

Pieter de la Court van der Voort. *Les Agrémens de la Campagne.* Paris, 1750. Dutch edition, Amsterdam, 1763.

Peter Walker. *Minimalist Gardens.* Washington, D.C., 1997.

Horace Walpole. *The History of the Modern Taste in Gardening.* Introduction by John Dixon Hunt. New York, 1995.

———. *Horace Walpole, Gardenist: An Edition of Walpole's "The History of the Modern Taste in Gardening."* Ed. I. W. U. Chase. Princeton, N.J., 1943.

———. *Visits to Country Seats.* Reprint, New York, 1982.

Charles Webster. *The Great Instauration: Science, Medicine, and Reform.* London, 1975.

Udo Weilacher. *Between Landscape Architecture and Land Art.* Basel, Berlin, and Boston, 1996.

Allen S. Weiss. *Mirrors of Infinity: The French Formal Garden and Seventeenth-Century Aesthetics.* Paris, 1992; New York, 1995.

James L. Wescoat, Jr. "Gardens of Invention and Exile: The Precarious Context of Mughal Garden Design During the Reign of Humayun." *JGH,* 10 (1990), 106-16.

———. "Picturing an Early Mughal Garden." *Asian Art,* 2 (1989), 59-79.

Thomas Whately. *Observations on Modern Gardening.* London, 1770.

Dora Wiebenson. *The Picturesque Garden in France.* Princeton, N.J., 1978.

George H. Williams. *Wilderness and Paradise in Christian Thought.* New York, 1962.

Raymond Williams. *The Country and the City.* New ed. London, 1985.

———. *Keywords: A Vocabulary of Culture and Society.* New York, 1976.

Tom Williamson. *Polite Landscapes: Gardens and Society in Eighteenth-Century England.* Baltimore, 1995.

———. "Some Early Geometric Gardens in Norfolk." Special double issue of *JGH,* 11, nos. 1 and 2 (1991).

———. *The Archaeology of the Landscape Park: Garden Design in Norfolk, England, c. 1680-1840.* British Archaeological Reports, British Series 268, Oxford, 1988.

Joachim Wolschke-Bulmahn. "The Ideology of the Nature Garden: Nationalistic Trends in Garden Design in Germany During the Early Twentieth Century." *JGH,* 12 (1992), 73-80.

———. "The 'Wild Garden' and the 'Nature Garden'—Aspects of the Garden Ideology of William Robinson and Willy Lange." *JGH,* 12 (1992), 183-206.

Denis Wood. "*Culture naturale*: Some Words About Gardening." *LJ,* 11, no. 1 (1992), 58-65.

———. *Poets in the Garden.* London, 1978.

Word & Image. Special double issue on "Garden and Architectural Dreamscapes in the *Hypnerotomachia Poliphili.*" 14, nos. 1 and 2 (1998).

———. Special issue on "Ekphrasis." 15, no. 1 (1999).

John Worlidge. *Systema Agriculturae.* London, 1669.

———. *Systema Horti-culturae.* London, 1677.

Henry Wotton. *The Elements of Architecture.* London, 1624.

William Wotton. *Reflections upon Ancient and Modern Learning.* 2nd ed., London, 1697.

Christopher Wren. *Parentalia.* 1750. Reprinted Farnborough, Hants., 1965.

INDEX